Ius Gentium: Comparative Perspectives on Law and Justice

Volume 123

Ius Gentium is a book series which discusses the central questions of law and justice from a comparative perspective. The books in this series collect the contrasting and overlapping perspectives of lawyers, judges, philosophers and scholars of law from the world's many different jurisdictions for the purposes of comparison, harmonisation, and the progressive development of law and legal institutions. Each volume makes a new comparative study of an important area of law. This book series continues the work of the well-known journal of the same name and provides the basis for a better understanding of all areas of legal science.

The *Ius Gentium* series provides a valuable resource for lawyers, judges, legislators, scholars, and both graduate students and researchers in globalisation, comparative law, legal theory and legal practice. The series has a special focus on the development of international legal standards and transnational legal cooperation.

Zhen Chen

Tourists, Consumer Contracts and Private International Law in China

Springer

Zhen Chen
Faculty of Law
University of Groningen
Groningen, The Netherlands

ISSN 1534-6781 ISSN 2214-9902 (electronic)
Ius Gentium: Comparative Perspectives on Law and Justice
ISBN 978-3-031-87914-2 ISBN 978-3-031-87915-9 (eBook)
https://doi.org/10.1007/978-3-031-87915-9

This Springer imprint is published by the registered company Springer Nature Switzerland AG
The registered company address is: Gewerbestrasse 11, 6330 Cham, Switzerland

To my beloved grandma Xiuying Jia (贾秀英)

Preface

This book is based on my doctoral project "Tourists, Consumer Contracts and Private International Law in the EU and China" conducted in the University of Groningen. This book will primarily focus on consumer jurisdiction and choice of law rules in China.

During my doctoral research, numerous people have helped me in one way or another and make my PhD journey special and memorable. First and foremost, I would like to thank my main supervisor Prof. Mathijs H. ten Wolde, for his support and guidance over these years. His expertise, advice, and suggestions have been invaluable in shaping both this book and my growth as a researcher. Without his dedication, completing this book would not have been possible. I would also like to thank my second supervisor, Prof. Qisheng He from Peking University, for supporting my pursuit of a PhD at the University of Groningen from the very beginning. His comments and feedback were very helpful in improving the chapters on Chinese law. I also appreciate the time and effort put by my co-supervisor Dr. Kirsten Henckel over the last two years. Her insights have helped me develop new perspectives.

My sincere thanks also go to my colleagues and friends, including Weidi, Margarita, Joe, Nischa, and Benedikt, who have always been supportive in both professional and personal matters. I am grateful to have worked together with many talented colleagues in the Private International Law Department. Additionally, I am fortunate to have met many excellent colleagues from the Law Faculty, including Adi, Stratis, Monique, Ida, Ana, Lauren, Carlijne, Sophie, Sophia, Nick, Martin, Lucas, Candan, Sena, Nina, Kostia, Tim, and Maartin. Special thanks go to Karien Galli, Anita Kram, and Marjolijn Both, for their help, coordination, and continuous support over these years.

I am grateful to have met a group of wonderful friends through the Reading Club founded by Zixiang, including Jinsheng, Yuhong, Yidan, Xuelai, Stephanie, Qihua, Siqi, Yubo, and others. A special thank you goes to my friends who make very delicious and authentic Chinese food: Xipeng, Qianyi, Weiwei, and Jie. Their food is a cure for homesickness. I am also fortunate to have very supportive and encouraging friends, such as Sijia, Qinuo, Xin, Ying, Chu, Shan, and others.

Last but not least, I would like to express my special gratitude to my family members. My parents have always valued education and supported me in every possible way. My grandparents raised me up with all the best care and love they could offer, for which I am incredibly grateful. Their unconditional love and unwavering support have been a constant source of strength and motivation for me. My heartfelt appreciation also goes to my partner, Stefano, for his love, support, and care over these years. In moments of self-doubt and anxiety, he has always been by my side, offering emotional support.

Groningen, The Netherlands Zhen Chen (陈珍)

Contents

Abbreviations

AI	Artificial Intelligence
B2B	Business-to-Business
B2C	Business-to-Consumer
DPC	District People's Court
GPCL	General Principles of the Civil Law
HCCH	Hague Conference on Private International Law
HPC	High People's Court
IPC	Intermediate People's Court
NPC	National People's Congress
OBOR	One Belt One Road
PRC	People's Republic of China
SAIC	State Administration for Industry and Commerce
SPC	Supreme People's Court
UN	United Nations

Chapter 1
Introduction

1.1 Tourism and the Protection of Tourists in Foreign-Related Civil Disputes

1.1.1 Booming Tourism Industry and International Tourists

Tourism is an important economic sector and provides an essential source of income for many countries and communities, as tourists spend money on accommodation, transport, food, activities, and shopping.[1] Jobs are created in the tourism industry and related sectors, such as hospitality, transport, and commerce, which helps boost the local economy.[2] It can also help preserve and promote a country's culture and heritage as tourists usually visit historical sites, museums, and local festivals.[3] In 2023, travel and tourism's direct contribution to GDP was approximately 9.9 trillion U.S. dollars, making up a 9.1% share of the total global GDP.[4] Tourism creates 1 in 10 jobs worldwide.[5]

The tourism industry is made up of companies that develop activities such as transport, cuisine, hotels, and those that create infrastructure to promote cultural exchange.[6] This industry can be further divided into different categories based on

[1] Barliza et al. (2024), p. 1.

[2] Barliza et al. (2024), p. 1.

[3] Ovallos and Zamora-Musa (2020), pp. 819–832.

[4] https://www.statista.com/statistics/233223/travel-and-tourism-total-economic-contribution-worldwide/, accessed on Jan 24, 2025.

[5] 10% of Jobs are Worldwide Connected to the Tourism Industry—What Does That Mean?, https://www.solimarinternational.com/10-of-jobs-are-worldwide-connected-to-the-tourism-industry-what-does-that-mean/, accessed on Jan 24, 2025.

[6] Florido-Benítez (2022), pp. 844–882; Barliza et al. (2024), p. 2.

Z. Chen, *Tourists, Consumer Contracts and Private International Law in China*, Ius Gentium: Comparative Perspectives on Law and Justice 123,
https://doi.org/10.1007/978-3-031-87915-9_1

various factors, such as mass tourism, social tourism, elite tourism, study tourism, voluntary tourism, backpacker tourism, package tourism, timeshare tourism, halal tourism, pilgrimage tourism, romantic tourism, honeymoon tourism, family adventure tourism, friendship tourism.[7] Based on travel purpose, there are leisure tourism, business tourism, medical tourism, and educational tourism. Based on geographic scope, there are domestic tourism, international tourism, and regional tourism. Based on tourism experience, there are cultural tourism, adventure tourism, ecotourism, and wellness tourism. Based on transportation method, there are air tourism, sea tourism, and land tourism. Based on economic impact, there are budget tourism, luxury tourism, and backpacking tourism. Today, the tourism industry uses technologies, such as artificial intelligence (AI), the Internet of Things, augmented reality, big data, and immersive environments, among others, in smart tourism to offer personalized services tailored to the needs of tourists, as well as to improve the efficiency and promotion of tourism services.[8] For instance, TikTok travel is becoming the new trend in young generations.[9]

Tourism has become an essential contributor to China's domestic economy, especially with the emergence of an affluent middle class.[10] In this sense, the law on the protection of the rights and interests of tourists (tourism law or related laws) will always remain to be middle class law.[11] In the context of outbound travel, it will involve the conflicts of laws in different jurisdictions. The Chinese tourism market has transformed into one of the world's most-watched inbound and outbound tourist markets. In particular, the One Belt One Road Initiative (OBOR)[12] launched in 2013, which spans more than 68 countries, encompasses 4.4 billion people, and accounts for 40% of the global GDP, has contributed to the development of Silk Road Tourism.[13] In 2012, the purchasing power of Chinese tourists outweighed that of the USA and Germany, ranking the first in the world with an expense of 678.6 billion RMB. In 2014, around four million Chinese travelers visited the EU.[14] In 2016, the Central and Eastern European (CEE) countries, such as Slovenia, Serbia, Hungary, Poland and the Czech republic, witnessed a 229% increase in outbound

[7] Zhang et al. (2023); Barliza et al. (2024), p. 2.

[8] Barliza et al. (2024), p. 2.

[9] Quaedvlieg L, Inside the Rise of TikTok Travel, August 14, 2024, https://www.cntraveler.com/story/rise-of-tiktok-travel?utm_source=chatgpt.com, accessed on Jan 22, 2025.

[10] Travel and tourism industry in China—statistics & facts, https://www.statista.com/topics/1210/tourism-industry-in-china/#editorsPicks, accessed on Jan 24, 2025.

[11] Chen (2020), p. 191.

[12] Chen (2020), p. 194. It is also known as the BRI, or Silk Road Initiative, connecting Europe, Asia and Africa not only in infrastructures, but also in resources. OBOR countries are rich in cultural and natural resources. In terms of the natural heritage, natural reserves and the world cultural heritage, those along the Belt and Road account for 34%, 53% and 74% respectively.

[13] Chen (2020), pp. 193–194.

[14] Facts and Figures on China's 'Golden Week' tourism boom, https://eng.yidaiyilu.gov.cn/p/30063.html, accessed on Jan 24, 2025.

travel for Chinese tourists.[15] Currently, only 10% of China's 1.4 billion population have passports. There is still a great potential in Chinese tourists in terms of outbound travel.

Meanwhile, China has also attracted more international tourists. From November 30, 2024 to December 31, 2025, ordinary passport holders from 38 countries can be exempted from Visa to enter China and stay for no more than 30 days for business, tourism, family visit, exchange visit and transit purposes.[16] Recently, 'Travel to China after work on Friday' became a trending topic on South Korean social media. Travel bookings from South Korea to China for the 2025 Spring Festival holiday have risen 452%, and South Korean tourists are flocking to Shanghai, drawn by its visa-free travel policy, luxury offerings, and cultural landmarks.[17] Data showed a significant increase in South Korean tourists traveling to China since China implemented a visa-free policy for South Korea on Nov. 8, 2024. In that month, 993,400 South Korean tourists visited China, up 47% from the same period in 2023.[18] Nearly 20.12 million inbound trips by foreigners were made visa-free in 2024, a year increase of 112.3%.[19] In short, tourism industry is booming in China. International travel can be pleasant, relaxing and memorable until a dispute arise. An efficient dispute resolution mechanism could enhance consumer's confidence and facilitate the development of tourism industry. The core question is how to effectively solve travel disputes and protect the interests of both domestic and foreign tourists in international dispute resolution.

[15] CEE tourism urged to be further tapped in China, https://eng.yidaiyilu.gov.cn/p/19981.html, accessed on Jan 24, 2025.

[16] Latest Notice- China will extend a unilateral visa-free policy for 38 countries and optimize entry policy in aspects of stay time and visit purposes, https://bio.visaforchina.cn/DEL3_EN/tongzhigonggao/327343163872251904.html#:~:text=From%20November%2030%2C%202024%20to,exchange%20visit%20and%20transit%20purposes, accessed on Jan 24, 2025. This involves visa-free treatment to travellers holding ordinary passport from 38 countries, namely, France, Germany, Italy, Netherlands, Spain, Malaysia, Switzerland, Ireland, Hungary, Austria, Belgium, Luxembourg, New Zealand, Australia, Poland, Portugal, Greece, Cyprus, Slovenia, Slovakia, Norway, Finland, Denmark, Iceland, Andorra, Monaco, Liechtenstein, Republic of Korea, Bulgaria, Romania, Croatia, Montenegro, North Macedonia, Malta, Estonia, Latvia, Japan and Negara Brunei Darussalam.

[17] Shanghai beats Tokyo as top winter destination for South Koreans, https://jingdaily.com/posts/shanghai-beats-tokyo-as-top-winter-destination-for-south-koreans, accessed on Jan 24, 2025.

[18] 'China travel' continues to heat up as impact of visa-free policies grows, http://en.people.cn/n3/2025/0123/c90000-20269722.html, accessed on Jan 24, 2025.

[19] Ibid.

1.1.2 Consumer Protection in Private International Law

When it comes to consumer protection, multiple dispute resolution mechanisms are available for cross-border disputes, be it traditional court procedures (international litigation), or new non-court procedures (Alternative Dispute Resolution or Online Dispute Resolution). International litigation could be very costly and time-consuming due to various factors, such as costs of translation and service of documents as well as delays in obtaining the recognition and enforcement of cross-border judgments.[20] Generally, consumers may prefer to redress their legitimate rights and interests before the courts of their home jurisdiction, as travel is not required, they do not have to engage foreign lawyers and the proceedings are usually held in a language they understand without the assistance of an interpreter. Unlike national litigation, a judgment issued in one country does not automatically take effect in another country, and the court in another country first has to validate the decision, declaring it enforceable.[21] This process may add further complexity and time to international legal proceedings. Despite this, international litigation might be still the last resort for consumers to redress their legitimate rights and interests, especially when the claim involves a large amount of money.

When a legal dispute over civil or commercial matters involves a foreign element, private international law comes into play. Determining which court is competent to hear the dispute and which law applies to solve the dispute can be challenging, as multiple jurisdictions may have a connection to the dispute based on various jurisdictional grounds and connecting factors. This often leads to conflicts of jurisdiction and choice of law rules. Private international law addresses three main issues: which court has jurisdiction over a foreign-related civil dispute, which law applies to this foreign-related civil dispute, and whether the judgment made in one country can be recognized and enforced in another country.

Private international law has become the center of discussion when it comes to the resolution of consumer disputes arising out of business to consumer (B2C) e-sales.[22] The jurisdictional issue relates to the determination of whether a court has legal authority to exercise its power over a defendant or a particular matter. The choice of law issue determines which law should apply when a dispute has a connection with two (or more) legal systems. Due to the unequal bargaining power and information asymmetry between consumers and businesses, businesses may prepare a standard contract containing jurisdiction and choice of law clauses that are to the benefit of the business. For instance, according to the general terms, when disputes arise out of a consumer contract, the consumer must go to the courts of the business's home country and invoke the law of the business's home country. In some

[20] Lima (2018), p. 143.

[21] Lima (2018), p. 143. The recognition and enforcement of judgments in Member States within the EU is an exception.

[22] Gillies (2006), pp. 359, 380; Schu (1997), pp. 192, 194; Svantesson (2016), p. 541; Yuthayotin (2015), p. 214.

circumstances, a consumer might be better-off litigating abroad, if the court fees in a foreign country is lower, the proceedings are quicker and the foreign law grants a higher level of protection or a foreign court will apply the substantive law of the consumer. However, in most cases, consumers are usually more familiar with their domestic court systems and domestic law in comparison with foreign ones. The hurdle for consumers to pursue their rights may be higher when they have to litigate abroad due to more uncertainties. For instance, it could be more expensive and time-consuming to launch a lawsuit in a foreign country and be subject to a foreign law, especially for individual consumers who are financially weaker than businesses. In this regard, compared to businesses, consumers are often in a disadvantaged position, having limited access to justice, because justice might be too costly, too difficult or comes too late.[23]

The term access to justice consists of two elements: access and justice. The wording 'access' stands for the chance to reach or accomplish something, whilst the wording 'justice' refers to fairness and reasonableness, embodying the concept that everyone's rights are safeguarded.[24] The notion of access to justice includes the right of access to a judicial process and the right to have appropriate legal remedies.[25] When it comes to consumer protection, it gives rise to the question how to facilitate consumers' access to justice in private international law and make litigation less costly and difficult for consumers. This question involves the examination of jurisdiction rules over consumer contracts, namely which court is competent to hear consumer disputes involving a foreign element. Another main research question is which law applies to a consumer contract which involves a foreign element. Different countries may have different substantive laws on consumers' rights, such as the right of withdrawal. The issue of applicable law determines what kind of protection consumers are granted with regard to their substantive rights.

Traditional jurisdiction and choice of law rules in private international law are primarily based on three main factors: the identity of the parties, the location of the parties, and the activities conducted by the parties. This book focuses on consumer jurisdiction and choice of law rules in China, which include special rules established on the ground of the identity of consumers as weaker parties, supplemented by the commercial activities conducted by businesses as criteria to apply such special rules. The law of the place of performance of the consumer contract applies as an exception under two scenarios.

In Chinese private international law, *actor sequitur forum rei,* as the general jurisdiction rule, is based on the location of the parties. The general jurisdiction rule of *actor sequitur forum rei* means that an individual should be sued in the court of the place where he is domiciled. If the general jurisdiction rule applies to consumer claims, a consumer has to file a lawsuit against a business in the jurisdiction of the

[23] Yuthayotin (2015), pp. 61, 65.

[24] Wrbka (2012), pp. 23, 27.

[25] Sotrskrubb and Ziller (2007), pp. 177–178; Yuthayotin (2015), p. 38.

business's domicile.[26] This may put consumers in a disadvantaged position and derogate consumers' access to justice, especially when the expensive costs of long-distance litigation far exceed the small amount of money involved in the dispute.[27] The businesses may preserve their advantage of suing at the courts of their home country through pre-drafted standardized terms by selecting the place of the business's domicile as the forum.[28] This leads to the questions of how China designs rules of private international law governing consumer contracts, how consumers' disadvantages as weaker contracting parties are compensated, and what special jurisdiction and applicable law rules are available for consumers in China.

1.2 Research Questions and Objectives

This book mainly examines the existing Chinese private international law rules over consumer contracts. It aims to determine how these protective private international law rules operate, whether they achieve their goals, would it be necessary to further improve them, and in the end whether it would be necessary to achieve a higher level of consumer protection. The main objective is to enhance consumer protection and facilitate consumers' access to justice in cross-border disputes.

To this end, first of all, it analyzes who is the so-called consumer and what kinds of consumer contracts are protected under the private international law in China. This is a basic and fundamental question, as the answer to this question determines the personal scope of protective jurisdiction and choice of law rules over consumer contracts. Second, it sheds light on what kind of jurisdiction and choice of law rules are applied to consumer contracts in China. What is the weakness of current private international law rules over consumer contracts? Is there a need to improve consumer protective rules, and if so, how to improve current rules in order to facilitate consumers' access to justice?

These questions can be simplified into three basic questions: who is the consumer, what is the consumer jurisdiction rule and which law applies to a consumer contract? Whether there is a need to revise existing rules, and if so, how may the notion of consumer and private international law rules over consumer contracts be further improved for the purpose of providing a better consumer protection in international civil litigation.

[26] Yuthayotin (2015), p. 94.

[27] Yuthayotin (2015), p. 94.

[28] Hill (2008), pp. 187–188; Yuthayotin (2015), p. 94.

1.2.1 Who Is the Consumer

The question of who is a consumer may give rise to several sub-questions. For instance, whether a legal person can be regarded as a consumer? Whether factors such as knowledge, regularity of activities, economic gain and the volume of transaction will deprive a person's consumer status? What if a person is acting partly for professional purpose and partly for private purpose and what criterion should be relied upon to classify a dual-purpose contract? What if a person changes the purpose after the conclusion of a contract? Whether the original purpose or the subsequent purpose should be decisive?

Even if a person is qualified as a consumer, does it mean that all consumers are subject to consumer jurisdiction and choice of law rules? Are certain types of consumer contracts excluded from the material scope of protective rules? For instance, nowadays, it is quite easy for a tourist to travel abroad by just booking a flight and a hotel online or via a travel agent. Once travel disputes arise and the tourist decides to initiate a lawsuit, the following questions include which court is competent and which law applies. In China, package travel contracts and timeshare contracts are not expressly classified as consumer contracts under the Chinese Conflict of Laws Act. The overarching question is could a tourist sue a foreign business before courts in the tourist's home country and be subject to the tourist's home law. The answer to that question depends on whether that tourist is qualified as a consumer.

Consumers are generally considered as weaker contracting parties because of the imbalance of bargaining power, information asymmetry and so forth. Tourists who travel abroad are even more vulnerable, as they are often located in a foreign country with a foreign culture, language and legal system. Being this said, it does not mean that all tourists are qualified as consumers under private international law. The concept of tourist and the concept of consumer overlap to a certain degree but are not equivalent. For instance, business tourists are not qualified as consumers. Not all tourists in a package travel contract (package travel tourists) are classified as consumers. Likewise, not all tourists who conclude a timeshare contract (timeshare tourists) are necessarily consumers. Through case analysis in China, Chap. 3 points out that package travel contracts and timeshare contracts are not protected as consumer contracts in Chinese private international law. Chapter 4 further analyzes whether, and if so, how package travel contracts and timeshare contracts could be protected as consumer contracts in China.

1.2.2 What Is the Jurisdiction Rule over Consumer Contracts

In China, in the absence of a specific consumer jurisdiction rule, what jurisdiction rules are applied to determine the competent court over consumer contracts? To answer this question, Chap. 3 conducts a case analysis to demonstrate what jurisdiction rules are applied to consumer contracts in judicial practice. In the context of the

Internet and E-commerce, what are the challenges to determine which court is competent to hear a consumer dispute? Are dispute resolution clauses in a consumer contract, such as jurisdiction clauses and arbitration clauses, valid and enforceable? For instance, in a take-it-or-leave-it situation for online shopping, does the fact of clicking the button 'agree' by a consumer mean consent to dispute resolution clauses drafted by a business? What are the conditions for a dispute resolution clause in a consumer contract to be valid? Is there a need to establish a consumer jurisdiction rule in China, and if so, under what conditions shall a consumer be granted with favorable jurisdiction rules? What lessons can be drawn from consumer choice of law rules in China?

1.2.3 Which Law Applies to a Consumer Contract

As to which law applies to a consumer contract, this question may involve the exercise of party autonomy and the application of mandatory provisions. For instance, how to limit the exercise of party autonomy and when the mandatory provisions are applicable. Chinese private international law limits the exercise of party autonomy and designates the law of the consumer's habitual residence as a default rule. The question is what are the conditions to apply such favorable consumer choice of law in China? What if the conditions are not met and which law applies in this situation? What is the interaction between choice of law rules over consumer contracts and general contracts? Since a consumer can unilaterally choose the law applicable to a consumer contract, does it mean a consumer can choose any favorable law? What are the limitations for the scope of the chosen law that applies to a consumer contract? Is the material scope of chosen law too narrow? Should the business also be allowed to choose the applicable law, and if so, under what conditions? How could the exercise of party autonomy be limited in determining the law applicable to consumer contracts? Could mandatory provisions and overriding mandatory provisions play a role in consumer protection, and if so, how? With these questions in mind, Chap. 5 endeavors to explore how consumer choice of law rules could be improved in China and how to limit the exercise of party autonomy for both parties in consumer contracts.

1.3 The Structure of the Book

Having the main research questions mentioned above in mind, this book consists of six chapters. Based on a thorough examination of the clarity and adequacy of existing definitions, jurisdiction and choice of law rules over consumer contracts in Chinese private international law, it aims to enhance consumer protection and access to justice in cross-border litigation. To this end, this book offers legislative recommendations for clarifying definitions, improving jurisdictional frameworks, and enhancing consumer protection in China. Chapter 1 introduces the background, research questions, and the structure of the book. Chapters 2–5 analyze jurisdiction and choice of law rules over consumer contracts in Chinese private international law, identifying existing legal barriers and challenges encountered by consumers in judicial practice, such as the lack of a consumer jurisdiction rule and unclear conditions for applying consumer choice of law rules.

To begin with, Chap. 2 will discuss the concept of consumer or consumer contract in Chinese private international law. The main question is who qualifies as a consumer. In the absence of a specific consumer jurisdiction rule in China, the analysis in Chinese private international law rules over consumer contracts starts with consumer choice of law rules. What is the current notion of a consumer under Article 42 of the Chinese Conflict of Laws Act and does it cover certain small or micro businesses? How is the term 'daily consumption needs' interpreted in China? What factors are considered relevant and irrelevant in determining whether a person qualifies as a consumer in China? How are persons establishing future businesses distinguished from consumers, and under what circumstances might a consumer activist be classified as a consumer? What role does the primary purpose of a contract play in determining the nature of dual purpose contracts? Based on the definitions in the Chinese Consumer Protection Law and relevant international instruments, what revisions or clarifications are needed in Article 42 of the Conflict of Laws Act to effectively define a consumer?

Chapter 3 examines what jurisdiction rules are applied to consumer contracts in China and what are the issues associated with applying general jurisdiction rules from the Chinese Civil Procedure Law to consumer contracts. Furthermore, whether it is necessary to establish a consumer jurisdiction rule, and if so, how could the Chinese Civil Procedure Law be further amended to implement such a rule? What considerations should be taken into account when determining the validity of choice of court agreements in standard consumer contracts, particularly regarding jurisdiction clauses that limit or deprive the consumer's jurisdictional interests?

Chapter 4 analyzes cases over package travel contracts and timeshare contracts in judicial practice, with regard to the conditions and obstacles to protect package travel tourists and timeshare tourists as consumers. It highlights several questions concerning the material scope and application of consumer choice of law rules under Article 42 of the Chinese Conflict of Laws Act. For instance, what are the implications of not referring to the existing definition of package travel contracts in Chinese substantive law? What are the specific conditions for applying consumer choice of law rules in China? How can Chinese courts ensure consistency in determining the presence of a foreign element in consumer contracts, particularly regarding the performance of the contract in a foreign country? In terms of the targeting test, what challenges are imposed by new technology and big data marketing adopted by tourism industry in the digital era?

Chapter 5 addresses questions regarding party autonomy in consumer choice of law rules under Article 42 of the Chinese Conflict of Laws Act. How does the unilateral grant of party autonomy to consumers impact the choice of applicable law in foreign-related consumer contracts? What are the implications of this limitation on party autonomy, particularly when goods or services are provided in the consumer's home country? Whether the material scope of the chosen law should be expanded? Whether bilateral party autonomy should be allowed, and if so, how can bilateral party autonomy be embraced to balance the interests of both consumers and businesses? How does the lack of interaction between special consumer choice of law rules (Article 42) and general contract choice of law rules (Article 41) affect the determination of applicable law in foreign-related consumer contracts? What is the distinction between mandatory provisions and overriding mandatory provisions in China? How can mandatory and overriding mandatory provisions be utilized to provide consumer protection in cross-border disputes?

Chapter 6 summarizes conclusions and proposed legislative suggestions resulting from this research.

References

Barliza AS et al (2024) Recommender systems applied to the tourism industry: a literature review. Cogent Bus Manag 1:1

Chen Z (2020) Jurisdiction and choice of law in foreign-related tourist-consumer disputes in China under the One Belt One Road Initiative. In: Wei D et al (eds) Innovation and the transformation of consumer law. Springer, p 191

Florido-Benítez L (2022) The impact of tourism promotion in tourist destinations: a bibliometric study. Int J Tourism Cities 8(4):844–882

Gillies L (2006) Adapting international private law rules for electronic consumer contracts. In: Rickett C, Telfer T (eds) International perspectives on consumers' access to justice. Cambridge University Press, pp 359, 380

Hill J (2008) Cross-border consumer contracts. Oxford University Press, pp 187–188

Lima M (2018) Traveller vulnerability in the context of travel and tourism contracts. Springer, Cham, p 143

Ovallos D, Zamora-Musa R (2020) Innovation, technology and user experience in museums: insights from scientific literature. In: Lecture notes in computer science, 12249, March 2021, pp 819–832

Schu R (1997) The applicable law to consumer contracts made over the internet: consumer protection through private international law. Int J Law Inf Technol 5(192):194

Sotrskrubb E, Ziller J (2007) Access to justice in European comparative law. In: Francioni F (ed) Access to justice as a human right. Oxford University Press, pp 177–178

Svantesson D (2016) Private international law and the internet, 3rd edn. Wolters Kluwer, p 541

Wrbka S (2012) European consumer protection law: quo vadis? Thoughts on the compensatory collective redress debate. In: Wrbka S et al (eds) Collective actions: enhancing access to justice and reconciling multilayer interest?. Cambridge University Press, pp 23, 27

Yuthayotin S (2015) Access to justice in transnational B2C e-commerce: a multidimensional analysis of consumer protection mechanisms. Springer

Zhang P et al (2023) Tourism-type ontology framework for tourism-type classification, naming, and knowledge organization. Heliyon 9(4):e15192

Chapter 2
The Notion of Consumer or Consumer Contract Under Chinese Private International Law

2.1 Introduction: Chinese Consumer Choice of Law Rules

The Law of the People's Republic of China on the Application of Laws to Foreign-Related Civil Relations (hereinafter referred to as the Chinese Conflict of Laws Act) was promulgated on 28 October 2010 and took effect from 1 April 2011.[1] The Chinese Conflict of Laws Act is the first code on private international law in China. Before the enactment of the 2010 Chinese Conflict of Laws Act, there is no specific choice of law provision on consumer contracts. In fact, there is no one single law on choice of law rules in China and relevant rules are scattered in various laws, such as the General Principle of Civil Law, Contract Law, Maritime Law, and Civil Aviation Law. On the one hand, they lack coordination on some common issues, and on the other hand, there are many repetitive or contradictory regulations on the same issue. Moreover, these provisions are only for special matters, lacking general provisions, and cannot cover all the content of civil relations. Thus, it is not surprising that consumer contracts are regarded as general contracts and subject to general contract choice of law rules.[2] These scattered choice of law rules can hardly meet the requirements of the contemporary international society and the need of the increasingly-developed civil and commercial transactions in China. In terms of consumer protection, the surge in the number of cross-border consumer disputes since the issue of opening-up policy in 1978 not only stresses the need to protect consumers' rights and obligations in substantive law, but also in the field of conflict of laws.[3]

[1] It was also referred to as "the Law Applicable to Foreign-Related Civil Relations", "the Chinese Private International Law Act", "the Chinese Choice of law Act", or "the Chinese Conflict of Laws Act".

[2] Article 145 of the General Principle of Civil Law and Article 126 of the Contract Law.

[3] Xiao (2016), p. 18. 肖雯:《跨境消费者合同法律适用问题研究》，西南政法大学博士论文，2016年，第18页。

Z. Chen, *Tourists, Consumer Contracts and Private International Law in China*, Ius Gentium: Comparative Perspectives on Law and Justice 123,
https://doi.org/10.1007/978-3-031-87915-9_2

This provides a factual basis for special consideration of consumer contracts by separating them from the general contracts.[4] Article 42 of the Chinese Conflict of Laws Act fills the gap by establishing a protective choice of law rule over consumer contracts and separates consumer contracts from general contracts.

As to why and under what basis the Chinese legislators established a separate consumer conflicts rule, the original drafts published on the official website offer very limited guidance and explanation. Without the guidance under an official explanatory report, the commentaries and interpretation given by Chinese scholars, such as Professor Jin Huang, Yongping Xiao, Zheng Tang, Zhengxin Huo, and Qisheng He, may offer some insights on the understanding of Article 42. In fact, the draft proposal for the 2010 Chinese Conflict of Laws Act was presented by the China Society of International Law, an academic association specializing in Chinese private international law.[5]

2.1.1 Legislative History of the 2010 Chinese Conflict of Laws Act

In July 1994, Depei Han[6] hosted a working conference in foreign affairs college and completed the first draft of Model Law of Chinese Private International Law. In 2000, the Society took 7 years to complete the Model Law of Chinese Private International Law (sixth draft), which was published by the Law Press. The model law is the crystallization of the collective wisdom of the Chinese society of international private law, and it is the first model law drafted by China's academic research organizations. The current 2010 Chinese Conflict of Laws Act is based on the Model Law of Chinese Private International Law.

The 2000 Model Law of Chinese Private International Law became one of the two primary sources of the Proposal Draft and Explanation of the Law of the People's Republic of China on the Application of Laws for Foreign-related Civil Relations.[7] It is an official draft proposal submitted to the legislature by the China Society of Private International Law, chaired by Professor Jin Huang, on the entrustment of the Legislative Affairs Committee of the Standing Committee of the National People's Congress as a collective result of the China Society of Private

[4] Xiao (2016), p. 18.

[5] History of China Society of Private International Law (中国国际私法学会), http://www.cspil.org/Plus/m_default/Cms/docDetail.php?ID=185, accessed on 17 January 2025. In August 1985, Wuhan University Institute of International Law and Law School of Guizhou University held first national academic seminars on private international law.

[6] Depei Han, Han was widely recognized as a famous jurist in China, a Chinese master on International Private Law as well as the pioneer and founder of Chinese Environmental and Resources Law.

[7] The Draft and Explanatory Notes on the Application of Law in Foreign-related Civil Matters of the People's Republic of China.

International Law.[8] Another source of the Proposal Draft of the Chinese Conflict of Laws Act was the ninth part of the Civil Code (Draft) on the 'law applicable to foreign-related civil relations', reviewed by the 31st meeting of the 11th National People's Congress Standing Committee on December 23, 2002. Moreover, the Proposal Draft also referred as widely as possible to recent foreign legislation and domestic practice. This Proposal Draft has a direct and significant impact on the final adoption of the 2010 Chinese Conflict of Laws Act.[9] Thus, it plays an important role in correctly interpreting the 2010 Chinese Conflict of Laws Act, including Article 42 on consumer choice of law rules. The predecessor of Article 42 of the Chinese Conflict of Laws Act is Article 56 of the Proposal Draft and Explanation of the Chinese Conflict of Laws Act.

2.1.2 Article 56 of the Proposal Draft and Explanation of the Chinese Conflict of Laws Act

Article 56 of the Proposal Draft and Explanation of the Chinese Conflict of Laws Act is about the choice of law rules over consumption contracts, which states that:

> For consumption contracts, the law of the consumer's habitual residence or the law of the place where goods or services are provided shall apply.
>
> The parties to a consumption contract may also choose a law that has a reasonable connection with consumption; if the operator has used any medium for marketing activities in the consumer's habitual residence, or has individually issued an invitation to the consumer in that place, or has received the consumer's order in that place, the parties' choice shall not violate the mandatory provisions of the law of the consumer's habitual residence, except that the consumer actively goes to the operator's place to receive services without the operator's marketing.[10]

---

[8] Ibid, http://www.cspil.org/Plus/m_default/Cms/docDetail.php?ID=226, accessed on 17 January 2025.

[9] Ibid.

[10] Article 56 of the Draft and Explanatory Notes on the Application of Law in Foreign-related Civil Matters of the People's Republic of China《中华人民共和国涉外民事关系法律适用法建议稿及说明》第56条【消费合同】:消费合同，适用消费者惯常居所地法律，或者货物或者服务提供地法律。

消费合同当事人也可以选择与消费有合理联系的法律；经营者在消费者惯常居所地利用任何媒介进行过营销活动的，或者在该地对消费者个别发出过邀请的，或者在该地收到消费者的订单的，则当事人的选择不得违反消费者惯常居所地法律的强制性规定，但消费者未经经营者进行营销而主动前往经营者所在地接受服务的除外。

This draft provision has drawn reference or inspiration from the Rome I Regulation, as expressly stated in the commentary and interpretation of Article 56 of the Proposal Draft and Explanation of the Chinese Conflict of Laws Act on choice of law rules over consumption contracts. 黄进主编:《 中华人民共和国涉外民事关系法律适用法建议稿及说明》，中国人民大学出版社，2011年6月第1版，第87页。Huang (2011), p. 87. The following text is the original Article 56 of the Proposal Draft and Explanation of the Chinese Conflict of Laws Act in Chinese. 说明: 给予弱方当事人以特殊保护,是当代国际私法的新价值观. 基于这一观念,考

Article 56 of the Proposal Draft is based on the distinction between active consumers and passive consumers, which will lead to different choice of law rules.[11] It uses the term 'consumption contract', instead of 'consumer contract'. The two primary connecting factors are the place of the consumer's habitual residence and the place of the provision of goods or services. Despite the fact that the two primary connecting factors remain unchanged, the distinction between active consumers and passive consumers is not adopted by the legislator in the end.

The final text in Article 42 of the Chinese Conflict of Laws Act is quite different from that in Article 56 of the Proposal Draft. Specifically, Article 42 of the Chinese Conflict of Laws Act states that:

> A consumer contract shall be governed by the laws of the habitual residence of the consumer; where the consumer chooses to apply laws of the place where goods or services are provided, or the business operator concerned does not engage in relevant business activities at the habitual residence of the consumer, laws of the place where goods or services are provided shall apply.[12]

It is for the first time in Chinese private international law that consumer contracts are separated from general contracts. The choice of law rules over general contracts are prescribed in Article 41 Chinese Conflict of Laws Act. Conflicts rules for special contracts such as consumer contacts constitute a derogation of general contract choice of law rules. Article 42 adopts a new connecting factor 'the consumer's habitual residence' as the primary connecting factor to replace the parties' party autonomy.[13] Meanwhile, it limits the exercise of party autonomy. What is the legal basis of establishing a consumer choice of law rule?

2.1.3 Weaker Party Protection and Substantive Justice

The parties in a consumer contract have asymmetric information over the goods or services provided and also have unequal footing or bargaining power in determining the price.[14] When disputes arise, consumers usually cannot get effective legal redress

---

虑到中国关于消费者保护尚处于初始阶段以及中国作为世界工厂的现状,并借鉴«中华人民共和国国际私法示范法»及欧洲议会和(欧盟)理事会«关于合同之债法律适用的第593/2008号(欧共体)条例» (罗马I)的相关规定,本条对消费合同法律适用的规定体现了如下特点:首先,本条规定消费合同适用消费者惯常居所地法律或者货物或者服务提供地法律;其次,有限度地赋予当事人选择法律的权利,即消费合同当事人也可以选择与消费有合理联系的法律,但当事人的选择不得违反消费者惯常居所地法律的强制性规定,除非消费者未经经营者进行营销而主动前往经营者所在地接受消费.

[11] Yu (2011), p. 68. 于颖:《〈涉外民事关系法律适用法〉第42条评析-我国国际私法对消费者之保护》，《法学评论》，2011年第2期，第68页。

[12] The original text is《中华人民共和国涉外民事关系法律适用法》第42条:消费者合同，适用消费者经常居所地法律；消费者选择适用商品、服务提供地法律或者经营者在消费者经常居所地没有从事相关经营活动的，适用商品、服务提供地法律。

[13] Yu (2011), p. 65.

[14] Yu (2011), p. 65; Ramsay (1989), p. 57.

because of expensive litigation cost and time-consuming procedure.[15] Thus, consumers need a special protection in private international law. In fact, how to protect the interests of weaker parties, such as consumers, employees, children and victims of product liability, was already a concern before the adoption of the Draft of the 2010 Chinese Conflict of Laws Act.[16]

The 2010 Chinese Conflict of Laws Act aims to protect the interests of socially and economically weaker parties.[17] Article 25 of the Chinese Conflict of Laws Act on the personal and property relationships between parent and child designates the law favoring protection of the rights and interests of the weaker party. Article 29 on maintenance designates the law favoring protection of the rights and interests of the person to be maintained. Article 30 on guardianship designates the law favoring protection of the rights and interests of the ward. Article 42 on consumer contracts and Article 43 on employee contracts generally favors protection of the rights and interests of consumers and employees. Likewise, 'the law of the place of habitual residence of the person whose right has been infringed upon' under Articles 45 and 46 favors the protection of the rights and interests of the infringed.

These choice of law rules have extensively used international conventions and practices for reference.[18] At international level, away from domicile and nationality, habitual residence has become the most important connecting factor in *lex personalis*, such trend is also reflected in the Chinese Conflict of Laws Act which also uses the habitual residence as the main connecting factor.[19] The designation of the law of the place of habitual residence of the weaker party is mainly because it is the legal system usually most familiar to the weaker parties and also the legal system upon which they may base their claims.[20]

The protection of weaker parties in private international law embodies the pursuit of substantive justice, instead of merely formal justice or conflict justice.[21] The conflict justice emphasizes the certainty and predictability of choice

---

[15] Yu (2011), p. 65.

[16] Fei (2010), p. 207. 费宗祎，《中国国际私法立法的十二个问题》，《武大国际法评论》，2010年第13卷，第207页。

[17] Chen (2014), p. 63.

[18] The Report of 23 August 2010 of the Law Committee of the National People's Congress on the Result of Its Declaration over the Draft of the Chinese Conflict of Laws Act, Gazette of the National People's Congress [中华人民共和国全国人民代表大会常务委员会公报], 2010, No. 7, pp. 634–644.

[19] Huang (2014), p. 10.

[20] Chen (2014), p. 63; Chen (2010), p. 118. 陈卫佐，《涉外民事法律适用法的立法思考》，《清华法学》，2010年第3期，第118页。

[21] Yu (2011), p. 66; Liu and Hu (2012), p. 41; 刘晓红，胡荻，《论我国〈涉外民事关系法律适用法〉的若干实践困境》，《中国国际私法与比较法年刊》，2012年第15卷，第41页；Xu (2006), pp. 67–72. 徐冬根，《论国际私法的形式正义与实质正义》，《华东政法学院学报》，2006年第1期，第67-72页。

of law rules, which examines whether a choice of law rule ensures that similar cases are treated similarly, regardless of the fairness of the result. The substantive justice examines whether the application of a certain law will lead to a proper or fair result, which offers more flexibility.[22] In private international law, the formal justice and substantive are not totally exclusive, instead, choice of law rules may not only emphasize certainty and predictability of the judgment, but also pay attention to the substantive justice of the result. There is a tendency to take into account substantive justice when making private international law rules since the beginning of twentieth century, especially towards the protection of weaker parties.[23] The 2010 Chinese Conflict of Laws Act also follows this tendency by establishing the principle of favoring weaker parties in Articles 25, 29 and 30 as well as separating consumer contracts, employee contracts and product liability from general contract and tort choice of law rules.[24] The legislators adopt the value of protecting the weaker parties and integrate such principle into the system of the 2010 Chinese Conflict of Laws Act.[25] Applying the law favorable to the weaker party is a choice of law rule resulting from the weaker party consideration.[26]

In terms of consumer contracts, consumers are often in a socially and economically disadvantaged position in comparison with the other party to the contract.[27] The general principle is applying the law of the consumer's habitual residence under Article 42 of the Chinese Conflict of Laws Act, provided that the business has engaged in relevant operative or commercial activities in the consumer's country of habitual residence. Meanwhile, the consumer has the unilateral right to choose the law of the place of provision of goods or services. However, in the absence of a clear definition of consumer, it is unclear who is qualified as a consumer under Article 42 of the Chinese Conflict of Laws Act. What kind of contracts can be considered as consumer contracts remains the most complicated and debatable question in the field of consumer protection law.[28]

---

[22] The substantive justice is a fairness value that pursues the most happiness of the majority of society members and regulates different people or situations differently. Qu (2011), p. 21; 屈广清，《国际私法之弱者保护》，商务印书馆，2011年版，第21页; Yu (2012), p. 58. 于飞，《国际私法"有利原则"之界定》，《中国国际私法与比较法年刊》，2012年第15卷，第58页.

[23] Xu (2006), pp. 67–72; Liu and Hu (2012), p. 41.

[24] Liu and Hu (2012), p. 41.

[25] Liu and Hu (2012), p. 41.

[26] Yu (2011), p. 66.

[27] Yu (2011), pp. 65–70; Du (2011), p. 145; 杜涛:《涉外民事关系法律适用法释评》，中国法制出版社 2011 年版，第 145 页。

[28] Different countries may define consumer contracts differently. Xiao (2002), p. 153. 肖永平，《欧盟统一国际私法研究》，武汉大学出版社，2002年，第153页。

2.1.4 Who Is the Consumer?

A choice of law rule may have judicial life only when the basic concept of that rule is clearly defined.[29] The consumer notion should not be too strict to overlook certain groups, nor too broad to overprotect certain groups.[30] It may also need a consistent interpretation with other related laws.[31] In order to understand Chinese private international law, it is crucial to understand the importance of judicial interpretations.[32] For instance, as to what constitutes a foreign element, habitual residence, mandatory provisions and other questions not addressed in the 2010 Chinese Conflict of Laws Act, the SPC Judicial Interpretation I of the 2010 Chinese Conflict of Laws Act has answered these questions.

Article 42 of the Chinese Conflict of Laws Act does not provide a definition of consumer or consumer contract. Some scholars did provide a specific definition of consumer contract in the commentaries of the Chinese Conflict of Laws Act by referring to the consumer definition in Article 5 of the Rome Convention and Article 120(1) of the Swiss Private International Law.[33] Specifically, a consumer contract refers to 'a contract in which one party purchases goods or services for the purpose of the consumer's personal or household use and the other party provides the goods or services; In short, it is a contract in which one party is a consumer.'[34] However, whether such definition proposed by scholars will be adopted by legislators and judges in judicial practice remains a question.

Meanwhile, there is also no specific provision in substantive law that defines the notion of consumer. As to who is the consumer or what kind of consumer contracts are covered under Article 42 of the Chinese Conflict of Laws Act, the SPC Judicial Interpretation I of the 2010 Chinese Conflict of Laws Act, unfortunately, does not provide a clear definition or explanation. In the absence of a specific definition of consumer, what constitutes a consumer or consumer contract is unclear both in substantive law and private international law. Despite this, Article 2 of the Chinese Consumer Protection Law stipulates that 'the rights and interests of consumers purchasing and using commodities or receiving services for daily consumption shall be protected by this Law'. This provision merely states the scope of application of this

[29] Xiao (2016), p. 145.

[30] Ma (2015), pp. 30–41; 马一德:《解构与重构:"消费者"概念再出发》,《法学评论》, 2015年第6期, 第30-41页; Wang (2021a), p. 29. 王芳:《涉外消费者合同的法律适用研究》，燕山大学硕士论文, 2021年, 第29页.

[31] Xiao (2016), p. 145.

[32] Under the constitutional law of the PRC, the Supreme People's Court has the power to issue interpretations of concrete problems arising from the implementation of laws and regulations in concrete cases. Huang (2014), p. 6; Huang (2005), p. 47.

[33] Huang and Jiang (2011), p. 231. 黄进、姜茹娇，《〈中华人民共和国涉外民事关系法律适用法〉释义与分析》，法律出版社，2011年，第231页。

[34] Huang and Jiang (2011), p. 230. 本条文消费者合同是指以消费者个人或家庭使用为目的，一方购买商品或服务而另一方提供该商品或服务所达成的合同。简言之，就是一方为消费者的合同。

law and does not provide a direct definition on who is the consumer. In fact, Article 2 contains a circular definition by defining consumers as consumers and the word 'person' is missing.[35] Despite this, it may be argued that the notion of consumer is indirectly provided in Article 2 of the Chinese Consumer Protection Law, according to which a consumer is a person who purchases and uses commodities or receive services for the needs of daily consumption. The Chinese notion of consumer is a positive definition, since it positively defines a consumer through limiting coverage to daily consumption needs.[36] Such definition has been subject to criticism as it is vague and at odds with the definition of consumer in many other jurisdictions.[37] Since the Chinese Consumer Protection Law does not introduce a clear definition of consumer, it might be considered as the most fundamental defect of the law. Several questions may arise.

First, it does not use the term 'a natural person'. This gives rise to the question whether a legal person can be regarded as a consumer. Whether a legal person that has needs for daily consumption is a consumer and thus invokes Article 42 of the Chinese Conflict of Laws Act? Second, the term 'for the needs of daily consumption', which is core to the notion of consumer, remains undefined. Whether the capacity of a person when concluding a contract should be examined? Whether the 'daily consumption needs' requirement is equivalent to the criterion of private, family or personal consumption? Despite the ambiguity of the term 'daily consumption needs', it is suggested that the so-called 'consumer' in Article 42 of the Chinese Conflict of Laws Act will follow the definition in Article 2 of the Chinese Consumer Protection Law.[38] A counter argument believes that whether the consumer definition in Article 2 can be used in the Chinese Conflict of Laws Act remains a question, since foreign-related consumer contracts usually are more complicated.[39] Despite this, it is held that the interpretation of the notion of consumer in private international law is based on the substantive law of a country.[40] If the definition of consumer contract in domestic substantive law is the foundation of applying choice of law rules over foreign-related consumer contracts, a harmonious interpretation of the same legal term in substantive law and conflicts law regarding consumer protection is required.[41]

---

35 Thomas (2022), p. 438.

36 Thomas (2018), p. 303.

37 Thomas (2018), p. 294; Thomas (2022), p. 436.

38 The same consumer definition is likely to be accepted to define the scope of Article 42. Tang et al. (2016), p. 233, para. 8.69.

39 Liu and Zhang (2021), p. 80.

40 Wang (2021a), p. 14.

41 Jiang (2019), p. 9. 江威：《涉外消费者合同法律适用问题研究》，郑州大学硕士论文，2019，第9页。Tang et al. (2016), p. 233, para. 8.69. Although the notion of consumer still contains some vagueness in Article 2 Chinese Consumer Protection Law, Professor Tang held that the same definition is likely to be accepted to define the scope of Article 42 Chinese Conflict of Laws Act.

Based on Article 42 of the Chinese Conflict of Laws Act, this chapter endeavors to answer the following questions: who is the consumer? whether a legal person can be regarded as a consumer? what is the meaning of 'daily consumption needs'? what are the criteria to determine the consumer status of a person? whether a professional consumer or a person acting partly for private purpose and partly for professional purpose can be considered as a consumer? what are the material scope of consumer choice of law rules? whether package travel contracts and timeshare contracts are included in the material scope of consumer contracts?

2.2 A Legal Person and a Natural Person in the Notion of Consumer?

2.2.1 Excluding or Including a Legal Person in Consumer Notion?

It is unclear whether the notion of consumer under Article 2 of the Consumer Protection Law covers merely natural persons or also includes legal persons and other organizations, such as small businesses and consumer institutions. Some jurisdictions do allow for the inclusion of certain types of legal persons under the umbrella of consumer protection legislation.[42] Although the majority of scholars held that Article 2 of the Consumer Protection Law only refers to natural persons and legal persons are not protected under Chinese Consumer Protection Law,[43] many local consumer protection legislations stipulate otherwise by covering legal persons such as work units. Specifically, there are 13 provinces in China that enact regulations to clarify the notion of consumer, only one expressly states that a

[42] Thomas (2018), p. 301. For example, the small-scale agricultural enterprises or fisheries that might objectively appear to be commercial enterprises are protected as consumers under the South Korean Consumer Protection Law. Rachagan (2010), p. 55; In Vietnam, the Philippines and India, small-scale producers are also explicitly included in the notion of consumer. United Nations Conference on Trade and Development (UNCTAD), Manual on Consumer Protection (2016), p. 6.

[43] This is primarily based on the weaker party protection theory. The inequality between the consumer and operator justifies an enhanced protection towards consumers. Legal persons generally are not weaker parties who require special protection and have more resources for legal remedy. If a legal person has disputes with a business operator, their disputes shall be regulated under the Contract Law, rather than Consumer Protection Law. Huang (2017), p. 4; 黄文秀,《论我国关于涉外消费者合同法律适用之规定》，华中师范大学硕士论文, 2017年, 第4页; Jiang (2019), pp. 8, 33; Liang (2001), p. 3; 梁慧星,《消费者权益保护法第49条的解释与适用》，《人民法院报》，2001年3月29日，第3页; Wang (2002), pp. 3–12; 王利明,《消费者的概念及消费者权益保护法的调整范围》，《政治与法律》，2002年第2期，第3-12页。 Wang (2021b), p. 7; 王璇:《我国涉外网络消费者合同的法律适用研究》，安徽财经大学硕士论文，2021年, 第7页.

consumer is a natural person.[44] Local regulations are normative documents enacted in accordance with the law by the local people's congresses and their standing committees. They have legal binding force within the local area and are not effective outside the specific defined geographic area. If there is a conflict between local regulations and national laws and regulations, the national laws and regulations take precedence.

2.2.1.1 Including Legal Persons in Consumer Notion Under Substantive Law

Only Article 2(1) of the Sichuan Consumer Protection Regulation expressly states that consumers refer to natural persons. Conversely, Article 2(1) of the Shanghai Consumer Protection Regulation defines that a consumer is a natural or legal person who purchases goods or receives services for material and cultural needs.[45] Likewise, Article 2 of the Hunan Consumer Protection Regulation, Article 2(1) of the Measures of Jiangxi Province to Implement the Chinese Consumer Protection Law, Article 2(1) of the Heilongjiang Consumer Protection Regulation, Article 2(1) of the Guizhou Consumer Protection Regulation, Article 2(1) of the Henan Consumer Protection Regulation, Article 2(1) of the Measures of Shenzhen to Implement the Chinese Consumer Protection Law, and Article 2 of the Measures of Hainan Province to Implement the Chinese Consumer Protection Law also explicitly include legal persons as consumers.[46]

These local regulations are formulated, in compliance with national laws and regulations issued by the National People's Congress, by the general standing meeting of the provincial (capital) city according to the local conditions, and are valid only in that jurisdiction. In principle, enterprises must comply with local regulations. Only in the absence of laws and regulations can local regulations be used as the basis for civil judgments. Currently, China has 34 provincial-level administrative regions, including 23 provinces, 5 autonomous regions, 4 municipalities directly under the Central Government, and 2 special administrative regions. When it comes to the interpretation of consumer concept in Article 2 of the Consumer Protection Law, 13 provinces enacted local regulations and 22 provinces did not. As to whether a legal person can be considered as a consumer, it is unclear whether the other 22 provinces will exclude or include legal persons. Such unclarity will increase legal uncertainty and unpredictability for both consumers and businesses. For instance, a company that purchases goods from the online business Alibaba may be considered as a consumer under Article 2(1) of the Shanghai Consumer Protection Regulation

[44] Huang (2018), p. 12; 黄子倩,《消费者概念研究》，扬州大学硕士学位论文，2018年，第12页.

[45] The provision does not use the term legal person per se, as the original text is work unit (单位). Since the term work unit is a concept in companion to individuals or natural person, the chapter will use legal person, instead of work unit to avoid confusion.

[46] Huang (2018), p. 12; Wang (2021a), p. 29.

and other 11 local regulations, but not as a consumer under Article 2(1) of the Sichuan Consumer Protection Regulation or unclear under other 22 provinces without local consumer regulations. It is unpredictable to determine a person's consumer status on the basis of territorial factor, namely where this person is domiciled or habitually resided.

In principle, the discrepancy in provincial regulations shall not affect the interpretation of consumer concept in private international law, because provincial regulations have a territorial limitation and only applies in one province. In practice, judges in a province which protects legal persons as consumers are more likely to reach a different conclusion from judges in another province which only protects natural persons as consumers. In this sense, the autonomous interpretation of consumer concept in provincial provisions may have an influence on the application of consumer choice of law rules in Chinese private international law. It is questionable that the same person will be protected as a consumer in one province but not as a consumer in another province in Chinese private international law. This could lead to forum shopping. The differences in substantive provincial provisions on consumer definition are not supposed to affect and thus lead to the application of different choice of law rules. To avoid such unsatisfactory situation, it is crucial to have a nationwide harmonious interpretation of consumer concept in private international law.

It is noticeable that in 2016, the State Administration for Industry and Commerce (SAIC) published the Draft for Soliciting Opinions on the Regulation for the Implementation of the Law of the PRC on the Protection of Consumer Rights and Interests,[47] which did clarify the notion of consumer. Article 2 stated that "*consumers who purchase or use goods, or accept services for personal, daily consumption needs, are protected under these regulations. However, this regulation does not apply to natural persons, legal entities, and other organizations, other than financial consumers, who purchase or use goods or accept services for profit-making purposes.*"[48] After soliciting public opinions, Article 2 of the 2016 Regulation for the Implementation of the Law of the PRC on the Protection of Consumer Rights and Interests (Draft for Review) made some minor amendment by avoiding mentioning financial consumers specifically. The notion of consumer in Article 2 was changed to "*Consumers who purchase or use commodities or receive services for their daily consumption needs shall have their rights and interests protected by this Regulation. However, this Regulation does not apply to natural persons, legal*

[47] The original text is 《中华人民共和国消费者权益保护法实施条例》(征求意见稿), which is available at http://iolaw.cssn.cn/flxw/201608/t20160815_4643541.shtml, accessed on Jan 21, 2025.

[48] The original text is《中华人民共和国消费者权益保护法实施条例》(征求意见稿)第二条: 消费者为生活消费需要而购买、使用商品或者接受服务的，其权益受本条例保护。但是金融消费者以外的自然人、法人和其他组织以营利为目的而购买、使用商品或者接受服务的行为不适用本条例。

persons or other organizations that purchase or use goods or receive services for profit".[49]

This provision indicates that whether a person is protected by this regulation is not based on whether this person is a natural person or a legal person, but whether the purpose of the person, when purchasing, using goods or receiving services, is for profit. The profit element is essential for determining whether a person is acting for daily consumption needs. This criterion implies that as long as a person is not concluding a contract for the purpose of making a profit, natural persons, legal persons as well as other organizations are also qualified as consumers and thus are protected by the regulation. It seems that the legislators intend to protect legal persons and other organizations that conclude a contract not for the purpose of making profits as consumers. If it was adopted, it means that legal persons not acting for the purpose of making a profit will be protected as a consumer nationwide. It will incur more debate as to whether legal persons can be considered as consumer under Article 42 of the Chinese Conflict of Laws Act. If the definition of consumer in Article 2 of the 2016 Regulation for the Implementation of the Law of the PRC on the Protection of Consumer Rights and Interests (Draft for Review) is adopted in Chinese private international law, it would considerably enlarge the notion of consumer. However, the final version of the 2024 Regulation for the Implementation of the Law of the PRC on the Protection of Consumer Rights and Interests, which came into effect on July 1, 2024, does not adopt this provision by not defining the notion of consumer explicitly in the very beginning. The absence of a specific definition of consumer will further fuel the debate over the criteria for determining the consumer status of a person.

2.2.1.2 Excluding Legal Persons in Consumer Notion Under Private International Law

The notion of consumer in Article 42 of the Chinese Conflict of Laws Act is a distinct concept as opposed to the notion of business operator. According to Jianwen Wang, in order to determine whether a person is a business operator, it is relevant to assess whether a person's behavior or activities are of commercial nature or for the purpose of making profits and whether these activities have stability or regularity.[50] If a person acts for the purpose of making a profit, but such activity is occasional, this person cannot be considered as a business operator. For instance, a person who occasionally sells his or her second-hand products or clothes online (e.g., eBay) is not a business operator, although such person may also make a profit.[51]

[49] The original text is《中华人民共和国消费者权益保护法实施条例 (送审稿)》，第二条:消费者为生活消费需要而购买、使用商品或者接受服务，其权益受本条例保护。但自然人、法人或者其他组织以牟利为目的购买、使用商品或接受服务的，不适用本条例。

[50] Wang (2014), p. 75; 王建文,《我国商法引入经营者概念的理论构造》，《法学家》，2014年第 3 期，第 75 页。

[51] Wang (2021b), p. 8.

Article 42 Chinese Conflict of Laws Act itself does not establish the criterion for making a profit.[52] Even for the classification of businesses, the criterion for making a profit is not decisive. It is also unclear that is the intention to make profits or the act of actually making profits that matters. If only the act of making profits that matters, it means that businesses that not making profits or for non-commercial purposes will not be classified as businesses. The non-profit organizations and companies not generating immediate economic profit may also qualify as businesses, rather than consumers. The fact that a natural person who purchases goods or services and makes a profit does not necessarily disqualify that person's consumer status. A natural person who acts outside of his trade or profession and concludes an investment contract in order to make a profit may also be considered as for private consumption.[53] Investing privately-held money or assets in any kind of investment for the hope of making a profit is a private matter.[54]

Based on Article 2 of the 2016 Regulation for the Implementation of the Chinese Consumer Protection Law (Draft for Review), although Chinese legislators tend to expand the notion of consumer to include legal persons and other organizations that purchase or use goods or receive services not for making profits, the concept of consumer in substantive law should not be equated with the concept of consumer in conflict of laws. The consideration of consumer protection is a general rule in Chinese Consumer Protection Law, but an exceptional rule in Chinese Conflict of Laws Act. Since the choice of law rules over consumer contracts, which is based on the doctrine of weaker party protection, constitutes an exception of the general contract choice of law rules, the concept of consumer in the conflict of laws, in principle, should be strictly interpreted. Legal persons or other organizations have roughly the same bargaining power as business operators. Given that legal persons or other organizations are generally on an equal footing with business operators,[55] even if they do not enter into contracts for the purpose of making profits, they should not be protected as consumers with special choice of law rules.

Another question is whether consumers should be protected from small businesses in private international law. For instance, an individual can register a business account and open an e-shop on a platform and sell products to consumers globally.[56] This small business may not have obviously stronger litigation and

[52] It is not required for a person to make a profit in order to be qualified as a business. Calliess (2020), p. 117, para. 26.

[53] Plender and Wilderspin (2020), p. 255, para. 9-013.

[54] Mankowski and Nielsen (2016), p. 466, para. 22.

[55] Despite this, some small and medium-sized enterprises might be still in a weaker position in comparison with cross-border enterprises. For instance, when it comes to complicated financial services provided by cross-border corporations, whether a small enterprise with limited professional knowledge and asymmetric negotiating power may invoke consumer choice of law rules on the basis of weak party protection principle? Fan (2014), p. 210. 范晓亮:《欧盟金融消费者合同法律适用规则研究》,《武大国际法评论》, 2014年第16卷第2期, 第210页。

[56] Tang (2015), p. 359.

bargaining power than individual consumers.[57] Despite the fact that small businesses are financially weak, consumers should be protected from small businesses on the basis of inequality of bargaining power.[58] Otherwise, it is impractical and unrealistic to give different treatments based on the financial status and classification of businesses.[59] Thus, consumers should be protected from small businesses in private international law.

The notion of consumer in Chinese private international law is subject to strict interpretation, as Article 42 of the Chinese Conflict of Laws Act on consumer choice of law rule constitutes an exception to and a derogation from the general contract choice of law rule in Article 41 of the Chinese Conflict of Laws Act. Natural persons are usually the end users of goods or services who are in a weaker position in terms of financial status, access to information and legal redress, whereas legal persons are generally not in a clearly weaker position.[60] Article 42 of the Chinese Conflict of Laws Act does not give a specific definition of consumer, and Article 2 of the Chinese Consumer Protection Law does not expressly include legal persons and other organizations. According to Professor Jin Huang, a strict interpretation of Article 42 of the Chinese Conflict of Laws Act would indicate that the notion of consumer in private international law only covers natural persons.[61]

2.2.1.3 Covering Only Natural Persons in Judicial Practice

The cases collected from the China judgments online indicate that Article 42 of the Chinese Conflict of Laws Act merely cover individual consumers who are natural persons. Meanwhile, Article 62 of Chinese Consumer Protection Law provides that this law applies to the purchase and use of production materials directly used in agricultural production by farmers.[62] Farmers are natural persons who own or manage a farm. This means that farmers are protected, by analogy, as consumers under substantive domestic law in China.

For instance, in *Chen Zhongdong v. Poettinger Landtechnik GmbH, et al,*[63] Chen Zhongdong, a Chinese citizen domiciled in Xinjiang province, bought an agricultural

---

[57] Tang (2015), p. 359.

[58] Tang (2015), p. 359.

[59] Tang (2015), p. 359.

[60] Wang (2021a), p. 29; Liu (2016), p. 30; 刘成,《对消费者概念的法律解析》，华东政法大学硕士学位论文, 2016年，第 30页.

[61] Wang (2021a), p. 29; Huang and Jiang (2011), p. 231.

[62] Article 62 of Chinese Consumer Protection Law: This Law shall apply, by reference, to farmers' purchase and use of means of production directly for agricultural production. Article 65 of the 2016 Regulation for the Implementation of the Chinese Consumer Protection Law: Farmers purchasing and using production materials directly used in agricultural production or accepting agricultural production technical services shall be governed by this Regulation.

[63] *Chen Zhongdong v. Poettinger Landtechnik GmbH, et al,* Shandong Province Qingdao Municipality Huangdao District's People's Court, [2019] Lu 0211 Min Chu No 8186. 陈忠东与奥

machinery from a company with a total price of 680,000 RMB (89,474 Euro) and later found out that this machinery was composed of two types of machines. The buyer, based on the Consumer Protection Law and Product Liability Law, sued the defendants that produced such machines for a compensation over this assembling machine. The first defendant was a company, domiciled in Qingdao, Shandong Province. The second defendant was a company domiciled in Austria. The court held that 'since the plaintiff filed a lawsuit on product liability or consumer rights protection, in accordance with the Chinese Conflict of Laws Act, Chinese law should be applicable'.[64] The court referred to Article 42 and Article 44 of the Chinese Conflict of Laws Act in the last paragraph of the judgment.[65]

Although the court did not specify which provision was relied on to designate Chinese law, Article 42 or/and Article 44 of the Chinese Conflict of Laws Act, the fact that Article 42 on consumer choice of law rule was invoked may indicate that farmers are protected, by analogy, as consumers in Chinese private international law. This case implies that the purchase of production materials directly used in agricultural production by farmers is considered as daily consumption.

2.2.2 'Daily Consumption' Test

The ambiguity of the core term 'daily consumption' in Article 2 of the Consumer Protection Law creates more uncertainty as regards the precise meaning of a consumer within Chinese law.[66] The local Consumer Protection Regulations in different provinces have interpreted the daily consumption need test differently, although there are more similarities than differences among local regulations.

Article 2(1) of the Shanghai Consumer Protection Regulation construes 'daily consumption needs' as for 'material and cultural needs'.[67] Article 2 of the Hunan Consumer Protection Regulation interprets 'daily consumption needs' as 'for the need of daily life'.[68] Article 2(1) of the Guizhou Consumer Protection Regulation emphasizes that consumers refer to a unit and an individual who obtains (not for

地博田农业科技(青岛)有限公司、奥地博田农机有限公司产品责任纠纷一审民事判决书, 山东省青岛市黄岛区人民法院,(2019)鲁0211民初8186号.

[64] Ibid.

[65] Some courts do not conduct a reasoning between the facts of a case and the provisions invoked, but directly refer to the legal provisions in the judgment result. Wang (2021a), p. 20.

[66] Wang (2021a), p. 20.

[67] The term 'material and cultural needs' is also used in Article 2(1) of the Guizhou Consumer Protection Regulation and Article 2 of the Measures of Hainan Province to Implement the Chinese Consumer Protection Law.

[68] The same term is used in Article 2(1) of the Measures of Jiangxi Province to Implement the Chinese Consumer Protection Law, Article 2(1) of the Heilongjiang Consumer Protection Regulation, Article 2(1) of the Henan Consumer Protection Regulation and Article 2(1) of the Measures of Shenzhen to Implement the Chinese Consumer Protection Law.

free) goods and receive services directly for material and cultural needs.[69] The wording 'directly' might intend to stress that a consumer is a final user or end user. In my opinion, this definition indicates that an individual who obtains goods and receive services for free is not protected as a consumer. It is understandable that the business operator should act for the purpose of making profits.[70] Nevertheless, whether a person has to pay equivalent price for the goods or services is a factor irrelevant to determine that person's consumer status or daily consumption needs. For instance, users of social networks such as WeChat and TikTok, are clearly consumers, although they are using the services for free.[71] Likewise, users of search engines, such as Google, or social networks, such as Facebook and Twitter, are also consumers, even if they are using the services for free.

Article 2(1) of the Sichuan Consumer Protection Regulation expressly states that consumers are natural persons who purchase goods or receive services for daily consumption or for improving life quality. In my opinion, all these differences in the interpretation of 'daily conception needs' increase legal unpredictability for both consumers and businesses. Having considered the dynamic and frequent movement of people from one province to another province within China, a person who purchases goods or services from one business in Shanghai may qualify as a consumer in Shanghai, but not as a consumer if he or she was in another province when purchasing the same goods or services. It would not be surprising that such inconsistency may also exist when it involves a foreign element, as it is more complicated in cross-border transactions.

2.2.2.1 Luxury or Profitable Consumption Considered as Daily Consumption?

What constitutes daily consumption is unclear in substantive law and private international law. Whether luxury or profitable consumption is to be considered as daily consumption? Whether receiving medical services, financial services,[72] tourism services, education services and consulting services can be considered as daily consumption?[73] The daily consumption needs test might be construed as household

[69] Article 2 (1) of the Guizhou Province Consumer Rights Protection Regulations: In this regulation, consumers refer to both entities and individuals who, for a fee, obtain goods and receive services directly for their material and cultural life needs. 《贵州省消费者权益保护条例》第2条第1款:本条例所指消费者是指有偿获得商品和接受服务直接用于物质、文化生活需要的单位和个人。

[70] Meng and Dai (2015), pp. 5–11; 孟勤国, 戴盛仪:《论"消费者"之界定要件》,《理论月刊》, 2015年第2期, 第5-11页.

[71] Although the users did not pay money to use such services, the users in fact are paying with their personal data by clicking on 'agree' button when signing up for using such services.

[72] For protection available for financial consumers, see Chan and Young (2016), p. 369.

[73] Wan (2011), p. 305. 万鄂湘主编:《〈中华人民共和国涉外民事关系法律适用法〉条文理解与适用》, 中国法制出版社2011年版, 第305页; Huang (2017), pp. 5, 28.

or family needs.[74] Again, what constitutes household or family needs? This might be determined by examining the subjective purpose and motivation of the person or by examining the objective activity of the person.[75] Article 2 of the Consumer Protection Law limits the object of contract to goods and services, without specifically covering finance, credits and other services.[76]

Does the daily consumption test focus exclusively on everyday purchases which would thus exclude luxury or exceptional purchases?[77] If the purchase of exceptional or luxury products is excluded from the scope of 'daily consumption', it would be unpredictable to tell who is a consumer and who is not. First of all, luxury is a relative concept, depending on the financial status of a person. What is luxury for one person might be normal for another person. Second, a person's financial status is dynamic or even unstable. A rich person might become very poor overnight, vice versa. If the daily consumption test rests upon the luxury factor, a person might be classified as a consumer when he is rich and not as a consumer when he is poor. The consumer status of a person is not supposed to be based on the financial status and differences among individuals as well as the prices they paid for similar products or services. The *Chen Zhongdong v. Poettinger Landtechnik GmbH, et al* case also shows the irrelevance of the price of the goods or services paid by a person, since a farmer who purchases an agricultural machinery with a price of 680,000 RMB (89,474 Euro) was protected as a consumer. The value of the transaction or the price of a product is not supposed to deprive a person of his or her consumer status. Instead, the nature of the transaction or the purpose of the activity matters.

As to whether the fact that a person is making a profit during the consumption can deprive his or her consumer status, Article 2 of the 2016 Regulation for the Implementation of the Law of the Chinese Consumer Protection Law (Draft for Review) would imply that as long as a person is concluding a contract for the purpose of making a profit, this person will be disqualified as a consumer.[78] In general, whether the activities of a person are for the purpose of making a profit may serve as a criterion to distinguish non-commercial activities from commercial activities.[79]

[74] Liu and Jiang (2004), pp. 156–176. 刘想树、江保国,《涉外消费者合同法律适用》，《武大国际法评论》，2004年第4期，第156-176页。

[75] Wang (2021a), p. 30.

[76] It is suggested that financial and credits services should be included. Gao (2016), p. 55; 高宏贵,《中国涉外民事法律关系法律适用法研究》，北京法律出版社 2016 年版，第 55 页。Wang (2021b), p. 9.

[77] Thomas (2022), p. 439.

[78] Such criteria is debatable, as it may exclude an individual investor or a financial consumer who concludes a contract mainly for the purpose of making a profit. This is different from the EU approach, according to which the factor of economic gain or economic loss should not disqualify a person as a consumer. Case C-208/18 *Petruchová v. FIBO*, ECLI:EU:C:2019:825, para. 59. More discussion can be seen in 'The Concept of Consumer or Consumer Contract in European Private International Law'. Chen (2024a), pp. 13–41. https://research.rug.nl/en/publications/tourists-consumer-contracts-and-private-international-law-in-the-, accessed on Jan 22, 2025.

[79] Huang (2017), p. 4.

Financial consumption is special in the sense that the nature of buying financial services is usually a behavior of investment, which, strictly speaking, is not daily consumption.[80] The financial consumption is usually for the purpose of increasing assets or capital, rather than for final consumption.[81] However, the financial consumers might be in a even weaker position than other consumers, having considered the information gap between financial institutions and individual investors. The customers of financial institutions may include natural persons, legal persons and other organizations. According to Xiaoliang Fan, only natural persons who purchase financial services for household or family needs are protected as consumers.[82]

2.2.2.2 The Experience of a Person and the Frequency of Activities

The ambiguity of daily consumption test may also give rise to the question whether the experience or expertise of a person may deprive his or her consumer status. Whether the regularity or frequency of the activities conducted by a person is relevant? In *Zhu Ying v. Hangzhou Junyi Automobile Sales and Services Ltd*,[83] the plaintiff Zhu Ying purchased a used Ferrari car from the defendant Hangzhou Junyi Automobile Sales and Services Ltd for a price of 2,080,000 RMB (297,143 Euro) and later found out that it had been involved in a fire accident before, which was caused by the quality problem of the vehicle itself. The buyer Zhu Ying deemed that the defendant deliberately concealed the fact that the vehicle had suffered a fire accident in the past, and the defendant's behavior was fraudulent. Hence, the buyer Zhu Ying asked for a full refund of the purchase price and also a punitive damage compensation of 2,080,000 RMB (297,143 Euro).[84] The defendant (car seller) argued that the plaintiff Zhu Ying (car buyer), as a person operating a used car business, was not a consumer within the meaning of the Consumer Protection Law. The defendant (car seller) provided evidences to prove that the claimant Zhu Ying purchased the vehicle for the purpose of resale, instead of personal use. In addition, the historical record of vehicle transfer under the name of the plaintiff Zhu Ying proved that Zhu Ying was engaged in second-hand car business and had an obligation to review the second-hand car transaction. Based on the experience of second-hand car

[80] Fan (2014), p. 210.

[81] Fan (2014), p. 224.

[82] Fan (2014), p. 210.

[83] *Zhu Ying v. Hangzhou Junyi Automobile Sales and Services Ltd,* (2014) Hang Shang Was Chu Zi No 27, Zhejiang Province Hangzhou Municipality Shangcheng District People's Court. 朱颖诉杭州骏意汽车销售服务有限公司买卖合同纠纷案，浙江省杭州市上城区人民法院,(2014)杭上商外初字第27号.

[84] Article 55 of Chinese Consumer Protection Law states that business operators engaged in fraudulent activities in supplying goods or services shall, on the demand of the consumers, increase the compensation for the consumers' losses; the increased amount of the compensation shall be three times the costs that the consumers paid for the goods purchased or services received, or 500 RMB if the amount of compensation is less than 500 RMB.

transactions of the buyer Zhu Ying, the defendant (car seller) held that the plaintiff Zhu Ying was not an ordinary consumer. Thus, the Consumer Protection Law was not applicable to the purchase of the vehicle. Meanwhile, the defendant (car seller) claimed that its business scope was the sale of new cars and did not have the qualification to sell used cars. The car sale involved in the case was only an act of disposing of its own assets and the defendant was not an operator within the meaning of the Consumer Protection Law. Therefore, the Consumer Protection Law should not be applied in this case.

As to whether the relationship between the plaintiff and the defendant constitutes a relationship between business operators and consumers (a B2C contract), the court held that, first of all, the defendant's business scope registered with the industrial and commercial department was as a dealer of imported automobile brands such as Ferrari and Maserati, engaging in the sales of automobiles of these brands, auto components and other related automobile products, providing after-sales service support, car display, management and technical services, technical consultation, automobile transmission, economic information consultation (except commodity intermediaries). Such business scope did not include the qualification of selling second-hand vehicles. Second, the defendant obtained the ownership of the vehicle from the second owner of the vehicle and registered it in its own name as the third owner of the vehicle. This indicated that 'the vehicle belonged to the defendant's fixed assets, not as a commodity for sale'. Therefore, the court took the view that the defendant's sale of the vehicle to the plaintiff should be identified as 'a behavior of disposing of its own assets', and should not be identified as an operator.[85] Given that selling second-hand vehicles was not within the operational scope of the auto shop, the court concluded that 'the sale and purchase of a second-hand vehicle in this case did not belong to the relationship between operators and consumers'. The contract in dispute was merely classified as a sale contract.[86]

As to whether the plaintiff Zhu Ying was entitled to claim a punitive damage compensation of 2,080,000 RMB (297,143 Euro) after the contract was revoked, the court held that 'although the plaintiff Zhu Ying was not a second-hand car dealer, the fact that there were dozens of vehicles in the plaintiff's name that had been traded as second-hand cars was sufficient to show that the plaintiff Zhu Ying had

[85] *Zhu Ying v. Hangzhou Junyi Automobile Sales and Services Ltd,* (2014) Hang Shang Was Chu Zi No 27, Zhejiang Province Hangzhou Municipality Shangcheng District People's Court.

[86] Ibid. 本院认为，本案原被告的争议焦点之一在于原被告之间是否构成经营者与消费者的关系。对此本院认为，首先，从工商部门登记的被告经营范围看，被告系作为法拉利、玛沙拉蒂进口汽车品牌经销商，从事上述品牌汽车的销售，汽车零配件及其他相关汽车产品的销售，提供售后服务支持，汽车展示、管理及其技术服务、技术咨询，汽车透信、经济信息咨询(除商品中介)。上述内容中并未包含有关被告可以经销二手机动车的经营资质。其次，被告从案涉车辆的第二任所有人取得车辆所有权后登记在自己名下，即被告系案涉车辆的第三任所有人，表明该车辆属于被告的固定资产，而非待售商品。因此被告将案涉车辆出卖给原告方，应认定为被告处置其自有资产的行为，不应认定为经营者。原被告之间就案涉二手机动车的买卖不属于经营者与消费者的关系。

relatively rich trading experience in second-hand car trading'.[87] The plaintiff was not entitled to claim punitive damages on the basis that the defendant had successfully presented evidence that the plaintiff had intended to purchase the Ferrari for resale purposes rather than for personal use.[88]

The court's statement of 'the plaintiff had relatively rich trading experience in second-hand car trading' indicates that a person's experience or expertise might be relevant for determining the consumer status of that person. Since the buyer had experience of second-hand car trading, he was not considered as acting for the needs of daily consumption. The application of this criterion may disqualify individuals who possess more experience or expertise than the average consumer, thereby potentially depriving them of their consumer status. The factor that a person has certain knowledge or expertise might be subjective and thus cannot be decisive in determining a person's consumer status.[89] Although the court did not mention it specifically, it seems that the court relied on the regularity or frequency of a person's activities to determine whether the purchase of goods (the used Ferrari) was related to or within that person's trade or profession. If the purchase and resale of second-hand vehicles have a certain regularity, it is not a daily consumption. The frequency of the second-hand car transactions conducted by the plaintiff may disqualify the plaintiff as a consumer. This case implies that a person acting with a certain degree of regularity for commercial purposes (resale purpose), rather than private purposes, is not be protected as a consumer.

Article 7 of the Provisions of the Supreme People's Court on Several Issues Concerning the Application of Law in the Trial of Online Consumer Disputes states that: *If consumers suffer damage from purchasing second-hand goods on an online trading platform, the people's court should support the consumer's claim that the seller should bear the responsibilities of an operator under the Consumer Rights Protection Law when, after considering factors such as the nature, source, quantity, price, frequency, presence of other sales channels, and income from the sale of goods, it can be determined that the seller is engaged in commercial activities.*[90]

---

[87] *Ibid.* 关于原告诉请被告按购车价款的一倍赔偿208万元，本院认为，就案涉二手车交易，原被告之间不成立经营者与消费者的关系，因此应适用合同法中关于合同被撤销后的相关规定。原告在本案中虽不认可系二手车经销者，但原告名下曾有数十辆车办理过二手车过户的事实，足以表明原告在二手车交易中具有相对丰富的交易经验。因此对于案涉买卖合同的被撤销，除被告未如实完整陈述交易车辆的状况构成欺诈外，原告未尽到审慎的审查义务，在未见到交易车辆、未对交易车辆进行必要的了解核实的情况下即与被告签订买卖合同，应认定原告对案涉交易被撤销也存在一定的过失。原告因此受到的损失应由其自行承担部分责任。

[88] See evidences in No 11 and No 18 provided by the defendant, which were confirmed by the court.

[89] Fan (2014), p. 224.

[90] This SPC provision is effective from 15 March 2022.《最高人民法院关于审理网络消费纠纷案件适用法律若干问题的规定(一)》于2022年2月15日由最高人民法院审判委员会第1864次会议通过，自2022年3月15日起施行。第七条: 消费者在二手商品网络交易平台购买商品受到损害，人民法院综合销售者出售商品的性质、来源、数量、价格、频率、是否有其他销售渠道、收入等情况，能够认定销售者系从事商业经营活动，消费者主张销售者依据消费者权益保护法承担经营者责任的，人民法院应予支持。The Provisions of the

This provision implies that a seller on an online second-hand product platform may be considered as an operator, depending on the nature, source, volume, price of the product as well as the regularity, earning and other factors. It can be seen that the regularity of a person's activities is a relevant factor to disqualify a person as a consumer.

2.2.2.3 A Person Acting in Pursuit of a Future Trade or Profession as a Consumer?

The ambiguity of the consumer notion in Article 2 Chinese Consumer Protection Law gives rise to the question whether a person who is acting in pursuit of a future trade or profession can be considered as a consumer. This question is different from the issue of time of assessment when a person changes his purpose after the conclusion of the contract and during the performance of the contract. It involves whether a person's intention at the time of concluding a contract or at the time of litigation is decisive. This question will be discussed later when comparing the static approach and the dynamic approach (at Sect. 2.2.4.3). This part focuses on whether a person who purchases goods or receives services to establish a new business can be classified as a consumer. For instance, a natural person is in the starting point of establishing a business and concludes some contracts for the purpose of setting up and operation of the future business. Whether such person should be regarded as a pre-professional or quasi-professional who concludes a business-to-business contract (B2B contract) with another professional, or, as a consumer who concludes a business-to-consumer contract (B2C contract) with another professional?

As to whether a person acting for the purpose of setting up a new business can be considered as a consumer, the case *Weihai Cuixianju Hotel v. Zhao Genzai & Weihai Lesheng Hotel Management*[91] may provide an answer. In this case, the plaintiff Weihai Cuixianju Hotel sued the defendants Zhao Genzai and Weihai Lesheng Hotel Management for unpaid fees, 106,698 RMB (14,039 Euro), on catering and use of cars of the hotel by the defendant Zhao Genzai since November 2014. The defendant Zhao Genzai had a Korean nationality and domiciled in Korea. The defendant Lesheng Hotel Management was registered in February 2015, solely invested by a legal person, and Zhao Genzai was the legal representative of the

---

Supreme People's Court on Several Issues Concerning the Application of Law in the Trial of Internet Consumer Dispute Cases (I) was passed by the 1864th meeting of the Judicial Committee of the Supreme People's Court on February 15, 2022, and came into effect on March 15, 2022. http://gongbao.court.gov.cn/Details/1f8888b3afdf77181ca8cf257dd361.html, accessed on 17 January 2025.

[91] *Weihai Cuixianju Hotel v. Zhao Genzai & Weihai Lesheng Hotel Management,* People's Court of Weihai Economic and Technology Development Zone, [2015] Wei Jing Ji Qu Shang Chu Zi No 178. 威海翠仙居大酒店有限公司与威海乐盛酒店管理有限公司、赵根在服务合同纠纷一审民事判决书, 威海经济技术开发区人民法院 (2015)威经技区商初字第178号.

enterprise.[92] The court stated that 'the plaintiff Weihai Cuixianju Hotel and the defendant Zhao Genzai had a relationship over a catering and consumption service contract'.[93] The court also referred to Article 42 of the Chinese Conflict of Laws Act in the last paragraph of the judgment.

(a) Is a 'Catering and Consumption Service Contract' Equivalent to a 'Consumer Contract'?

Since Article 42 of the Chinese Conflict of Laws Act is about choice of law rules over consumer contracts, does it mean that the 'catering and consumption service contract' classified by the court is regarded as a consumer contract? If so, Korean law might apply instead, if the business Weihai Cuixianju Hotel has conducted commercial activities in Korea, which is the habitual residence of the Korean consumer. If the business Weihai Cuixianju Hotel has not conducted commercial activities in Korea, the law where the services are provided (Chinese law) will apply under Article 42 of the Chinese Conflict of Laws Act.

It is noticeable that the concept of a 'catering and consumption service contract' (餐饮消费服务合同) is not equivalent to the concept of a 'consumer contract'(消费者合同). A catering and consumption service contract in essence is a service contract, which can be concluded between a consumer and a business, a business and another business, or a consumer and another consumer. A consumer contract is concluded between a consumer and a business, depending on the content of the contract, and could be a service contract or a sale contract in essence. On the one hand, the court did not expressly classify the contract in dispute as a consumer contract. On the other hand, the court did refer to Article 42 of the Chinese Conflict of Laws Act in the last paragraph of the judgment.[94] The reference to consumer choice of law rules may indicate that the court had regarded the contract as a consumer contract and Zhao Genzai as a consumer.

(b) Acting in the Name of or in Relation to a Future Business?

Whether Zhao Genzai can be qualified as a consumer and whether the service contract in dispute can be characterized as a consumer contract remains questionable. The court did state that the receipt of the catering consumption was signed before the establishment of the defendant Lesheng Hotel, there was no evidence to prove that the defendant Zhao Genzai was consuming in the name of the defendant Lesheng Hotel which was under establishment.[95] This does not mean that Zhao Genzai's consumption behavior in Weihai Cuixianju Hotel has nothing to do with the establishment of the defendant Lesheng Hotel, since the consumption of the defendant Zhao Genzai in Cuixianju Hotel was not totally for private purpose.

---

[92] Ibid.

[93] Ibid. 本院认为，被告赵根在认可其曾在原告处消费，且认可部分餐饮消费单据的真实性，故可以认定原告与被告赵根在之间存在餐饮消费服务合同关系。

[94] Ibid.

[95] Ibid. 原告提供的签有赵根在名字的单据载明的日期均在2015年2月28日即被告乐盛酒店成立之前，原告未提供其他证据证明被告赵根在签名的餐饮单据系被告乐盛酒店筹备过程中所产生的债务。

Of course, the defendant Zhao Genzai was not acting in the name of the defendant Lesheng Hotel, since the Lesheng Hotel was still not established yet at that time. The court's reasoning is well-grounded in terms of substantive rights of the parties,[96] but not very convincing when it comes to the qualification of a person as a consumer in the field of private international law. The fact that a person is not acting in the name of a future business does not mean the person is not acting in relation to the establishment of a future business. In fact, Zhao Genzai said he would like to invest $ 560 million on the villa where the Cuixianju Hotel was located, although only $ 3 million was invested in the end. The consumption in Cuixianju Hotel was for the establishment of the investment project and occurred before the establishment of the Lesheng Hotel Management, which had been in preparation since August 2014.

However, the fact that Lesheng Hotel Management was not qualified as a defendant does not mean the consumption of Zhao Genzai in the Cuixianju Hotel was not related to the Lesheng Hotel Management which was established later, especially considering that Zhao Genzai was the legal representative of the Lesheng Hotel Management. The substantive issue of whether the future business should take responsibility of activities conducted for the establishment of this business needs to be distinguished from the conflicts of law issue on whether a person establishing a future business should be considered as a consumer. In fact, all catering consumption and use of cars by the individual Zhao Genzai in the Cuixianju Hotel were essentially for the establishment of the Lesheng Hotel Management.

(c) Difficulty in Establishing the Burden of Proof for Persons Acting in the Name of a Future Business

From the perspective of the burden of proof on evidence, it is not possible for a person to act in the name of a future trade or business which has not been registered officially yet. Even though the consumption in the Cuixianju Hotel occurred before the establishment of the Lesheng Hotel Management, the purpose of such consumption is clearly not totally for private reasons but for commercial and professional reasons. Although the court held that the defendant company should not take responsibility for the service contract concluded by the defendant Zhao Genzai and

[96] *Weihai Cuixianju Hotel v. Zhao Genzai & Weihai Lesheng Hotel Management,* People's Court of Weihai Economic and Technology Development Zone, [2015] Wei Jing Ji Qu Shang Chu Zi No 178. Lesheng Hotel Management argued that the claims against Zhao Genzai had nothing to do with the company, as it was established on 28 February 2015 and qualified as a civil subject since then. The court held that the consumption receipts with the signature of Zhao Genzai were before the establishment of the Lesheng Hotel Management and there was no relevant information of the Lesheng Hotel Management showing on the receipts. There were no evidence to prove that Zhao Genzai was acting on behalf of the Lesheng Hotel Management which was in the process of preparation and formation. Therefore, the court held that Lesheng Hotel Management should not take any responsibility of Zhao Genzai's consumption, as the Lesheng Hotel Management was not a party to the concluded contract. 签有赵根在名字的餐饮消费单据均发生于被告乐盛酒店成立之前，并且相应的餐饮消费单据也没有出现被告乐盛酒店的相关信息，没有证据证明被告赵根在系以设立中的被告乐盛酒店的名义所进行的消费。故原告要求被告乐盛酒店承担责任，于法无据。

the plaintiff Cuixianju Hotel, it can be seen, based on the analysis of the facts of this case, that Zhao Genzai's consumption behavior was not completely independent of the business behavior of establishing Lesheng Hotel Management.

In the very beginning before consumption in the plaintiff's hotel, Zhao Genzai already promised that he will invest $ 560 million on the villa where the Cuixianju Hotel was located and the representative of the Cuixianju Hotel will be the Chinese representative of the new business Lesheng Hotel. The consumption in the Cuixianju Hotel was for the investment project. The defendant Zhao Genzai was a person acting for the purpose of preparing for the establishment of a new business, rather than for household, family or private consumption. Therefore, the catering consumption service contract concluded between the defendant Zhao Genzai and the plaintiff Cuixianju Hotel was not for daily consumption needs. Since the catering consumption service contract in dispute was not qualified as a consumer contract, the reference to Article 42 of the Chinese Conflict of Laws Act by the court in its judgment is questionable. The case *Weihai Cuixianju Hotel v. Zhao Genzai & Weihai Lesheng Hotel Management* implies that a person acting for the purpose of establishing a future trade or business might be considered as a consumer. In my view, this is questionable.

2.2.3 Are Professional Consumers or Consumer Activists Consumers?

The vagueness of the core term 'daily consumption needs' also increases uncertainty as to whether a professional consumer can be regarded as a consumer. For instance, it is unclear whether a professional consumer or consumer activist, whose main purpose is for economic gain can be regarded as a consumer purchasing goods or services for 'daily consumption'. A 'fake fighter (职业打假人)', also known as 'counterfeit hunter', 'counterfeit fighter', 'consumer activist' or 'professional consumer', refers to a person who seeks to exploit the punitive damage clauses in the Consumer Protection Law or the Food Safety Law by deliberately purchasing large quantities of fake or expired goods solely in order to claim punitive damages.[97] For instance, Article 148 of the 2015 Food Safety Law states that: *For the production of food that does not meet food safety standards or the sale of food known to violate such standards, consumers may, in addition to claiming compensation for damages, demand that the producer or seller pay compensation equal to ten times the purchase price or three times the amount of the loss. If the additional compensation is less than 1,000 yuan, it shall be set at 1,000 yuan. However, this does not apply to defects in food labels or instructions that do not affect food safety and do not*

[97] Thomas (2014); Thomas (2018), p. 312. Luo (2020), pp. 51–53; 罗元骏，《"知假买假"与消费者概念界定问题研究》，《西部学刊》，2020年第31期，第51-53页。

mislead consumers.[98] This provision means that professional consumers could make a profit by taking advantage of the provision on the punitive damage compensation. It is argued that consumer activists should not be protected as consumers because they are not acting in good faith.[99]

2.2.3.1 The Wang Hai Phenomenon: Fake Fighters as Consumers or Profit-Seekers?

The first and most famous 'counterfeit hunter (打假人士)' or 'fake fighter' in China is a person named Wang Hai, aka the 'Anti-Counterfeiting Hero'.[100] The Wang Hai Phenomenon refers to the act of knowingly buying fake goods and demanding compensation afterwards to get material benefits.[101] In March 1995, Wang Hai bought two pairs of Sony headphones at the Longfu Building in Beijing. He realized that they might be counterfeit goods and immediately purchased 10 more pairs. He made a claim for double compensation (2000 RMB) under Article 49 of the old Chinese Consumer Protection Law.[102] Subsequently, he bought counterfeit goods from major shopping centers in Beijing and received compensation through negotiation or complaints. That year, Wang Hai was awarded the first 'Consumer Anti-Counterfeiting Award (消费者打假奖)' issued by the Chinese Consumer Association, along with a prize of 5000 RMB. Wang Hai became the annual figure and his efforts in combating counterfeits made people realize the importance of consumer rights and the protective role of the law for consumers. Afterwards, similar actions to Wang Hai's fight against counterfeits emerged in various regions across China.

Fake-fighters believe it is their responsibility to highlight potential dangers in the marketplace, disseminate legal knowledge, and, crucially, prompt the government

---

[98] The original text of Art. 148 of the 2015 Food Safety Law reads: 生产不符合食品安全标准的食品或者经营明知是不符合食品安全标准的食品，消费者除要求赔偿损失外，还可以向生产者或者经营者要求支付价款十倍或者损失三倍的赔偿金；增加赔偿的金额不足一千元的，为一千元。但是，食品的标签、说明书存在不影响食品安全且不会对消费者造成误导的瑕疵的除外。The Food Safety Law of the PRC (《中华人民共和国食品安全法》) was promulgated on February 28, 2009 and came into effect on June 1, 2009. It was revised on April 24, 2015, which has been effective since October 1, 2015. The predecessor of Art. 148 is Art. 96 of the 2009 Food Safety Law, which states that: *For the production of food that does not meet food safety standards or the sale of food known to violate such standards, consumers may, in addition to claiming compensation for damages, demand that the producer or seller pay compensation equal to ten times the purchase price*. 生产不符合食品安全标准的食品或者销售明知是不符合食品安全标准的食品，消费者除要求赔偿损失外，还可以向生产者或者销售者要求支付价款十倍的赔偿金。生产不符合食品安全标准的食品或者销售明知是不符合食品安全标准的食品，消费者除要求赔偿损失外，还可以向生产者或者销售者要求支付价款十倍的赔偿金。

[99] Rui (2015), p. 68.

[100] Luo (2020), pp. 51–53; Wong (2012), p. 20.

[101] Wang (1996), p. 10.

[102] https://news.sohu.com/s2015/newsmaker323/index.shtml, accessed on Jan 20, 2025.

to enforce laws to better protect consumers.[103] Their intention in buying the fake goods is to fight against the bad merchants and sellers of the fake goods.[104] Fake-fighters depict themselves as consumer heroes.[105] They proclaim that they are the woodpeckers of the market economy, the more woodpeckers the less pests.[106] The majority of wronged consumers are isolated individuals fighting against manufacturers or sellers that are usually collective entities.[107] In this an asymmetric battle, the practice of professional fake fighting is the product of an imbalanced consumer environment that levels the playing field.[108] In the era of the internet and platform economy, with the rise of online shopping and livestream e-commerce (直播带货), a group of professional fake-fighters have been brought into the spotlight by exposing issues with well-known brands or top livestream influencers.

Are fake-fighters like Wang Hai consumer activists or morally dubious profit-seekers?[109] Do they make the marketplace safer for ordinary consumers by using the law to fight fake, dangerous and falsely advertised goods, or benefit only themselves through the exploitation of legal loopholes?[110] Compared with average consumers, fake-fighters usually have a better understanding of consumer protection laws and the processes for complaints and litigation. This means that they know how to take advantage of the laws protecting consumers' rights and make profits out of it. The purpose of fake-fighters like Wang Hai in purchasing goods is to seek compensation for profit rather than for private consumption. As no laws forbid such practice in China, it is controversial whether fake-fighters qualify as consumers who purchase goods or receive services for private consumption in daily life under Article 2 of the Consumer Protection Law. It may be argued that classifying them as consumers does not align with the definition of a consumer.[111] Fake-fighters are not consumers in the strictest sense. They buy fake products in the full knowledge and then present

---

[103] Kuever (2019), p. 1.

[104] Wang (1996), p. 10.

[105] Kuever (2019), p. 2.

[106] Kuever (2019), p. 17; Huang Z (2005), I Want To Be the 10,000th Egg (我愿意做第一万个鸡蛋): A Short Introduction to Huang Zhihong. https://news.sina.com.cn/c/2005-08-08/16337443810.shtml, accessed on 20 January 2025. 黄志宏:有些行业在经营中不够规范，时常侵犯消费者合法权　益。面对这些强劲的对手，告它们，无异于以卵击石。但是，如果用一万个鸡蛋同时碰一块石头，它会怎么样，可能经历过9999个鸡蛋碰撞后的石头，就差一个鸡蛋的撞击了!我愿做第一万个鸡蛋。Some industries operate in a non-compliant manner and frequently infringe upon consumers' legitimate rights and interests. Facing such powerful opponents, taking legal action against them can feel like striking a stone with an egg. However, if ten thousand eggs hit the stone at the same time, what might happen? Perhaps after being struck by 9999 eggs, the stone is just one egg away from breaking! I am willing to be that ten-thousandth egg.

[107] Is the Cause of Professional Fraud Fighters Authentic? April 9, 2015, Beijing Review, http://www.bjreview.com.cn/forum/txt/2015-04/07/content_682092.htm, accessed on Jan 20, 2025.

[108] Ibid.

[109] Kuever (2019), p. 1.

[110] Kuever (2019), p. 1.

[111] Shen and Lu (1999), p. 29. 沈玲萍，卢文道:《王海现象的法律分析与司法探究》，《法律适用》，1999年第3期，第29页。

themselves as victims, thus the action of these "fake consumers" may be just as morally questionable as those who produce and sell fake goods.[112] However, since laws in China do not explicitly clarify the legal status of fake-fighters, different courts may reach different conclusions in similar disputes.

2.2.3.2 Fake Fighting as a Profession

The Chinese Consume Protection Law introduced a fiscal incentive that made fake-fighting a viable career.[113] After earning the title of the first person to combat counterfeiting, Wang Hai established his business in 1996 and owns four professional anti-counterfeiting companies, located in Beijing, Tianjin, Nanjing, and Shenzhen.[114] These companies primarily engage in three types of business:

(a) Helping consumers protect their rights and identify counterfeits: This involves assisting consumers in identifying counterfeit and sub-standard products and safeguarding their legal rights.
(b) Knowledge-based purchasing of counterfeits: This business involves providing information about counterfeit products, allowing consumers to decide whether to purchase them knowingly.
(c) Working for companies to combat counterfeiting: The third type of business is the main focus of Wang's operations and constitutes more than one-third of the entire business. In this aspect, the companies are hired by other businesses to combat counterfeiting

The counterfeit products Wang Hai have targeted include fake drugs, questionable imported beef, defective autos and steels. Wang Hai held that China is still an enterprise-oriented society rather than a consumer-oriented society.[115] He established a laboratory and the primary research focus was illegal additives, including food, pharmaceuticals, disinfectant products, medical devices, and so on. One third of the businesses are conducting E-commerce. He used data to filter targeted businesses and also consider cost and benefit analysis.[116] When selecting potential counterfeit products, Wang Hai's team used the TOP 10 criterion in terms of total online sales. For instance, regarding facial masks, businesses with annual sales revenue lower than 30 million RMB on Taboo.com will not be considered.[117] Because of the profits in purchasing counterfeit products and claims punitive compensations later, many individuals, including university students and lawyers, have become consumer

[112] Is the Cause of Professional Fraud Fighters Authentic? April 9, 2015, Beijing Review, http://www.bjreview.com.cn/forum/txt/2015 04/07/content_682092.htm, accessed on Jan 20, 2025.

[113] Kuever (2019), p. 1.

[114] http://www.xinhuanet.com/politics/2015-03/23/c_127608513.htm, accessed on Jan 20, 2025.

[115] https://news.sohu.com/s2015/newsmaker323/index.shtml, accessed on Jan 20, 2025.

[116] http://www.xinhuanet.com/politics/2015-03/23/c_127608513.htm, accessed on Jan 20, 2025.

[117] http://www.xinhuanet.com/politics/2015-03/23/c_127608513.htm, accessed on Jan 20, 2025.

activists. Professional anti-counterfeiting individuals somewhat have become a profession. Many started their fake-fighting careers after seeking justice for a problem encountered in the market. Others entered the industry after witnessing regulatory failings in their own industries: Chen Xiaolan in medical devices, Ye Guang in alcohol, Gao Jingde in pharmaceuticals.[118] Despite this, they remain a small and scattered community.[119]

Since the Consumer Protection Law and the Food Safety Law allowed fake-fighters to profit from buying and returning fake, defective, or misrepresented goods, there were always doubts about the motives of fake-fighters.[120] As fake-fighting became an established career, much of the Chinese public came to see it not as activism or advocacy, but as the pursuit of profit and celebrity through the devious use of a legal loophole to extort money from retailers.[121] Indeed, as a profit-driven profession, professional fake-fighters who purchase problematic products to obtain punitive damage compensation as a strategy for making profit have positioned themselves more as business operators rather than consumers.

2.2.3.3 Knowingly Buying Expired Products

In case *SUN Yinshan v. Nanjing Auchan Supermarket Co, Ltd Jiangning Store,* the plaintiff SUN Yinshan bought 15 packs of sausages for 558.6 RMB (79 Euro) from the defendant Nanjing Auchan Supermarket Co, Ltd Jiangning Store, 14 of which were already past their expiration date.[122] After paying for the sausages at the counter, the plaintiff immediately went to the customer service desk to claim statutory compensation for 10 times of the purchasing price 5586 RMB (790 Euro) in accordance with Article 96 of the Food Safety Law.[123] The defendant argued that the plaintiff was not a consumer within the meaning of Article 2 of the Chinese Consumer Protection Law, since he purchased the goods solely for the purpose of claiming compensation rather than for the needs of daily consumption.

The court focused on whether the defendant could prove that the plaintiff had purchased the goods for any commercial purposes, such as resale, production or operation. Even if the plaintiff knowingly bought some expired products, since the defendant failed to provide any evidence that the plaintiff bought the sausages for

[118] Kuever (2019), p. 17.

[119] Kuever (2019), p. 17.

[120] Kuever (2019), p. 2.

[121] Kuever (2019), p. 2; Brandtstadter (2008), pp. 139–160.

[122] *SUN Yinshan v. Nanjing Auchan Supermarket Co, Ltd Jiangning Store,* Jiangsu Province Nanjing Municipality Jiangning District People's Court, (2012) Jiang Ning Kai Min Chu Zi No 646. It is a sale and purchase contract dispute. https://cgc.law.stanford.edu/guiding-cases/guiding-case-51/. Guiding case no 23 (2014). 指导案例23号:孙银山诉南京欧尚超市有限公司江宁店买卖合同纠纷案,江苏省南京市江宁区(县)人民法院, (2012) 江宁开民初字第646号.

[123] Ibid. Article 96 of the 2009 Food Safety Law provides that the seller should pay ten times the purchase price for any food which does not conform to food safety standards.

resale or business purposes, the court classified the plaintiff as a consumer who was entitled to statuary compensation under Article 2 of the Chinese Consumer Protection Law.[124]

2.2.3.4 For the Purpose of Personal, Family or Household Needs

In case *SUN Yinshan v. Nanjing Auchan Supermarket Co, Ltd Jiangning Store,* the court also clarified that '*the consumer concept is a concept as opposed to seller and producer*'.[125] The court further explained that '*as long as the purchase, use of goods or receipt of services by a person in market transactions is for the purpose of personal, family or household needs, rather than for the purpose of production and business or professional activities, such person should be identified as a consumer who is acting for the purpose of 'daily consumption needs' and thus falls within the scope of the Consumer Protection Law*'.[126] The court explained that since Article 96 of the Food Safety Law stipulates that consumers are entitled to receive compensation of ten times the price paid, the benefits obtained from the compensation are interests that should be protected by the law, and the law does not restrict consumers' subjective motivation of shopping.[127]

---

[124] Ibid. 本案中，原、被告双方对孙银山从欧尚超市江宁店购买香肠这一事实不持异议，据此可以认定孙银山实施了购买商品的行为，且孙银山并未将所购香肠用于再次销售经营，欧尚超市江宁店也未提供证据证明其购买商品是为了生产经营。孙银山因购买到超过保质期的食品而索赔，属于行使法定权利。因此欧尚超市江宁店认为孙银山"买假索赔"不是消费者的抗辩理由不能成立。

[125] *SUN Yinshan v. Nanjing Auchan Supermarket Co, Ltd Jiangning Store,* Jiangning District People's Court of Nanjing Municipality, Jiangsu Province, (2012) Jiang Ning Kai Min Chu Zi No 646. 消费者是相对于销售者和生产者的概念。

[126] *SUN Yinshan v. Nanjing Auchan Supermarket Co, Ltd Jiangning Store,* ibid. 只要在市场交易中购买、使用商品或者接受服务是为了个人、家庭生活需要，而不是为了生产经营活动或者职业活动需要的，就应当认定为"为生活消费需要"的消费者，属于消费者权益保护法调整的范围。

[127] *SUN Yinshan v. Nanjing Auchan Supermarket Co, Ltd Jiangning Store,* ibid. 《食品安全法》第九十六条第一款规定:"违反本法规定，造成人身、财产或者其他损害的，依法承担赔偿责任。"第二款规定:"生产不符合食品安全标准的食品或者销售明知是不符合食品安全标准的食品，消费者除要求赔偿损失外，还可以向生产者或者销售者要求支付价款十倍的赔偿金。" 当销售者销售明知是不符合安全标准的食品时，消费者可以同时主张赔偿损失和支付价款十倍的赔偿金，也可以只主张支付价款十倍的赔偿金。本案中，原告孙银山仅要求欧尚超市江宁店支付售价十倍的赔偿金，属于当事人自行处分权利的行为，应予支持。关于被告欧尚超市江宁店提出原告明知食品过期而购买，希望利用其错误谋求利益，不应予以十倍赔偿的主张，因前述法律规定消费者有权获得支付价款十倍的赔偿金，因该赔偿获得的利益属于法律应当保护的利益，且法律并未对消费者的主观购物动机作出限制性规定，故对其该项主张不予支持。When the seller sells food that he knows does not meet the safety standards, the consumer can claim compensation for the loss and ten times payment of the purchasing price at the same time, or only claim payment of the purchasing price. In this case, the plaintiff, Sun Yinshan, only asked the Supermarket Store to pay ten times the price as compensation, which is an act of disposing of the right of the party and should be supported. Regarding the claim of the defendant that the plaintiff knew that the food was expired and bought it, hoping to use

This case indicates that a buyer should be considered as a consumer unless the business can present evidence that the purchase was for business purposes or fell outside the scope of daily consumption needs.[128] Such approach adopted in this case would considerably widen the scope of consumer by potentially including the so-called professional consumers or consumer activists who knowingly purchase fake or counterfeit goods with the sole intention of economic gain by claiming punitive damages.[129] The broad interpretation might be based not only on the individual interest in protecting a consumer's rights but also on the public interest in safeguarding food safety. Nationwide cases involving the food or drug safety issues include the 2008 melamine-tainted milk scandal[130] and the 2018 vaccine scandal.[131]

Article 3 of the 2014 Provisions of the SPC on Several Issues Concerning the Application of Law in the Trial of Food and Drug Dispute Cases expressly states that: *In disputes arising from food or drug quality issues, if the purchaser asserts their rights against the producer or seller, and the producer or seller argues in defense that the purchaser knowingly bought the food or drugs despite being aware of the quality issues, the people's court shall not support such a defense.*[132] This provision remains unchanged in Article 3 of the 2021 amendment. As a result, a person who knowingly buys counterfeits and gains profits remains a consumers, and it does not matter "whether the purchase was for personal consumption", "whether the purchase was made knowingly of the counterfeit nature", or "whether it was a professional anti-counterfeiting action."

---

the supermarket's mistake to seek benefits or interests, and thus should not be compensated ten times as much, the court held that the benefits or interests obtained belong to the interests that should be protected by the law, and the law does not restrict consumers' subjective motives of shopping, so this claim is not supported.

[128] Thomas (2018), p. 307.

[129] Thomas (2018), p. 308. Although it is debatable whether the purchase of ten pairs of fake Sony-brand headphones could be objectively classified as for everyday or daily consumption needs if the term were to be interpreted strictly, the courts seem to tolerate such conduct with a broad interpretation of consumer in order to curtail widespread counterfeit goods and services.

[130] China dairy products found tainted with melamine, BBC News, July 9, 2010, https://www.bbc.com/news/10565838, accessed on January 20, 2025. Melamine is used to make plastics, fertilisers and concrete. When added to food products it indicates a higher apparent protein content but can cause kidney stones and kidney failure. Test samples from a dairy plant showed the milk powder carried up to 500 times the maximum allowed level of the chemical. In 2008, melamine was found in the products of 22 Chinese dairy companies -one out of every five suppliers in China. The use of melamine in milk in 2008 killed six babies and made 300,000 ill. More than 20 people were convicted for their roles in the scandal, and two people were executed.

[131] Kuever (2019), p. 8; Westcott B and Wang S (2018) Outrage in China over thousands of faulty vaccines for children, July 13, 2018, https://edition.cnn.com/2018/07/23/asia/faulty-vaccine-china-intl/index, accessed on January 20, 2025.

[132] 《最高人民法院关于审理食品药品纠纷案件适用法律若干问题的规定》 is available at https://law.pkulaw.com/chinalaw/ee2b5cc1ee8be0a1bdfb.html, accessed on Jan 21, 2025. 第三条: 因食品、药品质量问题发生纠纷，购买者向生产者、销售者主张权利，生产者、销售者以购买者明知食品、药品存在质量问题而仍然购买为由进行抗辩的，人民法院不予支持。

2.2.3.5 Malicious Complaints or Litigation by Professional Fake-Fighters

The problem with professional fake-fighters or consumer activists is that their primary motivations are allegedly only monetary gain and even fame.[133] Fake-fighting purely for the pursuit of profit is, to some extent, analogous to deliberately producing and selling fake products.[134] In recent years, issues such as intentional purchasing of counterfeit goods and malicious claims (恶意索赔) have been on the rise, leaving regulatory authorities overwhelmed.[135] Malicious complaints or litigation filed by professional fake-fighters (职业打假人恶意投诉或诉讼) have become problematic in certain circumstances. According to the China Chain Store & Franchise Association, in 2023, there were 24,000 professional fake-fighters initiating 730,000 claims and complaints. Among these, 220,000 malicious complaints were related to food.[136] Judicial resources are limited, and malicious litigation, which constitutes an abuse of litigation rights, waste these limited resources. The large number of malicious complaints or litigations may infringe upon the litigation rights of consumers who genuinely need remedies.

On February 23, 2024, the Regulation on Implementation of the Consumer Protection Law of the PRC (《中华人民共和国消费者权益保护法实施条例》) was approved and has been effective since July 1, 2024.[137] This Regulation addresses new consumer issues in areas of public concern, such as prepaid consumption, live-stream e-commerce, unfair clauses, big data pricing discrimination, automatic renewals, and bundled sales in the context of digital economy. It also includes provisions on the obligations of businesses regarding the protection of the rights and interests of elderly and minor consumers. With regard to professional fake-fighters, Art. 27 of the Regulation is very relevant. It provides that:

> Market supervision and other relevant administrative departments should ensure smooth and standardized channels for consumer complaints and reports, improve the complaint and reporting handling process, and timely accept and process complaints and reports in accordance with the law. They should strengthen the analysis and application of complaint and report information, conduct consumption warnings, and provide risk alerts.

---

[133] Is the Cause of Professional Fraud Fighters Authentic? April 9, 2015, Beijing Review, http://www.bjreview.com.cn/forum/txt/2015-04/07/content_682092.htm, accessed on Jan 20, 2025.

[134] Ibid.

[135] Goodbye! The road of "professional counterfeit fighting" has come to an end! (再见!"职业打假" 之路到头了!), Fujian Food Industry Association (福建省食品工业协会), August 1, 2024, https://mp.weixin.qq.com/s?__biz=MzA5MjQxNDg2NQ==&mid=2650639821&idx=4&sn=782d205c4a8d292d38d532099cbfcca4&chksm=892a8d8fb02975d89abaabdb99377bcbfd3246d87aca077dc872f27af942ed6f4e0ee9614978&scene=27, accessed on Jan 20, 2025.

[136] Are Professional Fake-fighters in the Dispute Seeking to Protect Rights or Make Profits? How Should the Boundaries of Their Actions be Defined? (争议中的职业打假人，是维权还是逐利？行为边界如何界定？), https://baijiahao.baidu.com/s?id=1820219184682951513&wfr=spider&for=pc, accessed on Jan 21, 2025.

[137] The original text of the Regulation (《中华人民共和国消费者权益保护法实施条例》, 简称《消法实施条例》) is available at https://faolex.fao.org/docs/pdf/chn224757.pdf, accessed on Jan 20, 2025.

> Complaints and reports should comply with laws, regulations, and relevant provisions, and should not be used to gain improper benefits, infringe upon the legitimate rights and interests of businesses, or disrupt the market economy order.[138]

This provision standardized consumer complaints and compensation claims, stipulating that complaints and reports must abide by laws, regulations and relevant provisions.[139] Furthermore, they shall not be used to seek improper benefits, infringe on the legitimate rights and interests of operators, and disrupt the market order.[140] For professional fake-fighters whose complaint volume and frequency significantly exceed normal levels, relevant administrative departments or courts may inform them of the reasons for rejecting their complaints or claims. This could help crack down on illegal activities such as extortion, malicious claims, and other unlawful actions under the guise of fighting fake products, and restrict the profit-making behavior of professional claimants, in order to effectively reduce the number of illicit profit-driven professional claim complaints. As a result, it will help allocate more timely administrative or judicial resources to handle complaints or claims, addressing urgent issues for consumers who genuinely need help in protecting their rights.

In this regard, the Chongyang Municipality Market Supervision Administration addressed the complaints and claims from some professional fake-fighters.[141] It analyzed that since the frequency of their purchases clearly exceeded a reasonable amount for daily consumption (购买商品的次数明显超出合理生活消费次数), and their intention was not for personal use but for profit-making (不是以生活消费为目的，而是以牟利为目的), the administration determined that their actions constitute malicious complaints and reports. This implies that professional fake-fighters whose purchases are not for personal use but for the purpose of making a profit might not qualify as consumers under the criterion of daily consumption need in Article 2 of the Consumer Protection Law.

---

[138] The original text of Art. 27 of the Regulation (《中华人民共和国消费者权益保护法实施条例》第27条) reads as follows: 市场监督管理部门或者其他有关行政部门应当畅通和规范消费者投诉、举报渠道，完善投诉、举报处理流程，依法及时受理和处理投诉、举报，加强对投诉、举报信息的分析应用，开展消费预警和风险提示。

投诉、举报应当遵守法律、法规和有关规定，不得利用投诉、举报牟取不正当利益，侵害经营者的合法权益，扰乱市场经济秩序。

[139] China unveils regulations on implementation of consumer rights protection law, https://english.www.gov.cn/policies/latestreleases/202403/19/content_WS65f974b2c6d0868f4e8e53d1.html#:~:text=Effective%20on%20July%201%2C%202024,and%20protection%20of%20consumers'%20personal, accessed on Jan 20, 2025.

[140] Ibid.

[141] The Chongyang Municipality Market Supervision Administration's unified response to the multiple complaints and reports filed by Zhang Yong, Zheng Siyuan, Chen Baolong, Zhang Huachao, and others against the operators in Chongyang. 崇阳市市场监督管理局关于张勇、郑思远、陈宝龙、张华超等人多次投诉举报崇阳县经营者的统一回复。

Notably, Article 12 of the SPC Judicial Interpretation on Several Issues Concerning the Application of Law in the Trial of Punitive Damages Disputes for Food and Drug Cases[142] expressly stipulates that:

> If a purchaser knowingly buys food that does not meet food safety standards and requests the producer or seller to pay ten times the purchase price as punitive damages in accordance with the second paragraph of Article 148 of the Food Safety Law, the people's court should legally support the purchaser's claim within the scope of reasonable daily consumption needs. The court may consider factors such as the product's shelf life and the typical consumption habits of ordinary consumers to determine the reasonable quantity of food required for the purchaser's daily consumption.[143]

In order to determine whether a person purchases food for personal or family consumption needs (购买者因个人或者家庭生活消费需要购买的食品) stipulated in Article 1 of the SPC Judicial Interpretation on Several Issues Concerning the Application of Law in the Trial of Punitive Damages Disputes for Food and Drug Cases, Articles 13 and 14 further explain that if the buyer knowingly purchases food that does not meet food safety standards multiple times within a short period (短时间内多次购买) and repeatedly files lawsuits requesting punitive damage compensation under Article 148 of the Food Safety Law, the people's court may support their claim within the scope of reasonable daily consumption needs.[144] Accordingly, the following factors are relevant in determining whether the purchase exceeds the daily consumption needs: (a) the typical consumption habits of ordinary consumers; (b) the buyer's purchase frequency in a short period; (c) the quantity and amount of food purchased; and (d) the buyer's frequency in filing litigation. If a buyer makes multiple purchases within a short period in large quantities or amounts, according to the usual habits of ordinary consumers, or frequently uses litigation to claim consumer fraud and punitive damages from businesses, these purchases may be considered as exceeding reasonable daily consumption needs.

[142] The Interpretation on Several Issues Concerning the Application of Law in the Trial of Punitive Damages Disputes for Food and Drug Cases issued by the Supreme People's Court, which came into effect on August 22, 2024. http://www.gaowenlawyer.com/index.php?id=144, accessed on Jan 20, 2025.

[143] 《最高人民法院关于审理食品药品惩罚性赔偿纠纷案件适用法律若干问题的解释》第十二条:购买者明知所购买食品不符合食品安全标准，依照食品安全法第一百四十八条第二款规定请求生产者或者经营者支付价款十倍的惩罚性赔偿金的，人民法院应当在合理生活消费需要范围内依法支持购买者诉讼请求。

人民法院可以综合保质期、普通消费者通常消费习惯等因素认定购买者合理生活消费需要的食品数量。

[144] 《最高人民法院关于审理食品药品惩罚性赔偿纠纷案件适用法律若干问题的解释》第十四条:购买者明知所购买食品不符合食品安全标准，在短时间内多次购买，并多次依照食品安全法第一百四十八条第二款规定就同一不符合食品安全标准的食品起诉请求同一生产者或者经营者支付惩罚性赔偿金的，人民法院应当在合理生活消费需要范围内依法支持其诉讼请求。

人民法院可以综合保质期、普通消费者通常消费习惯、购买者的购买频次等因素认定购买者每次起诉的食品数量是否超出合理生活消费需要

2.2.4 *Legal Nature of Dual Purpose Contracts or Mixed Contracts*

Compared to average consumers, it is controversial whether professional consumers should be classified as consumers. Similarly, it can be challenging to distinguish between professional and amateur sellers in the online trading model, especially considering the fact that the online model provides a convenient platform for many non-professionals to sell their second-hand goods.[145] In many online marketplaces, the lines between professional and amateur sellers often become blurred.[146] It might be difficult for a buyer to distinguish whether he is buying from a professional seller or from an amateur seller.[147] It is not always clear whether buyers and sellers are professional or amateur, or whether the products are used for personal household consumption.[148] Given the complex of cross-border transactions in the digital economy, the classification of professional consumers will be an ongoing issue.

A person may act as a professional in one situation and as a consumer in another situation. It is not always crystal clear whether the activity of a transaction is for private purpose or professional purpose in every situation. In modern society, it is difficult to classify a person's behavior as purely private or purely commercial, especially when the two purposes are mixed.[149] For instance, if a person purchases a camera for recording daily life as well as for commercial shooting, whether this person can be regarded as a consumer.[150] A contract concluded by a person with a combination of private purpose and professional purpose can be regarded as a mixed contract, or a dual-purpose contract. The classification of the nature of such dual purpose contracts or mixed contracts is very contentious in China. For instance, when a person's travel activities are mixed with business activities, or, a travel contract is concluded with dual purposes, one tricky question would be can these hybrid tourists be regarded as consumers and thus under the protection of more protective choice of law rules?

2.2.4.1 Primary Purpose Test in China?

In China, it is unclear whether a person must act solely for the needs of daily consumption in order to be qualified as a consumer.[151] The 'daily consumption needs' test in Article 2 Chinese Consumer Protection Law does not clarify the 'mixed

---

145 Xiao (2016), p. 98.

146 Xiao (2016), p. 98.

147 Xiao (2016), p. 98.

148 Xiao (2016), p. 98.

149 Wang (2021b), p. 7.

150 Wang (2021b), p. 7.

151 Thomas (2018), p. 304.

transactions' situation where goods or services are purchased partly for daily consumption needs and partly for business needs.[152]

In *Gu Weilong v. Xi'an Defang Investment Co., Ltd.*,[153] the plaintiff Gu Weilong participated in a business inspection tour to Japan organized by the defendant Xi'an Defang Investment Co., Ltd on the theme of 'elderly care real estate' with a price of 3, 2000 RMB (4210 Euro). The plaintiff sued the defendant for the return of travel fee on the ground of improper performance of contractual obligations.[154] The first-instance court held that the contract in nature was a travel contract for several reasons. First, the service programs provided by the defendant to the plaintiff included arranging entry and exit of borders, visas, catering and accommodation, tour buses, tour guides, attraction tickets, and other relevant issues. Second, although the defendant applied business visa for the plaintiff, most of the time spent in Japan was traveling and sightseeing. Third, the actual itinerary was different from the original one and the Japanese officials did not participate in the activities.[155]

Nevertheless, the second-instance court held that 'the contract was not a travel contract but a service contract, since it was significantly different from the travel contract stipulated by Chinese law in terms of the purpose, subject, and content of the contract (双方合同目的、主体、内容) between both parties'.[156] First, the purpose of the contract was to enable the participants to understand the relevant situation of Japanese pension real estate, not to travel to Japan for sightseeing, vacation, leisure and other forms of tourism activities.[157] Second, in terms of the content of the contract, Xi'an Defang Investment Company organized a delegation to investigate the situation of Japan's pension real estate and related pension service industry. The whole trip focused on the theme of business visit and the delegation visited many nursing homes and pension supplies exhibition halls in Japan, which is significantly different from the content of general travel contract. In this 7-day-trip to Japan, deducting the first day and the last day of the flight time, the actual inspection time is 5 days, in which two and half days were spent on four business inspection activities. The rest of the time was most spent on transportation. Visiting tourist

---

[152] Thomas (2018), p. 303.

[153] *Gu Weilong v. Xi'an Defang Investment Co., Ltd.*, Shaanxi Province Xi'an Municipality IPC, (2016) Shaan 01 Min Zhong No 3012; Shaanxi Province Xi'an Municipality Yanta DPC, (2015) Yan Min Chu Zi No 07364. 顾维龙与西安德方投资有限公司合同纠纷二审民事判决书, 陕西省西安市中级人民法院,(2016)陕01民终3012号; 西安市雁塔区人民法院(2015)雁民初字第07364号民事判决.

[154] Ibid. There were false elements in tourism product design, route arrangement and promotion (advertising, design and arrangement of the travel product was fraudulent), the tour guide did not pick up the tour group after 3 h landing of the flight, the accommodation standard did not reach five star as agreed in the contract, and no Kabukicho performances were arranged. In addition, the defendant was not professional travel organization and did not have the qualification for organizing tourism and foreign-related tourism. Thus, the service contract should be invalid and the defendant should return 23,000 RMB.

[155] Ibid.

[156] Ibid.

[157] Ibid.

attractions and shopping were only for the participants to understand the local customs and economic conditions of the Japanese society. The activity cannot be identified as a tourist activity because of the mere visit of tourist attractions.[158] Third, the participants of this inspection activities in Japan were either private entrepreneurs or senior managers of the company, which was obviously different from the tourists.[159] Fourth, GU Weilong and other members of the delegation held a short-term business visa issued by the Japanese Embassy in Beijing, not a tourist visa.[160] Fifth, Xi'an Defang Investment Company was a legal person established by law, not a tourism operator regulated under Chinese Tourism Law or Travel Agency Regulation.[161] The court held that the main purpose of the contract was not traveling but business visit.[162] The defendant organized a delegation to investigate pension real estate and related pension service industry in Japan. The activity cannot be identified as a tourist activity because of the mere interspersed tourist attraction visit.

Although the court did not establish a specific standard to examine the nature of a mixed contract, it can be seen from the reasoning that the nature of the contract is determined by the primary purpose of the contract. Still, it is debatable that the court reached a conclusion that the primary purpose of the contract was for business reasons by counting the portion of time allocated to different activities. The first-instance and second-instance courts analyze the same activity, based on different perspectives, the elements were put with different weights by different courts, and thus led to the discrepancy on the nature of the contract. Such difference implies that even if the primary purpose criterion is applied to the same case, different courts may reach different conclusions.

It remains a question whether the primary purpose criterion applied in judicial practice by the judges will be adopted by the legislature in the future. From a global perspective, the adoption of primary purpose criterion is in line with several international instruments, such as Article 3 of the UN Guidelines for Consumer Protection, Article 5(2) of the 2019 HCCH Judgments Convention and Article 2(1)

---

[158] Ibid.

[159] Ibid. 本案合同所涉及赴日考察活动的参团主体均为民营企业主或公司高级管理人员，与参加旅游团的游客存在明显不同。

[160] Ibid. 本案合同涉及的赴日考察活动中，顾维龙等所有团员持有的是日本驻北京大使馆签发的短期商用签证(商务签证)，并非旅游签证。通过本案所办理短期商用签证的情况也可看出双方合同与一般旅游合同存在明显区别。

[161] Ibid. 德方公司系依法成立的企业法人，并非旅游经营者，故不属于《中华人民共和国旅游法》、《中国公民出国旅游管理办法》及《旅行社条例》的规制对象。

[162] The trip focused on the theme of business visit and the delegation visited many nursing homes and pension supplies exhibition halls in Japan, which is significantly different from the content of general travel contract. In this 7-day-trip to Japan, deducting the first day and the last day of the flight time, the actual inspection time is 5 days, in which two and half days were spent on organizing four business inspection activities. The rest of the time was mostly spent on transportation. Visiting tourist attractions and shopping were only for the participants to understand the local customs and economic conditions of the Japanese society. 综上，本案合同的性质并非旅游合同，原审法院将涉案双方的合同认定为旅游合同有误。德方公司关于双方合同系服务合同而非旅游合同的上诉主张，本院予以支持。

(a) of the 2005 Hague Convention on Choice of Court Agreements. The 2005 Hague Convention on Choice of Court Agreements aspires to be one of the most significant private international law treaties of this century.[163] Its definition on consumer might influence many jurisdictions, including China. It is advisable for the Chinese legislator to take primary purpose criterion into account in the future when defining the notion of consumer in private international law.

2.2.4.2 Multi-party Contracts with Multiple Purposes

Apart from dual-purpose contracts, a more complicated scenario is when multiple parties who concludes the same contract with one operator have different purposes. In the context of multi-party contracts in which the parties have different purposes, the question is whose purpose should be decisive in determining the nature of the contract.

In *Zhu Kaili et al v. Guangzhou Baiyun District Fluent Education Training Centre,*[164] the four plaintiffs Zhu Kaili, Zhu Kaijia, Zhu Qingwen and Tan Peiyi signed a contract with the defendant for the plaintiff Zhu Kaili's performance on the stage to celebrate Chinese Spring Festival in the USA while other three plaintiffs accompanied Zhu Kaili as her family members. The plaintiffs sued the defendant for a refund of 64,700 RMB (8626 Euro) since the plaintiff Zhu Kaili did not perform on the stage as agreed in the contract, although they did travel to other American cities after that. The four plaintiffs held that they jointly signed the contract as one party with the defendant and the nature of such contract, in essence, was a service contract, since it was primarily about Zhu Kaili's performance on the stage of the Spring Festival Gala, although travel services were included.[165]

The defendant asserted that it had two different kinds of contractual relationships with different plaintiffs. First, the contract between Zhu Kaili and the defendant was a package travel contract, which included providing an opportunity to perform in the Spring Festival Gala, celebrating Chinese New Year with American children, visiting Disney, Hollywood and other American cities.[166] It provides a package travel contract with a series of tours, such as transportation, accommodation and entertainment, rather than a service contract. Second, it was merely a pure travel contract between the defendant and other three plaintiffs Tan Peiyi, Zhu Kaijia, Zhu Qingwen. They went to the USA only for the purpose of traveling. Since the entire itinerary of the American trip had been completed, the purpose of the travel contract

[163] Born (2021), p. 2080.

[164] *Zhu Kaili et al v. Guangzhou Baiyun District Fluent Education Training Centre*, Guangdong Province Guangzhou Municipality Baiyun DPC, (2014) Hui Yun Fa Min San Chu Zi No 15. 朱凯莉、朱凯嘉、朱庆文、谭佩仪与广州市白云区流利教育培训中心服务合同纠纷二审民事判决书, 广东省广州市中级人民法院,(2014)穗中法民四终字第137号; 广东省广州市白云区人民法院,(2014)穗云法民三初字第15号民事判决.

[165] Ibid.

[166] Ibid.

had been achieved. Thus, the request of the plaintiffs for the refund of travel expenses was unreasonable.[167]

The first-instance and second-instance courts both took the view that the contract, in nature, was a service contract (服务合同).[168] First, the concluded contract expressly stated that it included the four plaintiffs, among whom Zhu Kaili was the performer. The total price of 129,200 RMB (17,000 Euro) was the cost of the four plaintiffs' collective participation in the performance tour for the 2014 North American Spring Festival Gala.[169] Second, the participation of Zhu Kaijia, Zhu Qingwen, and Tan Peiyi, as family members of Zhu Kaili, was closely related to Zhu Kaili's performance on the stage of Spring Festival Gala. The plaintiffs chose the services provided by the defendant was also based on the condition of Zhu Kaili's performance on the stage, instead of visiting America only for the purpose of traveling.[170] Thus, the four plaintiffs had formed a service contract relationship with the defendant.[171]

This case involves a multi-party litigation in which several plaintiffs of one contract have different purposes when concluding the same contract. The defendant essentially advocated the separability or severability of the nature of the same contract between different parties. This would inevitably complicate the already tricky issue of classifying dual purpose contracts. It is not surprising that such argument is not upheld by the courts. Instead, the courts stated that the main purpose of the contract was for the performance of Zhu Kaili on the stage and other three plaintiffs, as family members, only concluded a contract with the defendant based on such

[167] Ibid. 本案中不同当事人之间存在两种不同性质合同关系，案由不应当定性为服务合同纠纷合并审理。1、流利中心与朱凯莉之间存在的是集提供登上北美国际电视春晚舞台机会以及参加校园手拉手与美国小朋友一起过新年、游玩迪斯尼、游览好莱坞、跨越旧金山、圣地亚哥、洛杉矶等城市旅行、品尝美食、提供交通、住宿等一系列游览活动的一揽子旅游合同，而非一审法院认定的提供登上北美国际电视春晚舞台机会的服务合同纠纷。2、流利中心与朱凯嘉、朱庆文、谭佩仪之间存在的是单纯的旅游合同关系。流利中心在宣传时已再三解释，本次北美之行有专人陪同，且登台的六名小朋友中，只有朱凯莉的家长和另外一名小朋友的家长选择跟团，而朱凯嘉并非演出人员也非家长，却也参与了此次旅行。可见，朱凯嘉、朱庆文、谭佩仪仅仅出于旅行的目的随团赴美，美国之行的全部行程均已游览完毕，即合同目的已经达到。在履行完毕的情况下，该三人要求退回旅游费用无理无据，一审判决没有查清事实，判决流利中心退款属于错误判决。

[168] Ibid.

[169] Ibid. 谭佩仪与流利中心签具"小明星美国星光之旅"报名表。报名表载明费用总额为129200元，包含朱凯莉、朱凯嘉、朱庆文、谭佩仪一行四人，朱凯莉为演出人员，包含住宿、交通、旅游景点门票、签证、演出人员服装、培训费用等。朱凯莉、朱凯嘉、朱庆文、谭佩仪主张该费用系朱凯莉团费35800元、朱凯嘉团费25800元、朱庆文团费33800元、谭佩仪团费33800元合计而来；流利中心主张该费用系朱凯莉团费33800元、朱凯嘉团费25800元、朱庆文团费33800元、谭佩仪团费33800元、演出服装、培训、录音制作费2000元合计而来.

[170] Ibid. 上诉人出具的《收款收据》确认上述报名费用是朱凯莉、朱凯嘉、朱庆文、谭佩仪共同参加2014年icn北美电视春晚演出之旅费用，可见，朱凯嘉、朱庆文、谭佩仪作为朱凯莉的家属参加此次旅行与朱凯莉参加演出是紧密相联的，其选择流利中心提供的服务亦是以朱凯莉参加演出为前提，因此朱凯莉、朱凯嘉、朱庆文、谭佩仪是共同作为合同的一方与流利中心形成了服务合同关系。

[171] Ibid.

precondition. The accessary purpose of the contract between the defendant and the three plaintiffs is subject to the main purpose of the contract between the plaintiff Zhu Kaili. Hence, the contract is a service contract. Just like the primary purpose criterion adopted in *Gu Weilong v. Xi'an Defang Investment Co., Ltd.*, the court also adopted main purpose criterion in *Zhu Kaili et al v. Guangzhou Baiyun District Fluent Education Training Centre*, which means the primary purpose rather than the accessary purpose of the contract determines the nature of a multi-party contract. Despite this, the court did not further clarify whether such service contract can be classified as a consumer contract.

2.2.4.3 A Dynamic Approach Towards the Time of Litigation

Prior to the determination of a dual-purpose contract, another preliminary question is which time point is decisive for examining the purpose of a contract. If a person's consumer status is to be determined by the time of conclusion of the contract, it is more predictable for the business. However, the remoteness and anonymity of online transactions make the determination of the identities of contract parties more difficult for both parties.[172] It may be difficult for a computer seller to know whether a computer buyer will use it for private purpose or business purpose. It is more likely that a person uses his or her computer for both private purpose and professional purpose. Moreover, what if the person changes his or her purpose after the conclusion of the contract? Neither Article 42 of the Chinese Conflict of Laws Act not Article 2 of the Consumer Protection Law provides a clear answer.

In *Qian Qinghua v. Lin Zhimin*,[173] Lin Zhimin borrowed 17,000 Euro from an individual lender Qian Qinghua and the legal relationship was established in Italy. The lender sued the borrower before a Chinese court for the return of the money and interests, since the borrower did not pay the debt later. The borrower Lin Zhimin argued that initially, it was not a loan, but a partnership investment fund. The lender Qian Qinghua quitted after joining the partnership and asked for the transfer of his share to her. She disagreed first and agreed later, but was unable to pay the debt. The court held that 'even though the parties initially had a creditor-debt relationship formed by the transfer of partnership rights, at the time of settlement, both parties agreed to perform the contract in accordance with the loan relationship'.[174] The defendant issued an IOU receipt to the plaintiff. Since the IOU reflected the true intention of the parties, it is thus effective.[175] The court did not invoke Article 42 of

[172] Xiao (2016), p. 98.

[173] *Qian Qinghua v. Lin Zhimin*, Zhejiang Province Ruian Municipality People's Court, [2020] She 0381 Min Chu No 1978. 钱青华与林芝民间借贷纠纷一审民事判决书，瑞安市人民法院(2020)浙0381民初1978号.

[174] Ibid. 即使原告钱青华与被告林芝最初存在合伙权益受让形成的债权债务关系，但在结算时，双方同意按借贷关系履行合同，被告由此出具借条交原告收执，该借条系当事人真实意思表示，其效力应予认定。

[175] Ibid.

the Chinese Conflict of Laws Act in determining the applicable law but referred to such provision in the last paragraph of the judgment.

The reference to Article 42 of the Chinese Conflict of Laws Act on consumer choice of law rules indicates that the court had considered the loan contract as a consumer contract based on the subsequent change of the legal relationship between the parties. It seems that the court adopted a dynamic approach by considering the nature of the contract at the time of litigation, rather than that at the time of conclusion of the contract. Regardless of whether the contract in dispute should be classified as a consumer contract or not, the fact that the court looked at the time of litigation how they would determine the parties' intention and qualify the contract has showed that the subsequent changes of the contract shall be taken into consideration. Is it also relevant to examine the parties' intention at the time of ligation for the classification of a contract? The requirement of legal certainty means that parties to a contract should be able to predict their legal positions. However, people's intention or purpose changes over time after the conclusion of the contract. The *Qian Qinghua v. Lin Zhimin* case shows that some Chinese courts have embraced a dynamic approach, albeit secondary to a static approach, in determining the nature of a contract.

2.2.4.4 Primary Purpose Criterion in Consumer Conflicts Rules?

The vagueness of the term 'daily consumption needs' in Article 2 of Chinese Consumer Protection Law does not make it easier for the classification of a consumer contract. Although both *Gu Weilong v. Xi'an Defang Investment Co., Ltd.* case and *Zhu Kaili et al v. Guangzhou Baiyun District Fluent Education Training Centre* case adopted primary purpose criterion in determining the nature of a contract, such primary purpose criterion has not been specifically prescribed in substantive law. In the absence of the word 'primarily' or 'primary', it may arguably be harder to qualify a person acting primarily for personal, household or family purposes as a consumer under Article 2 of Chinese Consumer Protection Law.[176] The lack of a definition of consumer in Article 42 of the Chinese Conflict of Laws Act makes such classification uncertain, which will inevitably derogate the function of this provision and increase legal unpredictability. If the primary purpose criterion is to be adopted in private international law, having considered the notion of consumer in Article 2 of the Consumer Protection Law, Article 3 of the UN Guidelines for Consumer Protection, Article 5(2) of the 2019 HCCH Judgments Convention as well as Article 2(1)(a) of the 2005 Hague Convention on Choice of Court Agreements, the concept of 'consumer' in Article 42 of the 2010 Chinese Conflict of Laws Act may be defined as '*a natural person who concludes a contract with*

[176] Thomas (2018), p. 304. The criteria in classifying dual purpose contracts have been discussed in Chen (2023), pp. 909–932.

another person, acting within his or her trade or profession, primarily for the purpose of private, household, family consumption'.

2.3 The Material Scope of Consumer Conflicts Rules in Chinese Judicial Practice

Since Article 42 of the Chinese Conflict of Laws Act does not explicitly state its material scope by excluding certain types of consumer contracts, whether this provision applies to all consumer contracts remains a question.[177] In Chinese judicial practice, there are only 19 judgments published on the China Judgments Online that invoke Article 42 of the Chinese Conflict of Laws Act.[178] Some of these contracts are not even classified as consumer contracts, but as service contracts, sale contracts, or loan contracts.

2.3.1 *Service Contracts*

Among these 19 judgments, 4 of them were about the dispute between Jin Bingzhou and two companies on the same dispute. In *Jin Bingzhou v. Sanhe Yanjiao Jinghua Golf Club Co., Ltd,*[179] Jin Bingzhou (English name: Dimsosik; Korean name: Kimbyeongju) signed a contract with Sanhe Yanjiao Jinghua Golf Club Company for purchasing a membership card of the club with a price of $25,000. The plaintiff claimed that the club company had transferred his membership card to another person without acknowledging him and asked for the continuing performance of the original contract. The court of first instance classified the case as 'a dispute over entertainment service contract' (娱乐服务合同纠纷). The court of second instance held that 'since the plaintiff Jin Bingzhou had a Korean nationality, it was a foreign-related civil and commercial case'.[180] Although the court did not classify the

---

[177] Liu and Zhang (2021), p. 80.

[178] Such data is collected by searching 'Article 42 of the Chinese Conflict of Laws Act' on the website China Judgments Online, the cases are uploaded until 25 May 2021.

[179] *Jin Bingzhou v. Sanhe Yanjiao Jinghua Golf Club Co., Ltd*, Hebei High People's Court, [2015] Ji Min San Zhong No 107; Hebei Province Langfang Municipality Intermediate People's Court, [2015] Lang Min San Chu Zi No 28. 金秉周与三河燕郊京华高尔夫俱乐部有限公司娱乐服务合同纠纷二审民事判决书，河北省高级人民法院，(2015)冀民三终字第107号；河北省廊坊市中级人民法院，(2015)廊民三初字第28号民事判决。

[180] Ibid, 本案上诉人金秉周系大韩民国国籍，本案为涉外民商事案件；本案双方当事人均选择适用中华人民共和国法律，故本案应适用中华人民共和国法律。 Article 1(1) of the SPC Judicial Interpretation of the Chinese Conflict of Laws Act stipulates what constitutes a foreign element.

contract as a consumer contract specifically, it did refer to Article 42 of the Chinese Conflict of Laws Act to determine the applicable law.[181]

Similarly, in *Xiao Rongzhao v. Zhongshan Tiffany Beauty & Hair Co., Ltd*,[182] Xiao Rongzhao, a resident of Hong Kong, domiciled in Hong Kong, initially bought a membership card of Zhongshan Tony Beauty Salon Center to enjoy beauty salon services there. The salon center was closed later and its members were informed to go to the defendant Zhongshan Tiffany Beauty & Hair Company to use the membership card. The defendant asked the plaintiff to top up 500 RMB to use the original membership card. The plaintiff Xiao Rongzhao, under the strong recommendation of the defendant, also bought the lifetime membership card of Tiffany (4500 RMB), moxibustion treatment (1980 RMB) and bathing treatment (2000 RMB) later. In 2017, the stores of the Tiffany Company were closed suddenly and the plaintiff Xiao Rongzhao did not have chance to use the prepaid money. Thus, the plaintiff filed a lawsuit against the Tiffany Company and its sole shareholder, Jia Meifu, before the court asking for the refund of prepaid 8980 RMB (1283 Euro). The court classified the case as 'a Hong Kong-related dispute over a service contract' (涉港服务合同纠纷) and referred to Article 42 of the Chinese Conflict of Laws Act specifically with full citation of the provision. The court further explained that the service was provided in Mainland China and the plaintiff chose to apply the laws of Mainland China. According to Article 42 of the Chinese Conflict of Laws Act, the place where the services were provided was in China, the laws of Mainland China should be the applicable law.[183] It can be seen that the service contract in dispute was regarded as a consumer contract and subject to consumer choice of law rules. However, the court did not expressly classify the case as a consumer contract dispute. Such practice may not cause problems in this case, but a clear dividing line needs to be drawn between consumer contracts and service contracts. A consumer contract could be a service contract, but not all service contracts are consumer contracts.

In *Li Lijun v. Guangzhou Yiyan Jiuding Catering Co., Ltd., et al*,[184] the court also did not classify the contract as a consumer contract but referred directly to consumer

---

[181] *Jin Bingzhou v. Huatang Yuanfang International Co., Ltd.*, Hebei High People's Court, [2015] Ji Min San Zhong No 108; Hebei Province Langfang Municipality Intermediate People's Court, [2015] Lang Min San Chu Zi No 27. 金秉周与华堂圆方国际有限公司娱乐服务合同纠纷二审民事判决书，河北省高级人民法院，(2015)冀民三终字第108号；河北省廊坊市中级人民法院，(2015)廊民三初字第27号民事判决。

[182] *Xiao Rongzhao v. Zhongshan Tiffany Beauty & Hair Co., Ltd*, Guangdong Province Zhongshan Municipality the First People's Court, [2017] Yue 2071 Min Chu No 1229. 萧容兆与中山市帝芙尼美容美发有限公司、贾美福服务合同纠纷一审民事判决书，广东省中山市第一人民法院，(2017)粤2071民初1229号 。

[183] Ibid, 依照《中华人民共和国涉外民事关系法律适用法》第四十二条…的规定，涉案服务提供地在内地，原告选择适用内地法律，因此本案服务合同纠纷应适用我国内地法律作为准据法进行裁决。

[184] *Li Lijun v. Guangzhou Yiyan Jiuding Catering Co., Ltd., et al*, Guangdong Province Guangzhou Municipality Intermediate People's Court, [2015] Hui Zhong Fa MIn Si Zhong Zi No 134; Guangdong Province Guangzhou Municipality Panyu District People's Court, [2015] Hui Pan Fa MIn Si Chu Zi No 12. 李丽君与广州市一盐酒鼎餐饮有限公司、李丹、赵平昭餐饮服务合同

choice of law rules. Specifically, the plaintiff Li Lijun was hospitalized for 2 days because of food poisoning after dining at the restaurant of the defendant Guangzhou Yiyan Jiuding Catering Co., Ltd. The catering company was operated by Li Dan, a resident of Hong Kong, and Zhao Pingzhao, without obtaining a catering service permit. The plaintiff was also pregnant for about 30 weeks and the food poisoning accident had caused great physical and mental damage to her. Thus, the plaintiff filed a lawsuit against the company and two operators for a compensation for physical and mental damages. The court of first instance held that the case was 'a dispute caused by personal injury suffered in the process of catering service'(在餐饮服务过程中遭受人身损害引起的纠纷). The court of second instance classified the case as 'a Hong Kong-related dispute', and should be addressed as 'a foreign-related commercial case'.[185] The court then referred to Article 42 of the Chinese Conflict of Laws Act and invoked the full text of it. The court further explained that 'since the food involved in this case was prepared and consumed in the Mainland China, and Li Lijun, as a consumer, voluntarily chose the laws of Mainland China as the governing law for dispute resolution, the laws of Mainland China should apply'.[186] Clearly, the catering service contract in dispute was protected as a consumer contract, although the court did not specifically classify such service contract as a consumer contract.

By contrast, in another case *Liu Mou v. Xiamen Education Technology Co., Ltd*,[187] the court expressly classified the case involving a service contract as a foreign-related dispute over consumer contract, and then referred to Article 42 of the Chinese Conflict of Laws Act. Specifically, Liu Mou, represented by his mother, signed a 'Magic Classroom Course Service Agreement' with Xiamen Education Technology Company for an annual courses with a total price of 25,000 RMB (3289 Euro). The company ceased operation after Liu taking 41 out of 264 class hours and the remaining tuition fee was 21,117 RMB (2778 Euro). Liu brought legal proceedings before the court for the refund of the remaining tuition fee. The court held that 'Liu was an American citizen, the case was a foreign-related dispute over consumer contract'(涉外消费者合同纠纷).[188] The court further explained that

纠纷2015民四终134二审民事裁定书，广东省广州市中级人民法院，(2015)穗中法民四终字第134；广东省广州市番禺区人民法院(2015)，穗番法民四初字第12号民事判决。

[185] Ibid. 本院认为，李丹是香港居民，本案属于涉港纠纷，应参照涉外商事案件处理。

[186] Ibid. 依照《中华人民共和国涉外民事关系法律适用法》第四十二条规定:"消费者合同，适用消费者经常居所地法律；消费者选择适用商品、服务提供地法律或者经营者在消费者经常居所地没有从事相关经营活动的，适用商品、服务提供地法律。"因涉案食品的生产消费地在中华人民共和国内地，且李丽君作为消费者自愿选择中华人民共和国内地法律作为解决纠纷的准据法，故本案应适用中华人民共和国内地法律作为准据法。

[187] *Liu Mou v. Xiamen Education Technology Co., Ltd*, Fujian Province Xiamen Municipality Intermediate People's Court, [2020] Min 02 Min Chu No 394. 刘某与厦门魔力课堂教育科技有限公司合同纠纷一审民事判决书，福建省厦门市中级人民法院，(2020)闽02民初394号。

[188] Ibid. 本院认为，原告刘某系美利坚合众国公民，本案属涉外消费者合同纠纷，因原告经常居所地、被告注册地与教育培训服务提供地均在中华人民共和国境内，根据《中华人民共和国涉外民事关系法律适用法》第四十二条规定:"消费者合同，适用消费者经常居所地法律；消费者选择适用商品、服务提供地法律或者经营者在消费者经常居所地没有从事

'since the plaintiff's habitual residence, the defendant's place of registration and the provision of education and training services were all within the territory of the People's Republic of China, in accordance with Article 42 of the Chinese Conflict of Laws Act, Chinese law should be applicable.' Although the court also stated that 'the parties in this case form a legal and effective education and training contractual relationship' (双方之间形成合法有效的教育培训合同关系), it is apparently that such education and training contract was classified as a consumer contract. Such classification is correct and consistent with the application of consumer choice of law rule. The judgment of *Liu Mou v. Xiamen Education Technology Co., Ltd* has set a good example for other Chinese courts regarding the classification of consumer contract and the reference to consumer choice of law rule.

2.3.2 Sale Contracts

There are five sale contracts which refer to Article 42 of the Chinese Conflict of Laws Act. In *Li Xiangqun v. Jiang Weifang*,[189] the plaintiff, a resident of Taiwan, bought some wood floorboard from a shop owned by the defendant Jiang Weifang in mainland China for the purpose of renovating her house. The plaintiff sued the defendant for refund and compensation on the ground that the type of the woods delivered were not the same type as agreed between the parties. The court of second instance classified the case as 'a dispute over a sale contract'(买卖合同纠纷) and invoked Article 42 of the Chinese Conflict of Laws Act with full text.[190] The court further analyzed that 'although the habitual residence of consumer Li Xiangqun in this case is in Taiwan, Jiang Yijun and Jiang Weifang, the suppliers of goods, have not engaged in relevant business activities in Taiwan. Moreover, the consumer Li Xiangqun filed a lawsuit in Guilin, where the supplier of goods is located, and asked the product providers Jiang Yijun and Jiang Weifang to bear liability for compensation under the laws of Mainland China. Thus, the substantive issue of this case should be governed by the laws of the place where goods are provided, that is, the laws of Mainland China.'[191] There is no doubt that the sale contract in dispute was

相关经营活动的，适用商品、服务提供地法律"，本案应适用中华人民共和国法律。刘某与魔力课堂公司签订的《魔力课堂课程服务协议》系双方当事人的真实意思表示，内容不违反法律、行政法规的强制性规定，应认定双方之间形成合法有效的教育培训合同关系。

[189] *Li Xiangqun v. Jiang Weifang,* Guangxi Zhuangzu Autonomous Region High People's Court, [2016] Gui Min Zhong No 34; Guilin Municipality Intermediate People's Court, [2015] Gui Shi MIn San Chu Zi No 18. 李湘群、蒋为芳买卖合同纠纷二审民事判决书，广西壮族自治区高级人民法院，(2016)桂民终34号；桂林市中级人民法院，(2015)桂市民三初字第18号民事判决。

[190] Ibid.

[191] Ibid. 本院认为，本案为买卖合同纠纷，本案上诉人李湘群为台湾地区居民，而台湾地区与大陆为同一国家之内的不同法域，其法律冲突问题应当参照我国涉外法律的相关规定进行审理。根据《中华人民共和国涉外民事关系法律适用法》第四十二条"消费者合同，适用消费者经常居所地法律；消费者选择适用商品、服务提供地法律或者经营者在消费者

treated as a consumer contract by referring to consumer choice of law rules, although the court did not specifically classify the sale contract as a consumer contract. More importantly, the court analyzed the criterion of targeting test by stating that the suppliers of goods have not engaged in relevant business activities in Taiwan. Even if the consumer's habitual residence was in Taiwan, the law of the place where the goods were provided applies under Article 42 Chinese Conflict of Laws Act. This analysis shows how Article 42 should be interpreted and applied in judicial practice.

In *Yuanyang Paint Co., Ltd v. Li Xingcai*,[192] Li Xingcai, domiciled in China, bought some materials from a paint company registered in Vietnam but did not pay the price. The Vietnam company sued the Chinese plaintiff before a Chinese court. The court classified the contract as a sale contract and the case as a foreign-related civil case. Such sale contract was not specifically characterized as a consumer contract, but Article 42 of the Chinese Conflict of Laws Act on consumer applicable law rules was referred to and the buyer Li Xingcai's consumer status was emphasized.[193] Likewise, in *Li Zhao v. Lizhu Construction Material Co., Ltd, et al*,[194] Li Zhao concluded a contract with Yu Feng, an individually-owned business, for purchasing some renovation materials. Yu Feng rent a business place at a shopping mall owned by Jinan Hongxing Company and signed an agency contract with Tian'an Company, which had been authorized by Lizhu Company to sell its products. Because of quality issues over the products delivered by the individual business Yu Feng, the consumer Li Zhao decided to sue the seller Yu Feng, the agency Tian'an Company and the producer *Lizhu Construction Material Co., Ltd* (a foreign business) before the court for compensation. The court of first instance classified the contract as 'a sale

经常居所地没有从事相关经营活动的，适用商品、服务提供地法律的规定"，虽然本案消费者李湘群的经常居所地在台湾地区，但商品的提供者蒋艺君、蒋为芳在台湾地区并未从事相关经营活动，且李湘群在商品提供者所在地桂林提起本案诉讼，根据大陆法律要求商品提供者蒋艺君、蒋为芳承担赔偿责任，故本案的实体处理应当适用商品提供地法律即大陆法律。

[192] *Yuanyang Paint Co., Ltd v. Li Xingcai,* Chongqing Free Trade District's People's Court, [2019] Yu 0192 Min Chu No 17788. 李永康远洋油漆投资有限责任公司与李兴才买卖合同纠纷一审民事判决书， 中华人民共和国重庆自由贸易试验区人民法院民事判决书， (2019)渝0192民初17788号.

[193] Chinese law was applied as the law of the consumer's habitual residence. 本院认为，远洋油漆公司系越南注册成立的公司，本案属于涉外民事案件。《中华人民共和国涉外民事关系法律适用法》第四十二条规定:消费者合同，适用消费者经常居住地法律。本案中，李兴才系中国公民，其住所地位于重庆市合川区，目前没有证据证明李兴才的经常居住地与住所地不一致，因此应当以住所地为准。本案系买卖合同纠纷，诉争对象为货物买卖，而李兴才属于货物的买方，其身份属于消费者。综上，本案应当适用中华人民共和国法律。

[194] *Li Zhao v. Lizhu Construction Material Co., Ltd, et al*, Shandong Province Jinan Municipality Intermediate's People's Court, [2020] Lu 01 Min Zhong No 8395; Jinan Municipality Tianqiao District People's Court, [2019] Lu 0105 Min Chu No 1689. 于峰与李照等买卖合同纠纷二审民事判决书， 山东省济南市中级人民法院民事判决书,(2020)鲁01民终8395号；李照与济南红星美凯龙世博家居生活广场有限公司等买卖合同纠纷一审民事判决书
山东省济南市天桥区人民法院，(2020)鲁0105民初1689号。

contract' (买卖合同) and referred to Article 42 of the Chinese Conflict of Laws Act. The court analyzed that 'since the provision of the goods was in Mainland China, in accordance with Article 42 of the Chinese Conflict of Laws Act, the dispute over the sale contract shall be governed by the laws of Mainland China'.[195] Despite the fact that the court merely characterized the case as a sale contract, the reference to consumer choice of law rules and the following analysis indicate that this sale contract was in essence considered as a consumer contract. Chinese law was applied on the basis that the place where the goods were provided was in China.

Moreover, consumer choice of law rules also apply to distance contracts concluded online. In *Wang Zhihao v. Li Guanhui*,[196] the plaintiff Wang Zhihao, a resident from Taiwan, domiciled in Guangdong, bought some clothes from an online shop owned by the defendant Li Guanhui, domiciled in Guangzhou, China. The plaintiff sued the defendant before the court for a refund because of delivery issues. The court characterized the case as 'a Taiwan-related dispute over an online shopping contract'(涉台网络购物合同纠纷) and invoked Article 42 of the Chinese Conflict of Laws Act in full text. Pursuant to consumer choice of law rules, the court analyzed that 'Wang Zhihao's habitual residence and the place where goods involved in the case are provided are both in mainland China. Wang Zhihao also chooses to apply the law of mainland China, so this case is governed by the law of mainland China'.[197] Again, the court did not specifically classify the contract as a consumer contract but referred to consumer choice of law rules.

Another online sale contract was *Hong Zhifu v. Guangdong Southern Shopping Co., Ltd, et al.*[198] Hong Zhifu, a resident of Hong Kong, bought several bottles of wine labeled as Extra.XO, produced in France, from Guangdong Southern Shopping Company for 3720 RMB. After scanning the QR code, Hong Zhifu found out that the place of production varied from America, Germany, France to even Jingdong, a Chinese E-commerce platform. Such wine was from the agent Shenzhen Trade Company and sold by Guangdong Southern Shopping Company via online pro-

---

[195] Ibid. 本案骊住通世泰建材(大连)有限公司系有限责任公司是外国法人独资企业。依照《中华人民共和国涉外民事关系法律适用法》第四十二条，涉案商品提供地在内地，本案买卖合同纠纷应适用我国内地法律作为准据法进行裁决。

[196] *Wang Zhihao v. Li Guanhui,* Guangzhou Internet Court, [2019] Yue 0192 Min Chu No 11265. 王志豪与李官辉网络购物合同纠纷一审民事判决书，广州互联网法院，(2019)粤0192民初11265号。

[197] Ibid. 本院认为，王志豪系台湾地区居民，本案为涉台网络购物合同纠纷。…《中华人民共和国涉外民事关系法律适用法》第四十二条规定:"消费者合同，适用消费者经常居所地法律；消费者选择适用商品、服务提供地法律或者经营者在消费者经常居所地没有从事相关经营活动的，适用商品、服务提供地法律。"王志豪经常居所地及涉案商品提供地均为中国大陆，王志豪亦选择适用大陆法律，故本案以大陆法律为准据法。

[198] *Hong Zhifu v. Guangdong Southern Shopping Co., Ltd, et al,* Guangdong Province Guangzhou Municipality Intermediate People's Court, [2018] Yue 01 Min Zhong No 21210; Guangdong Province Guangzhou Municipality Panyu District People's Court, [2017] Yue 0113 Min Chu No 6741. 洪致福、广东南方家庭购物有限公司合同纠纷二审民事判决书, 广东省广州市中级人民法院,(2018)粤01民终21210号; 广东省广州市番禺区人民法院，(2017)粤0113民初6741号民事判决。

grams. The court of first instance held that Hong Zhifu was a resident of Hong Kong, this case was 'a Hong Kong-related contract dispute'(涉港合同纠纷). It is noticeable that the court did classify the case as a 'consumption contract' (消费合同纠纷), instead of 'a consumer contract'(消费者合同). Regarding the issue of the applicable law, the court held that according to the provisions of Article 42 of the Chinese Conflict of Laws Act, the place where goods were provided was in mainland China. Moreover, Hong Zhifu did not submit evidence to the court of first instance to prove which place was his habitual residence. Thus, the court did not use Hong Zhifu's habitual residence as a connecting factor to determine the applicable law. Instead, the court held that since Hong Zhifu expressly chose to apply the law of the place where the goods were provided, the law of mainland China should be the applicable law.'[199] By contrast, the court of second instance merely classified the case as 'a Hong Kong-related civil and commercial case' (涉港民商事纠纷案件), rather than a consumer contract, although consumer choice of law rules were also invoked. The court of second instance analyzed that 'since both parties expressly choose the law of the provision of goods, the law of Mainland China shall be the governing law under Article 42 of the Chinese Conflict of Laws Act'.[200] The court referred to the law chosen by both parties, although Article 42 of the Chinese Conflict of Laws Act merely grants unilateral party autonomy to the consumer. When it comes to the burden of proof on substantive issues, the court of second instance did expressly state that it is 'a consumer contract dispute'(消费者合同纠纷).[201] In spite of the different classification given by the first-instance and second-instance courts, the sale contract in dispute was eventually regarded as a consumer contract.

2.3.3 Loan Contracts

Apart from service contracts and sale contracts, some loan contracts are also protected as consumer contracts. In *Xie Shixiong v. Qiu Lijuan et al*,[202] the borrower Qiu Lijuan singed a loan agreement with the lender Xie Shixiong and the guarantors

[199] Ibid. 原审法院认为:洪致福为香港公民，本案是涉港合同纠纷，参照涉外案件进行处理。本案是消费性合同纠纷，可按照合同之诉及侵权之诉确认管辖，洪致福购买案涉产品的收货地址在番禺，即侵权行为地在番禺，故原审法院对本案有管辖权。关于本案适用法律的问题，根据《中华人民共和国涉外民事关系法律适用法》第四十二条的规定，本案商品提供地在我国内地，洪致福未向原审法院提交证据证明其经常居所地，并明确选择适用商品提供地法律，故原审法院确认我国内地法律作为解决本案争议的准据法。

[200] Ibid. 本院认为，洪致福是香港特别行政区居民，本案属于涉港民商事纠纷案件，应参照涉外商事案件处理。讼争各方均明确选择适用商品提供地法律，根据《中华人民共和国涉外民事关系法律适用法》第四十二条的规定，本院确认我国内地法律作为准据法。

[201] Ibid. 洪致福以消费者合同纠纷作为案由提起诉讼，根据《中华人民共和国民事诉讼法》第六十四条第一款的规定:"当事人对自己提出的主张，有责任提供证据。"

[202] *Xie Shixiong v. Qiu Lijuan et al*, Guangdong Province Foshan Municipality Intermediate People's Court, [2018] Yue 06 Min Chu No 177. 谢世雄与邱丽娟、林昌华民间借贷纠纷一审

Lin Changhua, Songben Company and Gudi Company for 10 million RMB (1.4 million Euro).[203] The lender sued the borrower and the guarantors before the court because the borrower failed to pay the money and interest as agreed. The court classified the case as a private lending dispute. The defendant Lin Changhua, as a guarantor, was a Canadian citizen. The court, based on such foreign-related element, classified the case as 'a foreign-related civil dispute' (涉外民事纠纷). The court continued with the determination of applicable law. The place where the transfer in the loan agreement took place was within the territory of China, and the debt guaranteed by Lin Changhua as a guarantor was a loan between Chinese citizens. Moreover, during the trial, Xie Shixiong expressly chose to apply the laws of China, and none of the parties raised any objections. Therefore, this case shall be tried under the laws of China.[204] It is noticeable that the court did not refer to any specific provision in determining the choice of law issues, but in the last paragraph of the judgment, the court invoked Article 42 of the Chinese Conflict of Laws Act, among all other relevant legal provisions. The reference to consumer choice of law rules and the analysis of choice of law may indicate that a loan contract between two individuals is protected as a consumer. It is questionable whether such loan contract should be regarded as a consumer contract, considering the fact that the court did not analyze the capacity of both parties and the purpose of the loan contract. Another loan contract which was protected as a consumer contract by reference to Article 42 of the Chinese Conflict of Laws Act is *Qian Qinghua v. Lin Zhimin*, which has been discussed above (at Sect. 2.2.4.3).

2.3.4 Limited Categories of Contracts Are Protected as Consumer Contracts

In Chinese judicial practice, based on the cases published online, only very limited categories of contracts which involve a foreign element are protected as consumer contracts. Some cases that refer to Article 42 of the Chinese Conflict of Laws Act involve contracts that are actually not expressly included in the material scope.[205] The material scope of consumer choice of law rules in China is very

民事判决书, 民间借贷纠纷, 中华人民共和国广东省佛山市中级人民法院民事判决书,(2018)粤06民初177号。The other two defendants Lin Changhua and Matsumoto Electric Company (林昌华、广东松本电工公司) are the guarantors for Qiu Lijuan's debts.

[203] The court did not specify what is the purpose of this loan contract. It is unclear whether this 10 million RMB is for private purpose or professional purpose.

[204] Ibid. 本院认为， 本案为民间借贷纠纷。被告林昌华为加拿大国公民，本案具有涉外因素，属于涉外民事纠纷，应当适用涉外民事诉讼程序的特别规定审理。案涉《借款协议》中所涉转账行为发生地即借款行为发生在中华人民共和国境内，林昌华作为担保人所担保的债务为中华人民共和国公民之间所发生的借款；庭审中，谢世雄明确选择适用中华人民共和国法律，且各方当事人均未提出异议，故，本案适用中华人民共和国法律审理。

[205] Jiang (2019), p. 28.

narrow. There might be more cases not published online, but there are only 19 cases published on China Judgments Online over 11 years that expressly invoke Article 42 of the Chinese Conflict of Laws Act since its enactment in 2010. This limited case law shows that consumer choice of law rules in Article 42 of the Chinese Conflict of Laws Act have been underused in judicial practice. In my view, this unsatisfactory situation may be mainly attributed to the absence of the definition of the basic and core concepts of consumer and consumer contracts. The limited material scope of consumer contracts in judicial practice gives rise to the question of whether current material scope should be expanded, and if so, which kind of consumer contract should be included in the material scope. For instance, it is unclear whether package travel contracts and timeshare contracts are protected as consumer contracts. It may argue that travel service is not a daily consumption service under the definition of Article 2 of the Consumer Protection Law and thus tourists are not protected as consumers under Article 42 of the Chinese Conflict of Laws Act. In judicial practice, almost all foreign-related contracts involving package travel tourists and timeshare tourists are not considered as consumer contracts, as discussed below.

2.3.5 Excluded Package Travel Contracts and Timeshare Contracts

Tourists who travel abroad are more vulnerable than other consumers because they are in a foreign country with a different language, culture and legal system for a short period of time. There are four types of consumer vulnerability: technical vulnerability (the lack of knowledge regarding goods or services), legal vulnerability (the lack of legal knowledge), factual vulnerability (the lack of consumer economic, physical or even psychological capacity), and informational vulnerability (the lack of information concerning the goods or services that may influence consumers' choice).[206] The vulnerability of tourist consumers in cross-border litigation justifies the application of protective consumer choice of law rules.[207] Tourists, as individuals who conclude contracts with travel service providers for private, household or family purposes, should be protected as consumers in private international law.

[206] Lima (2018), pp. 25, 155.

[207] Lima (2018), pp. 158–171.

In judicial practice, Chinese courts classified a package travel contract as a civil contract, service contract, travel contract,[208] or even a commercial contract,[209] but not as a consumer contract.[210] Accordingly, general contract choice of law rules laid down in Article 41 of the Chinese Conflict of Laws Act apply, which designates first the law chosen by the parties, second the law of the country having the closest connection or best reflects the characteristic performance of the contractual obligation. Such conflicts rule fails to distinguish consumer contracts from commercial contracts and applies to all contracts. It does not offer tourist consumers with more favorable choice of law rules. Since package travel contracts and timeshare contracts are not expressly included in the material scope of consumer contracts, Article 42 of the Chinese Conflict of Laws Act does not play a role in protecting tourists.

In China, cruise tour contracts are not regarded as consumer contracts. In *Jiang Mou v. Royal Caribbean Cruises Company*,[211] the plaintiff Jiang Mou sued the two defendants RCL Cruises Ltd. and Zhejiang International Cooperative Travel Agency (Shanghai branch for a compensation of 141,527.84 RMB (20,218 Euro)) for her injury caused by the slippery floor on the cruise board. The plaintiff and her husband signed an outbound travel contract with the International Cooperative Travel Agency for a 5-day-4-night cruise travel from Shanghai to Okinawa, Japan. The court held that the outbound travel contract concluded between the plaintiff and the International Cooperative Travel Agency was a package travel contract. Nevertheless, the court did not further classify such package travel contract as a consumer contract. In *Huo Mou v. Sichuan China International Travel Agency*,[212] the first-instance

[208] The concept of travel contract is not equivalent to the notion of package travel contract nor consumer contract. In judicial practice, a travel contract may refer to a commission contract between commercial parties, a general service contract, or a package travel contract. In *Liu Chengqin v. Shenzhen Jiuzhou International Travel Agency*, the Shengdian Law Firm in which the 14 plaintiffs worked concluded a group outbound travel contract with the Shenzhen Jiuzhou International Travel Agency for a 6-day-5-night tour on a cruise ship to Japan. The court held that the case was a foreign-related travel contract dispute. Guangdong Shenzhen Qianhai Cooperation Zone People's Court, (2020) Yue 0391 Min Chu No 1620-1633. 刘承琴民事裁定书, 广东省深圳前海合作区人民法院,(2020)粤0391民初1620-1633号.

[209] In *Hu Siyuan et al v. Zhongnan International Travel*, the plaintiffs Hu Siyuan, Shu Sicong and five other tourists sued the defendant Zhongnan International Travel for the refund of travel fee for a 10-day-9-night travel in Australia. The court held that since the plaintiff Shu Sicong was a Hong Kong resident, the case should be regarded as foreign-related civil and commercial contract dispute. Hubei Province Wuhan Municipality Jiang'an DPC, (2018) 0102 Min Chu No 5680. 胡某、束某等与中南国际旅游湖北有限责任公司旅游合同纠纷一审民事裁定书, 湖北省武汉市江岸区人民法院,(2018)鄂0102民初5680号.

[210] Chen (2020), p. 217.

[211] *Jiang Mou v. Royal Caribbean Cruises Company*, Shanghai HPC, (2018) Hu Min Zhong No 85; Shanghai Maritime Court, (2017) Hu 72 Min Chu No 136. 上诉人蒋某某与上诉人皇家加勒比RCL游轮有限公司、被上诉人浙江省国际合作旅行社有限公司上海分公司海上人身损害责任纠纷案二审民事判决书, 上海市高级人民法院,(2018)沪民终85号; 上海海事法院,(2017)沪72民初136号.

[212] *Huo Mou et al v. Sichuan China International Travel Agency*, Shanghai First Intermediate People's Court, (2020) Hu 01 Min Zhong No 2977; Shanghai Changning DPC, (2019) Hu 0105 Min Chu No 16692. 四川省中国国际旅行社有限责任公司与李金发等生命权、健康权、身

court and appellate court also held that the travel contract in dispute, which included several travel services such as transportation, accommodation and catering, should be classified as a package travel contract. However, the courts did not further clarify whether package travel tourists should be protected as consumers with favorable choice of law rules provided in Article 42 of the Chinese Conflict of Laws Act.

Timeshare contracts are also not protected as consumer contracts. In *Wei Hong and An Yu v. Xi'an Diyawei Travel Tourism Project Development Co., Ltd., et al*,[213] the plaintiffs Wei Hong and An Yu, domiciled in Shaanxi Province, sued the defendants (1) Xi'an Diyawei Travel Tourism Project Development Co., Ltd., domiciled in Shaanxi, (2) Now Vacations, Co., Ltd., domiciled in HongKong, and (3) Hambesi Hotel Development (Shanghai) Co., Ltd., domiciled in Pudong, Shanghai. The plaintiffs signed a contract with the first and second defendants for being a member of the second defendant in order to participate travel activities organized by the second defendant in Thailand, Europe, Bali and other places. According to the contract, the membership price was 88,000 RMB and the plaintiffs had the right of 1-week vacation accommodation per year from January 2017 to December 2046. The court held that the second defendant was a company established in Hong Kong, thus the contract dispute was Hong Kong-related. The court referred to Article 41 of the Chinese Conflict of Laws Act directly without classifying the timeshare contract as a consumer contract.[214] The application of general contract choice of law rules to timeshare contracts is debatable.

It is questionable that package travel contracts and timeshare contracts are not protected as consumer contracts in judicial practice. In my view, tourists, including package tourists and timeshare tourists, who are individuals receiving tourism services for private, family or household purposes are qualified as consumers. Package travel contracts and timeshare contracts therefore should be protected as consumer contracts.[215] In particular, with the prevalence of E-commerce, it is easier for foreign travel service providers to sell their tourism products via Internet to tourists domiciled in China.[216] Tourists who travel abroad often find themselves in a foreign country with a foreign language, foreign culture and foreign legal system. They may expect that their home law will apply once disputes arise, as the foreign business has conducted commercial activities in their home country and is supposed to be familiar with the consumers' home law. Since tourists traveling to a foreign country are usually ignorant about the foreign law, the application of the tourist's home law may

体权纠纷二审案件二审民事判决书, 上海市第一中级人民法院,(2020)沪01民终2977号; 上海市长宁区人民法院,(2019)沪0105民初16692号.

[213] *Wei Hong and An Yu v. Xi'an Diyawei Travel Tourism Project Development Co., Ltd., et al*, Shaanxi Province Xi'an Municipality IPC, (2017) Shaan 01 Min Chu No 977. 魏红、安雨与西安地亚唯旅游项目开发有限公司、现代度假有限责任公司等确认合同效力纠纷一审民事判决书, 陕西省西安市中级人民法院 (2017)陕01民初977号。

[214] Ibid.

[215] Chen (2024b), pp. 68–69; Chen (2022), pp. 493–521; Chen (2021), pp. 879–899.

[216] Wu (2017), p. 19; 吴羿, 《沙巴沉船事件中的涉外管辖权和法律适用问题探析》, 西南政法大学法硕学术论文, 2017年, 第19页。

protect tourists' reasonable expectations. This favorable rule applies under the condition that the foreign business has targeted the tourist's home country in order to protect the business's reasonable expectation.

2.4 Conclusions

In this chapter, the main research questions are who is the consumer under consumer choice of law rules in Article 42 of the Chinese Conflict of Laws Act, what is the relation between consumer definition in substantive law and private international law, whether a legal person can be qualified as a consumer, how to interpret the term 'daily consumption needs', whether the transaction volume, economic gain, experience of a person or regularity of a person's activity is relevant to determine a person's consumer status, whether a person acting for the purpose of establishing a future business is a consumer, what is the legal nature of dual purpose contracts, which criteria is decisive to classify a dual purpose contract, what if a person changes his or her purpose after the conclusion of the contract, what is the material scope of consumer choice of law rules, what kind of contracts are considered as consumer contracts in judicial practice and whether the material scope of consumer choice of law rules is too narrow. Have these questions in mind, the following interim conclusions have been made for further research.

First, a harmonious interpretation of consumer notion is essential to ensure legal certainty and predictability, as the consumer definition is vague and subject to different interpretations in China. For the purpose of protecting the reasonable expectations of consumers and businesses, in principle, the notion of consumer in Article 42 of the Chinese Conflict of Laws Act only covers natural persons. As an exception, certain categories of small or micro businesses, such as agricultural workers, are included in the notion of consumer in China under the Chinese Consumer Protection Law. This may also apply to Article 42 of the Chinese Conflict of Laws Act. Although Article 2 of the 2016 Regulation for the Implementation of the Chinese Consumer Protection Law implies that legal persons or other organizations that purchase or use goods or receive services not for making a profit may also be protected as consumers, it was not adopted in the final text of the 2024 Regulation for the Implementation of the Chinese Consumer Protection Law. Even if the notion of consumer in Article 2 of the 2016 Regulation was adopted, the notion of consumer in Chinese private international law shall not be construed in exactly the same meaning as that in substantive law. Since the protection of consumer is a general principle in Chinese Consumer Protection Law and the consumer choice of law rules in Article 42 of the Chinese Conflict of Laws Act constitutes a derogation of general contractual choice of law rules, the notion of consumer in Article 42 of the Chinese Conflict of Laws Act should be interpreted strictly.

Second, the term 'daily consumption needs' in China can be construed as meeting a person's 'personal, family or household needs'. Whether the consumption involves luxury goods or services is irrelevant to determine whether a person is qualified as a consumer. The fact that an activity is for the professional purpose of setting up a trade in the future will deprive the consumer status of a person. This means a natural person who concludes a contract for the purpose of establishing a future business should not be protected as a consumer. The fact that a person is acting for the purpose of making a profit should not be considered as a key element to examine whether a person is a consumer. A natural person who concludes a contract in order to make a profit may also be considered as for private consumption.

Third, factors such as the economic gain and the special knowledge or expertise of a person are not relevant to determine a person's consumer status. Professional consumers, such as private investors and consumer activists, should be protected as consumers. Investing privately-held money or assets for the hope of making a profit could be considered as a private matter. Consumer activists whose main purpose is for making a profit could also be protected as consumers, as long as the purchase of goods is not for resale or other business purposes. When it comes to the distinction between a consumer and a professional, the regularity factor may serve as an evidence to disqualify a person's consumer status. For instance, a person who regularly sells second-hand products for profits may disqualify him for her as a consumer.

Fourth, as to the classification of dual purpose contracts, the Chinese judicial practice demonstrates that the nature of a dual purpose contract could rest upon the primary purpose of the contract. Accordingly, the primary purpose of a contract is decisive in determining the nature of the contract. In terms of multi-party litigation, the nature of the contract is not subject to separability. The primary purpose of one party may trump the accessary purpose of other parties. The adoption of primary purpose criterion, possibly in future legislative improvement, is also in line with several relevant international instruments. Meanwhile, since a person may change the initial private purpose to professional purpose, or vice versa, after the conclusion of the contract, a dynamic approach, albeit secondary to the static approach, should be adopted in order to make sure that consumer choice of law rules apply to the weaker party.

Having considered the consumer definition in Article 2 Chinese Consumer Protection Law and other relevant international instruments, a possible consumer definition in Article 42 of the Chinese Conflict of Laws Act may read '*a natural person who concludes a contract with another person primarily for the purpose of private, household, family consumption*'.

Fifth, the material scope of Chinese consumer choice of law rules is quite limited. In judicial practice, only some service contracts, sale contracts and loan contracts are protected as consumer contracts. Package travel contracts and timeshare contracts which should be regarded as consumer contracts are not protected as consumer contracts. This is due to the ambiguity of the core concepts of consumer and consumer contract. It is not surprising that the consumer choice of law rule in Article 42 of the Chinese Conflict of Laws Act is underused. This unsatisfactory situation gives rise to the question of whether current material scope should be expanded, and if so, which kind of consumer contract should be included in the material scope.

References

Born G (2021) The Hague Convention on choice of court agreements: a critical assessment. Univ Pa Law Rev 169:2080

Brandtstadter S (2008) Fakes: fraud, value-anxiety, and the politics of sincerity. In: Sykes K (ed) Ethnographies of moral reasoning. Palgrave Macmillan, New York, pp 139–160

Calliess GP (2020) Consumer contracts. In: Calliess GP, Renner M (eds) Rome regulations, 3rd edn. Wolters Kluwer, p 117, para. 26

Chan RSY, Young A (2016) Lack of regulatory safeguards for financial consumers in China: deficiencies in the Chinese consumer law. J Int Bank Law Regul 31:369

Chen W (2010) Legislative considerations of the Chinese Statute on the application of laws involving a foreign element in civil matters. Tsinghua Law J 3:118. 陈卫佐，《涉外民事法律适用法的立法思考》，《清华法学》，2010年第3期，第118页。

Chen W (2014) Selected problems of general provisions in private international law: the PRC perspective. In: Basedow J, Pissler K (eds) Private international law in Mainland China, Taiwan and Europe. Mohr Siebeck, p 63

Chen Z (2020) Jurisdiction and choice of law in foreign-related tourist-consumer disputes in China under the One Belt One Road Initiative. In: Wei D et al (eds) Innovation and the transformation of consumer law. Springer, p 217

Chen Z (2021) The Tango between Art. 17(3) Brussels Ibis and Art. 6(4)(b) Rome I under the Beat of Package Travel Directive. Maastricht J Eur Comp Law 6:879–899

Chen Z (2022) The Tango between the Brussels Ia Regulation and Rome I Regulation under the Beat of Directive 2008/122/EC on timeshare contracts towards consumer protection. J Private Int Law 3:493–521

Chen Z (2023) The classification of dual-purpose contracts in European private international law. Eur Rev Private Law 5:909–932

Chen Z (2024a) Tourists, consumer contracts and private international law in the EU and China. University of Groningen, pp 13–41

Chen Z (2024b) Consumer jurisdiction and choice of law rules in European and Chinese private international law. Chin J Transnatl Law 1:68–69

Du T (2011) Comments on Chinese Conflict of Laws Act. China Legal Publishing House, p 145. 杜涛:《涉外民事关系法律适用法释评》，中国法制出版社 2011 年版，第 145 页。

Fan X (2014) The law applicable to EU financial consumer contracts. Int Law Rev Wuhan Univ 16:210. 范晓亮:《欧盟金融消费者合同法律适用规则研究》，《武大国际法评论》，2014年第16卷第2期，第210页。

Fei Z (2010) Twelve issues in the legislation of private international law of China. Int Law Rev Wuhan Univ 13:207. 费宗祎，《中国国际私法立法的十二个问题》，《武大国际法评论》，2010年第13卷，第207页。

Gao H (2016) Research on the Chinese conflict of laws act. Beijing Law Press, p 55. 高宏贵,《中国涉外民事法律关系法律适用法研究》，北京法律出版社 2016 年版，第 55 页。

Huang J (2005) Private international law, 2nd edn. Beijing, p 47

Huang J (2011) The draft and explanatory notes on the application of law in foreign-related civil matters of the People's Republic of China. Renmin University of China Press, p 87. 黄进主编:《 中华人民共和国涉外民事关系法律适用法建议稿及说明》，中国人民大学出版社，2011年6月第1版，第87页。

Huang J (2014) New perspectives on private international law in the People's Republic of China. In: Basedow J, Pissler K (eds) Private international law in Mainland China, Taiwan and Europe. Mohr Siebeck, p 10

Huang W (2017) Provisions on the application of laws to foreign-related consumer contracts in China. Master's thesis, Huazhong Normal University, p 4. 黄文秀,《论我国关于涉外消费者合同法律适用之规定》，华中师范大学硕士论文, 2017年, 第4页

Huang Z (2018) Study on the consumer concept. Yangzhou University, p 12. 黄子倩,《消费者概念研究》，扬州大学硕士学位论文，2018年，第12页

Huang J, Jiang R (2011) Understanding Act of the PRC on the application of laws over foreign-related civil relationships. Law Press China, p 231. 黄进、姜茹娇，《〈中华人民共和国涉外民事关系法律适用法〉释义与分析》，法律出版社，2011年，第231页。

Jiang W (2019) Research on the application of law for international consumer contracts. Zhengzhou University, p 9. 江威:《涉外消费者合同法律适用问题研究》，郑州大学硕士论文，2019，第9页。

Kuever E (2019) If the people do not raise the issue, the officials will not investigate: moral citizenship among China's fake-fighters. J Curr Chin Aff:1. https://doi.org/10.1177/1868102619877325

Liang H (2001) Interpretation and application of Article 49 of the consumer rights protection law. People's Court Daily, 29 March 2001, p 3. 梁慧星,《消费者权益保护法第49条的解释与适用》，《人民法院报》，2001年3月29日，第3页

Lima MGS (2018) Traveller vulnerability in the context of travel and tourism contracts. Springer Nature Switzerland, pp 25, 155

Liu C (2016) Legal analysis of the concept of consumer. East China University of Political Science and Law, p 30. 刘成,《 对消费者概念的法律解析》，华东政法大学硕士学位论文, 2016年，第 30页

Liu X, Hu D (2012) Several issues arising from the judicial practice related to the "Law of application of law for foreign-related civil relations of the People's Republic of China". Chin Yearb Private Int Law Comp Law 15:41. 刘晓红，胡荻，《论我国〈涉外民事关系法律适用法〉的若干实践困境》，《中国国际私法与比较法年刊》，2012年第15卷，第41页。

Liu X, Jiang B (2004) The law applicable to foreign-related consumer contracts. Int Law Rev Wuhan Univ 4:156–176. 刘想树、江保国,《涉外消费者合同法律适用》，《武大国际法评论》，2004年第4期，第156-176页。

Liu X, Zhang Z (2021) Chinese private international law. Hart Publishing, p 80

Luo Y (2020) Study on the concept of consumer and knowingly purchasing counterfeit goods. Western J 31:51–53. 罗元骏，《"知假买假"与消费者概念界定问题研究》，《西部学刊》，2020年第31期，第51-53页。

Ma Y (2015) Deconstruction and reconstruction: new thinking of the concept of consume. Law Rev 6:30–41. 马一德:《解构与重构:"消费者"概念再出发》，《法学评论》, 2015年第6期, 第30-41页

Mankowski P, Nielsen P (2016) Jurisdiction over consumer contract: introduction to Articles 17-19. In: Magnus U, Mankowski P (eds) Brussels Ibis regulation. Otto Schmidt, p 466, para. 22

Meng Q, Dai S (2015) Criteria to define consumer. Theory Monthly 2:5–11. 孟勤国, 戴盛仪:《论"消费者"之界定要件》，《理论月刊》，2015年第2期，第5-11页

Plender R, Wilderspin M (2020) The European private international law of obligations, 5th edn. Sweet & Maxwell, p 255, para 9-013

Qu G (2011) The protection of the weaker parties in private international law. Commercial Press, p 21. 屈广清，《国际私法之弱者保护》，商务印书馆，2011年版，第21页。

Rachagan S (2010) Development and consumer law. In Ramsay G, Wilhelmsson T (eds) Handbook of research on international consumer law. Edward Elgar, p 55

Ramsay I (1989) Consumer law and policy. Weidenfeld and Nicolson Publishing, p 57

Rui G (2015) Should those who knowingly purchase fakes be protected by the consumer protection law? Contemp Law 6:68

Shen L, Lu W (1999) Legal analysis and judicial inquiry into the Wang Hai phenomenon. Law Appl 3:29. 沈玲萍，卢文道:《王海现象的法律分析与司法探究》，《法律适用》，1999年第3期，第29页。

Tang Z (2015) Electronic consumer contracts in the conflict of laws. Bloomsbury Publishing, p 359

Tang Z et al (2016) Conflict of laws in the People's Republic of China. Edward Elgar, p 233, para. 8.69

Thomas K (2014) The rebirth of the consumer activist in China: the Wang Hai phenomenon in the light of guiding case no. 23, 2014 China Guiding Cases Project

Thomas K (2018) Analysing the notion of 'consumer' in China's consumer protection law. Chin J Comp Law 6:303

Thomas K (2022) Amending China's notion of a "consumer": lessons from comparative analysis of the PRC consumer protection law. J Consumer Policy 45:438

Wan X (2011) Interpretation and application of provisions of the Chinese Conflict of Laws Act. China Legal Publishing House, p 305. 万鄂湘主编:《〈中华人民共和国涉外民事关系法律适用法〉条文理解与适用》，中国法制出版社2011年版，第305页。

Wang R (1996) On the phenomenon of Wang Hai. J Capital Normal Univ 2

Wang L (2002) The concept of consumers and the scope of consumer rights protection law. Polit Law 2:3–12. 王利明,《消费者的概念及消费者权益保护法的调整范围》，《政治与法律》，2002年第2期，第3-12页。

Wang J (2014) The theoretical construction of the introduction of the operator concept in China's commercial law. Jurist 3:75. 王建文,《我国商法引入经营者概念的理论构造》，《法学家》，2014 年第 3 期，第 75 页。

Wang F (2021a) Research on the application of law for foreign-related consumer contracts. Yanshan University, p 29. 王芳:《涉外消费者合同的法律适用研究》，燕山大学硕士论文, 2021年, 第29页。

Wang X (2021b) Study on the law applicable to foreign-related online consumer contract. Anhui University of Finance & Economics, p 7. 王璇:《我国涉外网络消费者合同的法律适用研究》，安徽财经大学硕士论文，2021年, 第7页.

Wong WWY (2012) The Panda Man and the anti-counterfeiting hero: art, activism and appropriation in contemporary China. J Visual Cult 11(1):20

Wu Y (2017) A study on the issues of jurisdiction over foreign cases and the application of law in Sabah boat sinking incident. Southwest University of Political Science and University, p 19. 吴羿，《沙巴沉船事件中的涉外管辖权和法律适用问题探析》，西南政法大学法硕学术论文，2017年，第19页。

Xiao Y (2002) Study on unified private international law in EU. Wuhan University Press, p 153. 肖永平，《欧盟统一国际私法研究》，武汉大学出版社，2002年，第153页。

Xiao W (2016) Research on the application of law for cross-border consumer contracts. Southwest University of Political Science and Law, p 18. 肖雯:《跨境消费者合同法律适用问题研究》，西南政法大学博士论文，2016年，第18页。

Xu D (2006) On formal justice and substantive justice of private international law. J East China Univ Polit Sci Law 1:67–72. 徐冬根，《论国际私法的形式正义与实质正义》，《华东政法学院学报》，2006年第1期，第67-72页。

Yu Y (2011) Analysis of Article 42 of the law on the application of laws in foreign-related civil relations - protection of consumers under Chinese private international law. Law Rev 2:68. 于颖:《〈涉外民事关系法律适用法〉第42条评析-我国国际私法对消费者之保护》，《法学评论》，2011年第2期，第68页。

Yu F (2012) On 'favor principle' in private international law. Chin Yearb Private Int Law Comp Law 15:58. 于飞，《国际私法"有利原则"之界定》，《中国国际私法与比较法年刊》，2012年第15卷，第58页。

Chapter 3
Jurisdiction Rules Over Consumer Contracts in China

3.1 Introduction

In Chinese private international law, specific jurisdiction rules over consumer contracts are absent. In the absence of a uniform statue on private international law, primary jurisdictional rules are derived from Chinese national laws, such as the Chinese Civil Procedure Law[1] and the Chinese Civil Code.[2] What are the general jurisdiction rules over a foreign-related contract? What are the grounds for Chinese courts to exercise jurisdiction over a foreign defendant? What if a foreign defendant has no domicile in China and on what basis a Chinese court may exert jurisdiction?

In China, the defendant's domicile is considered the basis for exercising jurisdiction in both domestic and foreign-related civil and commercial cases. Regarding general jurisdiction rules over foreign-related disputes, Part 4 of the Chinese Civil Procedure Law, titled 'Special Provisions on Foreign-Related Civil Procedures', outlines six basic principles for determining jurisdiction: (i) territorial jurisdiction principle, (ii) personal jurisdiction principle, (iii) exclusive jurisdiction principle, (iv) domicile principle, (v) freedom of choice principle, and (vi) principle of related location.[3]

[1] The Chinese Civil Procedure Law was enacted on 9 April 1991, amended in 2007, 2012, 2017 and 2021. The SPC Opinion on Several Questions in the Implementation of the Chinese Civil Procedure Law was issued by the SPC in 1992 to interpret the rules in the Civil Procedure Law, which was replaced by the 2015 SPC Opinion on Interpretation about the Application of the Civil Procedure Law. The amendment on 22 March 2022 has been effective since 10 April 2022. The latest 2023 amendment to the Civil Procedure Law involves 26 amendments, including 14 modified articles and 15 new additions. It will take effect on 1 January 2024.

[2] The Chinese Contract Law was modified and incorporated in the Civil Code which entered into force on 1 January 2021.

[3] Wang (2010), p. 87.

Z. Chen, *Tourists, Consumer Contracts and Private International Law in China*, Ius Gentium: Comparative Perspectives on Law and Justice 123,
https://doi.org/10.1007/978-3-031-87915-9_3

For foreign-related civil actions against a foreign defendant without domicile in China, Article 272 of the 2021 Chinese Civil Procedure Law specifies six jurisdiction grounds for Chinese courts.[4] Chinese courts may have jurisdiction over an action arising from a contractual relation or other property rights and interests in the following situations: (i) the subject matter of the action is located in China, (ii) there are seizable properties located in China, (iii) the tort occurs in China, (iv) the representative office of the defendant is located in China, (v) the place of conclusion of the contract was in China, (vi) the performance of the contract was in China.[5]

The jurisdiction rule in Article 272 of the 2021 Chinese Civil Procedure Law is simple and concise, but it may cause uncertainty and ambiguity in judicial practice.[6] First and foremost, it lacks specific conditions under which a particular jurisdiction ground shall apply. The question arises as to whether this jurisdiction rule is adequate for addressing foreign-related civil and commercial disputes, including consumer disputes. If not, what can be done to improve this provision? Furthermore, is there a need to establish a consumer jurisdiction rule, and if so, what insights can be gained from consumer choice of law rules stipulated in Article 42 of the Chinese Conflict of Laws Act? Finally, could the dis-targeting test employed in consumer choice of law rules be equally applicable in consumer jurisdiction rules?

To answer these questions, this Chapter will first explain the general jurisdiction rules over foreign-related contracts in China. It will delve into the jurisdiction rules applied in judicial practice to consumer contracts protected under the consumer choice of law rules set forth in Article 42 of the Chinese Conflict of Laws Act. Following a brief analysis of jurisdiction rules applied to consumer contracts in judicial practice, this chapter will specifically focus on what jurisdiction rules are applied to contracts that should have been protected as consumer contracts. In particular, the discussion will center on package travel contracts, which involve a

---

[4] The successor of Article 265 of the 2017 Civil Procedure Law and the predecessor of Article 276 of the 2023 Civil Procedure Law. The new provision deletes the wording 'contractual disputes or other property rights disputes' and replaces it with 'civil disputes' and 'litigation other than disputes involving personal relationships'. In addition, it adds a new jurisdiction ground, namely the 'reasonable connection' test, granting Chinese courts greater flexibility in exerting jurisdiction over disputes which have other reasonable connections with China. 《民事诉讼法(2023年修正版)》第二百七十六条：因涉外民事纠纷，对在中华人民共和国领域内没有住所的被告提起除身份关系以外的诉讼，如果合同签订地、合同履行地、诉讼标的物所在地、可供扣押财产所在地、侵权行为地、代表机构住所地位于中华人民共和国领域内的，可以由合同签订地、合同履行地、诉讼标的物所在地、可供扣押财产所在地、侵权行为地、代表机构住所地人民法院管辖。

除前款规定外，涉外民事纠纷与中华人民共和国存在其他适当联系的，可以由人民法院管辖。

[5] 《中华人民共和国民事诉讼法(2021年修正)》第二百七十二条:因合同纠纷或者其他财产权益纠纷，对在中华人民共和国领域内没有住所的被告提起的诉讼，如果合同在中华人民共和国领域内签订或者履行，或者诉讼标的物在中华人民共和国领域内，或者被告在中华人民共和国领域内有可供扣押的财产，或者被告在中华人民共和国领域内设有代表机构，可以由合同签订地、合同履行地、诉讼标的物所在地、可供扣押财产所在地、侵权行为地或者代表机构住所地人民法院管辖。

[6] Tang et al. (2016), p. 51, para.3.04.

combination of transportation, accommodation, and other travel services. The key question is which court has the competence to hear disputes related to package travel contracts? Given that this book focuses particularly on the protection of tourist consumers in private international law, the case law primarily revolves around package travel contracts. As discussed in Chap. 2, both package travel contracts and timeshare contracts should be protected as consumer contracts and thus enjoy favorable jurisdiction and choice of law rules. In the absence of a consumer jurisdiction rule in China, what are the common challenges faced by the Chinese courts and how to address these challenges? What lessons can be drawn from judicial practices and which rule can be improved to increase 'judicial credibility'[7] in practice with regard to jurisdiction over consumer contracts?

3.2 Jurisdiction Rules for Foreign-related Contracts in China

3.2.1 The Defendant's Domicile in General Jurisdiction Rules Over Domestic Cases

General jurisdiction is based on the domicile of the defendant, which means that a Chinese court has competence if the defendant has domicile in China.[8] The defendant's domicile is the main jurisdictional ground stipulated in Article 22 of the 2021 Chinese Civil Procedure Law.[9] This article stipulates that:

> a civil lawsuit brought against a citizen shall be under the jurisdiction of the people's court at the place of the defendant's domicile; if the defendant's place of domicile is inconsistent with the place of habitual residence, it shall be under the jurisdiction of the people's court at the place of habitual residence.
>
> A civil lawsuit brought against a legal person or other organization shall be under the jurisdiction of the people's court at the place where the defendant is domiciled.
>
> Where the domiciles and habitual residences of several defendants in the same lawsuit are within the jurisdiction of two or more people's courts, each of the people's courts shall have jurisdiction.[10]

[7] Xiao (2017), p. 3. 肖永平,《提升中国司法的国际公信力:共建"一带一路"的抓手》,《武大国际法评论》，2017年第1卷第1期，第3页。

[8] However, the concept of domicile differers in different countries. Tang et al. (2016), p. 73, para.3.51; Mann (1963), p. 1326; Weintraub (1965), p. 961.

[9] Article 21 of the 2017 Civil Procedure Law.

[10] The original text is《中华人民共和国民事诉讼法(2021年修正)》第二十二条:对公民提起的民事诉讼，由被告住所地人民法院管辖；被告住所地与经常居住地不一致的，由经常居住地人民法院管辖。

对法人或者其他组织提起的民事诉讼，由被告住所地人民法院管辖。

同一诉讼的几个被告住所地、经常居住地在两个以上人民法院辖区的，各该人民法院都有管辖权。

What constitutes the domicile for a legal person and a natural person? For a legal person, its domicile is determined by its principal place of business; if the principal place of business cannot be determined, the place of registration of the business is considered the legal person's domicile.[11] As for a natural person, their domicile is their place of registered residence.[12] Article 22 of the 2021 Chinese Civil Procedure Law states that when a person's habitual residence and domicile are inconsistent, the place of habitual residence takes precedence. The concept of habitual residence is defined as a place where a citizen has continuously lived for more than one year after leaving the place of residence until the filing a lawsuit, except for the place where the citizen is hospitalized for medical treatment.[13]

This general jurisdiction rule in Article 22 of the 2021 Chinese Civil Procedure Law is convenient for the defendant, reducing his burden in participating in litigation, and serves to prevent the misuse of legal procedure or vexatious lawsuits by the plaintiff.[14] However, it overlooks disparities between the parties in certain disputes, such as consumer disputes.[15]

3.2.2 General Jurisdiction Rules Over Domestic Contract Disputes

Consumer disputes are special civil disputes and thus are subject to special territorial jurisdiction rules.[16] Article 24 of the 2021 Chinese Civil Procedure Law[17] outlines the general jurisdiction rule for domestic contract disputes, stating that 'litigation arising out of contract disputes shall be under the jurisdiction of the people's court at the place where the defendant is domiciled or where the contract is performed'.[18] The claimant has the option to file a lawsuit before two or more courts

---

[11] Article 3 of the 2020 SPC Judicial Interpretation of the Civil Procedure Law.

[12] Article 3 of the 2020 SPC Judicial Interpretation of the Civil Procedure Law. The family registry system (household registration system) is unique in China. The Chinese notion of domicile of a natural person makes it difficult to sue a foreign citizen in China under general jurisdiction rule, since a foreign citizen is usually not registered in Chinese family system. The adoption of the concept of habitual residence in Article 15 of the 1986 GPCL (General Principle of Civil Law) adds more flexibility to this issue. Tang et al. (2016), p. 74, para.3.53.

[13] Article 4 of the 2020 SPC Judicial Interpretation of the Civil Procedure Law. The concept of habitual residence in the Civil Procedure Law is slightly different from that in the 2010 Chinese Conflict of Laws Act.

[14] Liu and Zheng (2015), p. 106; 刘学在、郑涛:《网购纠纷诉讼中的消费者住所地管辖规则》，《理论探索》，2015年第5期，第104页。

[15] Liu and Zheng (2015), p. 106.

[16] Chen (2008), p. 68; 陈文涛:《民事诉讼管辖中的"合同履行地"》，《法制与经济(上半月)》，2008年，第68页。

[17] Article 23 of the 2017 Civil Procedure Law.

[18] 《中华人民共和国民事诉讼法(2021年修正)》第二十四条:因合同纠纷提起的诉讼，由被告住所地或者合同履行地人民法院管辖。

which have jurisdiction over a case.[19] Article 32 of the 2022 SPC Judicial Interpretation of the Civil Procedure Law provides that in the situation where the jurisdiction agreement stipulates that the people's court of the place of the domicile of one party shall have jurisdiction, if the place of domicile of the parties changes after the agreement is concluded, the people's court of the place of domicile at the time of conclusion of the jurisdiction agreement shall have jurisdiction, unless otherwise agreed by the parties.[20] This means that a change in the domicile of one party after concluding the jurisdiction agreement does not affect the court's jurisdiction based on the party's old domicile. The place of the defendant's domicile reflects the general territorial jurisdiction, whereas the place of contract performance embodies special territorial jurisdiction.[21] How to determine the place of contract performance remains a debated issue.[22]

3.2.2.1 The Place of Performance in General Contracts

The Civil Procedure Law only states that the court at the place of contract performance shall have jurisdiction without specifying what constitutes 'the place of contract performance'. In this regard, the Supreme People's Court gives a further explanation in Article 18 of the 2022 SPC Judicial Interpretation of the Civil Procedure Law, which states that:[23]

> Where the contract stipulates the place of performance, the agreed place of performance shall be the place of performance of the contract.
>
> If the contract does not stipulate the place of performance or the stipulation is not clear, and the subject of the dispute is the payment of currency, the place where the party receiving the currency is located shall be the place where the contract is performed; where the real estate

[19] 《中华人民共和国民事诉讼法(2021年修正)》第三十六条:两个以上人民法院都有管辖权的诉讼，原告可以向其中一个人民法院起诉；原告向两个以上有管辖权的人民法院起诉的，由最先立案的人民法院管辖。Article 36 of the Chinese Civil Procedure Law: For a lawsuit with two or more people's courts having jurisdiction, the plaintiff may file a lawsuit before one of the people's courts; if the plaintiff files a lawsuit before two or more people's courts which have jurisdiction, the first filed people's court shall have jurisdiction.

[20] 《最高人民法院关于适用〈中华人民共和国民事诉讼法〉的解释(2022年修正)》第三十二条:管辖协议约定由一方当事人住所地人民法院管辖，协议签订后当事人住所地变更的，由签订管辖协议时的住所地人民法院管辖，但当事人另有约定的除外。

[21] Wang and Lei (2015), p. 39; 王亚新、雷彤:《合同案件管辖之程序规范的新展开——以<民事诉讼法>司法解释第18条的理解适用为中心》，《法律适用》2015年第8期，第39页。

[22] Ibid; Chen (2008), p. 68.

[23] 《最高人民法院关于适用〈中华人民共和国民事诉讼法〉的解释(2022年修正)》第十八条:合同约定履行地点的，以约定的履行地点为合同履行地。

合同对履行地点没有约定或者约定不明确，争议标的为给付货币的，接收货币一方所在地为合同履行地；交付不动产的，不动产所在地为合同履行地；其他标的，履行义务一方所在地为合同履行地。即时结清的合同，交易行为地为合同履行地。

合同没有实际履行，当事人双方住所地都不在合同约定的履行地的，由被告住所地人民法院管辖。

> is delivered, the place where the real estate is located shall be the place where the contract is performed; for other objects, the place where the party fulfilling the obligation is located shall be the place where the contract is performed. For a contract that is performed on the spot, the place of transaction is the place where the contract is performed.
>
> If the contract is not actually performed, and the domiciles of both parties are not at the place of performance agreed upon in the contract, the jurisdiction is subject to the people's court of the defendant's domicile.

The place of contract performance in Article 18 of the 2022 SPC Judicial Interpretation of the Civil Procedure Law refers to the place where the contractual obligations were performed, which could be a single place or multiple places.[24] The determination of the court of the place of contract performance involves three layers, depending on whether the parties made a choice, the types of subject matter in dispute, and whether the contract was actually performed.

Firstly, if the parties have chosen a specific place as the place of contract performance in their contract, the court at that specified place shall have jurisdiction. Secondly, if the parties have not agreed on the place of performance in the contract or the agreement is not clear, the determination of the place of performance depends on the nature of the subject matter in dispute within the contract. The subject matter of the dispute can be divided into three categories: (i) for contracts involving the payment of money, the place of the party receiving the money is considered the place of contract performance;[25] (ii) for contracts related to the delivery of immovable property, the place of the immovable property becomes the place of contract performance; (iii) for other contracts, such as those involving the delivery of movable properties or property rights, the place of contract performance shall be the location of the party fulfilling the obligation.

Thirdly, for a contract that is immediately executed, the place of transaction is considered the place where the contract is performed; if the contract is not actually performed, and the domiciles of both parties do not align with the agreed place of contract performance, the people's court in the place where the defendant is domiciled shall have jurisdiction. In judicial practice, the determination of the place of performance generally adheres to the characteristic performance principle, coupled with the consideration of the place of actual performance.[26] The inclusion of the actual performance criterion aims to emphasize the close connection between the

---

[24] In some contracts, such as loan contracts, both parties have the obligation to perform the contract, thus there may be two places of contract performance. Chen (2008), p. 68.

[25] The most typical contract is the loan contract. If the lender sues the borrower for the payment of principal and interest, the borrower has the obligation to pay the principal and interest to the lender. The party receiving the money is the lender. The place of the lender's domicile is the place of contract performance. The lender can file a lawsuit in the court of his domicile as the place of contract performance. By contrast, if the borrower fails to deliver the loan after the loan contract is signed and the borrower sues for the lender to grant the loan, the dispute is about the obligation of the lender to grant the loan to the borrower. The party receiving the money is the borrower. The place of the borrower's domicile is the place of contract performance. The borrower can file a lawsuit in the court of his domicile as the place of performance of the contract.

[26] Chen (2008), p. 68.

court of the place of actual performance and the contract, facilitating the identification of legal facts.[27] However, real-life transactions are more complicated, implying that the court of the place of actual performance does not necessarily have a closer connection with the contract.[28]

3.2.2.2 The Place of Performance for Online Sale Contracts

In China, the rise of online shopping platforms such as Taobao, JD.com, and Pinduoduo has become increasingly prevalent, with many people's lives intertwined with the Internet. Unlike traditional transactions, online transactions introduce greater uncertainty, and conventional jurisdiction rules, rooted in territorial factors, may prove inadequate for resolving online disputes.[29] It is more difficult to identity the place of conclusion or performance of the contract and the domiciles of the parties in online transactions, particularly those involving intangible products or services.[30] Thus, online contracts necessitate either a new jurisdiction rule,[31] or at the very least a new interpretation of the place of performance. In this regard, Article 20 of the 2022 SPC Judicial Interpretation of the Civil Procedure Law explains the meaning of the place of performance in a distance contract or online sale contract:[32]

> For a sale contract concluded by means of an information network, if the subject matter is delivered through the information network, the place of performance of the contract shall be the place of the buyer's domicile; if the subject matter is delivered by other means, the place of delivery shall be the place of performance of the contract. If the contract has an agreement on the place of performance, the agreement shall prevail.

In other words, the performance of a distance contract providing intangible products is at the place of the buyer's domicile. When the distance contract provides tangible products, the place of performance is the place where the product is delivered. Article 20 of the 2022 SPC Judicial Interpretation of the Civil Procedure Law, serving as a supplement to Article 24 of the 2021 Chinese Civil Procedure Law over jurisdiction rules for contract disputes, introduces the jurisdictional connecting factors of 'the buyer's domicile', thereby developing jurisdiction rules over online shopping disputes.[33]

---

[27] Chen (2008), p. 69.

[28] In such case, the parties should be given some freedom to choose the competent court. Chen (2008), p. 69.

[29] Tian(2021),p. 14; 田静怡:《网络购物合同纠纷管辖权的问题与建议探讨》，《法制博览》，2021年3月，第14页。

[30] Tian (2021), pp. 15–16.

[31] Tian (2021), p. 15.

[32] 《最高人民法院关于适用〈中华人民共和国民事诉讼法〉的解释(2022年修正)》第二十条：以信息网络方式订立的买卖合同，通过信息网络交付标的的，以买受人住所地为合同履行地；通过其他方式交付标的的，收货地为合同履行地。合同对履行地有约定的，从其约定。

[33] Liu and Zheng (2015), p. 104.

This new rule, to some extent, introduces the jurisdiction rule of the consumer' domicile for two reasons.[34] First, for the type of online performance of an online sale contract, the buyer's domicile as the place of contract performance is often the consumer's domicile. Second, for the type of offline performance of an online sale contract, in most cases, the place of delivery as the place of contract performance is also the consumer's domicile or has a close connection with the consumer's domicile.[35] It is a big step towards the protection of consumers' rights and interests in Chinese legislation.[36] However, this judicial interpretation only explains the place of performance of the contract, and does not make any special statement on other places with jurisdiction.[37] It still adheres to the traditional jurisdiction rules for contract disputes and cannot fundamentally solve the problems of the uncertainty of the jurisdiction over online shopping disputes, nor can it fully protect the consumers's legal rights and interests in the litigation procedure.[38]

It is noticeable that such a jurisdiction ground covers sales contracts with both intangible and tangible goods or products as the subject matter and does not take into account the distance contracts that provide services. Moreover, the distinction between 'online performance' and 'offline performance' is confusing for jurisdictional purposes, as some contracts may involve both online and offline performance.[39] It would be better for Article 20 of the 2022 SPC Judicial Interpretation of the Civil Procedure Law to explicitly state that the consumer's domicile shall have jurisdiction. This could simplify the process of determining the place of performance of the contract and make it easier for the parties to identify the competent court.[40]

3.2.2.3 The Place of Performance in Special Contracts

Article 18 of the 2022 SPC Judicial Interpretation of the Civil Procedure Law applies to all kinds of contract disputes other than lease contracts, insurance contracts, online sales contracts, and other contracts that are specially regulated by the Civil Procedure Law.[41] For instance, Article 28 of the Civil Procedure Law states

[34] Liu and Zheng (2015), p. 108.

[35] Liu and Zheng (2015), p. 108.

[36] Tian (2021), p. 16.

[37] Tian (2021), p. 16.

[38] Liu and Zheng (2015), p. 104.

[39] Liu and Zheng (2015), p. 108.

[40] China has the world's largest online shopping consumers, in order to take initiative in the future jurisdiction over foreign-related e-commerce contracts, it is advisable to adopt the consumer home jurisdiction rule to better protect the legitimate rights and interests of Chinese consumers in global market. Liu and Zheng (2015), p. 109.

[41] Articles 19-21 of the 2020 SPC Judicial Interpretation of the Civil Procedure Law set forth special provisions in determining the place of contract performances for lease contracts, online sales contracts, and insurance contracts. Still, if the parties in these contracts have chosen the place of

that lawsuits arising from disputes over railway, road, water, air transport, and combined transport contracts shall be under the jurisdiction of the people's court at the place of departure, destination, or the domicile of the defendant.[42]

Article 28 of the Chinese Civil Procedure Law, as the special rule, prevails over the general rule in Article 18 of the 2022 SPC Judicial Interpretation of the Civil Procedure Law.[43] Still, there are different kinds of nameless contracts or atypical contracts that are not specifically regulated under the Civil Procedure Law. The Chinese Contract Law sets forth 15 kinds of named contracts or typical contracts, which include sale contracts, loan contracts, guarantee contracts, lease contracts, transportation contracts.[44] The new Chinese Civil Code, which replaces the Contract Law, adds 4 more types of named contracts.[45] These named contracts are a summary of the most common contracts in Chinese market economy, but there are more nameless contracts in contractual transactions.[46] For instance, package travel contracts and timeshare contracts are nameless contracts. How to determine the jurisdiction of nameless contracts whose nature is more difficult to define?[47]

3.2.3 General Jurisdiction Rules Over Foreign-related Contract Disputes

When the defendant in a foreign-related civil action has no domicile in China, Article 272 of the 2021 Chinese Civil Procedure Law shall apply.[48] Article 272 provides six different kinds of jurisdiction grounds: (i) the place of conclusion of

performance of the contract, their agreement takes precedence. In the absence of choice, other special rules are applied to determine the place of performance of the contract. Wang and Lei (2015), p. 41.

[42] 《中华人民共和国民事诉讼法(2021年修正)》第二十八条:因铁路、公路、水上、航空运输和联合运输合同纠纷提起的诉讼，由运输始发地、目的地或者被告住所地人民法院管辖。

[43] Du and Hu (eds) (2015), p. 25; 杜万华、胡云腾主编:《最高人民法院民事诉讼法司法解释逐条适用解析》，人民法院出版社2015年，第25页。

[44] 《合同法》第9-23章分别规定了买卖合同，供用电、水、气、热力合同，赠与合同，借款合同，租赁合同，融资租赁合同，承揽合同，建设工程合同，运输合同，技术合同，保管合同，仓储合同，委托合同，行纪合同，居间合同。

[45] 《民法典·合同编》第二分编中规定了19种典型合同(有名合同)，包括买卖合同、供用电、水、气、热力合同、赠与合同、借款合同、保证合同、租赁合同、融资租赁合同、保理合同、承揽合同、建设工程合同、运输合同、技术合同、保管合同、仓储合同、委托合同、物业服务合同、行纪合同、中介合同、合伙合同。

[46] Chen (2014), p. 69.

[47] For instance, if Party A agrees to provide some clothes to Party B in exchange for Party B's two-week course training of Party A's son, whose performance best reflects the characteristic performance of the contract? Chen (2014), p. 69.

[48] The successor of Article 265 of the 2017 Civil Procedure Law and the predecessor of Article 276 of the 2023 Civil Procedure Law.

the contract, (ii) the place of contract performance, (iii) the place of location of seizable properties, (iv) the place of location of subject matter of the action, (v) the place of tort act, (vi) the place of the representative office of the defendant. If any of these connecting factors is in China, the people's court in China shall have jurisdiction. There is no hierarchy among these factors, nor specific conditions to apply these factors. These jurisdiction grounds apply to all types of cases, including general contracts and consumer contracts.[49] It is unclear under what conditions, to which kind of contract, and which jurisdiction ground should apply, respectively.

The jurisdiction ground of the place of conclusion of the contract might be weak, given that many contracts are concluded at a distance in the digital age.[50] Since the conclusion of a distance contract might be in any country or no country, such jurisdiction ground might be fortuitous and have no substantive connection with the contract or dispute.[51] Likewise, the location of seizable properties, in many cases, may also have no actual connection with the contract dispute. As to the jurisdiction ground of the place of contract performance, some contractual obligations may require continuous performance in more than one country, such as international carriage of goods or passengers.[52] It is difficult to determine one country of performance, especially when the breach of contract obligations is not within the territory of any country, such as on the high seas.[53]

Under Article 28 of the 2021 Chinese Civil Procedure Law, the people's court at the place of origin, destination or the domicile of the defendant has jurisdiction over disputes related to railway, road, water, air transport, and combined transport contracts. The jurisdiction based on the place of the representative office is specific, but a foreign business without a representative office in China may have a branch, agency, or other establishments in China engaged in commercial activities. In the digital age, soliciting consumers in China merely via a website is also possible. The jurisdiction ground of the place of tort act is more relevant to tort claims than contract claims. Such jurisdiction ground might be applicable when there are concurrent claims, and tort liability arises from or relates to the performance of a contract. The lack of clarity in Article 272 of the 2021 Chinese Civil Procedure Law shows that the rules relating to jurisdiction over foreign-related civil issues in China are still largely insufficient.[54]

---

[49] Tang et al. (2016), p. 77, para.3.58.

[50] Tang et al. (2016), p. 77, para.3.58.

[51] Tang et al. (2016), p. 77, para.3.58.

[52] Tang et al. (2016), p. 78, para.3.61.

[53] Tang et al. (2016), p. 79, para.3.61.

[54] Wang (2010), p. 87.

3.2.4 *Jurisdiction by Agreement*

Jurisdiction by agreement means that both parties to the transaction have negotiated and agreed on the issue of jurisdiction by reaching a consent.[55] In the event of a dispute, mutual agreement on jurisdiction enables efficient and quick dispute resolution.[56] If both parties agree to select a court before or after a dispute, it constitutes jurisdiction by agreement, which is only limited to express selection in written form rather than oral agreement.[57] In judicial practice, if the parties did not choose the court in advance, it might be difficult for them to reach an agreement after the dispute arises. Despite this, Chinese courts adopt presumptive jurisdiction to justify their jurisdiction during the trial. According to presumptive jurisdiction, when one party launches a lawsuit in a court and another party does not challenge the jurisdiction or mention counter-action, such court has presumptive jurisdiction. This is stipulated in Article 130 of the 2021 Chinese Civil Procedure Law, which states that the exercise of presumptive jurisdiction cannot violate exclusive jurisdiction and hierarchical jurisdiction. As to jurisdiction by agreement, the questions are: which courts can the parties choose from, what are the conditions for a choice of court agreement to be valid and enforceable, and which law applies to determine its validity?

3.2.4.1 Jurisdiction by Agreement Over Domestic and Foreign-related Contract Disputes

Article 35 of the 2021 Chinese Civil Procedure Law[58] provides that the parties to a dispute over a contract or other property rights and interests may reach a written agreement to select the people's court of the place of the defendant's domicile, the place where the contract is performed, the place where the contract is signed, the place of the plaintiff's domicile, the location of the subject matter, and other places that are actually related to the dispute, but such an agreement shall not violate the provisions of this law on hierarchical jurisdiction and exclusive jurisdiction.[59] Since Article 35 of the 2021 Chinese Civil Procedure Law does not specify which law

[55] Tian (2021), p. 16.

[56] Tian (2021), p. 16.

[57] Li (1996), pp. 58–64; 李浩培,《国际民事程序法概论》，法律出版社， 1996年， 第58-64页。

[58] Article 34 of the 2017 Chinese Civil Procedure Law. The so-called disputes over property rights and interests should be construed broadly to include all disputes other than those over legal status of a person. Zhou (2014), p. 458; 周翠,《协议管辖问题研究》，《中外法学》2014年第2期，第458页。

[59] 《中华人民共和国民事诉讼法(2021年修正)》第35条:合同或者其他财产权益纠纷的当事人可以书面协议选择被告住所地、合同履行地、合同签订地、原告住所地、标的物所在地等与争议有实际联系的地点的人民法院管辖，但不得违反本法对级别管辖和专属管辖的规定。

shall apply to determine the validity of a jurisdiction clause, most courts rely on the *lex fori* to determine the validity of a jurisdiction clause without considering choice of law issues.[60]

Article 35 of the 2021 Chinese Civil Procedure Law applies to jurisdiction agreements in all kinds of contract disputes, including employee contracts and consumer contracts.[61] It is noticeable that this provision mainly focuses on the parties' choice of people's court, instead of the parties' choice of foreign courts.[62] In this regard, Article 529 of the 2022 SPC Judicial Interpretation of the Civil Procedure Law expressly states that the parties to a dispute over a foreign-related contract or other property rights and interests may reach a written agreement to select the people's court of the place of the defendant's domicile, the place where the contract is performed, the place where the contract is signed, the place of the plaintiff's domicile, the location of the subject matter, the place of tort act, and other places that are actually related to the dispute.[63] This provision mainly adds the foreign-related element and the connecting factor of the place of tort act, comparing to Article 35 of the 2021 Chinese Civil Procedure Law.

In accordance with Article 35 of the 2021 Chinese Civil Procedure Law and Article 529 of the 2022 SPC Judicial Interpretation of the Civil Procedure Law, parties in a (foreign-related) contract can choose a competent court for jurisdiction under three conditions. First, it is a written agreement.[64] Second, the place of the chosen court has an actual connection with the dispute. Third, it is the result of the exercise of party autonomy. For standard contracts pre-drafted by the business party, the mandatory nature of jurisdiction clauses often violate the requirement of party autonomy and might be declared as invalid.[65]

As to what is the meaning of the term 'other places having an actual or practical connection with the dispute', there is no consensus.[66] According to traditional jurisdiction theory, jurisdiction grounds for contract cases stipulated in the Chinese Civil

---

[60] Tang et al. (2016), p. 66, para.3.37.

[61] Zhou (2014), p. 464.

[62] He (2016), p. 82; 何其生:《中国加入<海牙选择法院协议公约>的规则差异与考量》，《武汉大学学报(哲学社会科学版)》2016年第4期，第82页。

[63] 《最高人民法院关于适用〈中华人民共和国民事诉讼法〉的解释(2022年修正)》第529条:涉外合同或者其他财产权益纠纷的当事人，可以书面协议选择被告住所地、合同履行地、合同签订地、原告住所地、标的物所在地、侵权行为地等与争议有实际联系地点的外国法院管辖。

根据民事诉讼法第三十四条和第二百七十三条规定，属于中华人民共和国法院专属管辖的案件，当事人不得协议选择外国法院管辖，但协议选择仲裁的除外。

[64] In China, the written form of signing a contract includes the form of electronic data, and thus the legal status of the electronic contract is recognized. 《中华人民共和国民法典》第四百六十九条:当事人订立合同，可以采用书面形式、口头形式或者其他形式。

书面形式是合同书、信件、电报、电传、传真等可以有形地表现所载内容的形式。

以电子数据交换、电子邮件等方式能够有形地表现所载内容，并可以随时调取查用的数据电文，视为书面形式。

[65] Liu and Zheng (2015), p. 106.

[66] Tang et al. (2016), p. 69, para.3.42.

Procedure Law include the defendant's domicile, the place where the contract is performed, and the place agreed upon by the parties for jurisdiction.[67] If the jurisdiction agreement designates two or more courts with an actual connection to the dispute, the plaintiff may choose one of the courts in accordance with Article 30 of the 2022 SPC Judicial Interpretation of the Civil Procedure Law.[68] It is noticeable that according to Article 277 of the 2023 Civil Procedure Law, the chosen court does not have to have an actual connection with the foreign-related civil dispute. Deleting the 'actual connection' requirement means that Chinese courts could exercise jurisdiction over disputes without a practical connection with China, as long as the parties reach a choice of court agreement in writing.

3.2.4.2 The Validity of Choice of Court Agreement in Consumer Contracts

A choice of court agreement or forum selection clause is usually included in the general terms and conditions of a standardized consumer contract, pre-drafted by the business party for repetitive use without negotiation with the consumer. In prevalent online consumer contracts within electronic commerce, a jurisdiction clause might be part of a click-wrap contract or browse-wrap contract.[69] In these contracts, consumers cannot negotiate with the business operator during the registration process on online platforms, often requiring them to click 'agree' to proceed.[70] The language used in these general terms and conditions is often incomprehensible, unreadable and obscure. However, a business usually expects and presumes consumers to read these contracts, which are usually drafted in an unreadable way.[71] Since general terms and conditions in consumer contracts are usually (sometimes deliberately) written in a way that dissuades consumers from reading them, it is not surprising that consumers generally do not read these standard form contracts.[72] Moreover, it is unlikely that a choice of court agreement in a standard template would be drafted in a way to enable a consumer to sue in his or her home

[67] Liu and Zheng (2015), p. 105.

[68] 《最高人民法院关于适用〈中华人民共和国民事诉讼法〉的解释(2022年修正)》第30条:管辖协议约定两个以上与争议有实际联系的地点的人民法院管辖，原告可以向其中一个人民法院起诉。

[69] In a click wrap contract, there are usually two signs 'I agree' and 'I disagree' or 'I accept' and 'I don't accept' before concluding the contract. The consumer has to click the button 'I agree' or 'I accept' in order to enter into a contract. Wu (2005), p. 145; 吴伟光，《电子商务法》，清华大学出版社，2005年，第145页。

[70] Liu and Zheng (2015), p. 105.

[71] Since the business party does not generally have a duty to draft readable contracts, the average readability level of sign-in-wrap agreements used in companies such as Facebook, Amazon, Uber, and Airbnb is comparable to the usual score of articles in academic journals, which do not target the general public. Benoliel and Becher (2019), p. 2256.

[72] Benoliel and Becher (2019), p. 2256; Tian (2021), p. 16.

jurisdiction.[73] It seems counterintuitive for such agreements to incorporate a jurisdiction clause in the consumer's favour.[74] This gives rise to the question of whether a choice of court agreement reached before a consumer dispute arises is valid and enforceable. For electronic consumer contracts, where users, often less informed and in a weaker position, may not even notice the existence of a jurisdiction clause when clicking the 'agree' button, it becomes necessary for the court to examine the validity of the jurisdiction clause ex officio or upon the user's request.[75]

Chinese law does not expressly address the validity of a choice of court agreement reached before a dispute arises. In the absence of a uniform standard, courts may reach different conclusions on similar cases with regard to the validity of jurisdiction clauses inserted in standard contracts.[76] Given that businesses may use a forum selection clause to discourage consumers from taking legal action or indirectly evade the application of consumer protection laws by choosing a court other than the consumer's domicile, it gives rise to the question whether the right to choose a competent court should be restricted. If restrictions are deemed necessary, the inquiry then becomes why and how such restrictions should be implemented.

Business operators often incorporate jurisdiction clauses in standard clauses to improve efficiency, reduce costs, and prevent unfavorable situations without negotiating with the other party.[77] These pre-drafted clauses, including jurisdiction issues, usually only reflect the intention of the contract providers, leaving consumers in a passive status for either accepting or rejecting them. Typically embedded in lengthy general terms, these clauses are often overlooked by consumers. How many users will thoroughly read the lengthy general terms and conditions before signing up for social media networks or shopping apps? Furthermore, how many users are even aware of the existence of dispute resolution clauses in those general terms and

---

[73] The HCCH Report of the Experts' Group on the Cooperation and Access to Justice for International Tourists, para.73, Prel. Doc. 1 of February 2020. In very rare case, the business party may allow the consumer to choose the place of jurisdiction. For instance, Expedia, an online travel guidance website, allows its consumer to choose the place of jurisdiction. If the consumer chooses America, the consumer will stay in the website Expedia.com; if the consumer chooses Canada, the consumer will be directed to the website Expedia.ca; if the consumer chooses Mexico, the consumer will be reminded that it does not provide services there. Despite this, the consumer is still in a disadvantaged position and some consumers may provide misinformation in order to get access to the content of the website. Li (2009a), p. 206; 李智，《国际私法中互联网管辖权制度研究》，厦门大学出版社，2009年，第206页。

[74] The HCCH Report of the Experts' Group on the Cooperation and Access to Justice for International Tourists, para.73, Prel. Doc. 1 of February 2020.

[75] Li (2009b), p. 74; 李颖:《网站用户协议中协议管辖条款的效力》，《人民司法》，2009年8月，第74页。

[76] Liu and Zheng (2015), p. 108. 《北京市第二中级人民法院民事裁定书》(2015)二中民(商)终字 第02728号和《四川省郫县人民法院民事裁定书》(2014)成郫民管初字第38/39号认可了淘宝网络管辖协议，裁定被告管辖异议成立，由被告住所地管辖。而类似案情，在《江苏省南京市中级人民法院民事裁定书》(2014)宁民辖终字第463号和《安徽省合肥市中级人民法院民事裁定书》(2014)合管终字第00428号这两个裁定书中，法院认定淘宝管辖协议属于格式条款，协议无效，被告住所地没有管辖权。

[77] Tian (2021), p. 16; Liu and Zheng (2015), p. 107.

conditions? Even if consumers do notice them, they may have no choice but to click the 'agree' button to purchase goods or services from an online platform.[78] If the registration of an account by a user is considered consent to jurisdiction clauses in standard terms, it is difficult for consumers to prove that they disagree with the jurisdiction clauses once disputes arise.[79] Imposing limits on the exercise of party autonomy regarding jurisdiction clause may serve to protect the rights and interests of weak parties,[80] as businesses could easily choose a forum or applicable law without negotiating with consumers.

3.2.4.3 Applicable Law to Litigation Contracts or Choice of Court Agreements

Jurisdiction by agreement or choice of court agreement is itself one kind of litigation contract.[81] A litigation contract refers to an agreement reached between parties intended to directly or indirectly generate the effects on procedural law.[82] The assessment of the validity of the litigation contract itself needs to follow the relevant principles of contract law and other substantive laws, examining whether there is a defect in the expression of intention or whether it is obviously unfair.[83] While the Civil Procedure Law and the civil substantive laws belong to public law and private law separately, they both fall under the broader category of civil law, sharing some common values and principles.[84] Due to these commonalities, many issues in litigation contract, including the validity of jurisdiction clauses or choice of court agreements, may be analyzed using contract theory in private law.[85]

When procedural law provisions on litigation contracts are incomplete or absent, the validity of a pre-drafted jurisdiction agreement could be determined under the provisions in substantive law by analogy, such as the civil law, contract law and consumer protection law.[86] If a jurisdiction clause is invalid in form or substance, it cannot be enforced.[87] Article 496 of the Chinese Civil Code expressly states that:

> where standard terms are used to conclude a contract, the party providing the standard terms shall follow the principle of fairness to determine the rights and obligations between the parties, and take a reasonable approach to remind the other party to pay attention to the

[78] Tian (2021), p. 16.

[79] Tian (2021), p. 16.

[80] Wu (2017), p. 14; 吴羿，《沙巴沉船事件中的涉外管辖权和法律适用问题探析》，西南政法大学法硕学术论文，2017年，第14页。

[81] Li (2009b), p. 74.

[82] Chen (2002), p. 92; 陈桂明:《程序理念与程序规则》，中国法制出版社2002年版，第92页。

[83] Li (2009b), p. 74.

[84] Li (2009b), p. 74..

[85] Li (2009b), p. 74.

[86] Li (2009b), p. 74.

[87] Tang et al. (2016), p. 65, para.3.37.

exemption or mitigation of its liabilities and other terms that have a major interest in the other party. If the party providing the standard terms fails to perform the obligation of reasonable notice or explanation, so that the other party does not pay attention to or understand the terms of which it has a major interest, the other party may claim that these terms do not become part of the contract.[88]

Article 497 further explains that a standard clause is invalid in the following situations: if the party providing the standard terms unreasonably exempts or reduces its responsibility, aggravates the other party's responsibility, and restricts the other party's main rights; if the party providing the standard terms excludes the other party's main rights.[89] According to Article 498 of the Civil Code, in the case of a dispute regarding the interpretation of a standard clause, the clause should be interpreted in line with its common understanding. Where there are two or more interpretations of a standard clause, it should be interpreted in a manner unfavorable to the party providing the standard clause. Where a standard clause is inconsistent with a non-standard clause, the non-standard clause takes precedence.[90]

3.2.4.4 Defective Consent in the Take-It-or-Leave-It Situation

When it comes to the validity of a jurisdiction clause in a consumer contract, Article 31 of the 2022 SPC Judicial Interpretation of the Civil Procedure Law expressly states that when business operators use standard terms to enter into a jurisdiction agreement with consumers and fail to take reasonable measures to bring the jurisdiction agreement to the attention of consumers, if consumers claim that the jurisdiction agreement is invalid, the people's court shall uphold such claim.[91] The Chinese Supreme People's Court does not intend to invalidate all jurisdiction clauses in consumer contracts but aims to regulate asymmetric information.[92] The

[88] 《中华人民共和国民法典》第四百九十六条:格式条款是当事人为了重复使用而预先拟定，并在订立合同时未与对方协商的条款。

采用格式条款订立合同的，提供格式条款的一方应当遵循公平原则确定当事人之间的权利和义务，并采取合理的方式提示对方注意免除或者减轻其责任等与对方有重大利害关系的条款，按照对方的要求，对该条款予以说明。提供格式条款的一方未履行提示或者说明义务，致使对方没有注意或者理解与其有重大利害关系的条款的，对方可以主张该条款不成为合同的内容。

[89] 《中华人民共和国民法典》第四百九十七条:有下列情形之一的，该格式条款无效:

(一)具有本法第一编第六章第三节和本法第五百零六条规定的无效情形;

(二)提供格式条款一方不合理地免除或者减轻其责任、加重对方责任、限制对方主要权利;

(三)提供格式条款一方排除对方主要权利。

[90] 《中华人民共和国民法典》第四百九十八条:对格式条款的理解发生争议的，应当按照通常理解予以解释。对格式条款有两种以上解释的，应当作出不利于提供格式条款一方的解释。格式条款和非格式条款不一致的，应当采用非格式条款。

[91] 《最高人民法院关于适用〈中华人民共和国民事诉讼法〉的解释(2022年修正)》第31条:经营者使用格式条款与消费者订立管辖协议，未采取合理方式提请消费者注意，消费者主张管辖协议无效的，人民法院应予支持。

[92] Tang et al. (2016), p. 67, para.3.38.

requirement of reasonable notice presumes that once the consumer notices the jurisdiction clause and still decides to conclude the contract, it constitutes genuine consent.[93] Such presumption is problematic, since it is difficult to decide what amounts to 'reasonable notice'.[94]

Even if the business party has fulfilled the obligation of reasonable notice, it does not balance the inequality of bargaining power, since consumers are still in a take-it-or-leave-it position.[95] In my view, due to the unequal bargaining power and information asymmetry between consumers and businesses, the consent of the consumer over a jurisdiction clause in a standard contract is more likely to be a defective consent, rather than a genuine and free consent. Notwithstanding this, it is still an important development to recognize the necessity of protecting consumers with regard to choice of court agreements.[96] In order to fully respect the party autonomy in consumer contracts, Xuezai Liu and Tao Zheng propose that the pre-drafted jurisdiction clauses by large websites such as JD.com and Taobao should automatically pop up to remind consumers every time when they submit an order, with these words in eye-catching handwriting to attract consumers' attention.[97] More importantly, consumers should be given the right to choose, for instance, by providing a 'disagree' button, and also allow the consumer to negotiate or proceed with shopping if the consumer clicks the 'disagree' button.[98] The proposal of reminding consumers of the jurisdiction clause via a pop-up window every time they place an order seems unnecessary and not efficient for transactions. However, it is essential to allow consumers to continue shopping or negotiate undesirable terms even if they click the 'disagree' button.

3.2.5 *The 2005 Hague Convention on Choice of Court Agreements*

The 2005 Hague Convention on Choice of Court Agreements aspires to become a worldwide charter governing international forum selection agreements and national court judgments.[99] It is promoted as a significant milestone in the development of

---

[93] Tang et al. (2016), p. 67, para.3.38.

[94] Tang et al. (2016), p. 67, para.3.38. For instance, whether it is sufficient if the jurisdiction clause is highlighted or singled out? Whether the jurisdiction clause has to be interpreted to the consumer in person? Whether the jurisdiction clause has to be properly referred to and not buried in lengthy contract terms?

[95] Tang et al. (2016), p. 67, para.3.38. The level of consumer protection in jurisdiction issues is low and inadequate.

[96] Tang et al. (2016), p. 67, para.3.38.

[97] Liu and Zheng (2015), p. 109.

[98] Liu and Zheng (2015), p. 109.

[99] Born (2021a), p. 2126.

international civil procedure and global governance.[100] This Convention requires that Contracting States give effect to international choice-of-court agreements and enforce the resulting judgments.[101] It aims to enhance international judicial cooperation through 'uniform rules on jurisdiction and on recognition and enforcement of foreign judgments in civil or commercial matters'.[102] The 2005 Hague Choice of Court Convention would substantially alter existing rules in many jurisdictions, including China, governing the recognition and enforcement of both international choice-of-court agreements and judgments obtained in proceedings based on such agreements.[103]

China signed the 2005 Hague Choice of Court Convention on 12 September 2017 but has not acceded to it. As to the requirement of an actual connection between the chosen court and the dispute under Article 35 of the 2021 Chinese Civil Procedure Law and Article 529 of the 2022 SPC Judicial Interpretation of the Civil Procedure Law, it conflicts with the 2005 Hague Choice of Court Convention, which does not require an actual connection. This conflict may be resolved by a declaration of not accepting jurisdiction by agreement which designates courts having no actual connection with the dispute in accordance with Article 19 of the 2005 Hague Choice of Court Convention.[104]

Article 35 of the 2021 Chinese Civil Procedure Law remains the same in the 2023 amendment. For domestic disputes, an actual connection between the chosen court and the disputes is still required. Notably, for foreign-related disputes, Article 277 of the 2023 Civil Procedure Law has abolished the 'actual connection' requirement, the chosen court does not necessarily need an actual connection with the dispute. It is in line with the 2005 Hague Choice of Court Convention. Article 529 of the 2022 SPC Judicial Interpretation of the Civil Procedure Law, which requires an 'actual connection' between the chosen court and the foreign-related dispute, will no longer be effective after 1 January 2024. Without an 'actual connection' requirement, the scope of jurisdiction over foreign-related disputes for Chinese courts will be expanded.

In accordance with Article 2(1)(a)-(b) of the Choice of Court Convention, this Convention will not apply to choice-of-court agreements in which a consumer is a party or relating to contracts of employment. This means that this Convention primarily applies to choice of court agreements in commercial contracts.[105] In another list of exclusions, this Convention also excludes the carriage of passengers and

[100] Still, some terms of the Choice of Court Convention may suffer from serious flaws which make it unsuitable for adoption on a global scale. Born (2021a), p. 2126.

[101] Born (2021a), p. 2086.

[102] Preamble of the Choice of Court Convention.

[103] Born (2021a), p. 2080.

[104] Zhang (2015), p. 69; 张建:《涉外民事诉讼协议管辖规则的新发展》，《南都学坛(人文社会科学学报) 》2015年第6期，第69页。

[105] Schulz (2006), p. 248.

goods,[106] claims for personal injury to natural persons,[107] and non-contractual tort claims for damage to tangible property.[108] Since the Hague Choice of Court Convention excludes many issues, its scope of application has faced criticism.[109] It mainly applies to civil or commercial matters regarding Business to Business (B2B) agreements. However, distinguishing Business to Business agreements from Business to Consumer (B2C) agreements in the context of Internet and E-commerce poses challenges.[110] In this regard, the notion of consumer or consumer contract discussed in the previous Chapter will indirectly determine the scope of application of the 2005 Hague Choice of Court Convention.

3.3 Jurisdiction Rules Over Consumer Contracts in China

First of all, why is it important to analyze case law of the Chinese courts? The legal system in China largely belongs to the continental law system, which is based on the statutory law.[111] However, the judges in China and precedent law are playing an increasingly important role, especially after the opening-up policy.[112] In fact, judicial precedent may play a role in three ways in China.

First, the Supreme People's Court, based on judicial practice over foreign-related cases, has issued some judicial interpretations over certain specific issues.[113] These judicial interpretations, as the highest form of judicial precedent, have legal binding over Chinese courts and individuals.[114] Second, the Supreme People's Court may give formal opinions on some cases referred by courts of different levels. Although such opinions may not have universal value for other cases, they may still provide some guidance for other courts hearing similar cases.[115] Third, the Supreme People's Court will also publish some typical cases regularly. Although these cases do not impose legal binding power upon Chinese courts, they may still have some influence over courts hearing similar cases.[116] Likewise, cases heard by local courts may not have the same effect as guiding cases issued by the Supreme People's Court, but they may still provide some guidance for other courts hearing similar cases. The

[106] Article 2(2)(f) of the Choice of Court Convention.

[107] Article 2(2)(j) of the Choice of Court Convention.

[108] Article 2(2)(k) of the Choice of Court Convention.

[109] He (2016), p. 80.

[110] He (2016), p. 80.

[111] China is a civil law country with written laws. Wang (2010), p. 133.

[112] Tang (2010), p. 30; 汤唯，《大陆法系法典化之理性》，何勤华主编，《大陆法系及其对中国的影响》，法律出版社，2010年，第30页。

[113] Han and Xiao (2012), p. 24; 韩德培、肖永平,《国际私法(第二版)》，北京大学出版社和高等教育出版社，2012年，第24页。

[114] Han and Xiao (2012), p. 24.

[115] Han and Xiao (2012), p. 25.

[116] Han and Xiao (2012), p. 25.

pursuit of legal certainty and predictability means that Chinese courts shall treat similar cases similarly. The cases analyzed in this Chapter are mainly collected from the China Judgments Online.

To examine what jurisdiction rules are applied to consumer contracts in China, it is better to look at consumer contracts which have been subject to consumer choice of law rules under Article 42 of the Chinese Conflict of Laws Act. What jurisdiction rules have been applied to those consumer contracts falling within the material scope of Article 42 of the Chinese Conflict of Laws Act? Among the 19 judgments referring to Article 42 of the Chinese Conflict of Laws Act, only 5 judgments expressly provide reasoning on jurisdictional issues. This means that, for contracts governed by consumer choice of law rules, 14 out of 19 judgments do not touch upon jurisdiction issues. In the absence of a specific consumer jurisdiction rule in China, the question is how Chinese judges designate competent courts for consumer contracts and justify the exercise of jurisdiction by Chinese courts.

In *Jin Bingzhou v. Sanhe Yanjiao Jinghua Golf Club Co., Ltd,*[117] the Hebei Province Langfang Municipality Intermediate People's Court justified its jurisdiction by referring to a provision issued by the Supreme People's Court and a provincial legal document.[118] In *Chen Zhongdong v. Poettinger Landtechnik GmbH, et al,*[119] the Shandong Province Qingdao Municipality Huangdao District's People's Court held that it had jurisdiction over the dispute without referring to a specific provision. Specifically, the court analyzed that the defendant was a company registered in Austria, making the case a foreign-related civil litigation. Since the defendant's domicile was in Huangdao District of Qingdao Municipality (Shandong Province) and the plaintiff brought a tort action, this court had jurisdiction.[120] However, in the final paragraph of the judgment, the court did refer to Article 64 of the Civil Procedure Law and Articles 90-91 of the SPC Judicial Interpretation of the Civil Procedure Law. It is interesting that the court invoked both Article 42 and

[117] *Jin Bingzhou v. Sanhe Yanjiao Jinghua Golf Club Co., Ltd*, Hebei High People's Court, [2015] Ji Min San Zhong No 107; Hebei Province Langfang Municipality Intermediate People's Court, [2015] Lang Min San Chu Zi No 28. 金秉周与三河燕郊京华高尔夫俱乐部有限公司娱乐服务合同纠纷二审民事判决书，河北省高级人民法院，(2015)冀民三终字第107号；河北省廊坊市中级人民法院，(2015)廊民三初字第28号民事判决。

[118] Ibid. 本案为涉外民商事案件。根据《最高人民法院关于涉外民商事案件诉讼管辖若干问题的规定》第一条第一款第四项、第三条第一项的规定及《河北省高人民法院关于指定廊坊市中级人民法院管辖一审涉外、涉港澳台民商事案件的通知》，本院对本案有管辖权。

[119] *Chen Zhongdong v. Poettinger Landtechnik GmbH, et al,* Shandong Province Qingdao Municipality Huangdao District's People's Court, [2019] Lu 0211 Min Chu No 8186. 陈忠东与奥地博田农业科技(青岛)有限公司、奥地博田农机有限公司产品责任纠纷一审民事判决书，山东省青岛市黄岛区人民法院,(2019)鲁0211民初8186号.

[120] Ibid. 本院认为，被告奥地博田农机有限公司(PoettingerLandtechnikGmbH)系在奥地利共和国注册登记，因此本案属于涉外民事诉讼。被告奥地博田农业科技(青岛)有限公司(外国法人独资)的住所地在中华人民共和国山东省青岛市黄岛区，原告提起的是侵权诉讼，本院对该案有管辖权。

Article 44 of the Chinese Conflict of Laws Act to justify the application of Chinese Law. This case involves concurrent liability and the plaintiff chose tort liability as the cause of action. Even if the contract is a consumer contract and there is one consumer jurisdiction rule in Chinese law, jurisdiction rules over consumer contracts shall not apply since the cause of action was tort liability.

Another case that concerns concurrent liability is *Hong Zhifu v. Guangdong Southern Shopping Co., Ltd, et al.*[121] The first-instance court (Panyu District People's Court) held that Hong Zhifu is a Hong Kong citizen. This case is a Hong Kong-related contract dispute, which shall be handled with reference to foreign-related cases. It is a consumer contract dispute, and the jurisdiction can be determined based on both the contract lawsuit and the infringement lawsuit. The delivery address of the products involved in the case was in Panyu, indicating that the place of the infringement was in Panyu. As a result, the court of first instance stated that it had jurisdiction over this case.[122] The court did not refer to any legal provision to justify its jurisdiction.

However, it is noteworthy that the first-instance court refers to Article 42 of the Chinese Conflict of Laws Act and cites the consumer choice of law rules in full text when addressing the applicable law of the contract. Since the place of provision of goods was in mainland China, and Hong Zhifu expressly chose to apply the law of the place of provision of goods, the law of mainland China was applied.[123] On one hand, the jurisdiction of the first-instance contract is based on the place of tort. On the other hand, the law applicable to the contract is determined by consumer choice of law rules. In this regard, the reasoning on jurisdiction and choice of law appears inconsistent, if not self-contradictory. The second-instance court could have corrected such a mistake, however, it did not address the jurisdiction issue at all.

In *Wang Zhihao v. Li Guanhui*,[124] the buyer, Wang Zhihao, was a resident of Taiwan, and the Guangzhou Internet Court classified the case as a dispute over an online shopping contract. The court cited Article 23 of the Chinese Civil Procedure Law (replaced by Article 24 of the 2021 Chinese Civil Procedure Law) which prescribes that litigation arising from contract disputes shall be under the jurisdiction of the people's court in the place where the defendant is domiciled or where the

---

[121] *Hong Zhifu v. Guangdong Southern Shopping Co., Ltd, et al,* Guangdong Province Guangzhou Municipality Intermediate People's Court, [2018] Yue 01 Min Zhong No 21210; Guangdong Province Guangzhou Municipality Panyu District People's Court, [2017] Yue 0113 Min Chu No 6741. 洪致福、广东南方家庭购物有限公司合同纠纷二审民事判决书，广东省广州市中级人民法院，(2018)粤01民终21210号；广东省广州市番禺区人民法院，(2017)粤0113民初6741号民事判决。

[122] Ibid. 原审法院认为:洪致福为香港公民，本案是涉港合同纠纷，参照涉外案件进行处理。本案是消费性合同纠纷，可按照合同之诉及侵权之诉确认管辖，洪致福购买案涉产品的收货地址在番禺，即侵权行为地在番禺，故原审法院对本案有管辖权。

[123] Ibid.

[124] *Wang Zhihao v. Li Guanhui,* Guangzhou Internet Court, [2019] Yue 0192 Min Chu No 11265. 王志豪与李官辉网络购物合同纠纷一审民事判决书，广州互联网法院，(2019)粤0192民初11265号。

contract is performed. This case involves a lawsuit brought by Wang Zhihao on the grounds of a dispute over an online shopping contract. The defendant, Li Guanhui, is domiciled in Guangzhou, so this case falls under the jurisdiction of the Guangzhou Internet Court in accordance with the law.[125] It can be observed that the court referred to the general domestic jurisdiction rule over contracts to justify the exercise of jurisdiction over consumer contracts.

In *Li Lijun v. Guangzhou Yiyan Jiuding Catering Co., Ltd., et al,*[126] the plaintiff Li Lijun, a pregnant woman, was hospitalized for 2 days due to food poisoning after dining at the restaurant of the defendant Guangzhou Yiyan Jiuding Catering Co., Ltd. The catering company was operated by Li Dan, a resident of Hong Kong, and Zhao Pingzhao, without obtaining a catering service permit. In this case, the court also relied on the domicile of the defendant to justify its jurisdiction. This case also involved concurrent liability, and the plaintiff chose contract liability as the cause of action. The first-instance court (Panyu District People's Court) held that Li Dan is a Hong Kong resident, thus the case is a Hong Kong-related commercial dispute, which should be handled in the same way as a foreign-related dispute. The domicile of Yiyan Jiuding Company is within the jurisdiction of the first-instance court; thus, the first-instance court, as the court of the defendant's domicile, has jurisdiction over the case.[127] It is noticeable that no legal provisions were invoked to justify the jurisdiction of the first-instance court. The second-instance court does not mention the jurisdiction issue at all.

Based on the five judgments in which consumer choice of law rules are applied, the application of jurisdiction rules over consumer contracts, in general, is not satisfactory, let alone the contracts that are not protected as consumer contracts under Article 42 of the Chinese Conflict of Laws Act. The problems in the reasoning of jurisdiction over consumer contracts exist in package travel contracts, which should have been protected as consumer contracts. Moreover, there are more other problems in the reasoning of jurisdiction over package travel contracts.

---

[125] Ibid. 本院认为，王志豪系台湾地区居民，本案为涉台网络购物合同纠纷。《中华人民共和国民事诉讼法》第二十三条规定:“因合同纠纷提起的诉讼，由被告住所地或者合同履行地人民法院管辖。” 本案系王志豪以网络购物合同纠纷为由提起的诉讼，被告李官辉住所地在广州，故本案依法由本院管辖。

[126] *Li Lijun v. Guangzhou Yiyan Jiuding Catering Co., Ltd., et al,* Guangdong Province Guangzhou Municipality Intermediate People's Court, [2015] Hui Zhong Fa MIn Si Zhong Zi No 134; Guangdong Province Guangzhou Municipality Panyu District People's Court, [2015] Hui Pan Fa MIn Si Chu Zi No 12. 李丽君与广州市一盐酒鼎餐饮有限公司、李丹、赵平昭餐饮服务合同纠纷2015民四终134二审民事裁定书，广东省广州市中级人民法院，(2015)穗中法民四终字第134；广东省广州市番禺区人民法院，(2015)穗番法民四初字第12号民事判决。

[127] Ibid. 原审法院认为:李丹为香港居民，本案为涉港商事纠纷，应比照涉外纠纷处理。一盐酒鼎公司的住所地在原审法院辖区内，原审法院作为被告住所地法院对本案具有管辖权。

3.3.1 Skipping the Reasoning of Jurisdiction Ground

When it comes to foreign-related package travel contracts, some Chinese courts, consciously or unconsciously, skip the justification of jurisdiction issue and directly jump to the applicable law issue. It seems that, for some courts, there is no need to justify the exercise of jurisdiction over a foreign-related case that involves Chinese parties, even though these courts do elaborate on and justify why Chinese law should be the governing law. The absence of a consumer jurisdiction rule may have directly led to the omission of jurisdiction reasoning in Chinese courts. The lack of a specific provision on jurisdiction rules over consumer contract has become a common challenge for Chinese courts, as they have to resort to other provisions to justify their jurisdiction.

In *Foshan Guangzhilv International Travel Agency v Lin Jintian*,[128] the Guangdong Foshan Intermediate People's Court identified the case as Hong Kong-related, and directly invoked Article 551 of the 2015 SPC Judicial Interpretation of the Civil Procedure Law. This article stipulates that when hearing civil cases involving Hong Kong, Macao, and Taiwan, the People's Court may refer to special provisions applicable to foreign-related civil procedures. Although Hong Kong, Macao, and Taiwan are not foreign countries for mainland China, their legal systems are quite different from mainland China. In this sense, laws in Hong Kong, Macao, and Taiwan are different, unfamiliar, and foreign to the judges in mainland courts, just as laws of other foreign countries. The court merely pointed out that the factor of Hong Kong constituted a foreign element, without specifying why the court had jurisdiction over this dispute.

Similarly, in *Dr. Barsch-Supan v Xi'an Xindaya International Travel Agency and Zhang Li*,[129] two American tourists sued the Chinese travel agency and its deputy for the return of travel expenses after their cancellation of a Tibet trip. Shaanxi High People's Court classified the case as a foreign-related contract dispute and then jumped directly to the applicable law issue, without justifying why Chinese court has legitimate jurisdiction. There are also several other cases in which the courts did not mention the jurisdiction part and jumped directly to the choice of law part, such

[128] *Foshan Guangzhilv International Travel Agency v Lin Jintian*, Guangdong Foshan IPC, (2017) Yue 06 Min Zhong No 4445; Guangdong Foshan Nanhai District People's Court, (2016) Yue 0605 Min Chu No 9352. 佛山广之旅国际旅行社有限公司、林锦添旅游合同纠纷二审民事判决书，广东省佛山市中级人民法院，(2017)粤06民终4445号；广东省佛山市南海区人民法院，(2016)粤0605民初9352号民事判决。

[129] *Dr. Barsch-Supan v Xi'an Xindaya International Travel Agency and Zhang Li*, Shaanxi High People's Court, (2016) Shaan MIn Zhong No 511; Xi'an Municipality Intermediate People's Court, (2016) Shaan 01 Min Chu No 288. 西安信雅达国际旅行社有限公司、张立与Dr. Barsch-Supan,Axel Helmut、Dr. Blrsch-Supan Geb. Meuer,Martina Elisabeth旅游合同纠纷民事二审判决书，陕西省高级人民法院，(2016)陕民终511号；西安市中级人民法院，(2016)陕01民初288号民事判决。

as the cases *Tong Bo v Shandong Daxinhua Yuntong Travel Agency*,[130] *Feng Yunhai v Henan Feiyang Travel Agency*,[131] *Yongan Property Insurance Company Henan Branch v Yang Junya*[132] and *Liu Peilong et al v Kunming Kanghui Yonghui Travel Agency*.[133]

3.3.2 General Jurisdiction Rules Over Domestic Contracts Applied to Foreign-related Contracts

According to the general principle of private international law, the place of performance of a foreign-related contract is usually considered as the place of centre of gravity of the contract due to its significant connection with the contract.[134] This principle does not apply very well in the field of foreign-related tourism.[135] Specifically, in the context of cross-border travel contract, the place of performance of the contract is always in a foreign country or several foreign countries, different from the tourist's home country. A Chinese tourist entering into a package travel contract cannot rely on Article 272 of the 2021 Chinese Civil Procedure Law to sue a foreign business in the courts of the tourist's home country (Chinese courts), since the place of performance is in a foreign country.

Given that many cases involving cross-border travel disputes in judicial practice concern package travel contracts between Chinese tourists and Chinese travel agencies, with one or more foreign destinations, both the claimant (tourist) and the defendant (travel agency) share a common domicile or habitual residence in China. Consequently, the limitations of lacking a solid jurisdictional ground over a foreign

[130] *Tong Bo v Shandong Daxinhua Yuntong Travel Agency*, Shandong Province HPC, (2017) Lu Min Zhong No 1123; Shandong Province Qingdao Municipality IPC, (2016) Lu 02 Min Chu No 1146. 佟波、山东大新华运通国际旅行社有限公司旅游合同纠纷二审民事判决书，山东省高级人民法院，(2017)鲁民终1123号。

[131] *Feng Yunhai v Henan Feiyang Travel Agency*, Henan Province Zhengzhou Municipality IPC, (2015) Zheng Min San Chu Zi No 307. 冯运海与河南飞扬国际旅游有限公司、河南职工国际旅行社旅游合同纠纷一审民事判决书，河南省郑州市中级人民法院，(2015)郑民三初字第307号。

[132] *Yongan Property Insurance Company Henan Branch v Yang Junya*, Henan Province HPC, (2017) Yu Min Zhong No 540; Henan Province Zhengzhou Municipality IPC, (2014) Zheng Min Chu Zi No 203. 永安财产保险股份有限公司河南分公司、河南职工国际旅行社旅游合同纠纷二审民事判决书，河南省高级人民法院，(2017)豫民终540号；河南省郑州市中级人民法院，(2014)郑民三初字第203号民事判决。

[133] *Liu Peilong et al v Kunming Kanghui Yonghui Travel Agency*, Kunming Railway IPC, (2017) Yun 71 Min Zhong No 11; Kunming Railway Court, (2015) Kin Tie Min Chu Zi No 103. 刘佩龙、刘听燕旅游合同纠纷二审民事判决书，昆明铁路运输中级法院，(2017)云71民终11号；昆明铁路运输法院，(2015)昆铁民初字第103号。

[134] Xia (2015), p. 33; 夏雨:《涉外旅游纠纷管辖权规则研究》，《南昌师范学院学报(社会科学)》，2015年第1期，第33页。

[135] Xia (2015), p. 33.

business entering into a contract with a Chinese consumer for service provision are not yet prominently evident.

For instance, in *Xue Xiujuan v. Jiangxi Ganzhonglv International Travel Agency*,[136] the plaintiff Xue Xiujuan, domiciled in Nanchang City, Jiangxi, filed a lawsuit against the defendant Jiangxi Ganzhonglv International Travel Agency, also domiciled in Nanchang City, Jiangxi. A third party involved was China Dadi Property Insurance Company (Jiangxi Branch), also domiciled in Nanchang City, Jiangxi. The plaintiff Xue Xiujuan and 24 other tourists concluded a group outbound travel contract with the defendant for a 6-day trip to Thailand. Following the itinerary provided by the defendant, the plaintiff Xue Xiujuan took a speedboat to Jinsha Island in Pattaya, Thailand. Unfortunately, a sudden strong wind and wave during the journey led to continuous turbulence and severe back pain for Xue Xiujuan. Subsequently, the plaintiff Xue Xiujuan was sent to a local hospital in Thailand for examination and was diagnosed with a comminuted fracture of the thoracic spine.

The first-instance court held that the case involved a dispute arising out of a travel contract between a tourist and a tour operator.[137] Since the legal facts concerning travel contract relationship took place outside the territory of China, the case was classified as a foreign-related civil case. Given that the domicile of the defendant was in Nanchang City, Jiangxi Province, the court asserted jurisdiction in accordance with Article 23 of the 2017 Chinese Civil Procedure Law.[138] Nevertheless, the reliance on Article 23 of the 2017 Chinese Civil Procedure Law for justifying jurisdiction in a foreign-related case raises questions. On one hand, the Jiangxi Nanchang Intermediate People's Court classified the dispute as a foreign-related civil dispute. On the other hand, the court invoked an article addressing purely domestic jurisdiction rules (Article 23) to justify its jurisdiction over a foreign-related dispute. This practice introduces a level of self-contradiction. Using Article 23 of the 2017 Chinese Civil Procedure Law or other provisions dealing with foreign-related jurisdiction may lead to the same outcome, enabling the Chinese court to exert jurisdiction. Despite this, the conflicts justice is as important as

[136] *Xue Xiujuan v. Jiangxi Ganzhonglv International Travel Agency*, Jiangxi Province HPC, (2017) Gan Min Zhong No 248; Jiangxi Province Nanchang Municipality IPC, (2016) Gan 01 Min Chu No 229. 中国大地财产保险股份有限公司江西分公司、薛秀娟旅游合同纠纷二审民事判决书，江西省高级人民法院，(2017)赣民终248号；南昌市中级人民法院，(2016)赣01民初229号。

[137] The court did refer to Articles 11, 18 in the final paragraph of the judgment, although tourist is not explicitly mentioned as a consumer.

[138] This is also the case in *Xue Xiujuan v. Yongcheng Property Insurance Co.*, a foreign-related dispute between a tourist and an insurer operator regarding personal accident insurance of an overseas travel group, the court did not mention the fact that the tourist got injured in a speedboat when sailing in Pattaya, Thailand, instead, the court deemed that since the domicile of the defendant was in the jurisdiction of Nanchang, Jiangxi, the court had jurisdiction over the dispute in accordance with Article 23 of the 2017 Chinese Civil Procedure Law. *Xue Xiujuan v Yongcheng Property Insurance Co., Ltd.* Jiangxi Branch, Jiangxi Province Nanchang Municipality IPC, (2015) Hong Min Si Chu Zi No 30.

procedural justice and substantive justice, thus, a well-grounded reasoning on jurisdiction is essential. The importance of consistent reasoning in private international law cannot be overstated, as it concerns legal certainty and predictability.

In fact, Article 23 of the 2017 Chinese Civil Procedure Law has been widely used by judges to justify Chinese court jurisdiction over foreign-related travel disputes. For example, in *Zhu Kaili v. Guangzhou Baiyun District Fluent Education Training Centre*,[139] involving the United States and Hong Kong, and *Chen Yan v. Rizhao Oriental International Travel Agency*,[140] the courts justified their jurisdiction based on the defendant's domicile. In *Chen Yan v. Rizhao Oriental International Travel Agency*, where the travel contract between the tourist and the travel agency encompassed eight Western European countries, the tourist sued the travel agency for contractual liability after getting injured in Paris, France. Interestingly, what slightly different from the practice of other courts is that Shandong Rizhao Intermediate People's Court characterized the case as a travel contract dispute involving a foreign element, rather than a foreign-related dispute, thereby the case, in nature, was still a purely domestic case.[141] Despite the fact that the tourist was injured abroad, the court did not refer to jurisdiction rules over foreign-related cases. The domestic jurisdiction rule of Article 23 of the 2017 Chinese Civil Procedure Law was applied to justify the court's jurisdiction based on the defendant's domicile.[142] However, if the defendant lacks domicile in China, applying Article 23 of the 2017 Chinese Civil Procedure Law would be problematic.

In the absence of a specific jurisdiction rule for consumer contracts, package travel contracts have been considered as nameless contracts in judicial practice, governed by general contract jurisdiction rules. As a result, Article 23 of the 2017 Chinese Civil Procedure Law has been extensively used to justify Chinese court jurisdiction over disputes arising from or related to package travel contracts. Since most package travel contracts are performed in a foreign country, relying on the

[139] *Zhu Kaili v. Guangzhou Baiyun District Fluent Education Training Centre*, Guangdong Province Guangzhou Municipality IPC, (2014) Hui Zhong Fa Min Si Zhong Zi No 137; Guangdong Province Guangzhou Municipality Baiyun DPC, (2014) Hui Yun Fa Min San Chu Zi No 15. 朱凯莉、朱凯嘉、朱庆文、谭佩仪与广州市白云区流利教育培训中心服务合同纠纷二审民事判决书，广东省广州市中级人民法院，(2014)穗中法民四终字第137号；广东省广州市白云区人民法院，(2014)穗云法民三初字第15号。

[140] *Chen Yan v. Rizhao Oriental International Travel Agency*, Shandong Province Rizhao Municipality IPC, (2016) Lu 11 Min Xia Zhong No 95; Shandong Province Rizhao Municipality Donggang DPC, (2016) Lu 1102 Min Chu No 1480. 陈燕与日照东方国际旅行社有限公司、刘祥文旅游合同纠纷二审民事判决书，山东省日照市中级人民法院，(2016)鲁11民辖终95号；日照市东港区人民法院，(2016)鲁1102民初1480号。

[141] However, this classification is quite confusing and debatable, because in accordance with Article 1 of SPC Judicial Interpretation I of Conflict of Laws Act, this case is clearly 'foreign-related' as the tourist got injury in Paris, France. Then the question arises as to whether it should be a domestic travel dispute with a foreign element, or a foreign-related travel dispute in nature? Putting the wording 'foreign element' and 'foreign-related' in different order, the nature of the dispute differs and accordingly the jurisdiction and applicable law rules will follow varying trajectories.

[142] Regardless of whether this case should be identified as domestic or foreign-related in nature, at least the court was consistent in terms of classification and jurisdiction.

jurisdiction ground of the place of contract performance would lead to a foreign court. Referring to Article 23 of the 2017 Chinese Civil Procedure Law indicates that the domicile of the defendant becomes the primary jurisdictional basis over package travel contracts.

3.3.3 Multi-Party Litigation with Multiple Domiciles

In principle, Article 23 of the 2017 Chinese Civil Procedure Law doesn't apply when the defendant is a foreign travel service provider with no domicile in China. However, in judicial practice, Article 23 of the 2017 Chinese Civil Procedure Law has been used to justify the jurisdiction of a court based on one defendant's domicile in multi-party litigation, even when other defendants have domiciles in different places. An example of this is found in the case of *Liu Chengqin v. Shenzhen Jiuzhou International Travel Agency et al.*[143] In this case, 14 plaintiffs, including Liu Chengqin and Yi Jianguo, domiciled in Shenzhen City, Guangdong Province, sued three defendants: (i) Shenzhen Jiuzhou International Travel Agency, domiciled in Futian District, Shenzhen, Guangdong, (ii) Costa Crocieres.P.A, domiciled in Genoa, Italy, and (iii) Costa Cruises Shipping (Shanghai) Co., Ltd., domiciled in Hongkou District, Shanghai, before the Guangdong Shenzhen Qianhai Cooperation Zone People's Court.

The plaintiffs asked for a refund of 7, 550 RMB (1, 048 Euro) and three times the amount of the travel expenses as compensation (22, 650 RMB) (3, 146 Euro) for each plaintiff. The Shengdian Law Firm, where the 14 plaintiffs worked, concluded a group outbound travel contract with Shenzhen Jiuzhou International Travel Agency for a 6-day-5-night tour on a cruise ship to Japan with the itinerary 'Shenzhen-Okinawa-Miyako Island-Shenzhen'. On the day of departure, shortly after leaving the port, Costa Cruise Company notified the passengers that the destination would change from Japanese ports to Vietnamese ports due to bad wether without consulting the passengers. Despite the fact that the passengers onboard expressed their dissatisfaction and raised objections, the three defendants ignored their disagreements, gave no reasonable explanation, and proceeded directly to the ports of Vietnam. Ultimately, all tourists had to follow the new route with a changed itinerary 'Shenzhen-Da Nang-Nha Trang-Shenzhen', deviating completely from the tourists' original intention.

Later, the plaintiffs discovered that the defendants had known about the weather forecast before departure and had prepared a written notice in advance regarding the change in the tour route. This revelation indicated fraudulent provision of travel services by the operator. According to Article 55 of the Chinese Consumer Protection Law, the operator should pay three times the amount of the service fee. The

---

[143] *Liu Chengqin v. Shenzhen Jiuzhou International Travel Agency*, Guangdong Shenzhen Qianhai Cooperation Zone People's Court, (2020) Yue 0391 Min Chu No 1620-1633. 刘承琴民事裁定书, 广东省深圳前海合作区人民法院,(2020)粤0391民初1620-1633号.

defendant Shenzhen Jiuzhou International Travel Agency served as the travel operator, while the defendants Costa Crocieres.P.A and Costa Cruises Shipping (Shanghai) Company acted as assistant travel service providers. As professional cruise tour service providers, they were expected to pay close attention to weather conditions and fulfill the duty of providing sufficient notice to their passengers. The failure to fully fulfill this obligation of notification constituted a breach of contract.

The court held that Costa Crocieres.P.A was a foreign legal person,[144] thus the case involved a foreign-related travel contract dispute. According to the Approval of the Supreme People's Court on Approving the Establishment of the People's Court of Shenzhen Qianhai Cooperation Zone, the jurisdiction of this court includes: (i) first-instance civil and commercial cases falling under the jurisdiction of the grassroots court within the jurisdiction of Shenzhen Qianhai Cooperation Zone; (ii) first-instance foreign-related, Hong Kong, Macao, and Taiwan-related commercial cases falling under the jurisdiction of grassroots courts within Shenzhen's jurisdiction. While the case involved a foreign-related travel contract dispute, it was deemed a foreign-related civil case, rather than a foreign-related commercial case. Thus, the case did not fall within the scope of first-instance foreign-related commercial cases.[145]

In addition, the domicile of the defendant Shenzhen Jiuzhou International Travel Agency was in Futian District, Shenzhen, Guangdong, the domicile of the defendant Costa Crocieres.P.A was in Genoa, Italy, and the domicile of the defendant Costa Cruises Shipping (Shanghai) Co., Ltd., was in Hongkou District, Shanghai. The domiciles of these three defendants were not within the Shenzhen Qianhai Cooperation Zone. Consequently, the case was not a first-instance civil and commercial case that should be subject to the jurisdiction of grassroots courts within the Shenzhen Qianhai Cooperation Zone. Therefore, the Guangdong Shenzhen Qianhai Cooperation Zone People's Court lacked jurisdiction over this case.[146]

The Guangdong Shengdian Law Firm, as the employer of the 14 plaintiffs, signed the group outbound travel contract with the defendant Shenzhen Jiuzhou International Travel Agency in Futian District, Shenzhen, Guangdong, and made the travel fee payments in that district. Additionally, the domicile of the defendant Shenzhen Jiuzhou International Travel Agency was in Futian District, Shenzhen, Guangdong. Pursuant to Article 23 of the 2017 Chinese Civil Procedure Law, the People's Court of Futian District, Shenzhen, Guangdong, as the court in which the defendant was domiciled, should have jurisdiction. Therefore, the case should be transferred to the People's Court of Futian District, Shenzhen, Guangdong.[147]

---

[144] Ibid. The court did not mention Costa Cruises Shipping (Shanghai) Company as a foreign legal person.

[145] Ibid.

[146] Ibid.

[147] Ibid. The same reasoning was conducted in other cases concerning different plaintiffs against the same defendants on the same issue, see Guangdong Shenzhen Qianhai Cooperation Zone People's Court, (2020) Yue 0391 Min Chu No 1590-1599; (2020) Yue 0391 Min Chu No 1617-1619.

However, not all defendants had their domiciles in Futian District, Shenzhen, Guangdong. The other two defendants in this case had their domiciles in Shanghai (China) and Genoa (Italy) respectively. The application of Article 23 of the 2017 Chinese Civil Procedure Law is debatable in the sense that one of the defendants has a domicile in a foreign country.

Article 22 of the 2021 Chinese Civil Procedure Law states that where the domiciles and habitual residences of several defendants in the same lawsuit are within the jurisdiction of two or more people's courts, each of the people's courts shall have jurisdiction. However, this rule applies to purely domestic cases and allocates jurisdiction among Chinese courts, instead of addressing cross-border jurisdiction issues. Since the Chinese Civil Procedure Law does not expressly classify the relationship between domestic and international jurisdiction rules, it is unclear whether a domestic jurisdiction rule should be applied in foreign-related cases.[148] Given that the special jurisdiction rules specifically designed for international cases are simple and incomplete,[149] many Chinese courts are using domestic jurisdiction rules to determine the competent court for foreign-related cases.

3.3.4 The So-Called 'Relevant Provisions'

In *Zhu Kaili v Guangzhou Baiyun District Fluent Education Training Centre*,[150] the court held that according to 'relevant provisions' of the Answers of the SPC to Questions Concerning Economic Disputes Involving Hong Kong and Macau,[151] Article 4 of the Civil Procedure Law and Article 23 of the 2017 Chinese Civil Procedure Law,[152] the court where the domicile of the defendant was located has jurisdiction. At first glimpse, it seems well-grounded when the court invoked several articles from different laws to justify its jurisdiction. However, the quantity of legal reference does not necessarily guarantee the quality of legal reasoning. The court's reasoning is questionable for two reasons.

Firstly, the phrase 'according to relevant provisions' is notably ambiguous, as the court did not specify which provisions were relied upon. This lack of clarity makes it challenging for the parties involved to understand which specific provision justified the court's jurisdiction. In fact, the phrase 'according to relevant provisions' is

[148] Tang et al. (2016), p. 87, para.3.80.

[149] Tang et al. (2016), p. 87, para.3.80. Article 272 of the 2021 Chinese Civil Procedure Law on exorbitant jurisdiction is problematic.

[150] *Zhu Kaili v Guangzhou Baiyun District Fluent Education Training Centre*, Guangdong Province Guangzhou Municipality Baiyun DPC, (2014) Hui Yun Fa Min San Chu Zi No 15.

[151] The Answers of the SPC to Questions Concerning Economic Disputes Involving Hong Kong and Macau stipulates that the judicial proceeding of Hong Kong related case should refer to the special provisions of the Civil Procedure Law concerning foreign-related civil proceedings.

[152] As mentioned above, Article 23 of the 2017 Chinese Civil Procedure Law is mainly about jurisdiction rule on domestic issue, not dealing with jurisdiction regarding foreign-related civil issues.

widely used in Chinese courts when attempting to invoke various laws to support jurisdiction without explicitly identifying the specific article within that law. For instance, in another Taiwan-related travel contract dispute heard by Fujian Zhangzhou Xiangcheng District People's Court, namely, *Zheng Yangmei et al v. Zhangzhou Tengbang International Travel Agency*,[153] the court utilized the same wording. In this case, the tourist Huang Haizhong died during a group trip to Jinmen, Taiwan. The plaintiffs were the victim Huang Haizhong's wife, daughter, and son separately. Regarding the distribution of jurisdiction within Chinese domestic courts, the district court transferred the case to Zhangzhou Intermediate People's Court in accordance with Article 18 of the Civil Procedure Law and the 'relevant provisions' of the Minutes of the Intermediate People's Court of Zhangzhou City on the Acceptance of Foreign-related, Hong Kong-Related, or Macao-Related Cases.[154]

The court, however, did not specify the particular provisions of the Minutes referred to with the term 'relevant provisions'. This practice raises questions about how judges should justify the exercise of jurisdiction by one court. A more appropriate approach would involve first identifying a jurisdictional ground, then referring to a specific legal provision with appropriate interpretation, and subsequently explaining the connection between China and the dispute to justify why Chinese courts have jurisdiction. Unfortunately, this approach is not adopted in judicial practice, possibly due to the massive workload of the courts and a lack of sufficient knowledge of private international law for some judges.

Secondly, another provision invoked by the court in *Zhu Kaili v Guangzhou Baiyun District Fluent Education Training Centre* was Article 4 of the Civil Procedure Law.[155] This article is a general rule on the applicable law of civil proceedings, specifically stating that the law of the forum shall govern the civil proceedings conducted in that forum. This provision inherently concerns the applicable law of procedural issues within a domestic court, rather than a jurisdiction rule over foreign-related civil matters. Clearly, the court inappropriately applied a rule concerning the applicable law of procedural issues to address jurisdiction issues.

The court appeared to make an effort to invoke as many laws or regulations as possible without conducting a specific and in-depth analysis, as long as the legal document had a certain connection with the facts of the case in question. In this context, the court overlooked the need for cautious selection and detailed analysis, and the multiple laws or regulations may not have been correct or proper. It is better to refrain from referring to multiple but incorrect laws or regulations and instead focus on a single legal provision that genuinely justifies the court's exercise of jurisdiction.

[153] *Zheng Yangmei et al v Zhangzhou Tengbang International Travel Agency*, Fujian Province Zhangzhou Municipality Xiangcheng DPC, (2016) Min 0602 Min Chu No 6138. 郑杨梅、黄丽文等与王晓君等旅游合同纠纷一审民事裁定书，福建省漳州市芗城区人民法院，(2016)闽0602民初6138号。

[154] 《漳州市中级人民法院<关于涉外、涉港澳案件受理范围的纪要>的规定》。

[155] Article 4 of the Chinese Civil Procedure Law stipulates that this law (Chinese Civil Procedure Law) must be observed when civil proceedings are conducted in the territory of the PRC.

3.3.5 *Lack of Laws or Regulations to Support Legitimate Jurisdiction*

In contrast to situations where multiple but inappropriate laws or regulations are invoked, there is another situation in which the court does not refer to any law or regulation to justify its jurisdiction. In *Tong Bo v Shandong Daxinhua Yuntong Travel Agency*,[156] the tourist signed a travel contract with the travel agency for a 10-day, 5-European Country tour (France, Switzerland, Holland, Belgium, Germany), and sustained injuries in a traffic accident near Mount Tilex in Switzerland on a tour bus arranged by the travel agency. Shandong Qingdao Intermediate People's Court characterized the case as a travel contract dispute. Since the place of performance was overseas, the court heard the case according to foreign-related civil and commercial proceedings. Regarding the jurisdiction issue, the court held that the domicile of both the tourist and the travel agency was in Qingdao, Shandong, thus this granted the court jurisdiction. However, the court did not invoke any specific laws or regulations to justify its jurisdiction. This absence of legal invocation is also observed in *Lan Xinguo v Shandong Daxinhua Yuntong Travel Agency*.[157] Although there was no dispute over the court's exercise of jurisdiction, it remains necessary to invoke legal provisions before reaching such a conclusion.

3.4 Jurisdiction by Agreement Over Consumer Contracts

Most consumer contracts are standard contracts that include general terms and conditions, such as jurisdiction or arbitration clauses. Article 17 of the 2024 Regulation on Implementation of the Consumer Protection Law of the PRC states that:[158]

> Operators using standard terms and conditions should comply with the provisions of Article 26 of the Consumer Protection Law. Operators are not allowed to use standard terms to unreasonably exempt or reduce their responsibilities, increase the responsibilities of consumers, or restrict consumers' legal rights to modify or terminate the contract, choose litigation or arbitration to resolve disputes, or select products or services from other operators.

According to Article 17 of the Regulation, business operators should not use standard terms to restrict consumers' legal rights to choose between litigation and

[156] *Tong Bo v Shandong Daxinhua Yuntong Travel Agency*, Shandong Province Qingdao Municipality IPC, (2016) Lu 02 Min Chu No 1146.

[157] *Lan Xinguo v Shandong Daxinhua Yuntong Travel Agency*, Shandong Province Qingdao Municipality IPC, (2016) Lu 02 Min Chu No 1112. 兰新国、山东大新华运通国际旅行社有限公司旅游合同纠纷二审民事判决书，山东省高级人民法院，(2017)鲁民终1112号。

[158] The original text of Art. 17 of the Regulation (《中华人民共和国消费者权益保护法实施条例》第17条) reads as follows: 经营者使用格式条款的，应当遵守消费者权益保护法第二十六条的规定。经营者不得利用格式条款不合理地免除或者　减轻其责任、加重消费者的责任或者限制消费者依法变更或者解除合同、选择诉讼或者仲裁解决消费争议、选择其他经营者的商品或者服务等权利。

arbitration to resolve their disputes. It remains unclear whether jurisdiction clauses in a standard consumer contract should be declared invalid and, if so, under what basis.

3.4.1 The Validity of Jurisdiction Clause in a Consumer Contract

In accordance with Article 35 of the 2021 Chinese Civil Procedure Law and Article 529 of the 2022 SPC Judicial Interpretation of the Civil Procedure Law, the parties in a contract may choose the courts that have an actual connection with the dispute. Article 35 of the 2021 Chinese Civil Procedure Law remains unchanged in the 2023 amendment. For foreign-related civil relations, Article 277 of the 2023 Civil Procedure Law no longer requires an 'actual connection' between the chosen court and the dispute. However, there is no consensus as to the validity of a choice of court agreement inserted in a standard consumer contract. In principle, parties in a contract are allowed to choose a competent court. Given the inequality of parties in a consumer contract, it is questionable whether a forum selection clause inserted by the business party in a standard form contract without negotiating with the consumer can be considered valid and enforceable.

3.4.1.1 Highlighting Jurisdiction Clauses?

In *Lin Lin v. Beijing Ctrip International Travel Agency*,[159] the tourist Lin Lin booked a 6-day, 4-night independent trip to the Maldives on Ctrip.com, a Beijing-based company, and paid a total of 40,960 RMB (5,851 Euro). Because of an earthquake occurred in Indonesia and a subsequent tsunami warning issued by the Maldives, the trip was cancelled. The tourist Lin Lin requested a full refund, but the travel agency agreed to refund only 8,700 RMB (1,243 Euro). Lin Lin sued the online travel platform Ctrip before Beijing Municipality Dongcheng District People's Court, the court of the tourist and the travel agency's common domicile.

The defendant, Beijing Ctrip company, argued that when Lin Lin and Beijing Ctrip company entered into the contract, they had agreed that the disputes between the two parties would be under the jurisdiction of Shanghai Changning District People's Court. Therefore, Beijing Dongcheng District People's Court had no jurisdiction over this case.[160]

[159] *Lin Lin v. Beijing Ctrip International Travel Agency Company*, Beijing Municipality Second Intermediate People's Court, (2012) Er Zhong Min Zhong Zi No 17117; Beijing Municipality Dongcheng District People's Court, (2012) Er Zhong Min Zhong Zi No 8257. 林琳与北京携程国际旅行社有限公司纠纷二审民事裁定书，北京市第二中级人民法院，(2012)二中民终字第17117号；北京市东城区人民法院，(2012)东民初字第8257号。

[160] Ibid.

The first-instance court, Beijing Dongcheng District People's Court, held that the plaintiff and the defendant entered into a service contract through the Internet under the true manifestation of intention. The defendant Ctrip company provided dispute resolution clauses on the website page, and the plaintiff had to accept these clauses before proceeding with the booking process. The dispute resolution clause stipulated that any dispute over the performance of the contract shall be subject to the laws and regulations of the People's Republic of China and the jurisdiction of Shanghai Changning District People's Court. The first-instance court determined that since the plaintiff had accepted such a jurisdiction clause, the two parties should choose the competent court to resolve their dispute according to the agreement.[161] Moreover, if the parties did not agree on the place of concluding the contract, the place where the final signature or seal was signed is considered the place where the contract was signed. The first-instance court analyzed that the conclusion of contracts through the Internet is special. Since the defendant Ctrip company conducted the final signature or seal act through the Internet, and the location of the Internet server was in Shanghai Changning District,[162] the court concluded that the place of conclusion of the contract was in Shanghai Changning District. Since the parties' jurisdiction agreement did not violate relevant laws and regulations, the case should be transferred to Shanghai Changning District People's Court.[163]

The Beijing Second Intermediate People's Court held that the plaintiff Lin Lin, as a consumer, selected travel products on Ctrip.com, and she had to enter relevant information as required and click on the standard terms to complete the booking process.[164] Concerning the standard form contract provided by the business operator of the Ctrip website, the court found that the Ctrip website did not not draw consumers' attention to the jurisdiction clauses of the agreement in a special, highlighted, and reasonable manner, excluding consumers' right to negotiate and choose the competent court.[165]

In addition, the registered domicile of consumer Lin Lin and the domicile of Beijing Ctrip Company (the operator of travel products) were located in Dongcheng District, Beijing. However, the jurisdiction clause stipulated in the standard contract by Ctrip.com designated Shanghai Changning District People's Court, which was only the registered place, business place, and the location of the Internet server of Shanghai Ctrip Business Co., Ltd (the owner of the website of Ctrip.com).[166] The court deemed such a jurisdiction clause invalid since it contained unfair and unreasonable provisions for consumers, which seriously and unreasonably increased the

---

[161] Ibid.

[162] Ibid. Shanghai Ctrip Business Co., Ltd. is the website owner and operator of Ctrip.com. Its registered address and business address was Changning District, Shanghai. Entrusted by Beijing Ctrip Company, Shanghai Ctrip Business Co., Ltd. publishes relevant travel information and completes reservation process on the Ctrip Travel website free of charge.

[163] Ibid.

[164] Ibid.

[165] Ibid.

[166] Ibid.

litigation burden on consumers.[167] Instead, the court concluded that contract disputes should be subject to the courts of the defendant's domicile or the courts of the place of contract performance under Article 24 of the Civil Procedure Law. Since the domicile of the defendant Beijing Ctrip Company was in Beijing Dongcheng District, the second-instance court concluded that the case should be subject to the jurisdiction of Beijing Dongcheng District People's Court.[168]

It is evident that the second-instance court and the first-instance court had different opinions on the validity of the jurisdiction clause contained in a standard contract provided by an online travel platform. Article 34 of the Chinese Civil Procedure Law states that parties in contract disputes may choose the courts of the place of the defendant's domicile, the place of performance of the contract, the place of conclusion of the contract, the place of the claimant's domicile, the place of the location of the subject matter, and other places which have an actual connection with the dispute.[169] Although jurisdiction by agreement over contract disputes takes precedence, it cannot derogate from provisions on standard clauses in the Contract Law and special provisions on the protection of consumer rights and interests.[170]

The standard form contract states that when the user booked travel and vacation products on the Ctrip website, it indicated that the user has carefully read and accepted all terms of the agreement. Despite the fact that both the consumer's dormice and the business operator's domicile were in Beijing Dongcheng District, the jurisdiction clause chose the court of Shanghai Changning District, which was unfair and unreasonable for the consumer, since it unreasonably aggravated the litigation burden for consumers.[171] Moreover, Shanghai Changning District was only the registered place, business place and the location of the website owner of Ctrip.com (Shanghai Ctrip Business Co., Ltd.), rather than the place of domicile of Lin Lin and Beijing Ctrip, the counterparty to the contract.[172] It does not conform to the close connection principle set forth in the Chinese Civil Procedure Law regarding jurisdiction by agreement and is also obviously detrimental to the exercise and

---

[167] Ibid. Article 40 of the Contract Law states that standard clauses which exempts the provider's responsibilities, aggravates the other party's responsibility, or excludes the other party's main rights shall be invalid. 《合同法》第四十条:格式条款具有本法第五十二条和第五十三条规定情形的，或者提供格式条款一方免除其责任、加重对方责任、排除对方主要权利的，该条款无效。

[168] Ibid.

[169] 《中华人民共和国民事诉讼法(2021年修正)》第35条:合同或者其他财产权益纠纷的当事人可以书面协议选择被告住所地、合同履行地、合同签订地、原告住所地、标的物所在地等与争议有实际联系的地点的人民法院管辖，但不得违反本法对级别管辖和专属管辖的规定。

[170] Zhao and Zhou (2015), p. 57; 赵瑞罡、周 薇,《电子商务纠纷中协议管辖条款效力的认定》，《人民司法》，2015年8月，第57页。

[171] Zhao and Zhou (2015), p. 57.

[172] Zhao and Zhou (2015), p. 57.

protection of consumers' rights. Thus, it is invalid in accordance with Article 24 of the Consumer Protection Law.[173]

3.4.1.2 Website User Agreements

Likewise, in *Xuchun Wang v. Beijing Jingdong Century Trading Co., Ltd.*,[174] the Beijing Haidian District People's Court also held that the jurisdiction clause in a standard website user agreement was invalid. In this case, the plaintiff, Beijing Jingdong Century Trading Co., Ltd, domiciled in Beijing Haidian District, sued the consumer defendant Xuchun Wang for revoking a contract for the purchase of an air conditioner. The plaintiff Beijing Jingdong Century Trading Co., Ltd was the operator of the Jingdong website www.360buy.com, and the defendant Xuchun Wang, domiciled in Shanghai Pudong District, was the user of the website and had to sign the website user agreement before shopping on that website.[175]

The website user agreement stated that the parties may submit their dispute to the court of the place where the website is located, namely Beijing Haidian District People's Court. The user Xuchun Wang bought two air conditioners priced at 0 RMB on the website, which the website claimed was a mistake made by its staff. Based on the jurisdiction agreement, Jingdong company sued its user Xuchun Wang before Beijing Haidian District People's Court to revoke the air conditioner contract.[176] The defendant Xuchun Wang raised an objection over the jurisdiction clause, claiming that it severely limits or deprives his jurisdictional interests and thus should be invalid. Since the domicile of the defendant and the place of performance of the contract was in Shanghai Pudong District, the defendant claimed that the case should be transferred to Shanghai Pudong District People's Court.[177]

The Beijing Haidian District People's Court analyzed that the website user agreement was a standard contract. Although it designated the court of the location of the website, the defendant held that it does not exclude statutory jurisdiction. According to the interpretation principle of the Contract Law over the standard clauses, the court shall give an interpretation not favorable to the provider. In addition, that jurisdiction clause deprived the consumer's jurisdictional interests and unreasonably increased the consumer's jurisdictional burden. Since such a

[173] Zhao and Zhou (2015), p. 57. Art.24 of Consumer Protection Law expressly provides that the standard form contract which contains unfair or unreasonable provisions shall be invalid. 《消费者权益保护法》第二十四条:经营者不得以格式合同、通知、声明、店堂告示等方式作出对消费者不公平、不合理的规定，或者减轻、免除其损害消费者合法权益应当承担的民事责任。格式合同、通知、声明、店堂告示等含有前款所列内容的，其内容无效。

[174] *Xuchun Wang v. Beijing Jingdong Century Trading Co., Ltd.*, Beijing Haidian District People's Court, (2008) Hai Min Chu Zi No. 30043. 王旭春与北京京东世纪贸易有限公司管辖权纠纷案，北京市海淀区人民法院，(2008)海民初字第30043号。

[175] Ibid.

[176] Ibid.

[177] Ibid.

jurisdiction clause is obviously unfair for the consumer, especially considering the fact that Jingdong company sued the consumer to revoke the contract and the place of performance is in another place, the jurisdiction clause is invalid according to Article 40 of the Contract Law and Article 24 of the Consumer Protection Law.[178] The court ruled that the case should be transferred to Shanghai Pudong District People's Court.

3.4.2 *The Chosen Courts are Uncertain*

The exclusivity of a jurisdiction clause is important in that it determines whether the clause grants jurisdiction to a specific court or also derogates jurisdiction from other competent courts.[179] In *Cong Shuwan v. Zhongxin Travel Service Group*,[180] the contract stipulated that the courts in Dalian shall have jurisdiction. However, the court held that such a choice was not clear. Since the contract was signed in Xigang District (Dalian), the Xigang District People's Court, as the place of the conclusion of the contract, should exercise jurisdiction over this case. The court relied on the factor of the place of the conclusion of the contract as a jurisdiction ground, instead of the forum selection clause, to justify the exercise of jurisdiction. This means that if a choice of court clause does not refer to a specific court but rather to courts in a district in general, such a forum selection clause may be deemed invalid because of its uncertainty. Such a conclusion is debatable. If the parties reach an ambiguous choice of court agreement that designates courts of the PRC in general, the claimant is responsible for figuring out the competent domestic court by hierarchy and territory.[181]

3.4.3 *Two Courts Are Chosen*

Article 30 of the 2022 SPC Judicial Interpretation of the Civil Procedure Law states that if the jurisdiction agreement stipulates that the people's court in two or more places that have an actual connection with the dispute has jurisdiction, the plaintiff may file a lawsuit in one of the people's courts. However, what if one, or even both, of the two chosen courts are incompatible with hierarchical and domestic territorial jurisdiction? It may be suggested that such a forum selection clause is invalid since it violates Chinese law; however, it is an extra burden for the parties to require them

[178] Ibid.

[179] Tang et al. (2016), p. 67, para.3.38.

[180] *Cong Shuwan v. Zhongxin Travel Service Group*, Liaoning Province Dalian Municipality Xigang DPC, (2017) Liao 0203 Min Chu No 4798. 从树万、从哲峰与众信旅游集团股份有限公司旅游合同纠纷一审民事判决书，大连市西岗区人民法院，(2017)辽0203民初4798号。

[181] Tang et al. (2016), p. 72, para.3.49.

to fully understand the complicated Chinese domestic jurisdiction system, the cost of which would be inappropriate and inefficient in cross-border transactions.[182] Moreover, hierarchical jurisdiction is largely determined by the value of the dispute as well as the type and significance of the case, thus the parties cannot precisely predict it before the dispute arises.[183] Therefore, not all choice of court agreements that designate courts that are incompatible with hierarchical jurisdiction are invalid. If the chosen court is a lower or higher court in comparison with the otherwise competent court, the case can be transferred to the competent court in accordance with the Chinese Civil Procedure Law.[184]

In *Wu Xiaome v. Gangzhonglv International Chengdu Travel Agency (Cuihua Road Branch)*,[185] the plaintiffs Wu Xiaome and Li Yuening, domiciled in Qingdao City, Shandong Province, sued the defendant Gangzhonglv International Chengdu Travel Agency (Cuihua Road Branch), domiciled in Chengdu High-tech Zone, Sichuan Pilot Free Trade Zone.[186] The plaintiffs claimed that when signing the contract, what they really meant was that if the two parties had a dispute, it would be heard by the court with jurisdiction in Qingdao, not by the Chengdu District Court. In addition, the place of the plaintiff's domicile, the place where the contract was signed, and the place where the contract was performed were all in Qingdao. According to Article 34 of the Civil Procedure Law, the court of first instance should have jurisdiction over this case. Moreover, the travel agency violated Article 58 of the Tourism Law and failed to fulfill its obligation to explain the dispute resolution method to the plaintiffs in detail.

The court classified the case as a case over an objection to jurisdiction over a travel contract dispute.[187] The parties had reached an agreement on the dispute

[182] Tang et al. (2016), p. 73, para.3.50. In international transactions, most jurisdiction clauses are inserted in standard-term contracts. It is commercially unviable to require a more specific and correct designation of domestic courts.

[183] Tang et al. (2016), p. 73, para.3.50.

[184] Tang et al. (2016), p. 73, para.3.50.

[185] *Wu Xiaome v. Gangzhonglv International Chengdu Travel Agency (Cuihua Road Branch)*, Shandong Province HPC, (2020) Lu Min Xia Zhong No 66; Shandong Province Qingdao Municipality IPC, (2019) Lu 02 Min Chu No 2301. 吴晓梅、李悦宁旅游合同纠纷管辖民事裁定书，山东省高级人民法院，(2020)鲁民辖终66号；山东省青岛市中级人民法院，(2019)鲁02民初2301号。

[186] Ibid. The city Qingdao (Shandong province) is 1909 kilometers away from the city Chengdu(Sichuan province). It takes 21-hour driving from Qingdao to Chengdu.

[187] Ibid. The court of first instance held that the performance of the contract was overseas and classified the case as a foreign-related commercial case. The court did not classify the case as a travel contract dispute nor a consumer contract dispute. The tourists argued that the contract was a standardized contract provided by the travel agency. During the negotiation, the travel agency initially chose Chengdu as the place for arbitration and allowed the tourists to choose only one court. The tourists believed that it was clearly unfair to them and asked the change to courts in Qingdao where the tourists were domiciled. In the beginning the travel agency disagreed but then agreed after adding courts of the city in which it domiciled. The tourists held that regarding the choice of courts, the travel agency had taken advantage of being the provider of the standardized contract and its familiarity with relevant laws as the professional operator of travel business to deceive tourists.

resolution method in the outbound travel contract concluded between them, that is, after the occurrence of a dispute, the parties should file a lawsuit before Qingdao Municipality Shinan District People's Court or Chengdu Municipality High-Tech District People's Court, provided that negotiation or mediation failed.

The court held that although the plaintiff expressed her intention to submit their disputes to the District People's Court in Qingdao before the conclusion of the contract, the jurisdiction clause in the concluded outbound travel contract designated two courts, namely, Qingdao Municipality Shinan District People's Court and Chengdu Municipality High-Tech District People's Court. Since the plaintiffs signed their names in the outbound travel contract, such a signature indicated that the choice-of-court agreement, which designated the two courts, reflected the true intention of the plaintiffs, especially considering the plaintiffs did not explicitly express their intention to exclude the jurisdiction of the Chengdu Municipality High-Tech District People's Court. In addition, such a jurisdiction clause complied with Article 34 of the Civil Procedure Law; thus, it was binding on both parties. The agreed jurisdiction between the parties should precede; that is, the two courts agreed by both parties should exercise jurisdiction over the dispute.[188] In this case, the court equates the signature of the plaintiff on a standard travel contract as the expression of the true intention of the plaintiff. Such presumption is debatable, since tourists usually have no choice but to agree to all the general terms and conditions, including choice of law and choice of court clauses, inserted in a pre-drafted contract.

The court further explained that according to Article 1 of the Provisions of the Supreme People's Court on Several Issues Concerning the Jurisdiction of Foreign-Related Civil and Commercial Cases, centralized jurisdiction shall be implemented in foreign-related commercial cases. Since the performance of the travel contract at issue took place overseas, this case was a foreign-related commercial dispute and should be heard by a court having jurisdiction over the foreign-related commercial case. Among the two courts of jurisdiction agreed by both parties, only the Chengdu High-tech Zone People's Court was competent to hear foreign-related commercial cases, so the Chengdu High-tech Zone People's Court should exert jurisdiction over this case. The court of first instance was not one of the two courts agreed upon by the parties and thus did not have jurisdiction over this case. Therefore, the case should be transferred to the People's Court of Chengdu High-tech Zone for trial.[189]

There are two issues in the jurisdiction reasoning of the case. First, the classification of the dispute over a package travel contract as a commercial dispute is not correct. The tourists are consumers not acting in their trade or profession. It is a civil dispute, if not qualified as a consumer dispute. Second, this case indicates that the

---

The travel agency knew in advance that the choice of the court of the Qingdao Shinan District People's Court was invalid, such legal knowledge was generally unknown to the normal tourists, the abuse of this knowledge asymmetry by the travel agency was obviously unfair to the tourists. Despite this, the court still upheld the validity of choice of court clause in this standardized travel contract.

[188] Ibid.

[189] Ibid.

business party may take advantage of the consumer's ignorance of the law and designate the court which has no jurisdiction over foreign-related cases, together with another court that is convenient to the business. Thus, the consent of the consumer is not an informed consent because of asymmetry of knowledge and information in *Wu Xiaome v. Gangzhonglv International Chengdu Travel Agency* (Cuihua Road Branch). The consumer is forced to sue before the court of the business's domicile, instead of the consumer's domicile. The disadvantage of suing in the courts of the business' domicile is more obvious when the business is domiciled in a foreign country. It imposes a big burden on consumers who have less information, weaker bargaining power, limited litigation experience and financial resources to go to a distant and unfamiliar country where the business is domiciled, especially when the long-distance litigation costs far exceed the amount of the dispute.[190]

3.4.4 The Validity of an Arbitration Clause in a Consumer Contract

The related principles of party autonomy and consent are fundamental to contemporary private international law regimes concerning matters of international dispute resolution.[191] Both international commercial arbitration subject to the New York Convention and judicial proceedings subject to the Choice of Court Convention are based on consent.[192] Party autonomy does not mean giving effect to every alleged international arbitration clause or forum selection agreement.[193] Respect for party autonomy means giving effect to those dispute resolution agreements that commercial parties have in fact validly concluded.[194] The parties' consent to a particular forum for adjudication is of central importance.[195] Article 9(a) of the Choice of Court Convention gives the national legal system putatively chosen in a choice-of-court agreement the sole authority to decide on the existence and validity of that agreement, without the possibility of subsequent review in recognition proceedings in any other forum.[196]

What about the validity of an arbitration clause in a consumer contract? For instance, if a consumer sues a business before a court, and the business contests the court's jurisdiction on the basis of an arbitration agreement integrated into a standard contract, whether such an arbitration clause is valid? In principle, if the parties have reached an agreement on arbitration, Chinese courts shall not take

[190] Yuthayotin (2015), pp. 93–95.

[191] Born (2021a), p. 2114.

[192] Born (2021b), p. 3881.

[193] Born (2021a), p. 2115.

[194] Born (2021a), p. 2115.

[195] Born (2021a), p. 2115.

[196] Born (2021a), p. 2117.

jurisdiction.[197] Article 127(2) of the 2021 Civil Procedural Law[198] states that according to the law, if both parties have reached a written arbitration agreement to apply for arbitration and cannot file a lawsuit in a people's court, the plaintiff shall be notified to apply to an arbitration institution for arbitration. Such an arbitration agreement should be reached on a voluntary basis.

As to the validity of an arbitration clause, if one party requires the arbitration tribunal to make a decision and another party refers to the court for a ruling, the court's decision should be given priority in such concurrent proceedings.[199] Where a party brings an action in the Chinese court in breach of an arbitration agreement and the other party enters an appearance to make a defense on substantive issues, the Chinese court has jurisdiction.[200] Many jurisdictions consider consumer cases non-arbitrable and would thus not enforce such an arbitral award in tourism matters.[201] The main reason is that the consumers and businesses are not in an equal position.[202] It seems that Chinese courts have taken a different approach by admitting the validity of consumer arbitration clause.

In *Lin Mou v. Shandong Travel Agency International Travel Company*,[203] the plaintiff Lin Mou, domiciled in Jimou district, Qingdao City (Shandong Province), sued the defendants (i) Shandong Travel Agency International Travel Company, domiciled in Lixia District, Jinan City, Shandong Province, and (ii) Shandong Travel Agency International Travel Company (Qingdao branch) before the Shandong Qingdao Intermediate People's Court.

The plaintiff had a travel agreement with the defendant Shandong Travel Agency International Travel Company(Qingdao branch) for traveling to Australia. The plaintiff claimed that the travel agency did not provide travel services in accordance with the travel agreement and thus should take responsibility for the breach of the contract. Another defendant should also take responsibility. The court found out that 24 tourists, including the plaintiff, concluded an outbound travel contract with the parent company Shandong Travel Agency International Travel Company. Lan Mou and Li Yu, as representatives of these 24 tourists, signed the contract. The branch company affixed its special seal for confirmation on the contract. Article 26 of the travel contract stipulated that any disputes arising out of the performance of the contract shall be submitted to Qingdao Arbitration Commission for arbitration.[204]

---

[197] Tang et al. (2016), p. 93, para.4.10.

[198] Article 124(2) of the 2017 Civil Procedural Law.

[199] Article 20 of the Arbitration Law.

[200] Tang et al. (2016), p. 99, para.4.25.

[201] The HCCH Report of the Experts' Group on the Cooperation and Access to Justice for International Tourists, para.211, Prel. Doc. 1 of February 2020.

[202] McGill (2010), pp. 361–413.

[203] *Lin Mou v. Shandong Travel Agency International Travel Company*, Shandong Province Qingdao Municipality IPC, (2018) Lu 02 Min Chu No 1728. 林某与山东旅行社国际旅游有限公司、山东旅行社国际旅游有限公司青岛华威分公司旅游合同纠纷一审民事裁定书，山东省青岛市中级人民法院，(2018)鲁02民初1728号。

[204] Ibid.

The court held that Lan Mou and Li Yu signed the travel contract on behalf of 24 tourists, and the parent company and the branch company of the travel agency also confirmed by affixing its company seal. Thus, the arbitration clause in the travel contract, which represented the true intentions of both parties, was legal and effective.[205] Before the hearing of this case, the two defendants submitted the arbitration agreement and raised objections to the jurisdiction of this court. The court believed that the objections of the two defendants should be upheld in accordance with Article 26 of the Arbitration Law. Since the case was not within the jurisdiction scope of the court, the case was dismissed in accordance with Article 124 of the Civil Procedure Law.[206] The court affirmed the business's assertion and upheld the validity of the arbitration clause.

Notably, mutual consent from both parties is the foundation for arbitration.[207] One may argue that the signature in a traditional contract or click in a click-wrap contract also reflects the party's intention and constitutes consent.[208] The contractual clause should not be invalid only because one party is a stronger party. However, the mandatory arbitration clause in a consumer contract does not necessarily reflect the true intention of the consumer, especially for arbitration clauses in electronic consumer contracts. To compensate for the weak position of consumers, some scholars propose that three conditions have to be fulfilled for arbitration clauses in electronic standard form contracts to be valid.[209]

---

[205] Ibid.

[206] The same reasoning was conducted in *Chen Mou v. Shandong Travel Agency International Travel Company*, Shandong Province Qingdao Municipality IPC, (2018) Lu 02 Min Chu No 1715; 陈某与山东旅行社国际旅游有限公司、山东旅行社国际旅游有限公司青岛华威分公司旅游合同纠纷一审民事裁定书，山东省青岛市中级人民法院，(2018)鲁02民初1715号; *Lan Xiaobin v. Shandong Travel Agency International Travel Company*, Shandong Province Qingdao Municipality IPC, (2018) Lu 02 Min Chu No 1722; 兰晓彬与山东旅行社国际旅游有限公司、山东旅行社国际旅游有限公司青岛华威分公司旅游合同纠纷一审民事裁定书，山东省青岛市中级人民法院，(2018)鲁02民初1722号; *Liu Min v. Shandong Travel Agency International Travel Company*, Shandong Province Qingdao Municipality IPC, (2018) Lu 02 Min Chu No 1729; 刘敏与山东旅行社国际旅游有限公司、山东旅行社国际旅游有限公司青岛华威分公司旅游合同纠纷一审民事裁定书，山东省青岛市中级人民法院，(2018)鲁02民初1729号; *Dong Li v. Shandong Travel Agency International Travel Company*, Shandong Province Qingdao Municipality IPC, (2018) Lu 02 Min Chu No 1733; 董丽与山东旅行社国际旅游有限公司、山东旅行社国际旅游有限公司青岛华威分公司旅游合同纠纷一审民事裁定书，山东省青岛市中级人民法院，(2018)鲁02民初1733号; *Ma Jun v. Shandong Travel Agency International Travel Company*, Shandong Province Qingdao Municipality IPC, (2018) Lu 02 Min Chu No 1723; 马君与山东旅行社国际旅游有限公司、山东旅行社国际旅游有限公司青岛华威分公司旅游合同纠纷一审民事裁定书，山东省青岛市中级人民法院，(2018)鲁02民初1723号。

[207] Xiao and Tan (2014), p. 28; 肖永平、谭立:《论网上交易平台对概括性仲裁协议效力的影响》，《武大国际法评论》，2014年第2期，第28页。

[208] Casamiquela (2002), p. 476.

[209] Qiao and He (2007), p. 95; 乔仕彤、何其生,《电子格式合同中仲裁条款的效力-以中国消费者市场中Microsoft软件最终用户许可协议为例》，《武大国际法评论》，2007年第2期，第95页。

First, consumers should have the chance to check the substantive provisions and express 'yes' or 'no' in certain ways.[210] Second, the provider of the arbitration clause should draw the consumers' attention to the content of the clause in a reasonable way, or the arbitration clause should be conspicuous enough to attract consumers' attention.[211] Third, the arbitration clause should not be obviously unfair.[212] An arbitration clause in a standard contract is valid and enforceable only if the consumer expressly agrees.[213] In a unilaterally binding arbitration agreement, if the business and the consumer reach an optional arbitration clause, according to which the business can only submit the dispute to arbitration while the consumer can freely choose between arbitration and litigation, such a clause is valid since it provides protection to the weak party.[214] After the dispute arises, the consumer may choose to file a lawsuit before the courts. Once the consumer chooses litigation, the business cannot contest the court's jurisdiction based on the arbitration agreement, and the consumer cannot submit the same dispute to arbitration again.[215]

3.5 Concurrent Liability in Consumer Contracts

The *Lin Mou v. Shandong Travel Agency International Travel Company* case also gives rise to the concurrent liability in consumer contracts.[216] Article 26 of the travel contract stipulated that any disputes arising out of the performance of the contract shall be submitted to Qingdao Arbitration Commission for arbitration. The wording 'any disputes arising out of the performance of the contract' indicates that both contractual obligations and non-contractual obligations are subject to arbitration. Such dispute resolution clause may offer legal predictability in the context of concurrent liability, since the same tribunal is competent, regardless of the cause of action chosen by the claimant. In *Chen Caiyi v. Zhongshan China International Travel Agency*,[217] the court defines travel disputes as 'any contract disputes or tort

[210] Qiao and He (2007), p. 95.

[211] Qiao and He (2007), p. 95.

[212] Qiao and He (2007), p. 95.

[213] Chen (2018), p. 335. 陈珍，《涉外民商事合同中单边争议解决条款效力之争》，《中国国际私法与比较法年刊》，2018年第22卷，第335页。

[214] Xiao and Tan (2014), p. 39; Smit (2009), p. 391.

[215] Xiao and Tan (2014), p. 39.

[216] *Lin Mou v. Shandong Travel Agency International Travel Company*, Shandong Province Qingdao Municipality IPC, (2018) Lu 02 Min Chu No 1728.

[217] *Chen Caiyi v. Zhongshan China International Travel Agency*, Guangdong Zhongshan Municipality First People's Court, (2019) Yue 2071 Min Chu No 189. 陈财意与中山中国国际旅行社有限公司旅游合同纠纷一审民事判决书，广东省中山市第一人民法院，(2019)粤2071民初第189号。 The plaintiff Chen Caiyi, resident of Hong Kong SAR (Special Administrative Region), domiciled in Hong Kong, sued the defendant Zhongshan China International Travel Agency, domiciled in Zhongshan City, Guangdong province. The plaintiff and other 9 tourists signed an outbound travel contract with the defendant for a 6-day tour in Japan. The plaintiff, while

disputes arising from a travel contract between tourists and tour operators or auxiliary travel service providers'.[218]

3.5.1 Concurrent Claims in Package Travel Contracts

Concurrent liability in tourism disputes is more likely to happen when the breach of a package travel contract also incurs tort liability. This is often the case when personal injury or death occurs during the performance of a package travel contract in which the travel operators are negligent in fulfilling their obligations.[219] Article 1198 of the Chinese Civil Code states that "if the operators, managers of public places, such as hotels, shopping malls, banks, railway stations, airports, stadiums, entertainment venues, or organizers of mass activities, fail to fulfill their security obligations and cause damage to others, they shall be liable for infringement responsibility".[220] The omission to perform a required duty or the failure to act, which results in harm to a person or to property, may constitute nonfeasance tort.[221]

In *Liu Zhiwei et al v. Zhongshan Feixiang International Travel Agency*,[222] the three plaintiffs, as the deceased Liu Mou's family members, sued the travel agency for compensation of 409, 750 RMB (56, 909 Euro) for Liu Mou's death and 50,000 RMB (6, 944 Euro) for mental damage compensation.[223] The court held that the plaintiffs filed a lawsuit for the right to life on the ground that the travel agency had not fulfilled its obligations of guaranteeing the tourists' security through notification and reasonable warning. Since the plaintiffs required the defendant to bear tort liability, in accordance with Article 3 of the Provisions of the Supreme People's Court

---

staying in a hotel, was injured due to a slip and fall accident after enjoying hot spring. The plaintiff claimed that the defendant did fulfill the duty of guaranteeing the tourist's safety and thus was responsible for the injury. The plaintiff asked the defendant to pay a compensation of economic loss of 149903.5 RMB (20, 819 Euro).

[218] 所谓旅游纠纷，是指旅游者与旅游经营者、旅游辅助服务者之间因旅游发生的合同纠纷或者侵权纠纷。

[219] The nonfeasance tort is caused by the failure or omission to perform an obligatory or compulsory act. The law applicable to consumer concurrent claims has been discussed in Chen (2024), pp. 76–77; Chen (2021), pp. 626–647; Chen (2023), pp. 184–196.

[220] The Consumer Protection Law provides only some principles on the obligations of the operators, which is not very operational in judicial practice when it comes to the liability for tort by non-acting. Yang (2010), p. 454; 杨垠红，《我国侵权立法确立不作为侵权责任之探讨》，何勤华主编，《大陆法系及其对中国的影响》，法律出版社，2010年，第454页。

[221] Yang (2010), p. 453.

[222] *Liu Zhiwei et al v. Zhongshan Feixiang International Travel Agency*, Guangdong Zhongshan Municipality First People's Court, (2018) Yue 2071 Min Chu No 11424. 刘志伟、刘丽云等与中山飞翔国际旅行社有限公司旅游合同纠纷一审民事判决书，广东省中山市第一人民法院，(2018)粤2071民初11424号。

[223] The plaintiffs held that the defendant, as a tour operator, has the obligation to inform and warn the tourists about matters that may endanger the personal safety of the tourists in advance, and take necessary measures to prevent it from happening.

on Several Issues concerning the Application of Law in the Trial of Tourism Dispute Cases, the court should hear the case in line with the cause of action chosen by the parties. Article 3 of the SPC's Provisions states that 'where personal injury or property loss is caused to a tourist due to the same reason on the part of the tourist operator, and the tourist chooses to require the tourist operator to bear the liability for breach of contract or tort liability, the people's court shall conduct the trial according to the cause of action selected by the parties'.[224] Since the claimants chose tort liability as the cause of action, the court also resorted to Article 44 of the Chinese Conflict of Laws Act on tort choice of law rules to determine the applicable law. This is also the case in *Lu Jianfeng v. Zhongshan Feixiang International Travel Agency & Zhuhai Airline International Travel Agency*.[225] The difference is that, apart from Article 3 of the SPC's Provisions, the appellate court also invoked Article 122 of the Chinese Contract Law[226]

The tourist in a package travel contract may choose the travel operator to bear tort liability or contract liability. In *Li Mingqing v. Nanjing Tuniu International Travel Agency et al*,[227] the plaintiff signed a travel contract with Nanjing Tuniu International Travel Agency (Shantou Branch) for visiting Turkey but was injured

[224]《最高人民法院关于审理旅游纠纷案件适用法律若干问题的规定》第三条规定，因旅游经营者方面的同一原因造成旅游者人身损害、财产损失，旅游者选择要求旅游经营者承担违约责任或者侵权责任的，人民法院应当根据当事人选择的案由进行审理。

[225] *Lu Jianfeng v. Zhongshan Feixiang International Travel Agency & Zhuhai Airline International Travel Agency*, Guangdong Zhuhai Municipality Intermediate People's Court, (2020) Yue 04 Min Zhong No 3945; Guangdong Zhuhai Municipality Hengqin District People's Court, (2020) Yue 0491 Min Chu No 1404. 广东同程创游国际旅行社有限公司与陆健锋、珠海航空国际旅行社有限公司、广州市芳依电子商务有限公司、浙商财产保险股份有限公司珠海中心支公司侵权责任纠纷一案民事二审判决书， 广东省珠海市中级人民法院，(2020)粤04民终3945号；广东省珠海横琴新区人民法院，(2020)粤0491民初1404号。 The appellants/defendants were Guangdong TravelGo Chuangyou International Travel Agency, domiciled in Guangzhou and Zhuhai Airline International Travel Agency, domiciled in Zhuhai, the appellee/plaintiff was Lu Jianfeng, domiciled in Huangpu district, Guangzhou. The third parties were Zheshang Property Insurance Co., Ltd. (Zhuhai Branch), domiciled in Zhuhai City, and Guangzhou Fangyi Electronic Commerce Co., Ltd., domiciled in Guangzhou City. Lu Jianfeng was injured in his right foot due to a puncture of the tourist bus while in Cambodia and sued the organizing travel agency and the carrying travel agency before a Chinese court.

[226] Article 122 of the Chinese Contract Law: If one party's breach of contract violates the other party's personal or property rights, the injured party has the right to choose this law to require it to bear the liability for breach of contract or to require it to bear tort liability in accordance with other laws. Article 122 of the Chinese Contract Law has been replaced by Article 186 of the Chinese Civil Code.

[227] *Li Mingqing v. Nanjing Tuniu International Travel Agency et al*, Guangdong Shantou Jinping District People's Court, (2018) Yue 0511 Min Chu No 1194; 李明卿与南京途牛国际旅行社有限公司汕头分公司、南京途牛国际旅行社有限公司旅游合同纠纷一审民事判决书，广东省汕头市金平区人民法院，(2018)粤0511民初1194号。The plaintiff Li Mingqing, domiciled in Jinping District, Shantou City, Guangdong, sued three defendants Nanjing Tuniu International Travel Agency (Shantou Branch), domiciled in Jinping District, Shantou City, Guangdong, Nanjing Tuniu International Travel Agency, domiciled in Xuanwu District, Nanjing City, Jiangsu Province, and Chinese International Travel Agency, domiciled in Luhu District, Shenzhen City, Guangdong, before the Jinping District People's Court, Shantou City, Guangdong.

when taking a hot air balloon tour recommended by the travel agency in Cappadocia, Turkey. The tourist took the view that the tour guide did not provide safety tips or danger warnings to tourists other than advertising its safety, especially given that the weather was unfavorable on that day. In addition, the tour guide handed over tourists to a hot air balloon driver who did not speak Chinese or English. The hot air balloon crashed shortly after liftoff, causing the plaintiff's injury.

The plaintiff argued that the travel agency did not fulfill its contractual obligations to guarantee the tourist's safety, provide warnings of risks, and offer rescue, making them responsible for the injury. According to Article 402 of the Contract Law, the parent company of the travel agency should also take responsibility. The plaintiff thus sued these three defendants and sought compensation totaling 463, 221 RMB (64, 336 Euro), including mental damage compensation. Pursuant to Article 3 of the Provisions of the Supreme People's Court on Several Issues concerning the Application of Law in the Trial of Tourism Dispute Cases, the court held that since the plaintiff asserted that the tour operators' failure to guarantee the tourists' safety had violated the contractual agreement, thereby requiring the three defendants to bear liability for the breach of contract related to the plaintiff's personal injury, the case was considered a travel contract dispute.[228] The court did mention that the place of injury and the place of performance of the contract were in Turkey, but did not explain why Chinese courts had jurisdiction over the dispute, other than relying on the closest connection principle to designate Chinese law as the applicable law.[229]

3.5.2 *Jurisdiction Ground for Concurrent Claims*

Article 272 of the 2021 Chinese Civil Procedure Law provides six different jurisdiction grounds for all contract disputes and other disputes over proprietary rights and interests. It does not distinguish contractual claims from non-contractual claims by providing different claims with different jurisdiction grounds.[230] Certain jurisdiction grounds, such as the place of the conclusion of contract, the place of the performance of the contract, and the place of the subject matter of the contract, are more relevant to cross-border contracts.[231] By contrast, the

[228] Ibid. 本案原告李明卿以旅游经营者违反合同约定未尽到安全保障义务为由，要求三被告对原告的人身损害承担违约赔偿责任，故本案系旅游合同纠纷。

[229] Ibid. 因案涉热气球事故致原告受伤的法律事实及案涉合同的实际履行地均发生在中国域外的土耳其，依据《最高人民法院关于适用<中华人民共和国民事诉讼法>的解释》第五百二十二条第四款的规定,本案应为涉外民事纠纷。本案当事人未协议选择合同适用的法律，且原、被告的住所地、合同签订地均在中国境内，根据最密切联系原则，本案应适用中华人民共和国法律解决纠纷。

[230] Tang et al. (2016), p. 76, para.3.57.

[231] Tang et al. (2016), p. 86, para.3.77. The jurisdiction ground of the place where the defendant has distrainable property is unusual, since it may have no connections with the dispute. The only jus-

jurisdiction ground of the place of the occurrence of tort is more relevant to non-contractual claims. When a tortuous act takes place in China, Chinese courts may exercise special jurisdiction over such tort claims. Article 24 of the 2022 SPC Judicial Interpretation of the Civil Procedure Law provides that 'the place of the tortious act stipulated in Article 28 of the Civil Procedure Law includes both the place where the tortious act is carried out and the place where the result of the infringement occurs'. Both the place of wrong and the place of damage are considered the places where the tort takes place.[232] These jurisdictional grounds might be invoked in contractual claims only when there is a concurrent action involving both contract and tort, and the claimant chooses to bring the action based on contract.[233] Since the six jurisdiction grounds provided in Article 272 of the 2021 Chinese Civil Procedure Law are not explicitly tailored to six distinct claims respectively, it may be argued that they are equally applicable to both contractual and non-contractual claims.

When it comes to package travel contracts, concurrent contractual and non-contractual claims arise when package travel tourists suffer personal injury or even death during the performance of the contract. The jurisdictional grounds provided in Article 272 of the 2021 Chinese Civil Procedure Law do not adequately consider weaker party protection. This limitation also extends to the tort conflicts rules in Article 44 of the Chinese Conflict of Laws Act.

Article 61 of the Draft of the Chinese Conflict of Laws Act on the *lex loci delicti* states that if the place of wrong and the place of damage are in different locations, the law of the place which is more favorable to the victim shall apply. This provision lacks clarity on the specific criteria for assessing favorability. It does not specify in what regard one law is more favorable than another law, but it possibly refers to substantive rights. This reflects the consideration of protecting victims in tort claims and imposes constraints on judicial discretion. When consumers happen to be victims in tort claims, consumers theoretically have the right to choose between the law of the place of wrongful act and the law of the place of damage, selecting whichever is more favorable to them. However, the final text of Article 44 of the Chinese Conflict of Laws Act does not expressly include such a statement.[234] Consequently, being a consumer-victim may not significantly aid in choosing a more favorable law

tification is to facilitate the recognization and enforcement of judgments. The jurisdiction ground of the place where the defendant has his representative office is based on the extended personal connections with the defendant.

[232] Article 25 of the 2020 SPC Judicial Interpretation of the Civil Procedure Law stipulates that the place where the infringement on the information network is carried out includes the location of the computer and other information equipment that implements the alleged infringing act, and the place where the infringement result occurs includes the domicile of the infringed person.

[233] Such interpretation may expand the jurisdiction of Chinese courts, since Chinese courts could exercise jurisdiction as long as any relevant place is situated in China. Tang et al. (2016), p. 76, para.3.57.

[234] Tang et al. (2016), p. 293. Still, the increasing complicacy of tortious liability calls for the establishment of particular conflicts rules for particular types of torts apart from providing general tort conflicts rules.

when parties opt for tort liability as the cause of action in concurrent claims. The fact that a victim is also a consumer is irrelevant in terms of the law applicable to tort liability.

Article 26 of the 2022 SPC Judicial Interpretation of the Civil Procedure Law states that the people's court of the place where the product is manufactured, sold, the service is provided, the infringement is committed, or the defendant is domiciled shall have jurisdiction over lawsuits related to property or personal injury caused by the substandard quality of a product or service. Although Article 26 determines internal territorial jurisdiction for Chinese courts, Professor Zheng Tang argues that it could also be used as convincing evidence for interpreting jurisdiction rules in foreign-related product liability issues.[235] Despite this, in my opinion, it may still be argued that it does not necessarily apply to international disputes. However, many Chinese courts, in practice, resort to domestic jurisdiction rules to justify their jurisdiction over foreign-related cases. There is no exception with regard to jurisdiction over consumer contracts. This undesirable situation also demonstrates the necessity and urgency to establish a special consumer jurisdiction rule and to separate contractual jurisdiction rules from non-contractual jurisdiction rules in cross-border disputes.

3.6 Distribution of Jurisdiction Within the Framework of Chinese Domestic Courts

China has four levels of jurisdiction: the Grass-root People's Court, the Intermediate People's Court, the High People's Court, and the Supreme People's Court. The structure of the Chinese court system involves a two-parallel system under the Supreme People's Court, consisting of Local People's Courts and Special People's Courts. The Local People's Courts include the High People's Court, Intermediate People's Court and Grass-root People's Court. The Special People's Courts comprise the Maritime Court, Military Court, Railway Transportation Court, and Forestry Court. Due to the complexity of the domestic judicial system in China, questions may still arise when it comes to hierarchical jurisdiction and internal territorial jurisdiction even if the parties agree to submit their dispute to Chinese courts.[236]

Regarding foreign-related travel contract disputes, even though the parties agreed that a Chinese court has jurisdiction, one party may object to the jurisdiction level of the Chinese court. One question that might arise is whether the amount of the disputed object determines the competent court within the framework of China's domestic court. In most countries, the amount of disputed object serves as the basis

[235] Tang et al. (2016), p. 85, para.3.75.

[236] Tang et al. (2016), p. 72, para.3.49.

for dividing the range of jurisdiction within the domestic framework.[237] This is also the case in China for domestic cases, but in terms of foreign-related civil and commercial cases, these rules are not strictly followed.

In the case of *Feng Yunhai v Shenzhen Tese International Travel agency*,[238] heard by the Henan High People's Court,[239] Shenzhen Tese International Travel Agency was dissatisfied with the civil ruling[240] of the Zhengzhou Intermediate People's Court and raised objections to the jurisdiction. The primary reason was based on Article 2 of the Notification of the Supreme People's Court on Adjusting the Standard of the First-Instance Civil and Commercial Cases Heard by the High People's Court and the Intermediate People's Court. This provision stipulates that the Zhengzhou Intermediate People's Court has jurisdiction over the first-instance civil and commercial cases with a target amount of more than 3 million RMB. However, the object of this case did not exceed the standard amount of 3 million RMB; hence, the case should fall under the jurisdiction of the grass-root people's court. Accordingly, Shenzhen Tese International Travel Agency required to transfer the case to the Shenzhen Luohu District People's Court, where the travel agency was located, or the courts where other defendants were located. The Zhengzhou Intermediate People's Court held that the place of performance of the contract in this case was in Bali Island, Indonesia; thus, the case was foreign-related because of this foreign element. The jurisdiction of the Zhengzhou Intermediate People's Court complied with the relevant provisions of the Supreme People's Court on the Centralized Jurisdiction of Foreign-related Civil and Commercial Cases. Therefore, the claim to transfer the case on the ground that the amount of money involved in the case was small cannot be supported.

When the case was appealed to its superior court, the Henan High People's Court first classified the travel contract as an extraterritorial travel contract based on Article 522(4)[241] of the SPC Judicial Interpretation of the Civil Procedure Law. This

---

[237] Many legal systems have a simplified procedure in place that is designed to deal with disputes of small amounts. For instance, the EU has established a small claim procedure less than EUR 5,000. This means that certain claims of tourists might fall outside of the scope of this procedure. Having considered the advantages and disadvantages of small claim procedure, the implementation of this procedure should focus on giving tourists effective access to already existing small claim procedures, rather than establishing a completely new cross-border small claim procedure. The HCCH Report of the Experts' Group on the Cooperation and Access to Justice for International Tourists, paras.224-230, Prel. Doc. 1 of February 2020.

[238] *Feng Yunhai v Shenzhen Tese International Travel agency*, Henan High People's Court, (2016) Yu Min Xia Zhong No 71; Henan Province Zhengzhou Municipality IPC, (2015) Zheng Min San Chu Zi No 307. 冯运海与深圳市特色国际旅行社有限公司、河南新华飞扬国际旅行社有限公司旅游合同纠纷二审民事裁定书，河南省高级人民法院，(2016)豫民辖终71号；河南省郑州市中级人民法院(2015)郑民三初字第307号。

[239] The judgments based on the same dispute with the same defendant but with different plaintiffs also include (2016)Yu Min Xia Zhong No 68, (2016)Yu Min Xia Zhong No 69, (2016)Yu Min Xia Zhong No 70, (2016)Yu Min Xia Zhong No 72, (2016)Yu Min Xia Zhong No 73.

[240] (2015) Zheng Min San Chu Zi No 309.

[241] It is arguable that the court did not invoke Article 1 of the SPC Judicial Interpretation I of the Chinese Conflict of Laws Act, which is specially drafted and issued as a guidance for Chinese

classification was made because the traffic accident that led to the dispute occurred outside the territory of China. Therefore, the Provisions of the Supreme People's Court on Issues Concerning the Jurisdiction of Foreign-Related Civil and Commercial Cases should be applied as a legal basis to exercise centralized jurisdiction.

Although the disputed amount did not exceed 3 million RMB, there were no people's court in the economic and technological development zone established by the State Council, and no grass-root people's courts meeting the conditions for acceptance. Thus, Zhengzhou Intermediate People's Court, as the intermediate court located in the capital of Henan province, had jurisdiction over foreign-related first-instance civil and commercial cases according to Article 3 of the Provisions of the Supreme People's Court on Issues Concerning the Jurisdiction of Foreign-Related Civil and Commercial Cases.[242]

In the reasoning provided by the courts, it is clear that the disputed amount does not directly determine the competent court. In a travel dispute case with a foreign-related element, the domestic courts deviate from the strict domestic jurisdiction rule. A foreign-related element is an exceptional factor. In other words, the Intermediate People's Court can assert jurisdiction over foreign-related travel dispute even when the disputed amount is far below the regulated standard. Additionally, some Grass-root People's Courts may also be competent to hear transnational disputes that are classified as unimportant based on the value of the subject matter, complexity and impact.[243]

3.7 Travel Abroad, Sue at Home

To sum up, many challenges and problems arise when determining jurisdiction over foreign-related travel contract disputes in general, including in the case of package travel contracts. These jurisdictional problems cannot be addressed in isolation, since they are interconnected with, or arise from, other problems within the whole legal system in China.[244] When a package travel contract is concluded between Chinese tourists and Chinese travel service providers, Chinese courts may easily resort to domestic jurisdiction rules to justify their jurisdiction over cross-border travel disputes. However, if the travel service provider is a foreign company, under which ground the Chinese courts may exercise jurisdiction over a foreign business? Article 42 of the Chinese Conflict of Laws Act designates the consumer's home law.

---

domestic courts to apply the Chinese Conflict of Laws Act in foreign-related civil relations.

[242] The relevant judgements are (2016)Yu Min Xia Zhong No 68, (2016)Yu Min Xia Zhong No 69, (2016)Yu Min Xia Zhong No 70, (2016)Yu Min Xia Zhong No 71, (2016)Yu Min Xia Zhong No 72, (2016)Yu Min Xia Zhong No 73, which have almost the same reasoning and ruling with regard to the jurisdiction issue.

[243] Tang et al. (2016), p. 53, para.3.07.

[244] Tang et al. (2016), p.116, para. 4.67.

In the absence of a consumer jurisdiction rule in China, the application of traditional jurisdiction grounds, such as the domicile of the defendant and the place of performance of the contract, would designate the courts of a foreign country, rather than the consumer's home court, as the travel service provider is domiciled abroad and the package travel contract has been performed abroad.

As the HCCH Tourist Project points out, a significant challenge faced by tourists seeking redress against foreign travel service providers is the absence of a physical presence in the country of travel and the inadmissibility of pursuing a claim from abroad.[245] The jurisdictional reasoning of Chinese domestic courts is generally less than satisfactory, and there remains considerable progress to be made for Chinese courts to provide more compelling and well-founded justifications for jurisdiction. Since conventional bases of jurisdiction, such as the domicile of the defendant and the place of performance of the contract, often do not afford tourists the option of pursuing claims in their home jurisdiction, the establishment of a specific consumer jurisdiction rule becomes imperative.[246] One crucial step towards addressing these challenges is the implementation of a consumer home jurisdiction rule. The adoption of such a rule holds the potential to offer a solution to the existing jurisdictional issues concerning package travel contracts. Notably, tourists often qualify as consumers.[247] Consumers generally benefit from more favorable jurisdiction and choice of law rules. The complications associated with initiating legal proceedings in a foreign country could be circumvented if tourists had the option to file claims in their home jurisdiction.[248]

3.7.1 Jurisdiction of the Court of the Consumer's Domicile

In China, Article 42 of the Chinese Conflict of Laws Act has separated consumer choice of law rules from general contract choice of law rules, however, consumer jurisdiction rules have not been separated from general contract jurisdiction rules.[249] The legal basis for jurisdiction over transnational consumer contracts is scattered in Section 4 of the 2021 Chinese Civil Procedure Law, the 2022 SPC Judicial Interpretation of the Civil Procedure Law, and other legal documents.[250] Based on Article 266 of the 2021 Chinese Civil Procedure Law regarding China's legislative

[245] The HCCH Report of the Experts' Group on the Cooperation and Access to Justice for International Tourists, para.254, Prel. Doc. 1 of February 2020.

[246] Ibid, para.255.

[247] Ibid, para.255.

[248] Ibid, para.254.

[249] The level of consumer protection on jurisdiction issues in cross-border disputes is much lower than that in choice of law issues. Gao (2016), p. 348; 高宏贵,《中国涉外民事关系法律适用法研究》，法律出版社2016 年版，第348页; Liu (2022), p. 70; 刘阳,《跨国消费合同管辖权研究:欧盟经验及我国方案》，《武汉大学国际法评论》，2022年第1期, 第70页。

[250] Liu (2022), p. 70.

system of international civil jurisdiction,[251] jurisdiction rules over foreign-related consumer contracts in China have shown a tendency to apply domestic jurisdiction rules over consumer contracts by analogy,[252] complemented by the application of general contract jurisdiction rules.[253] Article 272 of the 2021 Chinese Civil Procedure Law encompasses six jurisdiction grounds without distinction, which may lead to a mixed usage of connecting factors.[254] It is necessary to separate jurisdiction grounds over contractual obligations from those over non-contractual obligations, clarifying the conditions to apply each jurisdiction ground.

More importantly, it is advisable for the Chinese Civil Procedure Law to adopt a specific jurisdiction rule over consumer contracts. The jurisdiction ground of the place of seizable property provided in Article 272 of the 2021 Chinese Civil Procedure Law has been on the blacklist in many countries, since the seizable property may have no actual connection with the dispute, potentially leading to political or legal revenge.[255] Other jurisdiction grounds might be difficult to be specified.[256] For instance, the place of the subject matter is useful in disputes involving immovable properties but has no special significance in other types of disputes.

In terms of foreign-related tourism, which involves catering, transportation, accommodation, sightseeing, shopping, and entertainment, the place of the subject matter may be in multiple countries.[257] Likewise, the place of performance of the contract might also be in several countries.[258] The place of conclusion of the contract may be fortuitous and have no actual connection with the dispute, especially in the context of E-commerce.[259] The other two jurisdiction grounds also have their limitations. The place of the representative office is specific but too narrow, as a foreign business having no representative office in China may have multiple other ways to target consumers in China in the digital age. The place of the tort act is not significant when the claim is based on contract liability, unless it concerns concurrent claims. Considering all these drawbacks, it is not surprising that the jurisdiction rule over foreign-related civil disputes in Article 272 of the 2021 Chinese Civil Procedure Law has been underused in judicial practice to justify the exercise of jurisdiction over consumer contracts by Chinese courts. The insufficiency of these jurisdiction grounds justifies the necessity to establish a consumer jurisdiction rule.

---

[251] Xiang (2019), pp. 183–184; 向在胜,《中国国际民事管辖权的立法体例研究》，《法律科学(西北政法大学学报)》，2019年第4 期，第183-184 页。

[252] Xiao (2020), p.238; 肖雯:《跨境消费者合同法律适用问题研究》，法律出版社2020 年版，第238 页。

[253] Liu (2022), pp.70, 72.

[254] Liu (2022), p. 73.

[255] It is noticeable that this jurisdiction ground only applies to foreign-related cases in China, not to domestic cases. Xia (2015), p. 35.

[256] Xia (2015), p. 35.

[257] Xia (2015), p. 35. If a tourist is unsatisfactory with several services, does it mean that the tourist has to file a lawsuit in one country or several countries where the subject matter is located?

[258] Xia (2015), p. 35.

[259] Xia (2015), p. 35.

In fact, Article 31 of the Draft Model Law of Chinese Private International Law (6th draft) provides that: *Chinese courts shall have jurisdiction over an action arising from a dispute in respect of consumer rights and interests, if the domicile or the habitual residence of the consumer is situated within the territory of the PRC.*[260] This provision does not specify further requirements for the application of consumer jurisdiction rules, other than providing the consumer's domicile or habitual residence as jurisdiction grounds.

The choice of the consumer's domicile or habitual residence as a jurisdiction ground is also in line with consumer choice of law rules in Article 42 of the Chinese Conflict of Laws Act, according to which the law of the consumer's habitual residence shall apply. Nevertheless, Article 31 of the Draft Model Law of Chinese Private International Law (6th draft) was not adopted in the final text of the Chinese Conflict of Laws Act. The reason why this provision is not adopted remains unclear, but it may be partly because the whole jurisdiction section in this proposal is not included in the Chinese Conflict of Laws Act. After all, the proposed jurisdiction rules under the Draft Model Law of Chinese Private International Law (6th draft) were drafted by the China Society of Private International Law. It is academic, not legislative, and aims to provide a reference for legislative, judicial organs, or other government departments engaged in foreign affairs, as well as law schools and legal research institutes. Despite this, it reflects academic efforts to facilitate the adoption of consumer jurisdiction rules that grant jurisdiction to the consumer's country of domicile or habitual residence.

Would the adoption of Article 31 of the Draft Model Law of Chinese Private International Law be a solution for addressing jurisdiction issues over consumer contracts? Many scholars in China have advocated the adoption of the consumer's home jurisdiction rule to compensate for the jurisdictional disadvantage of consumers.[261] In particular, consumer disputes usually involve a small amount of money,[262] and the financial cost of suing in a court other than the consumer's home country may dissuade most consumers from resorting to legal redress. Such a home jurisdiction rule in Article 31 of the Draft Model Law of Chinese Private International Law may protect consumers as the weaker party and enhance consumer confidence.[263] This being said, it does not mean that the business's interests and reasonable expectations should be totally ignored.

[260] The Chinese Society of Private International Law drafted a Model Law of Private International Law of the PRC with the aim to harmonize conflict of law rules in China. Article 31 of the 2000 Model Law of Chinese Private International Law (6th draft)《中华人民共和国国际私法示范法(第六稿)》第三十一条:【消费者权益】对因消费者权益纠纷提起的诉讼，如消费者住所地或者惯常居所地位于中华人民共和国境内，中华人民共和国法院享有管辖权。The original text of the 6th draft in Chinese is available at http://www.cspil.org/Plus/m_default/Cms/docDetail.php?ID=208, accessed on 17 January 2025.

[261] Tian (2021), p. 16; Liu and Zheng (2015), pp. 104, 107.

[262] Liu and Zheng (2015), p. 105.

[263] Xia (2015), p. 35.

The exercise of jurisdiction of the consumer's home country should also be under the condition that the dispute has a connection with the consumer's home country, and the business may anticipate the possibility of being subject to the jurisdiction of the consumer's home country. In this regard, the targeting test in Article 42 of the Chinese Conflict of Laws Act may be equally applicable in consumer jurisdiction issues to maintain a balance between the protection of consumers and businesses. To protect the reasonable expectations of the business party, the exercise of jurisdiction by the courts in which the consumer is domiciled should also be under the condition that the business has conducted commercial activities in the consumer's domicile.

The targeting test is used to examine whether a business has engaged in commercial activities in one country. The commercial activities of a business can be conducted via its agency or representative office. In this regard, Article 24 of the Model Law of Chinese Private International Law (6th draft) states that: *for a lawsuit brought about a dispute over commercial activities, if the defendant's branch or representative office is located within the territory of the People's Republic of China, and the lawsuit is caused by the commercial activities of the branch or representative office, the courts of the People's Republic of China shall have jurisdiction.*[264] Although this provision is not about consumer disputes, the fact that a dispute is arising out of the commercial activities conducted by a business's branch or representative office may justify the exercise of jurisdiction over a business could also, to some extent, illustrate the targeting test.

Having the consumer's domicile as the jurisdiction ground is particularly important for tourist consumers, since tourists who travel abroad usually have a short period of stay at the country of destination. It is not plausible to stay in a foreign country with a different language, culture, and legal system only for litigation.[265] If tourists have to sue in the country where the travel contract is performed, namely the country of destination, most tourists may simply just give up their rights due to financial costs.

3.7.2 Jurisdiction Clause in Package Travel Contracts

Even if Article 31 of the Draft Model Law of Chinese Private International Law on consumer jurisdiction rule is adopted, consumer issues do not fall within the scope of exclusive jurisdiction, which excludes party autonomy. Apart from the jurisdiction by the consumer's home country, parties in a consumer contract shall be allowed to choose the competent court based on party autonomy principle. If the parties in a

[264] The original text is《中华人民共和国国际私法示范法(第六稿)》第二十四条【分支机构或者代表机构】对因商业活动纠纷提起的诉讼，如被告的分支机构或者代表机构位于中华人民共和国境内，且该诉讼是由该分支机构或者代表机构的商业活动引起的，中华人民共和国法院享有管辖权。

[265] Wu (2017), p. 14.

consumer contract have reached an agreement on jurisdiction issues, their jurisdiction agreement prevails; in the absence of a jurisdiction agreement, the consumer contract is subject to the courts of the consumer's country of domicile.[266] It is advisable to give the parties in a consumer contract more freedom to choose the competent courts, as long as the chosen court does not violate provisions on the hierarchy of jurisdiction and exclusive jurisdiction.[267] This reflects the respect for party autonomy in consumer contracts. Meanwhile, to prevent unfair terms from undermining the legitimate rights and interests of consumers, the unfair jurisdiction clause could be considered as invalid.[268]

Consumer contracts, including package travel contracts, are usually standard form contracts pre-drafted by the business party. It is not advisable to invalidate all choice of court clauses in standard consumer contracts nor completely deprive the parties of the freedom to choose a court to hear their case. To avoid formal equality on party autonomy, the requirement of an actual connection in contract jurisdiction rules should also be extended to consumer jurisdiction rules.[269]

Moreover, Article 31 on consumer jurisdiction rule is not tailer-made for addressing disputes resulting from cross-border electronic consumer contracts, as the Internet lacks geographic boundaries.[270] Article 20 of the 2022 SPC Judicial Interpretation of the Civil Procedure Law regulates online sale contracts, but such provisions are still limited to general contract jurisdiction rules.[271] Article 31 of the Judicial Interpretation of the Civil Procedure Law regulates the choice of law agreement in a standard consumer contract. However, it is unclear as to what is the scope of the chosen forum and what constitutes reasonable notice.[272] For instance, because of the particularity of electronic standard contracts, the provider of choice of court clause may not draw the consumers' attention individually.[273] In such cases, it requires a certain degree of clarity or conspicuity of the forum selection clause among the general terms and conditions.[274] To protect consumers and the true value of agreed jurisdiction, it is necessary to clarify that the choice of court agreement made before the consumer dispute arises is invalid.

---

[266] Tian (2021), p. 17.

[267] Tian (2021), p. 17; Xie (2018), p. 21; 谢鑫媛:《网上购物发生争议后如何确定管辖问题——以淘宝购物平台为例》，《法制博览》，2018年1月，第21页。

[268] Tian (2021), p. 17.

[269] Xia (2015), pp. 33, 36.

[270] Wang (2010), pp. 80, 86.

[271] Article 20 of the Judicial Interpretation of the Civil Procedure Law in essence is about the jurisdiction of the place of performance of the contract. Moreover, the concept of online sale contract is not equivalent to consumer contract. Liu (2022), p. 71.

[272] Liu (2022), p. 72.

[273] Although the argument is originally on arbitration clause in electronic standard contracts, it equally applies to forum selection clauses. Qiao and He (2007), p. 95.

[274] It depends on the length and complicity of the standard contract, the longer or more complicated the standard contract is, the higher requirement for the degree of clarity or conspicuity of the forum selection clause. Qiao and He (2007), p. 95.

If the parties have reached an agreement on jurisdiction, the jurisdiction by agreement takes precedence; in the absence of a choice, the business operator may sue the consumer only before the consumer's country of domicile, whereas the consumer may choose to sue before the courts of the consumer's domicile or the business operator's domicile.[275] In short, the jurisdiction of consumer contracts could be based on the jurisdiction of the consumer' domicile, supplemented by the jurisdiction by agreement.[276]

3.8 Conclusions

This chapter focuses on the questions of which jurisdiction rules are applied to consumer contracts, particularly package travel contracts in China, what challenges and problems exist in judicial practice, and what can be done to enhance consumer protection. The most significant problem is the absence of a consumer jurisdiction rule in Chinese private international law. Since there is not even a specific provision on jurisdiction rules over consumer contracts, many problems exist in judicial practice regarding consumer jurisdiction issues.

Firstly, general jurisdiction rules over domestic contracts in the Civil Procedure Law are applied by Chinese courts to consumer contracts, while general jurisdiction rules over foreign-related contracts are not used. It is necessary to distinguish jurisdiction rules for domestic contract disputes from those applicable to foreign-related contract disputes and refrain from applying the former to the latter. In the absence of a specific consumer jurisdiction rule, Chinese courts may just skip the reasoning of jurisdiction issues and presume that Chinese courts have jurisdiction over foreign-related consumer contracts without any justification, or refer to multiple but incorrect local laws and regulations over domestic jurisdiction rules. The term 'relevant provisions' should be avoided in jurisdiction reasoning. A better way is to specify which provision was invoked and explain why this provision may justify the court's jurisdiction and what is the connection between the court and the dispute. Given that concurrent liability may occur in cross-border travel contract, especially when it comes to personal injury or death, the party in a consumer contract may choose to file an action based on tort liability or contract liability. In this regard, it is crucial to separate jurisdiction grounds over contractual obligations from those over non-contractual obligations set forth in Article 272 of the 2021 Chinese Civil Procedure Law. Additionally, the conditions for applying both tort and contract jurisdiction rules could be more specified to increase their functionality in judicial practice.

Secondly, as to the validity of choice of court agreements in standard consumer contracts, different courts may have different opinions. A choice of court agreement,

---

[275] The limitation of the location of lawsuit is to prevent the parties from abusing their rights of action and to reduce unnecessary burdens on the other party. Tian (2021), p. 16; Liu and Zheng (2015), p. 109.

[276] Liu and Zheng (2015), p. 109.

in nature, is a litigation contract, which will generate effects on procedural law. The examination of the validity of the litigation contract or choice of court agreement needs to follow relevant principles in substantive laws to see whether there is a defect in the expression of intention or whether it is obviously unfair. Although the validity of jurisdiction clause in a contract belongs to procedure issues, it cannot derogate provisions on standard clauses in substantive law, such as provisions in the Chinese Civil Code and Chinese Consumer Protection Law. If a jurisdiction clause severely limits or deprives the consumer's jurisdictional interests and unreasonably increases the consumer's jurisdictional burden, it is obviously unfair and unreasonable for the consumer. As a result, such a jurisdiction clause should be invalid. For choice of court agreements in electronic consumer contracts, consumers should be given reasonable notice of the jurisdiction clause and an option to disagree with such a clause without affecting the following purchasing process.

The choice of court agreement in a consumer contract does not have to be exclusive. If the court chosen is uncertain, the plaintiff should figure out which one is chosen. If there are two chosen courts which both have an actual connection with the dispute, the plaintiff is free to choose one of the courts. Moreover, the amount of disputed object does not directly determine which court is the competent court, as the foreign element in a travel dispute case may act as an exceptional factor to surpass hierarchical jurisdiction in China. Given the complexity of the Chinese legal system, if the parties' chosen court violates provisions of hierarchical jurisdiction, the case could be transferred to the competent court.

The mandatory arbitration clause in a consumer contract does not necessarily reflect the true intention of the consumer. To compensate for the weak position of consumers, the mandatory arbitration clause in standard consumer contracts is valid only when (i) consumers have the chance to check the substantive provisions and express 'yes' or 'no' in certain ways; (ii) the provider of the arbitration clause has raised the consumers' attention to the content of the clause in a reasonable way; and (iii) the arbitration clause is not obviously unfair.

Thirdly, it is crucial to establish a specific consumer jurisdiction rule in China, granting the consumer the right to sue at the consumer's home jurisdiction.[277] The adoption of Article 31 of the Draft Model Law of Chinese Private International Law on consumer home jurisdiction rule would largely solve the problems existing in judicial practice. Currently, this can be achieved by establishing a new provision or amending provisions in the Chinese Civil Procedure Law or the 2022 SPC Judicial Interpretation of the Civil Procedure Law. Such a consumer home jurisdiction rule is also in line with the favorable consumer choice of law rules set forth in Article 42 of the Chinese Conflict of Laws Act, which designates the home law of the consumer. In summary, when it comes to jurisdiction over consumer contracts, the court chosen by the parties takes precedence. If the parties cannot reach a choice of court agreement, the courts where the consumer is domiciled shall have jurisdiction. Jurisdiction by agreement reached by the parties prevails the jurisdiction of the consumer's home country.

[277] Chen (2024), p. 78.

References

Benoliel U, Becher SI (2019) the duty to read the unreadable. Boston Coll Law Rev 60:2256

Born G (2021a) The Hague convention on choice of court agreements: a critical assessment. Univ Pa Law Rev 169:2126

Born G (2021b) International commercial arbitration, 3rd edn. Kluwer Law International, p 3881

Casamiquela RJ (2002) Business law: electronic commerce: contractual assent and enforceability in cyberspace. Berkeley Technol Law J 17:476

Chen G (2002) Procedural Doctrines and procedural rules. China Legal Publishing House, p 92; 陈桂明:《程序理念与程序规则》，中国法制出版社2002年版，第92页。

Chen W (2008) The place of contract performance in civil litigation jurisdiction. Legal System and Economy (First Half Month): 68; 陈文涛:《民事诉讼管辖中的"合同履行地"》，《法制与经济(上半月)》，2008年，第68页。

Chen Z (2018) The analysis on the validity of unilateral dispute resolution clause in foreign-related civil and commercial contract. Chinese Yearb Priv Int Law Comp Law 22:335. 陈珍，《涉外民商事合同中单边争议解决条款效力之争》，《中国国际私法与比较法年刊》，2018年第22卷，第335页。

Chen Z (2021) Tort conflicts rules in cross-border multi-party litigation: which law has the closer or the closest connection? Maastricht J Eur Comp Law 5:626–647

Chen Z (2023) Tort choice-of-law rules in China: implications of the Rome II Regulation. Tort Law Rev 2:184–196

Chen Z (2024) Consumer jurisdiction and choice of law rules in European and Chinese private international law. Chinese J Transnatl Law 1:76–77

Du W, Hu Y (eds) (2015) Analysis of the application of judicial interpretation of the Supreme People's Court's on the civil procedure law Article by Article. People's Court Press, p 25; 杜万华、胡云腾主编:《最高人民法院民事诉讼法司法解释逐条适用解析》，人民法院出版社2015年，第25页。

Gao H (2016) Research on the Chinese conflict of laws act. Beijing Law Press, p 348; 高宏贵,《中国涉外民事关系法律适用法研究》，法律出版社2016 年版，第348页。

Han D, Xiao Y (2012) Private international law, 2nd edn. Peking University Press and Higher Education Press, p 24; 韩德培、肖永平,《国际私法(第二版)》，北京大学出版社和高等教育出版社，2012年，第24页。

He Q (2016) Evaluation of regulation differences for China to ratify the Hague Convention on Choice of Court Agreements. J Wuhan Univ (Philosophy Soc Sci) 4:82; 何其生:《中国加入<海牙选择法院协议公约>的规则差异与考量》，《武汉大学学报(哲学社会科学版)》2016年第4期，第82页。

Li H (1996) Introduction to international civil procedural law. Law Press China, pp 58–64; 李浩培,《国际民事程序法概论》，法律出版社， 1996年， 第58-64页。

Li Y (2009b) The validity of jurisdiction clauses in the website user agreement. People's Justice, p 74; 李颖:《网站用户协议中协议管辖条款的效力》，《人民司法》，2009年8月，第74页。

Li Z (2009a) Study on the jurisdiction system concerning internet cases in private international law. Xiamen University Press, p 206; 李智，《国际私法中互联网管辖权制度研究》，厦门大学出版社，2009年，第206页。

Liu X, Zheng T (2015) Rules on jurisdiction of consumers' domicile in online shopping dispute litigation. Theory Explor 5:106; 刘学在、郑涛:《网购纠纷诉讼中的消费者住所地管辖规则》，《理论探索》，2015年第5期，第104页。

Liu Y (2022) Research on Jurisdiction over international consumer contracts: EU experience and China's programme. Wuhan Univ Int Law Rev 1: 70; 刘阳,《跨国消费合同管辖权研究:欧盟经验及我国方案》，《武汉大学国际法评论》， 2022年第1期, 第70页。

Mann M (1963) The Seventh Report of the private international law committee on domicile. Int Comp Law Quart 12:1326

McGill S (2010) Consumer arbitration clause enforcement: a balanced legislative response. Am Bus Law J 47:361–413

Qiao S and He Q (2007) The analysis on the effect of the arbitration clause in microsoft end-user license agreement—from the point of view of chinese consumers. Wuhan Univ Int Law Rev 2: 95; 乔仕彤、何其生,《电子格式合同中仲裁条款的效力-以中国消费者市场中Microsoft软件最终用户许可协议为例》，《武大国际法评论》，2007年第2期，第95页。

Schulz A (2006) The Hague convention of 30 June 2005 on choice of court agreements. J Priv Int Law 2:248

Smit H (2009) The unilateral arbitration clause: a comparative analysis. Am Rev Int Arbitr 21:391

Tang W (2010) The rationality of the codification in the civil law system. In: He Q (eds) The influence of the civil law system over China. Law Press China, p. 30; 汤唯，《大陆法系法典化之理性》，何勤华主编，《大陆法系及其对中国的影响》， 法律出版社，2010年，第30页。

Tang Z et al (2016) Conflict of laws in the People's Republic of China. Edward Elgar Publishing, p 51, para.3.04

Tian J (2021) Discussion on issues and suggestions on jurisdiction over online shopping contract disputes. Legal Expo 3: 14; 田静怡:《网络购物合同纠纷管辖权的问题与建议探讨》，《法制博览》，2021年3月，第14页。

Wang FF (2010) Internet Jurisdiction and choice of law: legal practices in the EU, US and China. Cambridge University Press, p 87.

Wang Y, Lei T (2015) New development of procedural norms for jurisdiction of contract cases—focusing on the understanding and application of Article 18 of the Judicial Interpretation of the Civil Procedure Law. J Law Appl 8: 39; 王亚新、雷彤:《合同案件管辖之程序规范的新展开——以<民事诉讼法>司法解释第18条的理解适用为中心》，《法律适用》2015年第8期，第39页。

Weintraub RJ (1965) An inquiry into the utility of "Domicile" as a concept in conflicts analysis'. Mich Law Rev 63:961

Wu W (2005) Electronic commerce law. Tsinghua University Press, p 145; 吴伟光，《电子商务法》，清华大学出版社， 2005年，第145页。

Wu Y (2017) A study on the issues of jurisdiction over foreign cases and the application of law in sabah boat sinking incident. Southwest University of Political Science and University, p 14; 吴羿，《沙巴沉船事件中的涉外管辖权和法律适用问题探析》，西南政法大学法硕学术论文，2017年，第14页。

Xia Y (2015) Jurisdiction of foreign tourist disputes. J Nanchang Normal Univ(Soc Sci) 1:33; 夏雨:《涉外旅游纠纷管辖权规则研究》，《南昌师范学院学报(社会科学)》，2015年第1期，第33页。

Xiang Z (2019) Research on the legislative system of China's international civil jurisdiction. Legal Sci (J Northwest Univ Polit Sci Law) 4: 183–184; 向在胜,《中国国际民事管辖权的立法体例研究》，《法律科学(西北政法大学学报)》， 2019年第4 期，第183-184 页。

Xiao W (2020) Research on choice of law of cross-border consumer contracts. Law Press China, p.238; 肖雯:《跨境消费者合同法律适用问题研究》，法律出版社2020 年版，第238 页。

Xiao Y (2017) Enhancing international credibility of Chinese judiciary: the tongs to jointly promote the BRI. Int Law Rev Wuhan Univ 1: 3. 肖永平,《提升中国司法的国际公信力:共建"一带一路" 的抓手》，《武大国际法评论》，2017年第1卷第1期，第3页。

Xiao Y and Tan L (2014) A probe into online trading platforms' influence on the validity of general arbitration agreement. Wuhan Univ Int Law Rev 2: 28; 肖永平、谭立:《论网上交易平台对概括性仲裁协议效力的影响》，《武大国际法评论》，2014年第2期，第28页。

Xie X (2018) How to determine jurisdiction issues after online shopping disputes— taking Taobao shopping platform as an example. Legal Expo 1: 21; 谢鑫媛:《网上购物发生争议后如何确定管辖问题——以淘宝购物平台为例》，《法制博览》，2018年1月，第21页。

Yang Y (2010) Discussion on the establishment of inaction tort liability in China's Tort legislation. In: He Q (eds) (2010) The influence of the civil law system over China. Law Press China, p 454; 杨垠红，《我国侵权立法确立不作为侵权责任之探讨》，何勤华主编，《大陆法系及其对中国的影响》， 法律出版社，2010年，第454页。

Yuthayotin S (2015) Access to justice in transnational B2C e-commerce: a multidimensional analysis of consumer protection mechanisms. Springer, pp 93–95

Zhang J (2015) New development of jurisdiction rules for foreign-related litigation. Academic Forum of Nandu (J Human Soc Sci) 6: 69; 张建:《涉外民事诉讼协议管辖规则的新发展》，《南都学坛(人文社会科学学报) 》2015年第6期，第69页。

Zhao R and Zhou W (2015) Determination of the validity of jurisdiction clauses in E-Commerce disputes. People's Just 8: 57; 赵瑞罡、周 薇,《电子商务纠纷中协议管辖条款效力的认定》，《人民司法》，2015年8月，第57页。

Zhou C (2014) Research on jurisdiction by agreement. Chinese Foreign Legal Stud 2:458; 周翠,《协议管辖问题研究》，《中外法学》2014年第2期，第458页。

Chapter 4
Protecting Package Travel Tourists and Timeshare Tourists as Consumers in China

4.1 Introduction

In China there is no specific provision regulating jurisdiction rules over consumer contracts in the Civil Procedure Law. Although Article 42 of the Chinese Conflict of Laws Act establishes favorable choice of law rules over consumer contracts by ensuring that consumers are protected by the law of the country of the consumer's habitual residence, the vagueness of the core concept of consumer or consumer contract has limited its functionality. Since Article 42 of the Chinese Conflict of Laws Act does not explicitly state its material scope by excluding certain types of consumer contracts, whether this provision applies to all consumer contracts remains a question.[1] Although the definition of consumer is indirectly provided in Article 2 of the Chinese Consumer Protection Law,[2] the personal scope of the protection of consumer rights under the Chinese Consumer Protection Law remains uncertain.[3] The ambiguity of the main concept gives rise to the question of whether package travel tourists and timeshare tourists are protected as consumers in Chinese Private International Law.

The answer to this question largely depends on how widely the term 'daily consumption' is to be interpreted.[4] Whether tourism can be regarded as a daily consumption service remains uncertain, especially when considering outbound travel,

[1] Liu and Zhang (2021), p. 80.

[2] The PRC Consumer Protection Law, short for the Law of the PRC on the Protection of the Rights and Interests of Consumers, adopted on October, 31, 1993 at the 8th National People's Congress (NPC) Standing Committee 4th meeting, then first amended by the 11th NPC Standing Committee on August 27, 2009, second amended on October 25, 2013. The 2013 Amendment came into force as from March 15, 2014. It is also knowns as the Chines Consumer Protection Act.

[3] Binding (2014), p. 248.

[4] The notion of consumer or consumer contract has been discussed in Chap. 2.

Z. Chen, *Tourists, Consumer Contracts and Private International Law in China*, Ius Gentium: Comparative Perspectives on Law and Justice 123,
https://doi.org/10.1007/978-3-031-87915-9_4

which is generally considered as a luxury or middle class activity in China.[5] The 'daily consumption need' can be construed as private, household, or family purposes. Meanwhile, the amount of money involved in a contract is irrelevant for determining whether a person is a consumer. The concept of luxury in one country may be considered as normal in another country, and the concept of luxury for one individual may differ from another individual. Even if outbound travel is considered a luxury service in China, it does not mean that outbound tourists are not qualified as consumers. Travel service can be considered as daily consumption,[6] if a tourist concludes a contract with travel service providers for private, household, or family purposes, instead of for business or professional purposes. Tourists are individuals who receive services for daily consumption (private, household, or family purposes) rather than for the purpose of making profits.[7]

Tourists in cross-border situations could experience more vulnerabilities and challenges, including information gaps and language barriers which may cause difficulties in accessing justice.[8] In the tourism industry, standard contracts are often used by travel service providers to improve the efficiency of transactions. Such standard contracts are drafted without negotiation with tourists and may contain jurisdiction and applicable law clauses unfair to tourists. Tourists, including package travel tourists and timeshare tourists, are weaker contracting parties. The inequality and the imbalance of bargaining power between the tourists and travel service providers justify that tourists, including package travel tourists and timeshare tourists, are consumers, and travel service contracts have the nature of consumer contracts.[9]

Unlike transactions with the pattern of 'try first, pay later' or 'spot transactions'(钱货两清),[10] timeshare contracts adopt the 'pay first, use later' pattern, which may span 3 to 5 years for short terms or 30 to 50 years for long terms.[11] The realization

---

[5] Despite the fact that the parties in a package travel contract are individual tourists and professional tour operators, it is hard to say that overseas travel per se is a 'daily consumption' within the meaning of Article 2 of Chinese Consumer Protection Law.

[6] Wang (2018), pp. 103–106; 王群,《海外旅游消费者权利保护机制探讨—基于<涉外民事关系法律适用法>视角》，《九江学院学报(社会科学版)》，2018年第1期，第103–106页。

[7] Wang (2002), pp. 2–11; 王利明,《消费者的概念及消费者权益保护法的调整范围》，《政治与法律》2002年第2期，第2–11页。

[8] For instance, there may be an inability to commence or continue court proceedings, because the time spent by tourists in the visited country where the complaint lies is too short, or those non-resident complainants may have to provide security for costs in the case of judicial proceedings. Prel. Doc. No 3 of October 2018 - The HCCH Report of the Experts' Group on the Co-operation and Access to Justice for International Tourists (Tourism Project), Annex I, paras. 7–8. Xia (2010), p. 420; 夏雨:《论我国国际旅游法律制度的缺失与构建——以和平崛起为视角》，《武汉大学学报(哲学社会科学版)》，2010年第3期，第420页。

[9] Wang (2017), p. 571; 王利明,《合同法研究》(第四卷)，中国人民大学出版社2017年版，第571页。

[10] It can also be translated as transaction done upon completion of (both) payment and delivery.

[11] If the developer of a timeshare property goes bankrupt or the seller of the timeshare product absconds with money, the consumers' rights will be seriously damaged. Yao (2013), pp. 65, 67; 姚道艳,《刍议规制分时度假合同路径—以保护消费者的合法权益为视角》，《山东商业职业技术学院学报》，2013年第2期，第64页。

of contractual rights in timeshare contracts is in the long term. After the consumer pays the contract in full, ensuring that the consumer enjoys certain rights and interests in the uncertain future becomes a special concern for such contracts.[12]

Moreover, timeshare contracts are usually standard form contracts in which business operators may easily take advantage of their dominant position to formulate standard terms that are unfair to consumers.[13] Timeshare contracts are generally marketed and promoted on a one-to-one basis, during which sales staff may exaggerate timeshare vacations by guaranteeing the accessibility of any place in the world in the exchange system, the function of timeshare products as an investment, and assuming responsibility for visa applications on behalf of the consumer.[14] However, the timeshare contract the consumer actually signs may contain unfair terms, such as 'the business operator has no responsibility for applying a visa for the consumer, and the consumer may not cancel the contract or get a refund on this basis', 'the business operator does not guarantee that the consumer may get a room at any time', or 'the consumer cannot revoke the contract once it is signed'.[15] Chinese citizens usually travel abroad on public holidays such as the Labor Day, the National Day Holiday, and the Spring Festival Holiday, whereas the ambiguity of standard timeshare contracts regarding the date and room number of a timeshare property may lead to the result that timeshare tourists cannot get a room in peak seasons.[16]

In practice, due to the prevalence of choice of court and choice of law agreements inserted in a standard contract, tourists may be obliged to sue before courts where the travel service provider is domiciled and be subject to the law chosen by the travel service provider. As a result, tourists might be deprived of the right to sue at the courts where the consumer is domiciled and to invoke the law of the country where the consumer has habitual residence. The financial and time costs of suing in courts other than those of the consumer's domicile and applying a foreign law may increase litigation costs for tourist consumers in China. There is a need to reduce tourists' litigation costs, to improve the level of protection granted to tourists, and to facilitate their access to justice. To this end, this Chapter will first clarify the concept of package travel contract in China and then analyze what kinds of choice of law rules are applied to package travel contracts in judicial practice. Furthermore, whether, and if so, to what extent, current Article 42 of the Chinese Conflict of Laws Act may play a role in the protection of package travel tourists. What are the conditions to apply consumer choice of law rules and whether such conditions cause problems in judicial practice?

[12] Yao (2013), p. 65. Yang (2010), pp. 5–7; 杨雪飞,《消费者权益保障视角下的分时度假时权法律性质分析》，《理论前沿》，2010年第5期，第5–7页。

[13] Yao (2013), p. 65.

[14] Yao (2013), p. 65.

[15] Yao (2013), p. 65.

[16] Yao (2013), p. 66. Yang and Liu (2007), pp. 20–21; 杨清平、刘小蓉等:《影响我国分时度假消费需求阻碍因素分析》，《商业文化》2007年第5期，第20–21页。

4.1.1 The Notion of Package Travel Contracts

The Tourism Law of the PRC does not provide a definition for the term 'tourists'.[17] However, it explicitly defines the concept of a package travel contract as 'a contract where the travel agency arranges the tour in advance, provides, by itself or through its performance assistant, two or more tourism services, including transport, accommodation, catering, sightseeing, tour guide, or tour lead, and tourists make a total payment of the travel expenses'.[18]

For a contract to be classified as a package travel contract, it must have several components: (i) the tour is arranged in advance by a travel agency; (ii) two or more kinds of tourism services are provided, such as transport, accommodation, catering, sightseeing, tour guide, or tour lead; (iii) these tourism services can be provided by the travel agency or through its performance assistant; and (iv) the tourist makes an inclusive or total payment covering all travel expenses.[19] Article 2 of the Chinese Consumer Protection Law and Article 42 of the Chinese Conflict of Laws Act do not explicitly specify that package travel contracts are consumer contracts. Does this mean that these contracts are excluded automatically? To answer this question, it is necessary to examine what kinds of choice of law rules are applied to package travel contracts by Chinese courts in judicial practice.[20]

---

[17] The HCCH defines a tourist as a natural person who does not have his place of habitual residence in the State visited. The HCCH Report of the Experts' Group on the Cooperation and Access to Justice for International Tourists, para. 7, Prel. Doc. 1 of February 2020.: A traveller is defined as 'someone who moves between different geographic locations for any purpose and any duration'. Visitors are a subset of travellers as a 'visitor is a traveller taking a trip to a main destination outside his/her usual environment, for less than a year, for any main purpose (business, leisure or other personal purpose) other than to be employed by a resident entity in the country or place visited'. Tourists are a subset of visitors as a visitor is 'classified as a tourist (or overnight visitor) if his/her trip includes an overnight stay'. Guinchard, Study on the desirability and feasibility of further work on the Proposal on a Draft Convention on Co-operation and Access to Justice for International Tourists, Annex III to Prel. Doc. No 3 of October 2018.

[18] Article 111(3) of the Tourism Law of the PRC.

[19] The UNWTO Committee on Tourism and Competitiveness agreed upon the definitions of the following tourism categories: Cultural Tourism, Ecotourism, Rural Tourism, Adventure Tourism, Health Tourism, Wellness Tourism, Medical Tourism, Business Tourism (related to the Meetings Industry), Gastronomy Tourism, Coastal, Maritime and Inland Water Tourism, Urban/City Tourism, Mountain Tourism, Education Tourism and Sports Tourism. UNWTO, Report of the Secretary-General, Implementation of the General Programme of Work for 2016- 2017. Prel. Doc. No 3 of October 2018 - The HCCH Report of the Experts' Group on the Co-operation and Access to Justice for International Tourists (Tourism Project), Annex III, para. 10.

[20] The cases analyzed in this paper are collected via the official website China Judgements Online https://wenshu.court.gov.cn/ by typing in 'foreign-related' and 'travel/tourism contract' on 1 July 2021.

4.1.2 *The Notion of Timeshare Contracts*

Timeshare vacation, originating from the Europe and America in the twentieth century, is an emerging new life consumption pattern which integrates real estate, tourism, and financing.[21] Timeshare was introduced to the Chinese market in the 1990s.[22] However, due to the lack of relevant legal provisions, tourists' ignorance of the timeshare concept, and a lack of integrity awareness, timeshare almost became synonymous with fraud in China.[23] Consumers in China have filed many complaints about timeshare products.[24] Timeshare contracts can be divided into two categories: property-right timeshare contracts and time-right timeshare contracts.[25] This Chapter specifically focuses on time-right timeshare contracts.

There is no specific definition of timeshare contract in Chinese substantive law. Many Chinese scholars refer to the notion of timeshare in EU Law and American law to clarify such a notion.[26] Namely, timeshare refers to the purchase of the right to use a vacation property for a certain period of time.[27] Timeshare contracts are a combination of the sale of real estate property, lease contracts, and travel contracts.[28] Timeshare contracts are a mix of different contracts or a mixed contract (类型融合合同), which belongs to nameless contracts or atypical contracts.[29] The so-called a mixed contract refers to the contract in which each component of the contract belongs to other different types of contracts.[30]

In the absence of relevant laws and regulations, the resolution of timeshare contract disputes could refer to the relevant provisions on the sale of real estate, lease contracts, and travel contracts, as well as general principles in contract law, such as the principle of good faith.[31] In judicial practice, disputes over timeshare contracts are resolved in accordance with legal provisions in property law, contract law,

---

[21] Timeshare first emerges in France in the 1960s, goes to America in the 1970s and then becomes popular globally. Wang (2006), p. 131; 汪传才,《欧盟<分时度假指令>研究》，《河北法学》2006年第2期，第131页; Yao (2013), p. 64.

[22] Yao (2013), p. 64.

[23] Yao (2013), p. 64; Meng (2010), pp. 68–69; 孟洁:《我国分时度假的营销现状及对策》，《赤峰学院学报》，2010年第9期，第68–69页; Xue (2008), p. 168; Wang (2006), p. 134; 薛源,《欧盟对分时度假及相关产品的法律规制》，《河北法学》2008年第9期，第168页.

[24] Wang (2006), p. 134.

[25] Yao (2013), p. 65.

[26] Chen (2024b), pp. 127–172. https://research.rug.nl/en/publications/tourists-consumer-contracts-and-private-international-law-in-the-, accessed on Jan 22, 2025.

[27] Despite this, there is no consensus as to the legal nature of timeshare contracts. Han and Ming (2016), p. 7; 韩璐、明庆忠,《国内分时度假法律规制研究述评》，《河北旅游职业学院学报》, 2016年第4期，第8页。

[28] Yao (2013), p. 65.

[29] Yao (2013), p. 65.

[30] Yao (2013), p. 65.

[31] Yao (2013), p. 65.

consumer protection law, and other relevant laws.[32] Since the sale product in a timeshare contract is immovable property, the Property Law is the main basis, supplemented by the General Principles of Civil Law, the Contract Law, and the Consumer Protection law.[33] It is not efficient to refer to so many provisions scattered in different laws and the parties' rights and interests may not be properly protected.[34] This indicates that there is a need to establish relevant laws and regulations on timeshare contracts,[35] possibly within the Civil Code, Tourism Law, or Consumer Protection Law. In Chinese private international law, timeshare contracts are not expressly included in the material scope of consumer choice of law rules under Article 42 of the Chinese Conflict of Laws Act, raising the question of which choice of law is applicable to timeshare contracts.

4.2 General Contract Choice of Law Rules Applied to Package Travel Contracts

The issues of jurisdiction and applicable law are two relatively independent problems, and a case being heard in the courts of one country does not necessarily mean that the laws of that country shall automatically apply.[36] Given the absence of specific jurisdiction rules tailored for consumer contracts, all package travel contracts are governed by general contract jurisdiction rules. While protective consumer choice of law rules are stipulated in Article 42 of the Chinese Conflict of Laws Act, package travel contracts are not governed by such protective consumer conflict rules. Instead, general contract choice of law rules in Article 41 of the Chinese Conflict of Laws Act are widely used.[37]

Tourists involved in package travel contracts and timeshare contracts are more vulnerable than other consumers who are considered weaker parties, because they are often in a foreign country with a different language, culture, and legal system for only a short period of time. Applying consumer choice of law rules in Article 42 of the Chinese Conflict of Laws Act will make sure that package travel tourists are protected under the law of their habitual residence. Nevertheless, the general contract choice of law rules have been somewhat overused to determine the applicable law of package travel contracts. This might be attributed to judges treating travel contract cases as general contracts and subsequently applying general contract

[32] Han and Ming (2016), p. 8.

[33] Han and Ming (2016), p. 11.

[34] Han and Ming (2016), p. 8.

[35] Ibid; Yao (2013), p. 66.

[36] Huang and Du (2014), p. 25; 黄进、杜焕芳，《中国国际私法司法实践研究》，法律出版社，2014年，第25页。

[37] The same conclusion is reached in Zhuang (2020), p. 26; 庄允，《我国涉外旅游纠纷法律适用问题研究》，山东大学硕士学位论文，2020年，第26页。

choice of law rules.[38] In judicial practice, package travel contracts are merely considered nameless contracts or atypical contracts, falling under general contract jurisdiction and choice of law rules.

In China, two general principles are applied to determine the applicable law in contracts: (i) party autonomy principle, granting parties the freedom to choose the applicable law; and (ii) the closest connection principle, which applies in the absence of a choice by the parties.[39] Moreover, the Supreme People's Court of China has accepted the application of the characteristic performance doctrine to efficiently determine the applicable law which has the closest connection with the contract.[40] When it comes to contract disputes, the habitual residence of the parties, the place of contract conclusion, and the place of contract performance serve as the three main connecting factors.[41] Despite some scholars advocating for package travel contracts to be protected as consumer contracts under consumer choice of law rules, in absence of a clear clarification of the material scope of Article 42, package travel contracts continue to be subject to general contract choice of law rules in judicial practice.[42]

4.2.1 Two-Sided Party Autonomy Under Article 41 of the Chinese Conflict of Laws Act

Under Article 41 of the Chinese Conflict of Laws Act, *the law chosen by the parties prevails; in the absence of such a choice, the law of the habitual domicile of the party whose performance best reflects the characteristic of the contract or the law with the closest connection to the contract shall apply*.[43] This provision establishes a two-sided party autonomy approach where the law chosen by the parties takes precedence.

---

[38] Zhuang (2020), p. 27.

[39] Wang (2010), p. 133.

[40] Wang (2010), p. 133. The characteristic performance doctrine may make the determination more objective by limiting the courts' discretionary power and also provide more certainty, predictability and uniformity.

[41] Lu (2015), pp. 105–111; 卢月,《论<涉外民事关系法律适用法>中最密切联系原则的司法适用》，《时代法学》，2015年第4期，第105–111页。

[42] Wu (2017), p. 16; 吴羿，《沙巴沉船事件中的涉外管辖权和法律适用问题探析》，西南政法大学法硕学术论文，2017年，第16页。

[43] 《中华人民共和国涉外民事关系法律适用法》第四十一条:当事人可以协议选择合同适用的法律。当事人没有选择的，适用履行义务最能体现该合同特征的一方当事人经常居所地法律或者其他与该合同有最密切联系的法律。Article 41 of the Chinese Conflict of Laws Act: The parties may by agreement choose the law applicable to their contract. Absent any choice by the parties, the law of the habitual residence of a party whose performance of obligation is most characteristic of the contract or the law that most closely connected with the contract shall be applied.

4.2.1.1 Freedom to Choose Applicable Law

The party autonomy doctrine in the conflict of laws mirrors the substantive principle of freedom in private law, bringing certainty and efficiency, as parties and courts can easily know which law is applicable.[44] Most Chinese courts respect the applicable law chosen by the parties, whether stipulated in the contract terms or orally agreed upon by the parties during the trial, as long as it does not violate Chinese mandatory or forbidden regulations and international treaties acceded by China.[45] Unlike the choice of court agreement, which requires an 'actual connection' with the contract, a choice of law agreement does not necessitate an actual or material connection with the contract, as long as it does not violate public policy or social public interests of China.[46] Article 7 of the SPC Judicial Interpretation of the Chinese Conflict of Laws Act expressly states that:

> Where a party claims that the choice of law is invalid on the ground that the law agreed upon by the parties has no actual connection with the foreign-related civil relation at issues, the people's court shall not uphold such a claim.

4.2.1.2 Applying Party Autonomy in Choice of Law

Since Article 42 of the Chinese Conflict of Laws Act only allows the consumer to exercise one-sided party autonomy, it is more reasonable to invoke Article 41 when both parties unanimously choose the application of a certain law. In *Dr. Barsch-Supan v. Xi'an Xindaya International Travel Agency,*[47] two American tourists sued a Chinese travel agency and its agent Zhang Li for the return of travel fees following the cancellation of their Tibet trip. In accordance with the unanimous agreement of the parties, Chinese law was applied under Article 41 of the Chinese Conflict of Laws Act.

Similarly, in *Liu Peilong v Kunming Kanghui Yonghui Travel Agency* case,[48] the Kunming Railway Intermediate People's Court classified the case as a

[44] However, it does not mean that the parties may choose the governing law regardless of the type of their civil relations. Article 3 of the Chinese Conflict of Laws Act limits the exercise of party autonomy with the phrase 'according to law'. Article 6 of the SPC Judicial Interpretation of the Chinese Conflict of Laws Act further explains that the choice of law made by the parties for their civil relation shall be regarded as invalid if no law in the PRC has explicitly allowed them to do so. Tu (2015), p. 40, para. 71.

[45] Huang and Du (2014), p. 23; Wang (2010), p. 134.

[46] Wang (2010), p. 134.

[47] *Dr. Barsch-Supan v. Xi'an Xindaya International Travel Agency*, Shaanxi Province HPC, (2016) Shan Min Zhong No 511, Shaanxi Province Xi'an Municipality IPC, (2016) Shan 01 Min Chu No 288. 西安信雅达国际旅行社有限公司、张立与Dr. Barsch-Supan,Axel Helmut、Dr. Blrsch-Supan Geb. Meuer,Martina Elisabeth旅游合同纠纷民事二审判决书, 陕西省高级人民法院,(2016)陕民终511号; 西安市中级人民法院,(2016)陕01民初288号.

[48] *Liu Peilong et al v Kunming Kanghui Yonghui Travel Agency*, Kunming Railway IPC, (2017) Yun 71 Min Zhong No 11; Kunming Railway Court, (2015) Kin Tie Min Chu Zi No 103. 刘佩龙、刘

foreign-related civil dispute, because the plaintiff was an American citizen and the accident happened in Thailand. Chinese law was applied through the exercise of bilateral party autonomy stipulated in Article 41 of the Chinese Conflict of Laws Act, because both parties unanimously agreed to choose Chinese law as the applicable law to settle the dispute.

In *Zhu Kaili v Guangzhou Baiyun District Fluent Education Training Centre,*[49] involving a foreign-related and Hong Kong-related contract dispute, the first-instance court invoked Article 41 of the Chinese Conflict of Laws Act to justify the exercise of two-sided party autonomy. Chinese law was applied because the two parties unanimously agreed to choose it. However, the Court of Appeal invoked Article 3 of the Chinese Conflict of Laws Act to justify the application of the law chosen by both parties. Article 3 is a provision in the first chapter concerning the general provisions, ensuring that parties have the right to choose the governing law. This provision is a general principle applied to various foreign-related civil relations, not limited to the contract field.[50] The court relied on Article 3 to decide the applicable law, instead of Article 41, a decision that may lack some convincing rationale.

Apart from the unnecessary invocation of multiple legal provisions, there are instances where no legal documents were invoked to support the application of party autonomy. The absence of legal support documents could inevitably undermine the public credibility of the judicial judgment.[51] For example, in *Foshan Guangzhilv International Travel Agency v Lin Jintian,*[52] Guangdong Foshan Intermediate People's Court classified the case as a Hong Kong-related commercial dispute and determined that Chinese law should be applied. The court confirmed this decision without referencing any specific laws or regulations, stating that the parties had no objection to the application of the law of Mainland China. In comparison with the explicit consent mentioned earlier, the parties in this case tacitly accepted the application of Chinese law. This implied consent still embodies the principle of party autonomy.

昕燕旅游合同纠纷二审民事判决书, 昆明铁路运输中级法院 (2017)云71民终11号; 昆明铁路运输法院,(2015)昆铁民初字第103号.

[49] *Zhu Kaili v Guangzhou Baiyun District Fluent Education Training Centre*, Guangdong Province Guangzhou Municipality Baiyun DPC, (2014) Hui Yun Fa Min San Chu Zi No 15.

[50] Chen (2020), p. 209.

[51] Chen (2020), p. 210.

[52] *Foshan Guangzhilv International Travel Agency v Lin Jintian*, Guangdong Foshan IPC, (2017) Yue 06 Min Zhong No 4445; Guangdong Foshan Nanhai District People's Court, (2016) Yue 0605 Min Chu No 9352. 佛山广之旅国际旅行社有限公司、林锦添旅游合同纠纷二审民事判决书, 广东省佛山市中级人民法院 (2017)粤06民终4445号; 广东省佛山市南海区人民法院(2016), 粤0605民初9352号

4.2.2 The Closest Connection Principle Under Article 41 of the Chinese Conflict of Laws Act

When the parties have not chosen the applicable law, Chinese courts generally use the closest connection principle to determine the law applicable to a contractual dispute.[53] Apart from Article 41, the closest connection principle is also explicitly employed in other provisions.[54] This principle focuses on the centre of gravity of a legal relation by taking into account all objective connecting factors in that relation.[55] The closest connection principle has become the default choice of law rule for all kinds of foreign-related civil relations in accordance with Article 2 of the Chinese Conflict of Laws Act.[56] Since many Chinese judges are not experienced in addressing foreign-related cases, the expansion of this open-ended test has posed a challenge for inexperienced Chinese judges and might be applied unsatisfactorily in judicial practice.[57] The discretionary nature of the closest connection principle may lead to a tendency to apply Chinese law in most cases (the homeward trend) without conducting a proper analysis of the closest connection principle.[58] This is also the case when it comes to the determination of the applicable law for package travel contracts.

In *Xue Xiujuan v. Jiangxi Ganzhonglv International Travel Agency*,[59] a Chinese tourist who concluded a package travel contract with a Chinese travel agency was injured in Thailand. The Chinese court held that, since the parties did not choose the applicable law in the travel contract, according to the closest connection principle enshrined in Article 41 of the Chinese Conflict of Laws Act, Chinese Law should be applicable.[60] However, the court did not provide reasoning as to why Chinese law had the closest connection.

[53] Huang and Du (2014), p. 24.

[54] Articles 16, 17, 23 and 40 of the Chinese Conflict of Laws Act.

[55] Connecting factors may include the place of conclusion of the contract, the place of performance, the place of the breach of the contract, the domicile of both parties, the place of the location of subject matter. Tang et al. (2016), p. 227, para. 8.53.

[56] Tu (2015), p. 39, para. 69.

[57] Tu (2015), p. 40, para. 70.

[58] The flexibility of this principle may lead to the abuse of such principle for the purpose of applying Chinese law. In many cases, Chinese courts merely identify one factor relating to China and conclude that China has the closest connection with the contract, without considering and comparing other factors of weight. Tang et al. (2016), p. 227, para. 8.54.

[59] *Xue Xiujuan v. Jiangxi Ganzhonglv International Travel Agency*, Jiangxi Province HPC, (2017) Gan Min Zhong No 248; Jiangxi Province Nanchang Municipality IPC, (2016) Gan 01 Min Chu No 229. 中国大地财产保险股份有限公司江西分公司、薛秀娟旅游合同纠纷二审民事判决书, 江西省高级人民法院,(2017)赣民终248号; 南昌市中级人民法院;(2016)赣01民初229号.

[60] This is also the case in *Xue Xiujuan v. Yongcheng Property Insurance Company*, in which the legal fact and the claimant were the same, only the defendant was changed to an insurance company. The court classified the case as a foreign-related civil dispute. The parties didn't choose the applicable law. The court held that Chinese Law should be applied in accordance with the closest

In *Tong Bo v. Shandong Daxinhua Yuntong Travel Agency* case, the tourist suffered injuries in a traffic accident while taking a bus arranged by the travel agency in Switzerland.[61] The first-instance court resorted to the closest connection principle without referring to any laws or analyzing why China had the closest connection to the dispute. The appellate court, however, reasoned that since the place of performance of the contract was overseas and the parties' domicile was in Qingdao (Shandong province), Chinese Law should be applied according to the closest connection principle.[62] Nevertheless, the fact that the place of performance of the contract was overseas justifies the internationality of the case, such foreign-related element did not necessarily establish that Chinese law had the closest connection with the dispute.[63] It seems that the closest connection principle was mentioned first, leading directly to the application of Chinese Law, as long as some connecting factors were present in China.[64] This pattern is also observed in *Yang Junya v. Henan Zhigong International Agency,*[65] which was classified as a foreign-related contract dispute.

By contrast, in *Lan Xinguo v. Shandong Daxinhua Yuntong Travel Agency,*[66] involving the same dispute with different plaintiffs, the court considered the place of conclusion of the travel contract and the domicile of the parties (Qingdao, Shandong) to justify that China had the closest connection with the dispute. The factor of the place of performance of the travel contract, located outside the territory of China, was not mentioned. However, the court did not refer to Article 41 of the Chinese Conflict of Laws Act or other legal provisions.

---

connection principle in Article 41 of the Chinese Conflict of Laws Act. Xue Xiujuan v Yongcheng Property Insurance Co., Ltd. Jiangxi Branch, Jiangxi Province Nanchang Municipality IPC, (2015) Hong Min Si Chu Zi No 30.

[61] *Tong Bo v. Shandong Daxinhua Yuntong Travel Agency*, Shandong Province HPC, (2017) Lu Min Zhong No 1123; Shandong Province Qingdao Municipality IPC, (2016) Lu 02 Min Chu No 1146. 佟波、山东大新华运通国际旅行社有限公司旅游合同纠纷二审民事判决书，山东省高级人民法院,(2017)鲁民终1123号; 山东省青岛市中级人民法院, (2016)鲁民初1146号。

[62] Ibid.

[63] Chen (2020), p. 212.

[64] Chen (2020), p. 211.

[65] *Yang Junya v. Henan Zhigong International Agency*, Henan Province HPC, (2017) Yu Min Zhong No 540; Henan Province Zhengzhou Municipality IPC, (2014) Zheng Min Chu Zi No 203. 永安财产保险股份有限公司河南分公司、河南职工国际旅行社旅游合同纠纷二审民事判决书，河南省高级人民法院,(2017)豫民终540号; 河南省郑州市中级人民法院,(2014)郑民三初字第203号.

[66] *Lan Xinguo v. Shandong Daxinhua Yuntong Travel Agency*, Shandong Province HPC, (2017) Lu Min Zhong No 1112. 兰新国、山东大新华运通国际旅行社有限公司旅游合同纠纷二审民事判决书，山东省高级人民法院, (2017)鲁民终1112号。

4.2.2.1 Article 126 of the Chinese Contract Law

Before the enactment of the Chinese Conflict of Laws Act in 2010, the closest connection principle has played a role in determining the law applicable to contract disputes by virtue of Article 126 of the Chinese Contract Law. According to Article 126 of the Chinese Contract Law, *the parties to a foreign-related contract may choose the law applicable to the settlement of contract disputes, unless otherwise provided by the law. If the parties do not choose, the law of the country that has the closest connection with the contract shall apply*.[67]

After the Chinese Conflict of Laws Act took effect on 1 April 2011, it is sufficient to refer to Article 41 for contract choice of law rules to determine the law applicable to contract disputes. The reference to a provision in substantive laws, such as the Contract Law, becomes unnecessary and might cause confusion, as the application of the Contract Law itself already means that Chinese law should be applied.

In *Feng Yunhai v. Henan Feiyang Travel Agency*,[68] where a tourist was injured in a tour bus in Indonesia, the court justified that China had the closest connection with the case based on the factors that the domicile of the parties and the place of conclusion contract were in China. The court invoked both Article 41 of the Chinese Conflict of Laws Act and Article 126 of Chinese Contract Law, which provides the closest connection principle. However, it is unnecessary to invoke Article 126 of Chinese Contract Law, as the establishment of Article 41 of the Chinese Conflict of Laws Act has already considered relevant provisions in other laws, such as Article 142 and Article 126 of the 1999 Contract Law, Article 145 of the 1986 General Principles of the Civil Law (GPCL), and Article 5 of the 2007 SPC Rules on the Relevant Issues concerning the Application of Law in Hearing Foreign-Related Contractual Dispute Cases in Civil and Commercial Matters.

The court in *Cong Shuwan v. Zhongxin Travel Service Group*[69] also relied upon Article 126 of Chinese Contract Law, where the plaintiffs sued the defendant Zhongxin Travel Service Group for the compensation of Liang Huifang's death and the refund of the travel fee.[70] Article 126 of the Contract Law grants parties the

---

[67] 《中华人民共和国合同法》:第一百二十六条　涉外合同的当事人可以选择处理合同争议所适用的法律,但法律另有规定的除外。涉外合同的当事人没有选择的,适用与合同有最密切联系的国家的法律。

[68] *Feng Yunhai v. Henan Feiyang Travel Agency*, Henan Province Zhengzhou Municipality IPC, (2015) Zheng Min San Chu Zi No 307. 冯运海与河南飞扬国际旅游有限公司、河南职工国际旅行社旅游合同纠纷一审民事判决书,　　河南省郑州市中级人民法院　　(2015)郑民三初字第307号.

[69] *Cong Shuwan v. Zhongxin Travel Service Group*, Liaoning Province Dalian Municipality Xigang DPC, (2017) Liao 0203 Min Chu No 4798. 丛树万、丛哲峰与众信旅游集团股份有限公司旅游合同纠纷一审民事判决书, 大连市西岗区人民法院,(2017)辽0203民初4798号.

[70] The plaintiffs Cong Shuwan and Cong Zhefeng were the deceased Liang Huifang's husband and son respectively. The tourist Liang Huifang signed an outbound travel contract with the defendant for a 15-day-5-country travel. When traveling in Switzerland, Liang Huifang developed symptoms of fatigue, weakness and other discomforts. The tour guide thought it was a common cold and bought some medicine for her, but the symptoms did not relieve after taking the medicine. The next

freedom to the applicable law to a foreign-related contract, unless the law provides otherwise. In the absence of such a choice, the law of the country that has the closest connection to the contract shall apply. In this case, the parties did not reach an agreement on the applicable law. Since the domiciles of the plaintiff and the defendant were in China, and the place where the contract was signed was in China, Chinese law had the closest connection with the contractual relationship.[71] Thus, Chinese law should be applied to resolve the dispute in this case.

Although it is not wrong to invoke Article 126 of the Contract Law, it is more appropriate to rely on Article 41 of the Chinese Conflict of Laws Act to justify the application of the closest connection principle. It is noteworthy that the Contract Law has been repealed by the Chinese Civil Code, and the choice of law rules that overlap with Article 41 of the Chinese Conflict of Laws Act have been deleted. This means that, in the future, it is less likely for a Chinese court to invoke both Article 126 of the Contract Law and Article 41 of the Chinese Conflict of Laws Act, or merely the former, when applying the closest connection principle.

4.2.2.2 Analysis of Connecting Factors

Not all Chinese courts conduct an analysis of the connecting factors when applying the closest connection principle. In some cases, it is challenging to assert, based on the connecting factors in a case, that China has the closest connection with the case.[72] Verdicts lacking reasoning or analysis are not limited to contract cases but also extend to other fields.[73]

In this regard, the judgment of *Xue Xiujuan v. Jiangxi Ganzhonglv International Travel Agency* by the second-instance court serves as a good example of determining the applicable law under the closest connection principle in Article 41 of the

---

day her condition was getting more and more serious and stayed alone in the hotel. When arriving in Paris, she was already very ill. The tour guide left her in the hotel and took other tourists out to play. The next day she developed a high fever and coma and then the tour guide took her to the local hospital for treatment. After diagnosis, she was suffering from bacterial meningitis and died due to late hospitalization. The plaintiffs held that the products and services provided by the defendant failed to protect the personal and property safety of consumers, which caused Liang Huifang to be infected with meningitis bacteria during travel. After contracting the disease, the defendant failed to notify her family members in time, and did not send her to a hospital in time, which caused her condition to deteriorate rapidly and the rescue was ultimately ineffective. The defendant failed to fulfill his duty of care and security, which was a serious breach of contract.

[71] This reasoning means that most foreign-related package travel contracts will be subject to Chinese law, especially when the plaintiff and the defendant are both Chinese parties. Basically, it is not possible for Chinese consumers to rely on European law, since China has the closest connection, even if the European companies are liable.

[72] Huang and Du (2014), p. 25.

[73] Huang and Du (2014), p. 33.

Chinese Conflict of Laws Act.[74] The court analyzed that although the accident causing personal injury took place in Thailand, the parties involved were Chinese residents, a Chinese legal person, and a Chinese incorporated organization, respectively. Moreover, both the conclusion of the travel contract and the insurance contract took place in china.[75] Thus, the applicable law should be Chinese law.[76] Apparently, the court not only invoked the closest connection principle but also explained why China had the closest connection with the dispute.[77] Nonetheless, it is crucial to prevent judges from abusing the discretion granted by the closest connection principle to expand the application of the *lex fori*.[78]

4.2.3 The Characteristic Performance Under Article 41 of the Chinese Conflict of Laws Act

The characteristic performance doctrine is stipulated in Article 41 of the Chinese Conflict of Laws Act, running parallel to the closest connection doctrine. As to the relationship between the characteristic performance doctrine and the closest connection doctrine, there are mainly three different opinions.

The first opinion suggests that the characteristic performance doctrine serves as a test to assist in making a meaningful determination of the applicable law under the closest connection principle.[79] Essentially, this view holds that the characteristic performance doctrine is a sub-test of the closest connection test. The second opinion argues that the characteristic performance doctrine is used only when the place having the closest connection with the contract cannot be determined.[80] This opinion advocates that the application of the closest connection doctrine takes precedence over the characteristic performance doctrine, considering the characteristic performance doctrine supplementary. The third opinion asserts that the characteristic performance doctrine is applied in most cases, and the closest connection doctrine is used only when the characteristic performance test leads to a country with no substantive connection with the contract.[81] This opinion advocates that the characteristic

[74] *Xue Xiujuan v. Jiangxi Ganzhonglv International Travel Agency*, Jiangxi Province HPC, (2017) Gan Min Zhong No 248; Jiangxi Province Nanchang Municipality IPC, (2016) Gan 01 Min Chu No 229.

[75] Ibid. It is noticeable that the application of the consumer choice of law rules may lead to the application of the same law, but more convincing by relying on the consumer's habitual residence as the connecting factor.

[76] Ibid.

[77] Chen (2020), p. 211.

[78] Huang and Du (2014), p. 26.

[79] Tang et al. (2016), p. 228, para. 8.57; Huo (2010), p. 288; 霍政欣，《国际私法》，法律出版社，2010年，第288页。

[80] Tang et al. (2016), p. 229, para. 8.58.

[81] Tang et al. (2016), p. 229, para. 8.58.

performance doctrine prevails over the closest connection doctrine, and the closest connection doctrine is supplementary.

Regardless of the relation between these two doctrines, the objective is to find the law that has the closest connection with the contract. The application of the characteristic performance doctrine also reflects such consideration. The question then arises: how are the characteristic performance doctrine and the closest connection doctrine used in judicial practice, particularly in the context of package travel contracts?

In *Suzhou Youth Travel Agency v. Boss Egerhard*,[82] the plaintiff Suzhou Youth Travel Agency, domiciled in Suzhou City, Jiangsu Province, sued the defendants Boss Egerhard from Germany and Akpuaka Lily Ifeanyi Chukwu from the Federal Republic of Nigeria. The two defendants, who were husband and wife, signed a service contract with the plaintiff for a price of 25,606 RMB (3556 Euro), according to which the plaintiff provided services, including but not limited to accommodation, transportation, etc., to the defendants. Clearly, it constituted a package travel contract since more than two kinds of travel services are provided. After the conclusion of the contract, the plaintiff, upon the request of the defendants, provided two extra day services in Lhasa and bought flight tickets from Lhasa to Shanghai. The plaintiff fully fulfilled the contract obligations, but the two defendants still owe the plaintiff a service fee of 9409 RMB (1306 Euro).

The defendants argued that they could not enter the border of Nepal because of visa issues, which was caused by the fault of the plaintiff; thus, relevant loss should be borne by the plaintiff. The original Nepal schedule arranged by the plaintiff included a tour bus, tour guide, breakfast, lunch, and transportation to the airport; accommodation was not included. Despite this, it was still a package travel contract in accordance with Article 111(3) of the Tourism Law of the PRC. However, the court merely classified the contract as a travel service contract, instead of a package travel contract or consumer contract. As a result, Article 41 of the Chinese Conflict of Laws Act applied.[83] This case was the only instance in which a Chinese business sued foreign consumers for the payment of travel fees.

The court determined that, since the defendants were foreigners, the case constituted foreign-related civil litigation. As regards the application of procedure law, the Chinese Civil Procedure Law, as the *lex forum*, should be applicable. Regarding the application of substantive law, Article 41 of the Chinese Conflict of Laws Act should be applied to determine the governing law. The case concerned a travel service contract dispute, and the parties did not reach an agreement on the law applicable to the contract. The plaintiff's obligation in the contract was to provide travel services to the defendant, while the defendant's obligation was to make payment.[84] The

[82] *Suzhou Youth Travel Agency v. Boss Egerhard*, Suzhou Industrial Park District People's Court, (2014) Yuan Shang Wai Chu Zi No 00040. 苏州青年旅行社股份有限公司与AKPUAKALILYIFEANYICHUKWU、BOSSEGERHARD旅游合同纠纷一审民事判决书, 苏州工业园区人民法院,(2014)园商外初字第00040号.

[83] Ibid.

[84] Ibid.

plaintiff's obligations best reflected the characteristics of the contract, therefore, this case should apply the law of the country of the plaintiff's habitual residence, namely Chinese law.[85]

In the context of electronic commerce, many contracts, including travel contracts, are concluded online. These online contracts may be performed online or offline, depending on whether the provision of the contract involves goods or services.[86] It is argued that the determination of applicable law to electronic contracts should be treated exactly as ordinary paper contracts, unless the e-contracts do not involve any physical delivery.[87] Since this book focuses on the provision of travel services, all travel contracts, whether concluded online or offline, are to be performed offline. The way of electronic contracting does not affect the determination of the place of performance of the travel contract.

4.2.4 The Overuse of Article 41 on Contract Conflicts Rules and the Underuse of Article 42 on Consumer Conflicts Rules

It can be seen that Article 41 of the Chinese Conflict of Laws Act has been excessively used by Chinese courts to determine the applicable law in foreign-related travel contract disputes. However, Article 41 of the Chinese Conflict of Laws Act on general contract choice of law rules does not distinguish between consumer contracts (B2C contracts) and business contracts (B2B contracts). The overuse of Article 41 of the Chinese Conflict of Laws Act indirectly reveals the fact that Article 42 of the Chinese Conflict of Laws Act is underused. Before the enactment of the Chinese Conflict of Laws Act, there was no distinction between consumer contract and general contract regarding choice of law issues. This lack of distinction may be unjust to the weaker party.[88] The Chinese Conflict of Laws Act adopts the principle of protecting the supposedly weaker parties.[89] Article 42 of the Chinese Conflict of Laws Act separates consumer contracts from business contracts, providing favorable choice of law rules for consumer contracts.[90] Despite this, such favorable consumer applicable law rules have been underused in judicial practice. In order to

[85] Ibid.

[86] Wu (2005), p. 144; 吴伟光，《电子商务法》，清华大学出版社，2005年，第144页。

[87] Wang (2010), p. 136.

[88] Huo (2011), pp. 637, 674.

[89] Articles 25, 29 and 30 of the Chinese Conflict of Laws Act. Tu (2015), p. 42, para. 75.

[90] The protection of the interests of consumers is an international tendency, which has facilitated the establishment of consumer choice of law rules globally. Xiao (2007), p. 187; 肖永平，《国际私法原理》，法律出版社，2007，第187页。

understand why Article 42 of the Chinese Conflict of Laws Act does not play an important role in protecting consumers, more specifically concerning package travel tourists, it is necessary to examine the conditions under which Article 42 of the Chinese Conflict of Laws Act shall apply.

4.3 Conditions for Applying Protective Consumer Choice of Law Rules

Article 42 of the Chinese Conflicts Ac imposes several conditions for the application of protective consumer private international law rules. First, the contract in dispute is classified as a consumer contract. Second, the consumer contract involves a foreign element. Third, the business operator has engaged in relevant commercial or soliciting activities in the consumer's habitual residence. Fourth, the application of the law of the consumer's habitual residence is also under the condition that the consumer does not choose to apply the law of the place where goods or services are provided. The business party is deprived of the right to choose the applicable law for consumer contracts. Fifth, although Article 42 does not expressly state so, the consumer contract has to fall within the material scope of consumer choice of law rules. This consumer choice of law rule is more favorable to consumers, the question arises: why is it not fully used by Chinese courts?

In judicial practice, there are several reasons to explain why Article 42 of the Chinese Conflict of Laws Act is not fully used to determine the law applicable to package travel contracts. First, the distinction between travel contracts, service contracts, package travel contracts and consumer contracts is not clear. Most package travel contracts are classified as travel contracts or service contracts, but not as consumer contracts. Second, many package travel contracts involving a foreign element are classified as purely domestic cases and are subject to domestic rules. As to what constitutes a foreign element or international element with regard to package travel contracts, it lacks consensus among different courts in China. Third, the lack of specific criteria for 'engaging in relevant commercial activities' under Article 42 of the Chinese Conflict of Laws Act also undermines the function and operability of such consumer protective choice of law rule. Fourth, the total exclusion of two-sided party autonomy also limits the function of Article 42 of the Chinese Conflict of Laws Act. In practice, a consumer and a business may reach a choice of law agreement after a dispute arises. Since Article 42 of consumer choice of law rule only allows for one-sided party autonomy, Chinese courts have resorted to Article 41 of contract choice of law rule to justify the application of the law chosen by both parties.

4.3.1 Classification of Package Travel Contracts and Timeshare Contracts

The primary obstacle to applying favorable consumer choice of law rules in Article 42 of the Chinese Conflict of Laws Act to package travel contracts is the prevalent classification of package travel contracts as general contracts rather than consumer contracts.[91] Classification aims to characterize relevant facts and categorize them into the scope of a particular legal relation.[92] Article 42 of the Chinese Conflict of Laws Act fails to explicitly include package travel contracts within its material scope. The identification of the legal status of a consumer is the first step before applying consumer jurisdiction and choice of law rules.[93] The purpose criterion is the core element used to determine the legal status of a consumer.[94]

Article 2 of the Chinese Consumer Protection Law defines a consumer as 'a person who purchases and uses commodities or receives services for daily consumption'.[95] Due to the ambiguity of the notion of consumer or consumer contract and the unclear material scope of Article 42 of the Chinese Conflict of Laws Act, the vast majority of package travel contracts are not classified as consumer contracts. In judicial practice, a dispute arising from a package travel contract may be classified as a foreign related travel dispute, a contract dispute, a travel contract dispute, a commercial dispute,[96] a civil dispute, a civil tort dispute, a tourism dispute, or a service contract dispute.[97]

---

[91] The same conclusion is drawn in Zhuang (2020), p. 31.

[92] Han (2003), p. 126; 韩德培主编:《国际私法新论》，武汉大学出版社2003年版，第126页。

[93] Guo and Xiang (2002), p. 346; 郭玉军、向在胜,《欧盟电子消费合同管辖权问题研究》，《武汉大学学报(社会科学版)》, 2002年第3 期，第346页。

[94] Liu (2022), p. 59; 刘阳,《跨国消费合同管辖权研究:欧盟经验及我国方案》，《武汉大学国际法评论》， 2022年第1期, 第59页。

[95] The commercial demand is not covered under the concept of 'daily consumption' or 'meeting daily needs'. Binding (2014), p. 226.

[96] In *Hu Siyuan et al v. Zhongnan International Travel*, the plaintiffs Hu Siyuan, Shu Sicong and 5 other tourists sued the defendant Zhongnan International Travel for the refund of travel fee for a 10-day-9-night travel in Australia. The court held that since the plaintiff Shu Sicong was a Hong Kong resident, the case should be regarded as foreign-related civil and commercial contract dispute. *Hu Siyuan v. Zhongnan International Travel*, Hubei Province Wuhan Municipality Jiang'an DPC, (2018) 0102 Min Chu No 5680.

[97] Chen (2020), p. 217.

4.3.1.1 Distinction Between Package Travel Contracts and Travel Contracts

Many package travel contracts are often classified as regular travel contracts and are governed by general contractual choice of law rules under Article 41 Chinese Conflict Act. Since the enactment of the 1999 Chinese Contract Law, travel contracts, which are not specifically listed as a specific contract type (named contract), have been considered as general contracts and regulated under general contract principles and provisions.[98] This domestic law practice may have influenced the classification of package travel contracts as consumer contracts. Some argue that travel contracts inherently are consumer contracts, and thus Article 42 Chinese Conflict Act on consumer choice of law rules shall apply.[99] Others advocate that travel contracts should be divided into different types, including package travel contracts, self-service travel contracts, and agency travel contracts.[100] According to this perspective, only package travel contracts are protected as consumer contracts under Article 42 Chinese Conflict Act, whereas other travel contracts are subject to general contract choice of law rules.[101]

The concept of travel contract is not equivalent to the notion of package travel contract nor consumer contract. All package travel contracts are essentially travel contracts, but not all travel contracts are package travel contracts. In judicial practice, a travel contract may refer to a commission contract between commercial parties or a service contract, rather than a package travel contract or a consumer contract. In *Cong Shuwan v. Zhongxin Travel Service Group,* where a Chinese tourist passed away while traveling abroad,[102] the court held that this case was a dispute arising from a travel contract between a tourist and a tour operator. Since the place of performance of the contract and the place of the tourist's death were both outside the territory of China, it should be classified as a dispute over a foreign-related contract. Despite expressly stating that it was a dispute arising from 'a travel contract

---

[98] Xia (2010), p. 418.

[99] Wang (2018), pp. 103–106; Zhuang (2020), p. 26.

[100] 《中华人民共和国旅游法》第七十四条:旅行社接受旅游者的委托，为其代订交通、住宿、餐饮、游览、娱乐等旅游服务，收取代办费用的，应当亲自处理委托事务。Article 74 of Tourism Law of the People's Republic of China: Travel agencies accepting the entrustment of tourists to book transportation, accommodation, catering, tours, entertainment and other tourism services for them, and charge the agency fees, shall handle the entrusted affairs in person. The difference between package travel contracts and agency travel contract is that the travel operator determines the whole itinerary and travel service providers in a package travel contract, but only servers as an agent for individual tourists in an agency travel contract, which essentially is an entrustment contract.

[101] Guo (2018), pp. 86–91; 郭欢欢,《我国涉外旅游纠纷法律适用之偏差及其矫正-基于江苏省国际旅游案评析》，《时代法学》2018年第2期，第86–91页。

[102] *Cong Shuwan v. Zhongxin Travel Service Group*, Liaoning Province Dalian Municipality Xigang DPC, (2017) Liao 0203 Min Chu No 4789.

between a tourist and a tour operator', the court did not classify the contract as a package travel contract, but rather as a foreign-related contract. Hence, general contract choice of law rules applied, rather than consumer choice of law rules.

In certain instances, a contract concluded between two commercial parties might also be classified as a travel contract in judicial practice. An illustrative case is *Guangdong Goat City International Travel Agency v. Guangdong Changyou International Travel Agency.*[103] In this case, the plaintiff, Guangdong Goat City International Travel Agency, sued the defendant, Guangdong Changyou International Travel Agency, seeking termination of the contract and the return of 110,040 RMB (15,283 Euro) as part of the group fee. The plaintiff purchased a travel product for an 8-day trip to Hokkaido, Japan, from the defendant for seven tourists with a total price of 112,000 RMB (15,555 Euro). Due to the outbreak of Covid-19 and relevant prevention and control measures, the defendant was unable to provide the agreed-upon travel services. Following negotiations, the defendant initially agreed to refund 110,040 RMB to the plaintiff but later refused to do so.[104]

As to the nature of contract in dispute, the defendant asserted that the contract was an intermediary cooperation contract between travel agencies,[105] not a travel contract between consumers and travel agencies. The defendant contended that the travel contract between the plaintiff and the consumer for the 8-day trip to Japan was forced to be temporarily suspended due to the *force majeure* of the Covid-19 outbreak. This travel contract should not be confused with the cooperation contract between the defendant and the plaintiff. The subject matter of the contract in this case was an 8-day travel service in Japan, which could still be performed in the future. The relationship between the plaintiff and the defendant was essentially an intermediary entrustment relationship. By contrast, the plaintiff held that the relationship between the parties constituted a travel contract, instead of a commission contract.[106]

The court identified that one of the main disputes in this case was the determination of the legal relationship between the parties. Article 424 of the Contract Law of the PRC defines an intermediary contract as a contract in which the intermediary reports to the client an opportunity to conclude a contract or provides intermediary services for the conclusion of the contract, with the client paying a commission fee. The contract concluded between the plaintiff and the defendant for providing travel services did not contain the legal characteristics of an intermediary contract. Instead,

---

[103] *Guangdong Goat City International Travel Agency v. Guangdong Changyou International Travel Agency*, Guangdong Province Guangzhou Municipality Yuexiu District People's Court, (2020) Yue 0104 Min Chu No 43297. 广东羊城之旅国际旅行社有限公司番禺分公司与广东畅游国际旅行社有限公司旅游合同纠纷一审民事判决书, 广东省广州市越秀区人民法院, (2020)粤0104民初43297号.

[104] Ibid. The defendant argued that the travel contract cannot be performed because of the nation-wide lockdown measures caused by the Covid-pandemic. It was not caused by the defendant and should not be attributed to the defendant.

[105] Ibid.

[106] Ibid.

the contract in dispute was a travel contract.[107] In this case, the contract between the two travel agencies was a B2B contract, rather than a B2C contract.

A comparable case is *Born Eohy Ocean Tours & Rent A Car v. Jiangsu China Tour Travel Agency.*[108] In this case, the plaintiff, Born Eohy Ocean Tours & Rent A Car, domiciled in Sabah, Malaysia, filed a lawsuit against the defendant, Jiangsu China Tour Travel Agency, domiciled in Gulou District, Nangjing City (Jiangsu Province), before the Intermediate People's Court of Nanjing, Jiangsu. The plaintiff claimed that the defendant, with whom it had a long-term cooperation relationship, did not pay the group reception fee of 60,000 RMB (8333 Euro) for a tour group organized by the defendant. The parties signed an entrusted reception contract, according to which the defendant solicited tourists interested in visiting Malaysia, and the plaintiff would arrange local travel activities for the tour group organized by the defendant. The court held that, since the plaintiff was registered in Malaysia, the case was a foreign-related commercial dispute. In this instance, the contract concluded between these two commercial parties was classified as a commercial contract instead of a travel contract.

As mentioned above, many package travel contracts, which consist of more than two kinds of travel services, have been classified merely as travel contracts.[109] By contrast, in some other cases Chinese courts have conducted a correct classification of the package travel contracts. For instance, in *Huo Mou v. Sichuan China International Travel Agency*,[110] Huo Mou booked an '8-day-6-night Bangkok-Phuket-Phi Phi Island, Thailand' travel product for herself and her husband on the Ctrip website operated by the Ctrip Commercial Company. Both the online booking

[107] Ibid.

[108] *Born Eohy Ocean Tours & Rent A Car v. Jiangsu China Tour Travel Agency*, Jiangsu Province Nanjing Municipality Intermediate People's Court, (2019) Su 01 Min Chu No 79. 79沙巴海洋精品旅游及租车有限公司与江苏省中旅旅行社有限公司旅游合同纠纷一审民事判决书，江苏省南京市中级人民法院,(2019)苏01民初79号.

[109] *Wang Xuerong v. Kunming Kanghui Yonghui Travel Agency*, Yunnan Province Kunming Municipality Intermediate People's Court, (2017) Yun 01 Min Zhong No 7280; 昆明康辉永辉旅行社有限公司、王雪蓉旅游合同纠纷二审民事判决书，云南省昆明市中级人民法院 (2017)云01民终7280号；昆明市五华区人民法院,(2016)云0125民初第1890号；*Suzhou Youth Travel Agency v. Boss Egerhard*, Suzhou Industrial Park District People's Court, (2014) Yuan Shang Wai Chu Zi No 00040; *Xue Xiujuan v. Jiangxi Ganzhonglv International Travel Agency,* Jiangxi Province HPC, (2017) Gan Min Zhong No 248.

[110] *Huo Mou v. Sichuan China International Travel Agency*, Shanghai First Intermediate People's Court, (2020) Hu 01 Min Zhong No 2977; Shanghai Changning DPC, (2019) Hu 0105 Min Chu No 16692. 四川省中国国际旅行社有限责任公司与李金发等生命权、健康权、身体权纠纷二审案件二审民事判决书, 上海市第一中级人民法院,(2020)沪01民终2977号；上海市长宁区人民法院,(2019)沪0105民初16692号. Thc plaintiffs Li Jinfa, Xic Xiurong, Huo Mou ct al, domiciled in Tongzhou District, Beijing, sued the defendants (i) Sichuan China International Travel Agency, domiciled in Wuhou District, Chengdu, (ii) Shanghai Ctrip Commercial Company, domiciled in Changning District, Shanghai, and (iii) Beijing Ctrip International Travel Agency, domiciled in Chaoyang District, Beijing. The plaintiffs Huo Mou and Li Mou were the deceased Li Mou's wife and daughter. The plaintiffs Li Jinfa and Xie Xiurong were the deceased Li Mou's parents.

page and the itinerary order explicitly stated that 'this product was solicited by Beijing Ctrip Company, with Sichuan China International Travel Company serving as the entrusting agency responsible for specific travel services and operations.' Huo Mou paid a total of 16,552 RMB (2365 Euro) through the payment channel of Ctrip.com, covering round-trip air tickets, hotel accommodation, meals, exclusive use of cars, tickets, and other costs for additional activities like the yacht 'Big White' Emperor Island activity (deep diving and snorkeling). The couple took the Phoenix tour boat to visit the Emperor Island. The Phoenix tour boat capsized in the Andaman sea area of Phuket, Thailand when returning from the Emperor Island, leading to the drowning of Li Mou. This case involved more than two kinds of travel services.

The court of first instance held that, since the Phoenix tour boat capsized in the Andaman sea area of Phuket, Thailand, the case involved a foreign element. Beijing Ctrip Company, acting as the agent of Sichuan China International Travel Company, concluded a travel contract with Huo Mou and Li Mou, encompassing transportation, accommodation, catering, and other travel services. Such a contract was classified as a package travel contract.[111] The appellate court also held that the travel contract in dispute, which included several travel services such as transportation, accommodation and catering, should be classified as a package travel contract.[112] This correct classification is not only legally sound but also justifies the application of Article 42 of the Chinese Conflict of Laws Act when determining the applicable law.

Another case with correct classification of the package travel contract is *Jiang Mou v. Royal Caribbean Cruises Company.*[113] The plaintiff and her husband signed an outbound travel contract with the International Cooperative Travel Agency for a 5-day-4-night cruise travel from Shanghai to Okinawa, Japan. Unfortunately, on the return journey to the Shanghai port, the plaintiff slipped on the deck, resulting in injuries. The plaintiff held that Royal Caribbean Cruises, as the operator, and the International Cooperative Travel Agency, as the contracting party of the travel contract, did not fulfill the duty of guaranteeing the plaintiff's safety and thus should be liable for the personal injury caused by the slip-and-fall accident. The court correctly determined that the outbound travel contract concluded between the plaintiff and the International Cooperative Travel Agency was a package travel contract.[114] Although the court did not specify the content of the outbound travel contract in the judgment, the 5-day-4-night cruise tour inherently encompassed transportation, accommodation, and various entertainment services, justifying the classification made by the court.

[111] Ibid.

[112] Ibid.

[113] *Jiang Mou v. Royal Caribbean Cruises Company*, Shanghai HPC, (2018) Hu Min Zhong No 85; Shanghai Maritime Court, (2017) Hu 72 Min Chu No 136. 上诉人蒋某某与上诉人皇家加勒比RCL游轮有限公司、被上诉人浙江省国际合作旅行社有限公司上海分公司海上人身损害责任纠纷案二审民事判决书, 上海市高级人民法院,(2018)沪民终85号; 上海海事法院,(2017)沪72民初136号.

[114] Ibid.

4.3.1.2 Distinction Between Package Travel Contracts and Service Contracts

Travel contracts and package travel contracts are fundamentally two types of service contracts. However, not all service contracts are qualified as package travel contracts. A case that illustrates this distinction is *Zhu Kaili v. Guangzhou Baiyun District Fluent Education Training Centre.*[115] The plaintiffs, Zhu Kaili, Zhu Kaijia, Zhu Qingwen, and Tan Peiyi, sued the defendant, Guangzhou Baiyun District Fluent Education Training Centre, for the return of 64,700 RMB (9243 Euro). Zhu Kaijia, was a resident of Hong Kong, domiciled in Huangpu District, Guangzhou (Guangdong). The other plaintiffs were all domiciled in Guangdong.

The plaintiff Tan Peiyi signed a registration form titled "Little Star American Starlight Journey" with the defendant, according to which the defendant was to organize Zhu Kaili and other performers for rehearsals of a program and to perform at the 2014 North America Spring Festival Gala for Chinese New Year. The total price for the four plaintiffs was 129,200 RMB (18,457 Euro), covering transportation, accommodation, visas, tourist destination tickets, performing costumes, and training fees for Zhu Kaili. Since Zhu Kaili didn't perform in the Gala as promised by the defendant, the plaintiffs sued the defendant for contract fraud, even though they had visited San Francisco, San Diego, Los Angeles, and other places afterward.[116]

Although both parties agreed that the four plaintiffs collectively constituted one contracting party in the contract concluded with the defendant, their opinions on the nature of the contract differed. The four plaintiffs held that they, as one party, jointly signed the contract with the defendant, and the nature of such contract was essentially a service contract. Although travel services were included, the contract was primarily about Zhu Kaili's stage performance at the Spring Festival Gala.[117] The main content or primary purpose of the contract was Zhu Kaili's stage performance organized by the defendant, whilst Zhu Kaijia, Zhu Qingwen, and Tan Peiyi, as family members, accompanied Zhu Kaili and engaged in travel activities in other cities after the performance.

In contrast, the defendant asserted that it had two different kinds of contractual relationships with different plaintiffs. First, the contract between Zhu Kaili and the defendant was a package travel contract, which included providing an opportunity to perform at the Spring Festival Gala, celebrating Chinese New Year with American children, and visiting Disney, Hollywood and other American cities (San Francisco, San Diego, and Los Angeles). This package travel contract encompassed a series of travel activities, such as transportation, accommodation, and catering. The defendant asserted that the contract in dispute was not a service contract which only

[115] *Zhu Kaili v. Guangzhou Baiyun District Fluent Education Training Centre*, Guangdong Province Guangzhou Municipality IPC, (2014) Hui Zhong Fa Min Si Zhong Zi No 137; Guangdong Province Guangzhou Municipality Baiyun DPC, (2014) Hui Yun Fa Min San Chu Zi No 15.

[116] Ibid.

[117] Ibid.

provided the opportunity to perform on the stage. Second, the contract between other three plaintiffs and the defendant was a pure travel contract.[118] The defendant had repeatedly clarified in its publicity that the trip to North America was accompanied by a special person. Among the six children who were to perform on the stage, only the parents of Zhu Kaili and the parents of another child chose to join the group. Zhu Kaijia, who was neither a performer nor a parent, also joined the trip, suggesting a purpose focused solely on travel. It can be seen that these three plaintiffs went to America only for the purpose of traveling. Since the entire itinerary of the trip to America had been completed, the purpose of the contract had been achieved.[119]

Both the first-instance and second-instance courts concurred the that the contract, in nature, was a service contract.[120] First, the contract expressly stated the inclusion of the four plaintiffs, with Zhu Kaili being the performer, and the total price of 129,200 RMB (17,944 Euro) reflected the collective cost of the four plaintiffs' participation in the performance tour for the 2014 North American Spring Festival Gala. Second, the participation of Zhu Kaijia, Zhu Qingwen, and Tan Peiyi, as family members of Zhu Kaili, was closely related to Zhu Kaili's performance on the stage of Spring Festival Gala. The plaintiffs chose the services provided by the defendant was also based on the condition of Zhu Kaili's performance on the stage, instead of visiting America only for the purpose of traveling. Thus, the four plaintiffs had formed a service contract relationship with the defendant.[121] This reasoning indicates that, in a multi-party contract, if several parties' activities or purposes are intricately linked to one party' activity or purpose, the latter takes precedence.

The court did not classify the plaintiffs as consumers but did refer to Article 49 of the Chinese Consumer Protection Law. Despite the higher cost of traveling to other American cities for Zhu Kaili's three family members compared to the service fee for Zhu Kaili to perform on the stage of Spring Festival Gala, the court held that the package travel service was secondary to the primary service of Zhu Kaili's stage performance.[122] The primary purpose of the contract was Zhu Kaili's stage performance, with the package travel service in other American cities being supplementary to the primary service. Even if the cost for the secondary service is higher than the primary service, the nature of the contract still depends on the primary service.

The case of *Zhu Kaili v. Guangzhou Baiyun District Fluent Education Training Centre* shows that not all classifications of package travel contracts are beneficial for the parties concerning substantive rights. This case involves a multi-party litigation, in which the four plaintiffs as one party to the contract have different purposes. Although the contract encompassing more than two kinds of travel services should be classified as package travel contracts, the court ultimately classified the contract

[118] Ibid.

[119] Ibid. Thus, the claim of the three plaintiffs for the refund of the travel expenses was unreasonable.

[120] Ibid.

[121] Ibid.

[122] Ibid.

as a service contract. From a substantive law perspective, such classification favors the plaintiffs. As the primary contractual obligation, Zhu Kaili's stage performance, remained unfulfilled, the defendant was obligated to return the fee, despite the fact the plaintiffs did visit other American cities. However, from a private international law perspective, if the defendant is a foreign business, classifying the contract as a service contract does not ensure consumer protection under the law of the consumer's habitual residence, as outlined in Article 42 of the Chinese Conflict of Laws Act.

4.3.1.3 Distinction Between Package Travel Contracts and Consumer Contracts

Despite some courts classifying travel contracts that include more than two kinds of travel services as package travel contracts, the identity of a package travel tourist as a consumer is usually overlooked by Chinese judges. As a result, package travel tourists are not protected as consumers in Chinese private international law.

For instance, in *Dr. Barsch-Supan v. Xi'an Xindaya International Travel Agency,*[123] the status of the two American tourists in a package travel contract as consumers was totally ignored, and the package travel contract was classified as a foreign-related contract, rather than a consumer contract. What if the two American tourists argued that American law, as the law of the tourists' habitual residence, should be applicable in accordance with Article 42 of the Chinese Conflict of Laws Act, would American law be applicable?[124] In this scenario, the business may need to prove that it has not engaged in relevant commercial activities in America and invoke Chinese law as the law of the place where the travel services are provided under Article 42 of the Chinese Conflict of Laws Act.

In *Xu Yan v. Shenyang Overseas International Travel Agency,*[125] a tourist died abroad during the performance of a package travel contract for a cruise tour.[126] The court explicitly stated that the victim was a consumer and should be protected as a consumer when participating travel activities organized by travel agencies. The legal status of a package travel tourist as a consumer was expressly mentioned in this case.[127] Despite this, the court did not refer to consumer choice of law rules,

---

[123] *Dr. Barsch-Supan v. Xi'an Xindaya International Travel Agency*, Shaanxi Province HPC, (2016) Shan Min Zhong No 511.

[124] Chen (2020), p. 209.

[125] *Xu Yan v. Shenyang Overseas International Travel Agency*, Liaoning Province Shenyang Municipality Heping District People's Court, (2018) Liao 0102 Min Chu No 1848. 徐波、徐利等与中国旅行社总社(辽宁)有限公司辽阳分公司、沈阳市海外国际旅行社有限公司等生命权、健康权、身体权纠纷一审民事判决书, 沈阳市和平区人民法院,(2018)辽0102民初1848号.

[126] The court did not classify the case as a foreign-related case, although the performance of the contract was outside the territory of China.

[127] *Xu Yan v. Shenyang Overseas International Travel Agency*, Liaoning Province Shenyang Municipality Heping District People's Court, (2018) Liao 0102 Min Chu No 1848.

potentially due to the absence of explicit inclusion of package travel contracts in the material scope of Article 42 of the Chinese Conflict of Laws Act.

However, not all package travel contracts should be automatically protected as consumer contracts in private international law, especially when a package travel contract is primarily concluded for business purposes or is closely related to business activities. This is illustrated in *Liu Chengqin v. Shenzhen Jiuzhou International Travel Agency*,[128] where 14 lawyers from a Chinese law firm sued three defendants (a Chinese travel agency, an Italian cruise company, and its branch in Shanghai) for a refund of the travel fee of 7500 RMB (1071 Euro) and three times the punitive compensation fee for providing fraudulent services. The law firm where these 14 plaintiffs work concluded a group outbound travel contract with the travel agency for a 6-day-5-night tour on a cruise ship to Japan. The cruise company, based on bad weather, changed the destination to Vietnam immediately after the cruise left the port and without notifying the plaintiffs in advance. In this case, since this package travel activity was arranged by the law firm, which was closely related to the lawyer's profession, such a package travel contract should not be subject to consumer choice of law rules under Article 42 of the Chinese Conflict of Laws Act.

In Chinese civil law, travel contracts, package travel contracts, or even service contracts are considered nameless contracts or atypical contracts, as they are not included in the 19 kinds of contracts stipulated in the Chinese Civil Code. In substantive law, issues relating to nameless contracts or atypical contracts are governed by rules concerning general contracts. The same principle applies in private International law when it comes to nameless contracts or atypical contracts, such as package travel contracts. Generally, the classification of package travel contracts as travel contracts or general contracts has led to the overuse of Article 41 of the Chinese Conflict of Laws Act, which constitutes the primary legal barrier to applying consumer conflicts rules in Article 42 of the Chinese Conflict of Laws Act to determine the law applicable to package travel contracts. Therefore, it is necessary to expressly include package travel contracts in the material scope of consumer choice of law rules in Article 42 of the Chinese Conflict of Laws Act.

4.3.1.4 Timeshare Contracts

Just as package travel contracts are not protected as consumer contracts in Chinese private international law, timeshare contracts, being considered nameless contracts or atypical contracts, are also not afforded protection as consumer contracts in China. Article 2 of the Tourism Law of the PRC outlines the scope of application of the Tourism Law, including 'tours, vacations, leisure activities, and other forms of tourism activities organized within the territory of or beyond the territory of the

[128] *Liu Chengqin v. Shenzhen Jiuzhou International Travel Agency*, Guangdong Shenzhen Qianhai Cooperation Zone People's Court, (2020) Yue 0391 Min Chu No 1620-1633. 刘承琴民事裁定书, 广东省深圳前海合作区人民法院,(2020)粤0391民初1620–1633号.

PRC' as well as 'business operations providing relevant tourism services'.[129] Although timeshare contracts are not expressly mentioned, they can be covered through a broad interpretation of 'other forms of tourism activities'. Despite this, the absence of a specific definition of timeshare contracts may give rise to the question of whether timeshare contracts are protected as consumer contracts under Article 42 of the Chinese Conflict of Laws Act. Given the lack of a precise definition of timeshare contracts in the Tourism Law and the Chinese Civil Code, it is more likely that timeshare contracts are regarded as nameless contracts or atypical contracts.

It may be argued that timeshare contracts are contracts related to a right in rem in immovable property or a tenancy of immovable property. As a result, Article 36 of the Chinese Conflict Act would apply, designating the law of the place where the immovable property is located. However, timeshare contracts, in their nature, differ from contracts related to a right in rem in immovable property or a tenancy of immovable property.[130] Article 34 of the 2021 Chinese Civil Procedure Law[131] states that litigation for disputes over an immovable property shall be under the exclusive jurisdiction of the people's court where the immovable property is located. The exercise of exclusive jurisdiction over certain disputes aims to protect fundamental economic and social interests of a country, preserve state sovereignty, and safeguard national interests.[132] It is impractical to allow any other country to adjudicate disputes on the title of land located in China, as it goes against Chinese public policy.[133] The question arises as to whether timeshare contracts are subject to exclusive jurisdiction.

Although it is acknowledged that the court where an immovable property is situated shall have exclusive jurisdiction over disputes related to the immovable property, the key question is what constitutes 'disputes related to the immovable property'.[134] Article 28 of the 2020 SPC Interpretation of the Application of the 2017 Civil Procedure Law explains that disputes over immovable properties stipulated in Article 33 of the 2017 Civil Procedure Law refer to disputes arising from the confirmation, division, and adjacent relationship of the rights of immovable properties. The rights of using an immovable property during a certain period of time for certain years under a timeshare contract do not fall within the material scope of exclusive jurisdiction, since the timeshare right has legal binding only between the contracting parties and is not binding on a third party.

---

[129] Article 2 of the Tourism Law of the PRC, The law applies to the tours, vacations, leisure activities and other forms of tourism activities organized within the territory of or to go beyond the territory of the People's Republic of China, and the business operations providing relevant tourism services.

[130] See the discussion in the previous Chapter on the tango between Brussels Ibis Regulation and Rome I Regulation under the beat of the Timeshare Directive.

[131] Article 33 of the 2017 Chinese Civil Procedure Law.

[132] Wagner (1952), p. 111; Cloherty (1994), p. 1287.

[133] Tang et al. (2016), p. 57, para. 3.17.

[134] Tang et al. (2016), p. 57, para. 3.18.

Nevertheless, an argument could be made that a timeshare contract is akin to a lease contract. Article 19 of the 2020 SPC Interpretation of the Civil Procedure Law states that the place of performance of a lease contract is where the property subject to lease is situated. If a timeshare contract is classified as a lease contract, the courts where the property is situated would have jurisdiction, instead of the courts where the timeshare tourist is domiciled.

(i) General contract choice of law rules applied to timeshare contracts

Since the concept of timeshare contracts is not explicitly provided in the Chinese Tourism Law, disputes over timeshare contracts are usually addressed as contractual disputes. This is the case in *Wei Hong and An Yu v. Xi'an Diyawei Travel Tourism Project Development Co., Ltd., et al.*[135] The plaintiffs, Wei Hong and An Yu, domiciled in Shaanxi Province, entered into a contract in Xi'an with the first defendant, Xi'an Diyawei Travel Tourism Project Development Company, domiciled in Shaanxi, and the second defendant, Now Vacations Company, domiciled in HongKong, to become members of the second defendant and participate in travel activities organized by the second defendant in Thailand, Europe, Bali, and other places. According to the contract, the membership price was 88,000 RMB (12,222 Euro), granting the plaintiffs the right to one-week vacation accommodation per year from January 2017 to December 2046.

The first defendant acted as the second defendant's authorized dealer.[136] The third defendant, Hambesi Hotel Development (Shanghai) Company, domiciled in Shanghai, was the second defendant' service center in Shanghai, handling membership matters on its behalf. The membership of the second defendant's club entitled the plaintiffs to accommodation, exchange, gifting, rent, transfer, and inheritance rights. The second defendant was responsible for providing room reservation, exchange, and related services during the membership's validity period. The membership card should be issued by Resort Fiduciary Service Co., Ltd in the UK within 30 working days after the conclusion of the contract, but the defendants did not fulfill their contractual obligation. The plaintiffs did not receive their membership cards after paying the membership fee. Consequently, the plaintiffs asked the court to confirm the invalidity of the contract signed with the first and second defendants, and demanded that the three defendants return the contract payment of 88,000 RMB and compensate them for their loss of 4528 RMB (628 Euro).[137]

[135] *Wei Hong and An Yu v. Xi'an Diyawei Travel Tourism Project Development Co., Ltd., et al*, Shaanxi Province Xi'an Municipality IPC, (2017) *Shaan 01 Min Chu No* 977.

[136] Ibid. The first defendant provided leasing and commercial services, and its business projects include tourism project development, business information consulting, etc., and it did not have administrative licensing projects for operating travel agencies.

[137] Ibid. Article 28 of the Tourism Law stipulates that to set up a travel agency, solicit, organize, and receive tourists, and provide tourism services to them, the following conditions shall be met, the permission of the tourism authority shall be obtained, and the business registration shall be handled in accordance with the law. Since the first defendant did not obtain the qualification for operating travel agencies and violated the mandatory provisions of Tourism Law and Travel Agency Regulations, the plaintiffs claimed that the travel contract between the three parties was invalid.

The first defendant argued that its operating projects included tourism project development, business information consultation, hotel management, and reservation of air tickets or train tickets. The products operated by the second defendant' club involved rights to vacation accommodation, not travel agency business. The plaintiffs had purchased the right to one-week vacation accommodation per year for 30 years and 30 weeks. The first defendant asserted that it merely assisted the second defendant's club in arranging family travels for its club members, emphasizing that the products operated by travel agencies were two completely different businesses.[138]

The court held that the second defendant was a company established in Hong Kong, thus the contract dispute was Hong Kong-related. Article 41 of the Chinese Conflict of Laws Act stipulated that the parties may choose the applicable law for the contract, and Article 19 of the SPC Judicial Interpretation of the Chinese Conflict of Laws Act states that Hong Kong-related cases should refer to the Chinese Conflict of Laws Act. Since both parties in this case chose to apply the laws of mainland China, the laws of mainland China shall apply.[139]

As regards the validity of the contract, the court held that the contractual obligation of the second defendant was to provide holiday accommodation and related services for the purchaser, namely, one-week holiday accommodation right per year from January 2017 to December 2046. The second defendant had the obligation to provide holiday accommodation services to the plaintiffs during the contractual period, which had a different nature from the travel contract alleged by the plaintiffs. Since the first and second defendants did not conduct travel service activities within the territory of China, Chinese Tourism Law and Travel Agency Regulation should not apply.[140]

(ii) Protecting timeshare contracts as consumer contracts

It can be seen that the timeshare contract in *An Yu v. Xi'an Diyawei Travel Tourism Project Development Co., Ltd., et al* was not classified as a travel contract nor a consumer contract. The court mentioned the domicile of the second defendant, which was in Hong Kong, as a foreign element. The fact that the place of performance of the timeshare contract was in several foreign countries, such as Thailand, Bali, and other European countries, was not explicitly mentioned.

However, when it comes to the application of Chinese substantive law, such as the Chinese Tourism Law and Travel Agency Regulation, the court did mention the fact that the first and second defendants did not conduct travel service activities within the territory of China.[141] Since the place of performance of the timeshare

[138] Ibid. The first defendant claimed that it was an authorized distributor of the second defendant and was qualified to engage in the distribution and promotion of vacation accommodation rights. Therefore, the first defendant did not violate the mandatory provisions of the Tourism Law and Travel Agency Regulation.

[139] Ibid.

[140] Ibid.

[141] Ibid.

contract was in foreign countries, Chinese law shall not apply.[142] Such reasoning is questionable, as Chinese law may still be applicable as the law that has the closest connection with the dispute, the law of the timeshare tourist's habitual residence, or the law chosen by the parties.

Due to the fact that Chinese law, including the Chinese Tourism Law and the Chinese Conflict of Laws Act, does not provide a specific definition of timeshare contract, the court resorted to general contract choice of law rules set forth in Article 41 of the Chinese Conflict of Laws Act, instead of consumer choice of law rules in Article 42 of the Chinese Conflict of Laws Act. Although the application of contractual choice of law rules may lead to the same law designated under consumer choice of law rules, the rationale behind contractual and consumer choice of law rules is different, especially with regard to the protection of weaker contracting parties.

Just like package travel tourists, timeshare tourists should also be protected as consumers. It is necessary to distinguish timeshare contracts from service contracts and contracts related to immovable properties.[143] Otherwise, it is confusing when it comes to the application of jurisdiction and choice of law rules over timeshare contracts. In order to improve consumer protection efficiently, substantive and procedural mechanisms are interdependent and needed to develop in parallel.[144]

The marketing strategy is often aggressive in the timeshare industry, and the contracts concluded are usually standard contracts. It is suggested that relevant industry associations and government agencies may provide some model standard contracts for consumers and businesses when it comes to timeshares and related products.[145] In addition, it is essential to prescribe a cooling-off period to ensure consumers' right of withdrawal in purchasing timeshare or timeshare-related products,[146] since consumers usually conclude such contracts under the business's aggressive marketing strategy and may be irrational. During the cooling-off period, consumers are prohibited from paying in advance to sellers or third parties.[147] Consumers may cancel the contract without any reason during the cooling-off period and only need to pay the legal fees that are necessary to cancel the contract.[148] If a timeshare contract is the result of a business's behavior of 'covering illegal purposes in a legal form', such a contract should be invalid as it harms the social public interest and violates the public order and good faith principle.[149] Therefore, it is essential to provide a specific definition of timeshare contract in the Chinese Tourism Law or Consumer Protection Law first, establishing relevant

---

[142] Ibid.

[143] Article 36 of the Chinese Conflict of Laws Act states that the law at the place where the immovable is situated shall apply to the right to the immovable.

[144] Cseres (2007), pp. 123, 125–126, 132.

[145] Xue (2008), p. 168.

[146] Xue (2008), p. 168.

[147] Xue (2008), p. 168.

[148] Xue (2008), p. 168.

[149] Yao (2013), p. 66.

provisions in substantive law, in order to protect timeshare contracts as consumer contracts under Article 42 of the Chinese Conflict of Laws Act.

4.3.2 The Conclusion of a Contract

Article 42 of the Chinese Conflict of Laws Act does not specify whether a contract must have been concluded for the application of consumer choice of law rules. This gives rise to the question of whether the conclusion of a contract is a hidden or unwritten condition in the provision. In the case of *Gao Jin v. Shaanxi Shouxin International Travel Agency,*[150] the plaintiff entered into an outbound travel contract with a third party, Sichuan Huashi International Travel Agency, for a 7-day-5-night trip to Thailand. The travel fee was paid to the defendant, Shaanxi Shouxin International Travel Agency, who then transferred the fee to the third party, Sichuan Huashi International Travel Agency. The plaintiff was injured while participating in a skydiving activity in Thailand, where she fell into the water and was towed by a yacht floating around an island for a circle.

The court of first instance pointed out that the plaintiff did not enter into an outbound travel contract with the defendant, the parties did not have a contractual relationship, the plaintiff cannot sue the defendant before the court.[151] The appellate court found that the name 'Gao Jin' in the outbound travel contract was not signed by herself. The court held that the tourist paid the defendant group fee, visa fee, and airport fee, establishing a travel contract relationship with the defendant, even though the defendant transferred the money to Sichuan Huashi International Travel Agency. The defendant failed to inform the tourist that it was entrusted by Sichuan Huashi International Travel Agency to collect relevant fees. Thus, it was improper for the court of first instance to conclude that there was no contractual relationship between Gao Jin and Shaanxi Shouxin International Travel Agency.[152]

In *Huang Ningnan v. Sichuan Oriental International Travel Agency et al*,[153] the plaintiffs Liu Yulan and Huang Ningnan, domiciled in Chengdu, Sichuan, sued the defendants (i) Sichuan Oriental International Travel Agency, domiciled in Chengdu, Sichuan, and (ii) Sichuan Oriental International Travel Agency (Guanghan Branch),

---

[150] *Gao Jin v. Shaanxi Shouxin International Travel Agency*, Shaanxi Province Xianyang Municipality Intermediate People's Court, (2018) Shaan 04 Min Zhong No 114; Shaanxi Province Xianyang Municipality Qindu District People's Court, (2017) Shaan 0402 Min Chu No 4074. 高瑾与陕西首信国际旅行社有限公司旅游合同纠纷二审民事判决书, 陕西省咸阳市中级人民法院, (2018)陕04民终114号; 咸阳市秦都区人民法院,(2017)陕0402民初4074号。

[151] Ibid.

[152] Ibid.

[153] *Huang Ningnan v. Sichuan Oriental International Travel Agency*, Sichuan Province High People's Court, (2018) Chuan Min Zhong No 676; Sichuan Province Deyang Municipality Intermediate People's Court, (2017) Chuan 06 Min Chu No 73. 刘玉兰、黄宁楠旅游合同纠纷二审民事判决书, 四川省高级人民法院,(2018)川民终676号; 四川省德阳市中级人民法院;(2017)川06民初73号.

domiciled in Guanghan City, Sichuan, and iii) Sichuan Global International Travel Agency, domiciled in Chengdu, Sichuan. The tourist Huang Kang paid a travel fee to the second defendant for traveling to Thailand. Huang Kang participated in a tour group organized by the third defendant to travel to Thailand. While staying in a hotel in Thailand, Huang Kang's physical condition suddenly deteriorated. He was sent to a local hospital in Thailand but died in that hospital.[154] The plaintiffs Liu Yulan and Huang Ningnan were the deceased's wife and son respectively. The plaintiffs asked the defendants to take responsibility for the death of Huang Kong with compensation of 550,575 RMB (76,468 Euro).

The first and second defendants argued that Huang Kang formed a travel contract relationship with the third defendant. Since the second defendant signed contracts and collected payments on behalf of the third defendant, the third defendant should bear liability. By contrast, the plaintiffs asserted that Huang Kang established a travel contract relationship with the first defendant, who transferred the travel business to another travel agency with the tourist's authorization; thus, both travel agencies should take responsibility. The court held that Huang Kang established a travel contract relationship with the second defendant, as Huang Kang signed the travel contract with this travel agency. However, this agency transferred the travel business to another travel agency without the consent of the tourist, so both travel agencies should be liable.[155] Although it is about the substantive rights between different travel agencies, it may be argued that such reasoning is equally applicable to choice of law issues, especially when the contracting travel agency transferred the business to another travel agency without the consent of the tourist.

In *Huang Xiang v. Guizhou Overseas International Travel, et al*,[156] the plaintiff Huang Xiang sued the defendants (i) Guizhou Overseas International Travel, (ii) Guizhou Zhongyi International Travel Agency; (iii) Wang Renxiong, all domiciled in Guiyang City, Guizhou Province. The third defendant was the first defendant's salesman who organized a group travel to Thailand. The plaintiff contacted the third defendant via his son and followed the travel group to visit Thailand. The first defendant bought insurance for the plaintiff, and the second defendant addressed issues of declaration of exit, border inspection, and other procedures for taking the flight. During the travel in Thailand, the vehicle carrying the plaintiff and other tourists had a traffic accident, which caused injury to the plaintiff. The plaintiff was hospitalized in Thailand and received medical treatment in a local hospital in Guiyang after coming back to China. The plaintiff asked the defendant to pay compensation of the medical treatment of his injury.[157]

---

[154] Ibid. The court did not mention this foreign element.

[155] Ibid.

[156] *Huang Xiang v. Guizhou Overseas International Travel*, Guizhou Province Guiyang Municipality Intermediate People's Court, (2017) Qian 01 Min Zhong No 6187; Guizhou Province Guiyang Municipality Yunyan District People's Court, (2017) Qian 0103 Min Chu No 5336. 贵州海外国际旅游有限公司、黄祥旅游合同纠纷二审民事判决书, 贵州省贵阳市中级人民法院, (2017)黔01民终6187号; 贵州省贵阳市云岩区人民法院;(2017)黔0103民初5336号.

[157] Ibid.

As regards whether the plaintiff and the first defendant had a travel contract, the court held that although the parties did not conclude a written travel contract, since the plaintiff was guided by the tour guide of the first defendant and the first defendant also bought insurance for the plaintiff and addressed relevant issues during the plaintiff's stay in the hospital in Thailand, the plaintiff and the first defendant had formed a de facto travel contract relationship.[158] The court further explained that if the plaintiff was traveling in a group at his own expense, how could the profit-oriented defendant allow the plaintiff to travel with the tour group organized by the defendant? How could the plaintiff be allowed to follow the itinerary of the tour group arranged by the defendant? Why would the defendant buy outbound travel accident insurance for people who are not related to the tour group? Why would the defendant handle hospitalization issues for people who have no contractual relationship with the defendant? Therefore, the defendant's argument that the plaintiff and the defendant did not form a travel contract cannot be upheld.[159] The appellate court agreed with the first-instance court. Since the plaintiff and the first defendant had formed a travel contract relationship, the defendant should take responsibility and guarantee the personal safety of the tourists.[160]

This case implies that even if the parties did not conclude a written travel contract, the defendant is responsible for the tourist's personal injury as long as the parties had formed a de facto travel contract relationship. Admitting the existence of a de facto travel contract relationship in the field of private international law may prevent a foreign business that targets consumers from a country but does not conclude a written contract with the consumer in bad faith from escaping favorable consumer choice of law rules.

Moreover, not requiring the conclusion of a written contract for the application of consumer conflicts rules may also protect the consumers from the complicated relations between the travel agency and its agent or travel service assistants. In *Li*

---

[158] Ibid.

[159] Ibid.

[160] The plaintiff was injured in Thailand due to car accident, the first defendant should bear liability for the breach of contract. The second defendant was not the contracting party of the travel contract, thus should not take responsibility of the contractual obligation. *Huang Xiang v. Guizhou Overseas International Travel*, Guizhou Province Guiyang Municipality Yunyan District People's Court, (2017) Qian 0103 Min Chu No 5336. The same reasoning is conducted in the following cases *Ma Yun v. Guizhou Overseas International Travel*, Guizhou Province Guiyang Municipality Yunyan District People's Court, (2017) Qian 0103 Min Chu No 5338; 马芸、贵州海外国际旅游有限公司旅游合同纠纷二审民事判决书， 贵州省贵阳市中级人民法院 (2017)黔01民终6612号，贵州省贵阳市云岩区人民法院,(2017)黔0103民初5338号； *Peng Shiqi v. Guizhou Overseas International Travel*, Guizhou Provincc Guiyang Municipality Yunyan District People's Court, (2017) Qian 0103 Min Chu No 6610; 贵州海外国际旅游有限公司、彭某1旅游合同纠纷二审民事判决书, 贵州省贵阳市中级人民法院 (2017)黔01民终6610号; 贵州省贵阳市云岩区人民法院(2017)黔0103民初5337号； *Peng Qi v. Guizhou Overseas International Travel*, Guizhou Province Guiyang Municipality Yunyan District People's Court, (2017) Qian 0103 Min Chu No 5335. 彭琪与贵州海外国际旅游有限公司、贵州中意国际旅行社有限公司旅游合同纠纷一审民事判决书, 贵州省贵阳市云岩区人民法院,(2017)黔0103民初5335号.

Qiuping v. Shenyang Jinqiao International Travel Agency,[161] the Chinese tourist who was injured in Malaysia sued three Chinese travel agencies and one Chinese insurance company in China. The court held that although the plaintiff and the first defendant did not conclude a written travel contract, the parties had formed a *de facto* travel contract relationship, and the Malaysian mosque was the assistant travel service provider. Thus, the travel agency, as the tour operator, had the obligation to guarantee the personal safety and property of its tourists, including the plaintiff.[162]

In *Wang Xuerong v. Kunming Kanghui Yonghui Travel Agency*,[163] the plaintiff Wang Xuerong sued the defendant Kunming Kanghui Yonghui Travel Agency, both domiciled in Kunming City, Yunnan Province, for the return of the group travel fee of 6660 RMB. The plaintiff paid the group travel fee of 53,280 RMB, for a 6-day-4-night trip to Bali Island, Indonesia, to Xu Hongling, who then issued a receipt with the seal of the defendant. Because of passport issues, the plaintiff did not manage to travel to Bali Island, and the travel fee was not refunded to the plaintiff.[164]

The court held that the seal of the defendant was on the receipt issued by Xu Hongling, an individual employee. Since tour operators usually cannot be individuals, it was logical for the plaintiff to believe that the party who concluded a travel contract with her was the defendant instead of the individual Xu Hongling. Although the defendant did not conclude a travel contract with the plaintiff, the plaintiff and the branch of the defendant had formed a travel contract relationship. The defendant, as the parent company of its branch which had a travel contract with the plaintiff should take responsibility.[165]

The defendant appealed, claiming that its operation scope did not include outbound travel and it had not conducted any foreign-related travel project. In addition, the sales department of its branch did not have the capacity to conclude travel contracts, and the collection of group fees by Xu Hongling was merely an individual behavior. The appellate court took the same view as the first-instance court and held that the branch of the defendant had formed a travel contract relationship.[166] This case indicates that the reasonable expectations of a tourist should be protected when

[161] *Li Qiuping v. Shenyang Jinqiao International Travel Agency et al*, Liaoning Province Shenyang Municipality Huanggu District People's Court, (2018) Liao 0105 Min Chu No 1462. 原告李秋平诉被告沈阳金桥国际旅行社有限公司韩国新城门市部、金桥(沈阳)国际旅行社有限公司、深圳市海外国际旅行社有限公司沈阳分公司、中华联合财产保险股份有限公司深圳分公司旅游合同纠纷一案一审民事判决书，辽宁省沈阳市皇姑区人民法院,(2018)辽0105民初1462号.

[162] Ibid.

[163] *Wang Xuerong v. Kunming Kanghui Yonghui Travel Agency*, Yunnan Province Kunming Municipality Intermediate People's Court, (2017) Yun 01 Min Zhong No 7280; Yunnan Province Kunming Municipality Wuhua District People's Court, (2016) Yun 0125 Min Chu No 1890. 昆明康辉永辉旅行社有限公司、王雪蓉旅游合同纠纷二审民事判决书，云南省昆明市中级人民法院 (2017)云01民终7280号; 昆明市五华区人民法院,(2016)云0125民初第1890号.

[164] Ibid.

[165] Ibid.

[166] Ibid.

the tourist concludes a contract with another individual who is acting on behalf of a travel company.

In *Jiang Mou v. Royal Caribbean Cruises Company*,[167] the plaintiff Jiang Mou sued the two defendants RCL Cruises Ltd. and Zhejiang International Cooperative Travel Agency (Shanghai branch for compensation of 141,527.84 RMB (20,218 Euro) for her injury caused by the slippery floor on the cruise board. The International Cooperative Travel Agency was the organizing travel agency, and the Wenzhou Overseas Travel Company was the local travel agency. Since the Royal Caribbean Cruises had a relationship of a sale contract for a cruise ticket with Wenzhou Overseas Travel Company and had actually provided cruise tour services, it was a performance assistant who assisted in fulfilling the obligations of the package travel contract. Since the performance assistant does not conclude a contract with a tourist, it is debatable whether protective consumer choice of law rules in Article 42 of the Chinese Conflict of Laws Act also apply to the proceedings against the performance assistant.

4.3.3 The Other Party to the Contract Is a Natural Person or a Legal Person

Given that Article 42 of the Chinese Conflict of Laws Act does not specify the other party in a consumer contract, the question arises whether the other party is only limited to a legal person or also includes a natural person in Chinese private international law. The other party to a consumer contract comprises manufacturers, retailers, service providers, and business entrepreneurs.[168] Sometimes, it is challenging to distinguish a consumer-to-consumer contract (C2C contract) from a business-to-consumer contract (B2C contract). This issue also arises when it comes to package travel contracts, as seen in *Guo Li v. Liang Hong*.[169] The plaintiff, Guo Li, domiciled in Kunming, Yunnan, sued the defendants: (i) Liang Hong, domiciled in Hancheng, Shaanxi, and (ii) Yunnan Jimei Adventure Outdoor Sports Company, domiciled in Kunming, Yunnan. The plaintiff sought the return of 20,000 RMB (2857 Euro) from Liang Hong for the cancellation of the travel activity, and joint liability from the Yunnan Jimei Adventure Outdoor Sports Company.

The defendant Liang Hong argued that the Tourism Law regulates tourists and tour operators, and the law applied by the court of first instance was wrong. As a natural person, he was not a tour operation business and only provided consultation,

[167] *Jiang Mou v. Royal Caribbean Cruises Company*, Shanghai HPC, (2018) Hu Min Zhong No 85; Shanghai Maritime Court, (2017) Hu 72 Min Chu No 136.

[168] Binding (2014), p. 228.

[169] *Guo Li v. Liang Hong*, Yunan Province Kunming Municipality Railway Transport Intermediate Court, (2017) Yun 71 Min Zhong No 36; Yunan Province Kunming Municipality Railway Transport Court, (2017) Yun 7101 Min Chu No 101. 梁宏、郭立旅游合同纠纷二审民事判决书, 昆明铁路运输中级法院,(2017)云71民终36号; 昆明铁路运输法院,(2017)云7101民初101号.

assistance, and communication services. In addition, the case involved a general civil contract relationship, rather than a travel contract legal relationship. Article 2 and Article 28 of the Tourism Law provide a broad material scope of application of this law, but they mainly focus on the organization of travel activities by travel agencies with the qualification of a legal person regarding the regulation of tour operation behaviors and travel service contracts. The parties in this contract were both natural persons, and the activity was a self-guided tour, or self-driving tour with an AA system, rather than conventional tourism activities in the form of excursions, vacations, and leisure. Liang Hong argued that he was not an operator providing relevant services for travel activities, thus, the case should be subject to the Consumer Protection Law, Contract Law, Tort Liability Law, and other relevant laws, instead of the Tourism Law.[170]

In addition, Liang Hong contended that the travel activities regulated under the Tourism Law were normal travel activities, rather than unusual high-risk activities. The nature of the activity in this case was not conventional tourism, but an adventure activity, or a mixed activity of tourism and adventure, primarily an adventure. This did not conform to the conventional definition of tourism in the Tourism Law. The name 'Expedition to the South American Aconcagua' also indicated that the nature of this activity was not traveling but corresponded to the definition of outdoor mountaineering.[171] Liang Hong emphasized that he was not a foreign-related tour operator, nor the organizer or initiator of the activity. As a natural person, he did not acquire business registration and a tourism operation license, had no qualifications for foreign-related outbound tourism, and no right to provide tourism services for tourism activities. There was no evidence to prove that he had conducted business activities in this case. In summary, Liang Hong argued that this case was a civil act between equal subjects and should be considered a legal relationship of a 'mutual assistance contract' (互助合同).[172]

The first-instance court held that the second defendant was established after the formation of relations between the plaintiff and the first defendant. Since the second defendant had no contract with the plaintiff, it was deemed an improper defendant in this case. The plaintiff participated in the 25-day activity with a schedule of Argentina climbing-Tierra del Fuego -Great Glacier organized by the first defendant after consulting with the first defendant. The plaintiff paid fees to Liang Hong, who then arranged relevant issues and acted as a guide and leader of this adventure activity. Although the parties did not conclude a written travel contract, Liang Hong issued the travel itinerary offer, and Guo Li chose the route and paid fees in advance. Liang Hong accepted the advance payment, arranged the relevant itinerary, and booked air tickets and hotels, all of which met the formal requirements of a travel contract. Thus, Guo Li established a travel contract relationship with Liang Hong.[173]

[170] Ibid.

[171] Ibid.

[172] Ibid.

[173] Ibid.

Regarding the applicability of the Tourism Law in this case, the appellate court held that according to Article 1 of the Tourism Law, it regulates the order of the tourism market, with one of the main subjects being tourism operators. However, the scope of tourism operators is not limited to travel agencies. The definition of tour operator under Article 1 of the Provisions of the Supreme People's Court on Several Issues concerning the Application of Law in the Trial of Tourism Dispute Cases refers to a person who provides travel services to the public in his or her own name, and this does not exclude natural persons. Therefore, the appellate court also concluded that the plaintiff and the second defendant had established a travel contract relationship in accordance with the Tourism Law.[174]

However, it is questionable whether the notion of package travel contact is equally applicable to consumer choice of law rules. Provisions contained in different legal documents are not completely coherent and consistent.[175] The need to establish systematic conflict of law rules for consumer contracts requires the adoption of a consistent concept of consumer. Although the main dispute concerns whether the Tourism Law applies to a travel contract concluded between an individual with another individual, the reasoning about whether a natural person is qualified as the other party to a package travel contract can be easily applied to consumer choice of law rules. As long as a natural person is acting within his or her trade or profession, that person can be regarded as the other party to a consumer contract.

4.3.4 Identification of a Foreign Element or Internationality

The involvement of a foreign element or an international factor is a prerequisite for the application of private international law rules in cross-border civil litigation.[176] The question is what element can be regarded as foreign or foreign-related and to what extent it constitutes the internationality of a consumer contract. Pursuant to Article 1 of the SPC Interpretation on Certain Issues Concerning the Application of the 'Law of the People's Republic of China on Application of Law to Foreign-Related Civil Relations',[177] a foreign element is involved if one of the parties is a foreign person, the habitual residence of either party is outside China, the subject matter is outside China, or the establishment, change, or termination of a legal fact takes place outside China. A foreign element might be established in many ways, for instance, if the place of performance is outside the consumer's habitually resided country.

[174] Ibid.

[175] Huo (2010), p. 287.

[176] Article 1 of the Chinese Conflict of Laws Act.

[177] The SPC Judicial Interpretation I of the Chinese Conflict of Laws Act was adopted by the SPC Judicial Committee at its 1563th meeting on December 10, 2012 and came into force as from January 7, 2013.

The vast majority of cases collected concern a Chinese tourist who concludes an outbound travel contract with a domestic travel agency for traveling to a foreign country. If the travel dispute involves the cancellation of a cross-border travel contract, the only foreign element is that the place of performance is outside the territory of China. It may be argued that such case is a purely domestic case.[178] For similar cases in which a Chinese tourist got injured in a traffic accident occurred in a foreign country while traveling abroad, some courts held that the case was foreign-related, whereas some courts held that it was a domestic case.

4.3.4.1 Personal Injury and Death of Tourists in a Foreign Country

In *Peng Shiqi v. Guizhou Overseas International Travel Agency,*[179] the Chinese tourist was injured in a traffic accident while taking a tour coach provided by the defendant in Thailand. The tourist filed a lawsuit in a Chinese court based on contractual liability, instead of tortious liability. The court held that since the travel contract was concluded in Guizhou, China, the foreign-related jurisdiction rules didn't apply to this case.[180] The first defendant argued that the case should be under the jurisdiction of the courts where the traffic accident occurred, but this claim cannot be established. Similarly, in *Huang Ningnan v. Sichuan Oriental International Travel Agency et al,*[181] the performance of the travel contract was in Thailand, and the death of the tourist took place in Thailand. Both the first-instance court and the appellate court did not explicitly mention the foreign element.[182]

In *Chen Yan v. Rizhao Oriental International Travel Agency,*[183] a Chinese tourist concluded a package travel contract with a Chinese travel agency for traveling to 8 European countries. The tourist was injured in Paris, France, and sued the Chinese

[178] Zhuang (2020), p. 25.

[179] *Peng Shiqi v Guizhou Overseas International Travel Agency*, Guiyang Municipality Yunyan District People's Court, (2017) Qian 0103 Min Chu No 5337.

[180] The same reasoning is conducted in *Huang Ningnan v. Sichuan Oriental International Travel Agency*, Sichuan Province High People's Court, (2018) Chuan Min Zhong No 676; Sichuan Province Deyang Municipality Intermediate People's Court, (2017) Chuan 06 Min Chu No 73. The court held that since the formation of the travel contract was in Guizhou province, the case should not apply foreign-related jurisdiction procedures.

[181] *Huang Ningnan v. Sichuan Oriental International Travel Agency*, Sichuan Province High People's Court, (2018) Chuan Min Zhong No 676; Sichuan Province Deyang Municipality Intermediate People's Court, (2017) Chuan 06 Min Chu No 73.

[182] This is also the case in *Guo Li v. Liang Hong,* Yunan Province Kunming Municipality Railway Transport Intermediate Court, (2017) Yun 71 Min Zhong No 36; Yunan Province Kunming Municipality Railway Transport Court, (2017) Yun 7101 Min Chu No 101. Although the place of performance of the travel contract was abroad, the courts did not mention the foreign element and regarded it as a purely domestic case.

[183] *Chen Yan v. Rizhao Oriental International Travel Agency*, Shandong Province Rizhao Municipality IPC, (2016) Lu 11 Min Xia Zhong No 95. 陈燕与日照东方国际旅行社有限公司、刘祥文旅游合同纠纷二审民事判决书，山东省日照市中级人民法院,(2016)鲁11民辖终95号；日照市东港区人民法院，(2016)鲁1102民初1480号。

defendant in a Chinese court. Interestingly, the court did characterize the case as a travel contract dispute involving a foreign element, rather than a foreign-related dispute. Thus, the case was still a purely domestic dispute in nature. Such characterization is confusing, as it seems that the court played a word game by stating 'a travel contract dispute involving a foreign element' is not 'a foreign-related travel contract dispute', whereas under Article 1 of SPC Judicial Interpretation I of the Chinese Conflict of Laws Act, the factor that the performance of the travel contract or the personal injury in a foreign country is sufficient to justify the internationality of the case.

There are more tourist disputes in which the tourist died or suffered personal injury in a foreign country. In *Xu Yan v. Shenyang Overseas International Travel Agency,*[184] the place of performance of the package travel contract was in Japan and South Korea, and the tourist died in Japan. In *Chen Guanglan v. Shandong China Travel Agency (Tai'an branch) et al,*[185] the performance of the travel contract involved Hong Kong and Macau, and the death of the tourist occurred in Hong Kong. In *Yu Na v. Jiangsu Shuntian Overseas Travel Company,*[186] the place of performance of the package travel contract was in Thailand, and the death occurred in Thailand. The tourist' family members sued the travel agency for compensation of 1,088,819.5 RMB(155,545 Euro).[187] These disputes concern the performance of a package travel contract in a foreign country and thus involve a foreign element.

In *Zhang Qiang v. China Youth Travel Agency,* the tourist Zhang Qiaozhu signed a travel contract with Ctrip Travel Agency and paid travel fees to China Youth Travel Agency for visiting Singapore and Malaysia.[188] The tourist died in Singapore during the performance of the travel contract. Although the case clearly involves a foreign

---

[184] *Xu Yan v. Shenyang Overseas International Travel Agency*, Liaoning Province Shenyang Municipality Heping District People's Court, (2018) Liao 0102 Min Chu No 1848.

[185] *Chen Guanglan v. Shandong China Travel Agency (Tai'an branch)*, Shandong Province Tai'an Municipality Intermediate People's Court, (2016) Lu 09 Min Zhong No 81; Shandong Province Tai'an Municipality Taishan District People's Court, (2014) Taishang Shang Chu Zi No 81. 陈光兰、郝群等与中国平安财产保险股份有限公司山东分公司、山东省中国旅行社泰安分社旅游合同纠纷二审民事判决书, 山东省泰安市中级人民法院, (2016)鲁09民终81号; 山东省泰安市泰山区人民法院,(2014)泰山商初字第888号.

[186] *Yu Na v. Jiangsu Shuntian Overseas Travel Company*, Jiangsu Province Nanjing Municipality Intermediate People's Court, (2014) Ning Shang Zhong Zi No 1546; Jiangsu Province Nanjing Municipality Qinhuai District People's Court, (2014) Qin Shang Chu Zi No 405. 上诉人江苏舜天海外旅游有限公司与被上诉人顾春生、周群、于娜旅游合同纠纷一案的民事判决书,江苏省南京市中级人民法院,(2014)宁商终字第1546号; 南京市秦淮区人民法院,(2014)秦商初字第405号.

[187] The plaintiffs held that the defendant did not fulfill its obligation of ensuring the personal safety of the tourist and investigating the cause of Gu Peng's death, the rescuers had not taken first aid measures in time, and the assistant travel service providers were not carefully selected.

[188] *Zhang Qiang v. China Youth Travel Agency*, Sichuan Province Yibin Municipality Intermediate People's Court, (2020) Chuan 15 Min Zhong No 1651; Sichuan Province Yibin Municipality Cuiping District People's Court, 2019 Chuan 1520 Min Chu No 5080. 张强、刘大奇旅游合同纠纷二审民事判决书, 四川省宜宾市中级人民法院, (2020)川15民终1651号, 四川省宜宾市翠屏区人民法院, (2019)川1502民初5080号.

element, namely the death of the tourist taking place in Singapore and the performance of the travel contract being in Singapore and Malaysia, the courts did not classify the case as foreign-related. Accordingly, jurisdiction and applicable law issues were not addressed. The same goes for *Li Qiuping v. Shenyang Jinqiao International Travel Agency*,[189] in which the plaintiff paid the tour fee to the first defendant for traveling to Singapore and Malaysia. The first defendant entrusted this outbound travel matters to the third defendant, who bought insurance for tourists from the fourth defendant. The plaintiff fell down and was injured while visiting a Malaysian mosque due to the slippery ground of the church. The plaintiff sued the defendants for the compensation of medical cost for such injury. The court did not mention the foreign element in this case and treated it as a purely domestic case. This is also the case in *Liu Lu v. Shaanxi Yuntong International Travel Agency*,[190] where the tourist signed an outbound travel contract with the defendant for traveling to Malaysia and died because of drowning during the stay in the hotel arranged by the defendant.

In *Guan Jingjing v. Yunnan International Travel Agency (Baitalu Branch),*[191] the tourist signed an outbound travel contract with the first defendant for a 14-day-12-night travel in America.[192] The first defendant, based on the tourism reception cooperation agreement signed with the third defendant, entrusted a tour group of 16 people to the third defendant to lead the tour group to America. On the way from Los Angeles to San Diego, the tourist died on the bus.[193] The first-instance court held that this case was related to foreign tourism. The second-instance court also mentioned that the case was foreign-related travel when addressing whether the

---

[189] *Li Qiuping v. Shenyang Jinqiao International Travel Agency et al*, Liaoning Province Shenyang Municipality Huanggu District People's Court, (2018) Liao 0105 Min Chu No 1462. 原告李秋平诉被告沈阳金桥国际旅行社有限公司韩国新城门市部、金桥(沈阳)国际旅行社有限公司、深圳市海外国际旅行社有限公司沈阳分公司、中华联合财产保险股份有限公司深圳分公司旅游合同纠纷一案一审民事判决书, 辽宁省沈阳市皇姑区人民法院, (2018)辽0105民初1462号.

[190] *Liu Lu v. Shaanxi Yuntong International Travel Agency*, Shaanxi Province High People's Court, (2018) Shaan Min Shen No 634; Shaanxi Province Xi'an Municipality Intermediate People's Court, (2017) Shaan 01 Min Chu No 11500. 陕西运通国际旅行社有限责任公司与刘胜利、刘璐旅游合同纠纷民事裁定书, 陕西省高级人民法院, (2018)陕民申634号; 西安市中级人民法院,(2017)陕01民终11500号.

[191] *Guan Jingjing v. Yunnan International Travel Agency (Baitalu Branch)*, Kunming Railway Transport Intermediate Court, (2017) Yun 71 Min Zhong No 20; Kunming Railway Transport Court, (2017) Yun 7101 Min Chu No 5. 云南省国际旅行社白塔路分社、官静静旅游合同纠纷二审民事判决书, 昆明铁路运输中级法院, (2017)云71民终20号; 昆明铁路运输法院,(2017)云7101民初5号.

[192] The defendants were (i) Yunnan International Travel Agency (Baitalu Branch), domiciled in Panlong District, Kunming City, Yunnan Province, (ii) Yunnan International Travel Agency, domiciled in Kunming City, Yunnan Province, (iii) MIngyou Tianxia International Travel Investment (Shanghai branch), domiciled in Changning District, Shanghai.

[193] During the travel, Peng told the group leader of third defendant that she was unwell and had to go to the local hospital for treatment. The leader informed Peng that the local medical expenses were high, and asked Peng to call 911 on her own.

defendants are responsible for the death of the tourist.[194] Although the place of performance of the contract was in America and the death occurred in America, the court did not classify the case as foreign-related.

These cases demonstrate that one barrier for applying Article 42 of the Chinese Conflict of Laws Act to package travel contracts is the failure to identity the foreign element in an outbound package travel contract. In *Zhao Chengwu v. Guangdong Nanhu International Travel Agency,*[195] the tourist was injured in a traffic accident that took place in Spain. Although the case is obviously foreign-related because the place of performance of the contract and the place of injury were in a foreign country, the court did not classify the case as foreign-related on one hand. On the other hand, the court referred to the Chinese Conflict of Laws Act to determine the applicable law. The classification and the choice of law rule are inconsistent in nature.[196] Such practice is self-contradictory, since the Chinese Conflict of Laws Act does not apply to purely domestic cases.[197]

By contrast, some courts held that the fact that the place of the performance of the contract and the place of injury were in a foreign country constitutes a foreign element, even if both parties of the contract are domiciled in China. For instance, in *Tong Bo v Shandong Daxinhua Yuntong Travel Agency,* where the tourist was injured in a traffic accident in Switzerland, the case was characterized as a travel contract issue. Since the place of performance was overseas, the court heard the case according to foreign-related civil and commercial proceedings.[198] Likewise, in *Hao Lingzhen v. Shandong China Travel Agency (Qingdao Branch) et al,*[199] the plaintiff signed an outbound travel contract with the first defendant. While traveling abroad, the plaintiff was bitten by a monkey. The plaintiff held that the defendant did not fulfill its duty to remind tourists of safety issues and to rescue tourists, thus, the

[194] *Guan Jingjing v. Yunnan International Travel Agency (Baitalu Branch)*, Kunming Railway Transport Intermediate Court, (2017) Yun 71 Min Zhong No 20; Kunming Railway Transport Court, (2017) Yun 7101 Min Chu No 5.

[195] *Zhao Chengwu v Guangdong Nanhu International Travel Agency*, Guangdong Foshan Shunde District People's Court, (2017) Yue 0606 Min Chu No 11502. 赵成武与广东南湖国际旅行社有限责任公司、佛山市南湖国际旅行社股份有限公司旅游合同纠纷一审民事判决书，广东省佛山市顺德区人民法院,(2017)粤0606民初11502号.

[196] It is similar to the jurisdiction reasoning mentioned above, while some courts classify a case as a domestic dispute but invoke international jurisdiction rule to determine the competent court.

[197] Chen (2020), p. 213.

[198] *Tong Bo v Shandong Daxinhua Yuntong Travel Agency*, Shandong Province HPC, (2017) Lu Min Zhong No 1112.

[199] *Hao Lingzhen v. Shandong China Travel Agency (Qingdao Branch)*, Shandong Province Qingdao Municipality Intermediate People's Court, (2017) Lu 02 Min Chu No 1653. 郝凌珍与山东省中国旅行社青岛第一分社、中国旅行社总社(青岛)有限公司旅游合同纠纷一审民事裁定书，山东省青岛市中级人民法院,(2017)鲁02民初1653号. the plaintiff Hao Lingzhen sued three defendants (i) Shandong China Travel Agency (Qingdao Branch), (ii) China Travel Agency Head Office (Qingdao), (iii) China Pacific Property Insurance Company (Qingdao branch). The plaintiff asked the first defendant to cover fees for medical treatment, return travel fee and pay three times the compensation for travel expenses. The second and third defendants should be jointly and severally liable for the above compensation.

defendant should take responsibility. The court held that the injury to the plaintiff occurred outside the territory of China, making the case a foreign-related civil and commercial case.[200]

4.3.4.2 Cancellation of an Outbound Travel Contract

In comparison with personal injury sustained by tourists during the performance of an outbound travel contract, cases involving the cancellation of an outbound travel contract with a destination in foreign countries are more likely to be classified as purely domestic cases. In *Chen Hedan v. Ningbo China Youth Travel Agency,*[201] the plaintiffs, Chen Hedan, Lin Jicheng, and Lin Jingyan, sued the defendant Ningbo China Youth Travel Agency to terminate the contract and return the travel fee of 19,440 RMB (2777 Euro). The plaintiffs and the defendant, who were introduced by friends, confirmed by telephone that the whole family would participate in a 4-day tour in Boracay, Philippines, and paid relevant travel fees. The plaintiffs waited nearly 6 hours in the small cabin, and the plane was still unable to take off. In desperation, the plaintiffs got off the plane and ended the trip.[202] The defendant argued that the trip was a package travel. The delay of the flight was not caused by the defendant but by *force majeure*, and the flight delay did not lead to the unfulfillment of the contractual purpose. After a 19-hour flight delay, all other tourists in the tour group continued to travel and had completed the trip to Boracay Island.[203] In this case, the court did mention that the outbound travel contract was about a 4-day-3-night travel in Boracay, Philippines, but did not classify the case as foreign-related.

In *Zhang Huimin v. Tang Fei,*[204] the plaintiff Zhang Huimin sued the defendants: (i) Luoyang Xiangshida Travel Agency, (ii) Luoyang Zhonglv Travel Agency, (iii) Tang Fei. The third party was Henan Zhongqiao International Travel Company. The plaintiff stated that he went to the office of the first defendant consulting about travel issues to Thailand. The defendant Tang Fei verbally stated that he could travel to Thailand during the first seven days of the Chinese lunar new year. Tang Fei

[200] Ibid. Since the plaintiff did not provide relevant translation materials and provide evidence within the time period, the subject of the litigation was unclear, it should be regarded as not meeting the statutory conditions for litigation. Thus, the action was dismissed by the court.

[201] *Chen Hedan v. Ningbo China Youth Travel Agency*, Zhejiang Province Ningbo Municipality Haishu District People's Court, (2015) Yong Hai Min Chu Zi No 93. 陈荷丹、林吉升等与宁波中国青年旅行社有限公司旅游合同纠纷一审民事判决书， 宁波市海曙区人民法院,(2015)甬海民初字第93号.

[202] Ibid.

[203] Ibid.

[204] *Zhang Huimin v. Tang Fei*, Henan Province Luoyang Municipality Jianxi District People's Court, (2014) Jian Min San Chu Zi No 64. 张会民与唐菲、洛阳祥仕达旅行社有限公司、洛阳市中旅旅行社有限公司、河南省中侨国际旅游有限公司旅游合同纠纷一审民事判决书， 河南省洛阳市涧西区人民法院,(2014)涧民三初字第64号.

received the travel fee of 10,800 RMB (1500 Euro) for the plaintiff and his wife and stamped on the receipt with a special seal from the second defendant.[205]

Arriving at the terminal of Zhengzhou Xinzheng Airport, the plaintiff was notified by the tour guide to meet at a hotel. In that hotel, the tour guide said that the flight was cancelled due to the hazy weather and could not fly to Thailand. The delay time was uncertain, thereby the travel time needed to be postponed and changed. The plaintiff proposed that if the flight could not take off, a refund should be given, but such a proposal was refused. The plaintiff returned to Luoyang after staying for a few hours. Later, the plaintiff complained to relevant departments and learned that the first and second defendants did not have the qualifications to organize overseas travel. The behavior of these two defendants violated the provisions of the Tourism Law of the PRC, which constituted consumer fraudulent behavior. The plaintiff asked the defendants to return the group travel fee of 10,800 RMB and compensate the plaintiff for various economic losses totaling 32,400 RMB (4288 Euro).[206] The court did not mention the foreign element in this case and addressed the case as a purely domestic case.

In *Yang Guang et al v. Nanjing Dahua International Travel Agency*,[207] the plaintiff Yang Guang, Li Jing (Xuanwu District, Nanjing), Li Lan, Yang Mou (Jiangning District, Nanjing) et al (7 plaintiffs in total), sued the defendant Nanjing Dahua International Travel Agency, for the return of the travel fee due to flight delay. The plaintiff Li Jing, as the representative of 7 plaintiffs, concluded a group outbound travel contract with the defendant for traveling from Nanjing to Hong Kong and Palau.[208] Due to flight delay caused by a typhoon, the plaintiff Yang and his family cancelled the itinerary, and the plaintiff Li Jing and her family changed the itinerary. The seven plaintiffs believed that although there was a typhoon, the defendant, as a professional travel agency, failed to perform its duty of reasonable care and thus constituted a breach of contract.[209] The court did not mention the factor that the performance of the travel contract was in Hong Kong and Palau and thus constituted a foreign element. Instead, the court applied Chinese law directly.[210]

The question arising in these cases is whether a package travel contract, whose performance is in a foreign country but the contract is not actually performed, can be regarded as foreign-related. As mentioned above, the mere fact that the place of performance is in a foreign country may serve as a sufficient international element, regardless of whether the contract is performed or not, albeit such a conflict might constitute a false domestic conflict.

---

[205] Ibid.

[206] Ibid.

[207] *Yang Guang v. Nanjing Dahua International Travel Agency*, Jiangsu Province Nanjing Municipality Xuanwu District People's Court, (2017) Su 0102 Min Chu No 7050.

[208] Ibid.

[209] Ibid. The Central Meteorological Observatory issued the first typhoon red warning signal one day before the departure, but the travel agency did not notify the plaintiff of such factor.

[210] Ibid.

Overall, Chinese courts share diverging opinions on the identification of a foreign element for cross-border travel disputes. Nevertheless, the legal certainty and predictability require a judicial practice of treating alike cases alike and treating different cases differently. The reality is that different Chinese courts treat similar cases differently. The opposing views held by Chinese courts on the identification of a foreign element in similar cases have derogated legal certainty and predictability for both tourists and tour operators or travel service providers. To enhance legal certainty and predictability, a unified or harmonized approach should be taken to ensure similar cases are treated similarly in terms of classification and applicable law.[211]

4.3.5 The Targeting Test and Causal Link with Concluded Contract in Digital Economy

Another reason for the underuse of consumer choice of law rules is the lack of criteria in determining what constitutes targeting activities in the consumer's country of habitual residence. In particular, in the context of the Internet and E-commerce, it is difficult to determine whether a business has engaged in relevant commercial activities in a consumer's country of habitual residence. The targeting activities conducted by a business will establish a strong connecting factor with the consumer's home country. Under Article 42 of the Chinese Conflict of Laws Act, a consumer contract is governed by the law of the consumer's habitual residence (home country), provided that the business has targeted consumers from that specific country. If the business does not target consumers from that specific country (dis-targeting context), the law of the place where goods or services are provided will apply. In the context of cross-border travel, it means that the tourist's home law will not apply; instead, the law of the place where the travel services are provided (typically a foreign law) will apply. The non-engagement of relevant commercial activities in one country protect businesses from being subject to the law of that particular country. In the context of targeting activities, Article 42 does not explicitly require a causal link between the conclusion of a consumer contract and the business's targeting activities.[212] Despite this favorable condition, it remains unclear as to what constitutes engaging in relevant commercial activities, particularly in the digital age, where emerging technologies and new marketing strategies are used to target consumers globally.

211 Chen (2020), p. 223.

212 A deeper comparative analysis about the targeting test and the requirement of a causal link with the concluded consumer contract in China, the EU, and the USA can be seen in Chen (2024a), p. 71; Chen (2022), pp. 328–350; Chen (2023), pp. 23–44.

4.3.5.1 Recommendation System and Personalized Targeting in Big Data Era

The rapid proliferation of mobile devices has essentially served to personalize our digital media consumption.[213] Consumers are increasingly willing to share personal information, a trend amplified by social media. People now openly share details about their lives, preferences, locations, and activities.[214] This user-generated data has become a valuable resource for marketers and businesses to create personalized advertising. When a consumer click 'cookies' before using search engines and travel apps, the website or app could store the browsing history and personal data from a consumer. Based on the collected data, it is possible to conduct personalized advertising or customized advertising.

In big data era, recommendation system (推荐系统) has been widely applied to many domains and the most typical domain is the e-commence.[215] Recommendation system can integrate deep learning algorithms, data analytics, and optimization techniques with collaborative tourism features to provide innovative solutions in terms of personalization of recommendations.[216] Internationally, well-known e-commerce websites include Amazon and eBay, with Amazon's recommendation algorithm considered highly successful.[217] Domestically, major e-commerce platforms such as Taobao, JD.com, Dangdang, and Suning.com, have utilized recommendation systems to recommend relevant products to potential consumers based on their browsing history and shopping habits. These systems can also perform retargeting by using consumers' purchasing history and preferences. When it comes to services, such as travel services, recommendation system and personalized advertising have also been used in popular travel websites and apps in China and internationally. In 2017, 60% of the revenues from the global travel and tourism market came from online sales channels.[218] According to the forecasts made by Statista, in 2027 online sales channels will represent 74% of revenues and rise to over one trillion U.S. dollars by 2030.[219]

Popular travel websites and apps in China Ctrip (携程旅行网), Qunar (去哪儿网), Fliggy (飞猪), Mafengwo (马蜂窝), Tuniu (途牛), Meituan (美团), and LY.com (同程旅游).[220] According to a report released by the China Internet Network

---

[213] Nesamoney (2015), p. 3.

[214] Nesamoney (2015), p. 3.

[215] Li (2015), p. 16. 李翠平等:《大数据与推荐系统》，《大数据》，2015年第1期，第16页。

[216] Barliza et al. (2024), p. 1.

[217] Li (2015), p. 16.

[218] Popsa (2023), p. 182.

[219] Popsa (2023), p. 182.

[220] Ctrip is China's largest travel platform offering flight, train tickets, hotels, and vacation packages. Qunar is a comprehensive platform for booking flights, hotels, train tickets, and tourist attractions. Fliggy is Alibaba's travel platform focusing on younger travelers with deals on flights, hotels, and visa services. Mafengwo is popular for user-generated travel guides, reviews, and rec-

Information Center, the number of internet users had reached 940 million as of June 2020[221] and 932 million (99.2%) users can access the internet by phone.[222] In May 2019, Qunar released a 'report on the travel data of college students in 2019' and 2.6 million college students registered on the website.[223] Travel applications are the seventh most popular category of most downloaded apps and over 60% of the global smart phone users have downloaded some kind of travel app.[224] The days of guide-books, maps and other printed stuff have been replaced by travel apps that come loaded with functionalities.[225] Popular international travel websites and apps include Booking.com, Expedia, Tripadvisor, Airbnb, Skyscanner, Kayak, Google Travel, Agoda, Hopper, and Turo.[226] These platforms cater to a range of travel needs, from planning and booking to reviews and recommendations. With the easy accessibility of these platforms via mobile phones and the rise of livestream commerce on social media, Chinese travel businesses can effortlessly target international consumers, while international businesses can just as easily reach Chinese consumers.

4.3.5.2 New Targeting Strategies with Technology and Data in Tourism Industry

International travel websites and apps employ various targeting strategies, including but not limited to the following, to effectively target global consumers:

(1) Multilingual and Multi-currency Support. This approach aligns with the 'digital transformation'[227] in the travel industry by offering services in multiple

ommendations. Tuniu focuses on packaged tours and customized travel services. Meituan is primarily a lifestyle app, offering hotel bookings, attraction tickets, and dining deals. LY.com provides a full range of travel services, including tickets, hotels, and vacation packages.

[221] The 46th Statistical Report on the Status of Internet Development in China (第46次《中国互联网络发展状况统计报告》). China Internet Network Information Center. http://www.cac.gov.cn/2020-09/29/c_1602939918747816.htm, accessed on Jan 22, 2025.

[222] Tang et al. (2022), p. 12.

[223] Wu et al. (2022), p. 1.

[224] How mobile app benefits travel and tourism industry, Goodwork labs, June 26, 2015, https://www.goodworklabs.com/how-mobile-app-benefits-travel-and-tourism-industry/, accessed on Jan 22, 2025.

[225] Ibid.

[226] Booking.com is a leading platform for hotels, apartments, and vacation rentals worldwide. Expedia offers flights, hotels, car rentals, and vacation packages. Tripadvisor is known for travel reviews, guides, and recommendations. Airbnb is popular for vacation rentals and unique accommodations. Skyscanner is a search engine for flights, hotels, and car rentals. Kayak provides travel comparisons for flights, hotels, and cars. Google Travel is an all-in-one platform for planning trips and tracking reservations. Agoda specializes in hotel bookings, especially in Asia. Hopper predicts flight and hotel prices and helps users book at the best times. Turo is a peer-to-peer car rental service available in various countries.

[227] Popsa (2023), p. 184. For instance, digital transformation among accommodation businesses in Europe 2022 includes social media marketing and online advertising.

languages and currencies to enhance accessibility for a diverse user base and a global audience. Popular international travel websites and apps that have Chinese versions include: Booking.com (缤客), Airbnb (爱彼迎), Expedia (智游网), Tripadvisor (猫途鹰), Skyscanner (天巡) and Travelocity (旅游百事通). These platforms cater to Chinese-speaking users, making it easier for them to plan and book their travel online. Likewise, some popular Chinese travel websites and apps also have international versions: Ctrip (Trip.com), Qunar (Multilingual), and Fliggy (Alibaba Travel). In these travel platforms, users can pay with different currencies. In addition, the rapid development of artificial intelligence (AI) and the adoption of Generative AI-powered AI in marketing enables travel business operators to effortlessly target consumers globally. AI-powered Chatbots or conversational AI, as valuable tools for customer service, can provide 24/7 availability, rapid responses, and multilingual support.[228]

(2) Personalization Through Data Analysis. Mobile apps can analyze user behavior based on factors such as individual personality, age, and gender to provide tailored recommendations, thereby influencing users' travel intentions.[229] User's location can be used in location-based systems to improve the relevance and personalization of recommendations for products and services in the tourism industry.[230] For instance, by offering localized information and services, mobile apps play a significant role in destination marketing.[231] Multi-objective genetic algorithms used in tourism recommender systems could personalization in the tourism sector could optimize different objectives in tourism recommender systems.[232]

(3) Geo-targeting Technology. Geolocation technologies allow the identification of the geographical location of a user accessing the Internet.[233] Geo-blocking technologies disallow a user's access to certain internet applications, such as websites, social media platforms and search engines, from certain countries.[234] Geo-location and geo-blocking, also known as geo-identification, geo-filtering, or geo-targeting, refer to technologies used to pinpoint the geographical location of those active on the internet.[235] Implementing geolocation and geo-blocking technology allows platforms to offer or restrict region-specific content and services based on the user's location.[236]

---

[228] Generative AI in Marketing: Benefits & Use Cases in 2025, https://research.aimultiple.com/generative-ai-in-marketing/, accessed on Jan 23, 2025.

[229] Wu et al. (2022), pp. 5–6.

[230] Barliza et al. (2024), p. 10.

[231] Szollosi and Benedek (2022), p. 95.

[232] Barliza et al. (2024), p. 11.

[233] Svantesson (2012), p. 478; Hörnle (2021), p. 448.

[234] Hörnle (2021), p. 448.

[235] Svantesson (2016), p. 521.

[236] A more detailed discussion on the determination of dis-targeting test by using geolocation and geo-blocking can be seen in Chen (2024a), pp. 93–95.

(4) Social Media and Influencer Marketing. Leveraging social media platforms and influencers helps in reaching a broader audience. The rise of platforms like Rednote (小红书) and TikTok (抖音) has transformed traditional approach of travel planning, with users seeking inspiration and information through blogs and short-form videos. Since its global launch in 2018, TikTok has emerged as a global entertainment platform with over 1 billion users.[237] The generation dubbed 'digital natives (数字原住民)', who have lived in a world where any destination is just a few clicks away, uses TikTok as a search engine for holiday-planning.[238] 71% of European users on TikTok say they're likely to book a holiday based on recommendations they have seen on TikTok.[239] 70% of Spanish users agree that seeing travel content on TikTok helps them decide which travel product or activity to choose, with 51% of TikTok users in Spain purchasing a holiday or travel-related product after seeing it on TikTok.[240] Apart from social media marketing, travel businesses could also use influencer marketing, a superb, cost-efficient tourism marketing channel.[241] By taking these new marketing strategies, international travel platforms can effectively engage and serve a global consumer base.

4.3.5.3 Challenges in Determining the Constitution of Targeting Activities in PIL

In big data era, the usage of recommendation system and personalized targeting in the travel and tourism industry has posed challenges in determining whether a foreign business has targeted consumers from a particular country. Compared with traditional marketing approach, the new advertising strategies are more technology-oriented and data-based. Big data marketing (大数据营销) through websites, social media, and travel apps does not require the physical presence of a foreign business in the country where its targeted consumers habitually reside. Questions may arise as to whether the adoption of generative AI, social media and influencer marketing strategies is sufficient to constitute the test of engaging in relevant commercial

[237] TikTok World 2024, https://newsroom.tiktok.com/en-us/tiktok-world-2024, accessed on Jan 23, 2025.

[238] Quaedvlieg L, Inside the Rise of TikTok Travel, August 14, 2024, https://www.cntraveler.com/story/rise-of-tiktok-travel?utm_source=chatgpt.com, accessed on Jan 22, 2025.

[239] TikTok Marketing Science UK Travel Survey 2023 conducted via AYTM (Among TT users who intend to travel in the next 12 months); How travel brands can stay top of mind on TikTok, https://ads.tiktok.com/business/en-GB/blog/travel-on-tiktok, accessed on Jan 22, 2025.

[240] Ibid. TikTok Marketing Science EU Travel Vertical Research 2021 conducted by Walnut Unlimited.

[241] Macro influencers are the big names. Brands think of them as long-term ambassadors who stand for the same values the brand represents. Micro-influencers usually have 1000–500,000 followers and specialise in a specific niche within their industry. Tourism Marketing: Your Guide to Success Within The Tourism Industry, https://profiletree.com/tourism-marketing-strategies/?utm_source=chatgpt.com#10-engage-macro-and-micro-influencers, accessed on Jan 22, 2025.

activities in the country of the consumer's habitual residence. The answer to this question, at least, not clear under Article 42 of the Chinese Conflict of Laws Act.[242]

Based on the domicile or habitual residence of the parties, there are three types of package travel contracts in the cases discussed above in Chinese judicial practice: (1) both tourists and travel service providers are domiciled in mainland China, and the place of performance is in a foreign country or in Hong Kong, Taiwan or Macao; (2) tourists are domiciled in China, and travel service providers are domiciled in a foreign country, while the travel service is provided in China; (3) tourists are domiciled in a foreign country, and travel service providers are domiciled in China, while the travel service is provided in China.

To determine whether a tourist consumer has been targeted by a business, it is necessary to identity the domicile or habitual residence of the tourist consumer. In the context of the digital economy and e-tourism, online transactions have caused problems for determining the domicile of the parties and whether a business has engaged in relevant commercial activities in a consumer's home country. Factors such as the domain name and email address of the parties might be misleading.[243] Factors like languages and currencies become less relevant in determining which country has been targeted, particularly with the convenience of online payment and the development of generative AI, which enables the production of a multilingual promotional videos for products or services within seconds. With the development of geo-location and geo-blocking technologies, businesses using websites may filter users or visitors based on their location. The geo-location of users, or the habitual residence of a tourist, is relevant if the content accessed via a website is targeted for users from certain countries or if users located in particular countries are prevented from interacting with the website.[244] Given the countless ways in which contracting parties can hide or distort identifying personal or geographic information, it is more difficult to determine whether a business has targeted consumers from a certain country. It is unclear what constitutes the dis-targeting test according to Article 42 of the Chinese Conflict of Laws Act. Although Article 42 of the Chinese Conflict of Laws Act does not require a causal link specifically, the consumer may still need to prove that there is a connection between the business's commercial activities and the conclusion of the consumer contract.

The legal framework of Chinese private international law and consumer protection standards in Consumer Protection Law and other laws do not currently provide

[242] Even in the field of private international law in the EU, in which the Rome I Regulation and the Brussels Ibis Regulation along with the CJEU judgments are more specific about the criteria in determining what constituting targeting activities, the answer to this question is also not crystal clear. A detailed discussion about the targeting test can be seen in Chen (2023), pp. 23–44; Chen (2022), pp. 328–350.

[243] Xiao (2016), p. 99. 肖雯:《跨境消费者合同法律适用问题研究》，西南政法大学博士论文，2016年，第99页。

[244] Wang (2010), p. 88.

adequate protection for consumers in China.[245] It would be useful to strengthen legal precedents to address gaps in the existing legal system, allowing courts to respond more effectively to future developments.[246] The legal precedents involving the package travel tourists demonstrate the necessity of harmonizing jurisdiction and choice of law rules over consumer contracts in general. In this regard, the Supreme People's Court may consider issuing guiding cases on the application of consumer choice of law rules for package travel contracts and timeshare contracts. Guiding cases issued by the Supreme People's Court hold significant reference value for other Chinese courts.[247] This can contribute to a more consistent and predictable legal framework, offering enhanced protection for consumers involved in such contracts. In addition, to address the new development of marketing strategies in big data era, the Supreme People's Court could issue judicial interpretations to clarify the targeting test in Article 42 of the Chinese Conflict of Laws Act.

4.4 Conclusions

This chapter contends that package travel contracts and timeshare contracts should be expressly included in the material scope of Article 42 of the Chinese Conflict of Laws Act and protected as consumer contracts. However, the case law in China demonstrates that consumer choice of law rules are not applied to package travel contracts involving a foreign element. Instead, general contractual conflicts of law rules are applied to determine the competent court and the governing law of a package travel contract. In particular, Article 41 of the Chinese Conflict of Laws Act on contract choice of law rules is excessively used. The law applicable to package travel contracts is determined by applying the two-sided party autonomy principle, the closest connection principle, and the characteristic performance principle in contract conflicts rules, whereas consumer choice of law rules in Article 42 of the Chinese Conflict of Laws Act are not used at all.

To fully employ Article 42 of the Chinese Conflict of Laws Act, the material scope of consumer choice of law rules needs clarification. It is necessary to establish a separate provision under Article 42 of the Chinese Conflict of Laws Act to expressly include package travel contracts set forth in Article 111(3) of the Tourism Law of the PRC as well as timeshare contracts. Alternatively, the Supreme People's Court may issue a judicial interpretation of Article 42 of the Chinese Conflict of Laws Act and clarify the notion of consumer contracts by explicitly including package travel contracts and timeshare contracts. More importantly, it is crucial to

[245] The Chinese Consumer Protection Law provides few protections specifically for consumers pursuing their rights under the legislation, especially considering the high cost of litigation. Binding (2014), p. 250.

[246] Binding (2014), p. 251.

[247] Gu and Li (2020), pp. 134–146; 顾培东、李振贤:《当前我国判例运用若干问题的思考》，《四川大学学报(哲学社会科学版)》，2020年第2期，第134–146页。

provide a specific definition of timeshare contract and establish relevant provisions for timeshare contracts in Chinese substantive law by virtue of the Tourism Law, the Consumer Protection Law or the Chinese Civil Code.

As to the conditions for applying consumer choice of law rules in Article 42 of the Chinese Conflict of Laws Act, the conclusion of a written consumer contract should, in principle, be a pre-condition. However, other factors may substitute for the lack of a written contract and justify the existence of a de facto contractual relationship. The other party to a consumer contract, including a package travel contract, is not limited to a legal person but also includes a natural person. A package travel contract concluded between a tourist and a natural person who acts as a retailer or service provider is not a consumer contract (C2C contract) but a business to consumer contract (B2C contract).

Moreover, a distinction needs to be drawn between a service contract, a travel contract, and a package travel contract. Travel contracts and package travel contracts, in essence, are service contracts, but only some service contracts and travel contracts are classified as package travel contracts. As to the determination of a foreign element, the fact that the performance of a contract is in a foreign country may constitute a foreign element under Article 1 of the SPC Judicial Interpretation of the Chinese Conflict of Laws Act, regardless of whether the contract is performed or not. In this regard, Chinese courts should be more consistent when identifying a foreign element to ensure that alike cases are treated likely. When the place of performance of a package travel contract is in a foreign country, the dispute over the contract shall be considered foreign-related. Meanwhile, the criteria of dis-targeting test may be construed in combination with the criteria of the targeting test to increase the operability of Article 42 of the Chinese Conflict of Laws Act. With the development of new personalized advertising strategies, such as recommendations system, Generative AI, social media, and influencer marketing in the digital economy, the Supreme People's Court could issue judicial interpretations to clarify what constitutes the targeting test.

References

Barliza AS et al (2024) Recommender systems applied to the tourism industry: a literature review. Cogent Bus Manag 1:1

Binding J (2014) Consumer protection law in the People's Republic of China. China-EU Law J 3:248

Chen Z (2020) Jurisdiction and choice of law in foreign-related tourist-consumer disputes in China under the One Belt One Road Initiative. In: Wei D et al (eds) Innovation and the transformation of consumer law. Springer, p 209

Chen Z (2022) Jurisdiction and choice of law rules over electronic consumer contracts: the nexus between the concluded contract and the targeting activity. Maastricht J Eur Comp Law 3:328–350

Chen Z (2023) Internet, consumer contracts and private international law: what constitutes targeting activity test. Inf Commun Technol Law 1:23–44

Chen Z (2024a) Consumer jurisdiction and choice of law rules in European and Chinese private international law. Chin J Transnatl Law 1:71

Chen Z (2024b) Tourists, consumer contracts and private international law in the EU and China. University of Groningen, pp 127–172

Cloherty DJ (1994) Exclusive jurisdiction and the eleventh amendment: recognizing the assumption of the state court availability in the clear statement compromise. Calif Law Rev 82:1287

Cseres KJ (2007) Enforcement of collective consumer interests: a competition law perspective. In: Boom W, Loos M (eds) Collective enforcement of consumer law. Europa Law Publishing, pp 123, 125–126, 132

Gu P, Li Z (2020) Reflections on several issues regarding the application of precedents in China. Sichuan Univ J (Philos Soc Sci Ed) 2:134–146; 顾培东、李振贤:《当前我国判例运用若干问题的思考》，《四川大学学报(哲学社会科学版)》，2020年第2期，第134-146页。

Guo H (2018) Deviation and correction of the applicability of Chinese foreign-related tourism dispute laws - based on an analysis of international tourism cases in Jiangsu Province. Contemp Jurisprud 2:86–91; 郭欢欢,《我国涉外旅游纠纷法律适用之偏差及其矫正-基于江苏省国际旅游案评析》，《时代法学》2018年第2期，第86-91页。

Guo Y, Xiang Z (2002) Research on jurisdiction of EU electronic consumer contracts. J Wuhan Univ (Soc Sci Ed) 3:346; 郭玉军、向在胜,《欧盟电子消费合同管辖权问题研究》，《武汉大学学报(社会科学版)》, 2002年第3 期，第346页。

Han D (2003) New perspectives on international private law. Wuhan University Press, p 126; 韩德培主编:《国际私法新论》，武汉大学出版社2003年版，第126页。

Han L, Ming Q (2016) A review of legal regulation of timeshare vacation in China. J Hebei Tour Vocat Coll 4:7; 韩璐、明庆忠,《国内分时度假法律规制研究述评》，《河北旅游职业学院学报》, 2016年第4期，第8页。

Hörnle J (2021) Internet jurisdiction law and practice. Oxford University Press, p 448

Huang J, Du H (2014) Research on the judicial practice of China's private international law. Law Press, p 25; 黄进、杜焕芳，《中国国际私法司法实践研究》，法律出版社，2014年，第25页。

Huo Z (2010) Private international law in China. Law Press China, p 288; 霍政欣，《国际私法》, 法律出版社，2010年，第288页。

Huo Z (2011) Highlights of China's new private international law act. Revue Juridique Themis 45(637):674

Li C (2015) Big data and recommendation system. Big Data Res 1:16. 李翠平等:《大数据与推荐系统》，《大数据》，2015年第1期，第16页。

Liu Y (2022) Research on jurisdiction over international consumer contracts: EU experience and China's Programme. Wuhan Univ Int Law Rev 1:59; 刘阳,《跨国消费合同管辖权研究:欧盟经验及我国方案》，《武汉大学国际法评论》，2022年第1期, 第59页。

Liu X, Zhang Z (2021) Chinese private international law. Hart Publishing, p 80

Lu Y (2015) Judicial application of the closest connection doctrine of law in the application of law for foreign-related civil relations. Contemp Jurisprud 4:105–111; 卢月,《论<涉外民事关系法律适用法>中最密切联系原则的司法适用》，《时代法学》，2015年第4期，第105-111页。

Meng J (2010) Marketing status and measures of timeshare vacation in China. J Chifeng Univ 9:68–69; 孟洁:《我国分时度假的营销现状及对策》，《 赤峰学院学报》，2010年第9期，第68-69页。

Nesamoney D (2015) Personalized digital advertising: how data and technology are transforming how we market. Pearson Education, p 3

Popsa RE (2023) Digitalization: a strategic approach for the travel and tourism industry. Expert J Market 2:181–187

Svantesson D (2012) Time for the law to take internet geolocation technologies seriously. J Priv Int Law 8:478

Svantesson D (2016) Private international law and the internet, 3rd edn. Wolters Kluwer, p 521

Szollosi T, Benedek I (2022) The role of mobile apps in destination marketing and branding. Territ Identity Dev 7(1):95–108

Tang Z et al (2016) Conflict of laws in the People's Republic of China. Edward Elgar Publishing, p 227, para. 8.53

Tang J et al (2022) Can tourism development help improve urban liveability? An examination of the Chinese case. Sustainability 14:11427

Tu G (2015) Private international law in China. Springer, p 40, para. 71

Wagner WJ (1952) The original and exclusive jurisdiction of the United States SPC. La Univ Law J 2:111

Wang L (2002) The concept of consumer and the application scope of the consumer rights protection law. Polit Law 2:2–11; 王利明,《消费者的概念及消费者权益保护法的调整范围》，《政治与法律》2002年第2期，第2-11页。

Wang C (2006) Study on the EU Timeshare Directive. Hebei Law Sci 2:131; 汪传才,《欧盟<分时度假指令>研究》，《河北法学》2006年第2期，第131页.

Wang FF (2010) Internet jurisdiction and choice of law: legal practices in the EU, US and China. Cambridge University Press, p 133

Wang L (2017) Research on contract law. China Renmin University Press, p 571; 王利明,《合同法研究》(第四卷)，中国人民大学出版社2017年版，第571页。

Wang Q (2018) Discussion on the protection mechanism of overseas tourist-consumer rights—based on the perspective of the law applicable to foreign-related civil relations. J Jiujiang Univ (Soc Sci Ed) 1:103–106; 王群,《海外旅游消费者权利保护机制探讨—基于<涉外民事关系法律适用法>视角》，《九江学院学报(社会科学版)》，2018年第1期，第103-106页。

Wu W (2005) Electronic commerce law. Tsinghua University Press, p 144; 吴伟光，《电子商务法》，清华大学出版社，2005年，第144页。

Wu Y (2017) A study on the issues of jurisdiction over foreign cases and the application of law in Sabah Boat Sinking Incident. Southwest University of Political Science and University, p 16; 吴羿，《沙巴沉船事件中的涉外管辖权和法律适用问题探析》，西南政法大学法硕学术论文，2017年，第16页。

Wu S et al (2022) Experience with travel mobile apps and travel intentions—the case of university students in China. Sustainability 19:5–6

Xia Y (2010) On the deficiency and construction of the international tourism legal system in China. Wuhan Univ J (Philos Soc Sci) 3:420; 夏雨:《论我国国际旅游法律制度的缺失与构建——以和平崛起为视角》，《武汉大学学报(哲学社会科学版)》，2010年第3期，第420页。

Xiao Y (2007) The theory of private international law. Law Press China, p 187; 肖永平，《国际私法原理》，法律出版社，2007，第187页。

Xiao W (2016) Research on the application of law for cross-border consumer contracts. Southwest University of Political Science and Law, p 99. 肖雯:《跨境消费者合同法律适用问题研究》，西南政法大学博士论文，2016年，第99页。

Xue Y (2008) Analysis on EU's regulation of timeshare and relevant products. Hebei Law Sci 9:168; 薛源,《欧盟对分时度假及相关产品的法律规制》，《河北法学》2008年第9期，第168页。

Yang X (2010) Analysis of the legal nature of timeshare vacation rights from the perspective of consumer rights protection. Front Theory 5:5–7; 杨雪飞,《消费者权益保障视角下的分时度假时权法律性质分析》，《理论前沿》，2010年第 5期，第5-7页。

Yang Q, Liu X (2007) Analysis of obstructive factors affecting China's timeshare consumption demand. Bus Cult 5:20–21; 杨清平、刘小蓉等:《影响我国分时度假消费需求阻碍因素分析》，《商业文化》2007年第5期，第20-21页。

Yao D (2013) Discussion on the path of the regulation of timeshare contract: from the perspective of protecting the legitimate rights and interests of consumers. J Shandong Inst Commerce Technol 2:65, 67; 姚道艳,《刍议规制分时度假合同路径—以保护消费者的合法权益为视角》，《山东商业职业技术学院学报》，2013年第2期，第64页。

Zhuang Y (2020) Research on the application of laws concerning foreign tourism disputes in China. Shandong University, p 26; 庄允,《我国涉外旅游纠纷法律适用问题研究》，山东大学硕士学位论文，2020年，第26页。

Chapter 5
Party Autonomy in Consumer Choice of Law Rules in China

5.1 Introduction: Consumer Choice of Law Rules in China

In Chinese private international law, a consumer contract is, in principle, governed by the law of the consumer' habitual residence, as stipulated in Article 42 of the Chinese Conflict of Laws Act.[1] Such general rule of applying the consumer's home law may be deviated from under certain circumstances. Specifically, if the consumer chooses to apply the law of the place where goods or services are provided, or if the business operator does not engage in relevant business activities at the consumer's habitual residence,[2] then the consumer contract is subject to the law of the place where goods or services are provided. This implies that party autonomy regarding the applicable law of consumer contracts is limited and only the consumer can unilaterally choose the applicable law. Although the exercise of party autonomy of the business party is deprived, it does not mean that the consumer can select any law that is most favorable to them, since the material scope of chosen law is confined to the consumer's home law and the law of the place of provision of goods or services. Moreover, if the business has not engaged in relevant commercial activities in the consumer's home country, the law of the place of provision of goods or services applies as a default rule. However, Article 42 does not further specify whether the otherwise applicable mandatory rules that protect the consumer's interests must still be applied or not.[3]

Article 42 of the Chinese Conflict of Laws Act is a special choice of law rule compared to its Article 41 which addresses general contract choice of law rule.

[1] The Law of the PRC on the Application of Laws to Foreign-Related Civil Relations, enacted on 28 October 2010, was effective from 1 April 2011.

[2] However, it is unclear what constitutes 'related commercial activities'. Tang et al. (2016), p. 233.

[3] Tu (2016), p. 102, para. 193.

Z. Chen, *Tourists, Consumer Contracts and Private International Law in China*, Ius Gentium: Comparative Perspectives on Law and Justice 123,
https://doi.org/10.1007/978-3-031-87915-9_5

Protective consumer conflicts rules, as a derogation of general contract conflicts rules, are supposed to be more favorable to consumers in terms of the freedom to choose applicable law and substantive rights granted under the chosen law. Is it the case that consumers enjoy more freedom in choosing applicable law under Article 42 on consumer choice of law rules than that under Article 41 on general contract choice of law rules? Is the application of the so-called protective consumer conflicts rules more favorable to consumer protection, and if not, why? What are the considerations and conditions for applying the law of the consumer's habitual residence as the primary rule? Why is the law of the place of provision of goods or services is of particular significance to consumer contracts, and what are the conditions for applying this law? Why is the exercise of party autonomy limited, how is it limited, and to what extent does such limitation justify its cause? Is it necessary to embrace bilateral party autonomy and if so, should such bilateral party autonomy be limited by virtue of mandatory provisions?

Furthermore, when a business has not conducted relevant commercial activities in the consumer's country of habitual residence, the law of the place of provision of goods or services applies as a secondary default rule under Article 42, instead of applying the law designated under general contract choice of law rules in Article 41 of the Chinese Conflict of Laws Act. Does the law of the place of provision of goods or services always have the closest connection with the consumer contract and correspond to the parties' reasonable expectations in the dis-targeting context? If not, what can be improved to ensure that the law applicable to consumer contract in the dis-targeting context has the closest connection with the contract and corresponds to the parties' reasonable expectations? What is the relation and interaction between Article 41 and Article 42 of the Chinese Conflict of Laws Act, and if there is a lack of interaction, is it necessary to establish a connection between these two provisions? With these questions in mind, this Chapter will shed light on the consumer choice of law rule, the exercise and limitation of party autonomy, the material scope of chosen law under Article 42 of the Chinese Conflict of Laws Act, the possibility of embracing bilateral party autonomy, the role of (overriding) mandatory provisions, and the interplay between special consumer conflicts rule and general contract conflicts rule.

5.2 The Law of the Consumer's Habitual Residence as the Default Rule

5.2.1 Weaker Party Protection Doctrine

The application of the law of the consumer's habitual residence as the default rule is mainly based on the unequal bargaining power between parties and the doctrine of protecting the weaker party. Consumers are regarded as the weaker contracting parties.[4] This weakness isn't limited to just bargaining power, but also with regard to financial status and access to information.[5] In the context of e-commerce, consumers often find themselves subject to unfair contract terms in standardized contracts with 'take-it-or-leave-it' clauses. Standard contracts prioritize transaction convenience, aligning with the core principles of commercial law, which aim to maintain transaction order, reduce transaction risks and improve transaction efficiency. In contrast to commercial law, civil law pursues substantive justice by providing special protection to weaker parties, such as consumers and employees.[6] Typically, consumers have limited knowledge of the laws of other countries and may not fully understand the meaning of choice of law clauses in standard contracts. They generally assume that they will be protected by their own country's domestic laws.[7] This disadvantage justifies the special protection afforded to consumers through the default rule of applying the consumer's home law in Chinese and European private international law. Furthermore, the use of the consumer' habitual residence as a subjective connecting factor is not easily manipulated by business operators.[8]

5.2.2 *Ascertainment of Foreign Law*

Consumers are more likely to be familiar with their home law than with foreign laws. Applying the consumer' home law could save the cost of ascertaining a foreign law, especially for small consumer claims.[9] Article 10 of the Chinese Conflict of Laws Act states that if the parties choose to apply the laws of a foreign country, they should ascertain or provide these laws to the court; if the foreign law cannot be ascertained or lacks relevant provisions, Chinese law will be applied instead.[10] The

[4] Rosler (2010), p. 729.

[5] Rühl (2011), p. 231; Qu (2009), p. 8; 曲波，《国际私法本体下弱者利益的保护问题》，法律出版社，2009年，第8页。

[6] Barnhizer (2005), pp. 139–241.

[7] Tang et al. (2016), p. 231.

[8] Yang (2012), p. 119; 杨月萍:《论我国涉外消费者合同的法律适用及其完善》，《重庆工商大学学报(社会科学版)》，2012年第1期，第119页。

[9] Yang (2012), p. 119.

[10] Article 10 of the Chinese Conflict of Laws Act: The foreign law applicable to a foreign-related civil relation will be ascertained by the relevant people's court, arbitration institution or the administrative agency. Where the parties have chosen a foreign law to be applicable, they shall adduce the law of that country.

Where the foreign law cannot be ascertained or the law of that country does not have a relevant provision, the PRC law shall be applied.

《中华人民共和国涉外民事关系法律适用法》第十条:涉外民事关系适用的外国法律，由人民法院、仲裁机构或者行政机关查明。当事人选择适用外国法律的，应当提供该国法律。

不能查明外国法律或者该国法律没有规定的，适用中华人民共和国法律。

parties are obligated to provide the foreign law within a reasonable period of time. Pursuant to the second paragraph of Article 15 of the SPC Judicial Interpretation I of the Chinese Conflict of Laws Act,[11] if the parties are required to provide a foreign law but fails to do so without a justifiable reason within the reasonable time limit set by a people's court, the court may rule that the foreign law cannot be ascertained. The provisions in Article 10 of the Chinese Conflict of Laws Act and Article 15 of the SPC Judicial Interpretation I of the Chinese Conflict of Laws Act indicate that the parties shall bear the primary responsibility for ascertaining a foreign law. However, it does not mean that the judges have no responsibility at all in this matter, as they still take a secondary role in ascertaining the foreign law.[12] If the parties fail to provide the foreign law they have chosen to apply, it does not necessarily mean that the foreign law cannot be ascertained.[13] If the judge knows the content of the foreign law chosen by the parties or can easily ascertain its content through a certain channel, the judge should ascertain the foreign law and rely on it for adjudication.[14] If the parties do not choose a foreign law but a foreign law applies according to conflicts rules in the absence of the parties' choice, the Chinese courts have the primary responsibility to ascertain the foreign law.[15] Regarding specific methods for ascertaining foreign law, the Supreme People's Court explains this in the first paragraph of Article 15. When a foreign law should be applied, the court shall consider the opinions of all parties with regard to the content, interpretation and application of the foreign law.[16]

[11] Article 15 of the SPC Judicial Interpretation of the Chinese Conflict of Laws Act: Where a people's court fails to ascertain a foreign law through reasonable channels, such as those provided by the parties or Chinese and foreign legal experts, or specified by international conventions effective in the PRC, the court may rule that the foreign law cannot be ascertained.

If the parties are required to provide a foreign law under Article 10(1) of the Chinese Conflict of Laws Act but fails to do so without justifiable reason within the reasonable time limit designated by a people's court, the court may rule that the foreign law cannot be ascertained.

《最高人民法院关于适用〈中华人民共和国涉外民事关系法律适用法〉若干问题的解释(一)》第十五条: 人民法院通过由当事人提供、已对中华人民共和国生效的国际条约规定的途径、中外法律专家提供等合理途径仍不能获得外国法律的，可以认定为不能查明外国法律。

根据涉外民事关系法律适用法第十条第一款的规定，当事人应当提供外国法律，其在人民法院指定的合理期限内无正当理由未提供该外国法律的，可以认定为不能查明外国法律。

[12] Xiao (2017), p. 16; 肖永平，《提升中国司法的国际公信力:共建"一带一路"的抓手》，《武大国际法评论》，2017年第1期，第16页。

[13] Xiao (2017), p. 16.

[14] Xiao (2017), p. 16. The Supreme People's Court has cooperated with some universities and a court in Shenzhen to establish research center to ascertain foreign laws, including laws in Hong Kong, Taiwan and Macao.

[15] Han and Xiao (2014), pp. 153–154; 韩德培、肖永平,《国际私法》(第三版)，高等教育出版社，2014年，第153–154页。

[16] Article 16 of the SPC Judicial Interpretation of the Chinese Conflict of Laws Act: the people's court shall listen to the opinions of all parties with regard to the content of a foreign law that should be applied as well as its interpretation and application. If the parties have no objection to the con-

5.2.3 Conditions for the Application of the Consumer' Home Law

The application of the consumer' home law as a default rule aims to protect the reasonable expectations of consumers. However, the consumer protection provided in Article 42 of the Chinese Conflict of Laws Act is not absolute.[17] The goal of consumer protection is not to make consumers the stronger party in every aspect, but to restrain advantages that businesses may have and maintain a balance between the two parties.[18] The default rule of applying the consumer's home law can be deviated in two circumstances. First, the application of the law of the consumer's habitual residence is subject to the condition that the business has engaged in relevant commercial or soliciting activities in the consumer's habitual residence. Second, this default rule may not apply if the consumer chooses the law of the place of provision of goods or services instead.

5.2.3.1 The Targeting Test Is Fulfilled

Article 42 of the Chinese Conflict of Laws Act does not specifically set a positive condition under which the consumer's home law shall apply. However, it does explicitly establish a negative condition under which the consumer's home law shall not apply. The consumer's home law does not apply if the dis-targeting test is fulfilled, indicating that the consumer's home law only applies when the targeting test is met. If the targeting test is met, the consumer may choose between the two laws, opting for whichever is more favorable. This condition implies that the consumer contract has a connection with the country where the consumer is habitually domiciled, aligning with the consumer's reasonable expectations.[19] Allowing the consumer to choose any law with no connection to the parties or the contract could increase both the business's information collection costs and transaction costs, potentially passing those costs onto consumers.[20]

When the dis-targeting test is fulfilled, the law of the place of provision of goods or services applies. This dis-targeting test in Article 42 of the Chinese Conflict of

tent, interpretation and application of the foreign law, the people's court may confirm it; if the parties have objections, the people's court shall make an examination and determination.

《最高人民法院关于适用〈中华人民共和国涉外民事关系法律适用法〉若干问题的解释(一)》第十六条：人民法院应当听取各方当事人对应当适用的外国法律的内容及其理解与适用的意见，当事人对该外国法律的内容及其理解与适用均无异议的，人民法院可以予以确认；当事人有异议的，由人民法院审查认定。

[17] Tu (2016), p. 102, para. 193.

[18] Liu (2005), p. 234; 刘益灯，《国际消费者保护法律制度研究》，中国方正出版社，2005，第234页。

[19] Yang (2012), p. 119; Xu (2004), p. 18; 徐冬根，《人文关怀与国际私法中弱者利益保护》，《当代法学》，2004年第5期，第18页。

[20] Yang (2012), p. 120.

Laws Act is intended to protect the reasonable expectations of the business party that does not target the consumer's home country. One advantage of implementing the dis-targeting test in China is that courts do not have to examine whether there is a causal link between the targeting test and the conclusion of the consumer contract.[21] In this regard, the dis-targeting test in the Chinese Conflict of Laws Act is more consumer-friendly. In cases where a business does not conduct commercial activities in a specific country or the consumer is a mobile or active consumer who travels to the business's domicile to purchase goods or services, it would be unpredictable for the business to apply the law of the consumer's habitual residence.[22] Such a condition aims to provide legal certainty and predictability for the business party and reduce its legal or commercial risk.[23] It also strikes a balance by leaning towards the business in situations where the consumer is excessively protected and the business's interests are unduly sacrificed.[24]

The targeting test and dis-targeting test determine whether a business is considered an active business or a passive business. The territorial scope of the business' operational or commercial activities determines whether the consumer's country of habitual residence applies and which country's laws apply. The targeting test and dis-targeting test also indirectly help distinguish between active consumers and passive consumers. In today's modern and globalized society, consumers increasingly go abroad to consume.[25] It becomes necessary to apply different choice of law rules based on this distinction between active and passive consumers.[26] When a consumer actively goes abroad to consume, the arbitrary application of the law of the consumer's country of habitual residence might be unreasonable or even cause substantive unfairness.[27]

5.2.3.2 The Criteria of Targeting Test

Based on the targeting and dis-targeting test, consumer choice of law rules may strike a balance between protecting consumers and business operators. However, the current consumer conflicts rule, which is based on the scope of targeting activities, is still too rigid and does not get rid of the mindset of territorial connection.[28]

---

[21] Chen (2022), p. 406.

[22] Tang et al. (2016), p. 232.

[23] Tang et al. (2016), p. 232.

[24] Tu (2016), para. 193.

[25] Yu (2011), pp. 65–70. 于颖:《〈涉外民事关系法律适用法〉第42条评析-我国国际私法对消费者之保护》，《法学评论》，2011年第2期，第65–70页。

[26] Yu (2011), p. 68.

[27] Liu and Hu (2012), p. 42; 刘晓红，胡荻,《论我国〈涉外民事关系法律适用法〉的若干实践困境》，《中国国际私法与比较法年刊》，2012年第15卷，第42页。

[28] Huang(2017),p.31;黄文秀,《论我国关于涉外消费者合同法律适用之规定》，华中师范大学硕士论文, 2017年, 第31页。

Moreover, there is a lack of clarity regarding what constitutes relevant operational or commercial activities?

The term 'operator's operational or commercial activities' refers to actions that involve the direct provision of goods or services.[29] The following factors might be relevant: whether the operator has registered its company or place of business in one place, whether it conducts activities such as manufacturing, selling, and providing services in that place, whether it seeks to realize its interests in that place, and other factors which have a close connection with the consumer contract.[30] Specifically, it is relevant to assess whether a foreign operator has established an agency in the consumer's home country for selling products or provide services, whether it provides goods or services via a website, or whether it operates through a subsidiary or affiliate company in the consumer's home country.[31] These factors are relevant because they may have a close connection with the contract.[32] However, with respect to the criteria for determining operational or commercial activities, Chinese private international law or substantive law lack specific provisions for clarification. This absence of clarification also leads to a lack of clear reasoning in judicial practice.[33]

5.2.4 *Insufficiency of Substantive Consumer Law in China*

The existing substantive consumer law in China is insufficient and presents challenges for consumers seeking protection in cross-border transactions. Article 42 of the Chinese Conflict of Laws Act stipulates that a consumer contract is governed by either the consumer's home law or the law of the place of provision of goods or services in Chinese private international law. When the targeting test is not met, the law of the place where goods or services are provided shall apply. However, the application of the consumer's home law under the targeting test may not always favor consumers, especially considering the fact that the substantive law on consumer protection in China is still less developed than that in the EU and the USA.[34] In China, consumer protection provisions are scattered across various laws and

[29] Huang (2017), p. 29.

[30] Huang (2017), p. 30.

[31] Huang (2017), p. 30; Hong and Zong (2014), pp. 282–283; 洪莉萍，宗绪志,《国际私法理论与实践探索》，中国法制出版社，2014年，第282–283页。Based on the principle of privity of contract, the operational or commercial activities conducted by the subsidiary or affiliated company of an operator cannot be equivalent to the operator's activities.

[32] Wang (2021a), p. 30; 王芳,《涉外消费者合同的法律适用研究》，燕山大学硕士论文，2021年, 第30页。These factors are comparable to the criteria in determining the targeting test under the Brussels Ibis Regulation and Rome I Regulation. See Chen (2023), pp. 23–44.

[33] Wang (2021b), p. 15.

[34] Yang (2012), p. 121.

regulations and may not offer comprehensive coverage for all aspects of a consumer's daily life and consumption.[35]

For instance, a Chinese consumer bought a product from an American company in the USA and that company has conducted relevant commercial activities in China. If disputes arise, Chinese law should apply in accordance with Article 42 of the Chinese Conflict of Laws Act.[36] Whether the application of Chinese law would correspond to the consumer's reasonable expectations? When compared to American law, whether the application of Chinese law will offer the same level protection to the consumer?[37] If the consumer does not choose the law of the place of provision of goods or services, the less favorable law of the consumer' habitual residence will apply instead.[38] The mandatory application of the consumer's home law could potentially result in reduced consumer protection, particularly when the business targeting Chinese consumers is based in the EU or the USA. Furthermore, due to the insufficiency of Chinese consumer law, such as tourism law, when consumer choice of law rules lead to the application of Chinese substantive law, it may lead to no applicable law.[39]

5.3 Limiting the Exercise of Party Autonomy

In the targeting context, the condition of applying the consumer's home law is that the consumer does not choose the law of the place of provision of goods or services. The consumer' choice of law takes precedence over the consumer's home law. Article 42 of the Chinese Conflict of Laws Act introduces limited party autonomy by allowing the consumer to choose the law of the place where goods or services are provided. Business operators or service providers have no right to choose an applicable law other than being subject to the law chosen by the consumer.[40] This limitation prevents the exercise of party autonomy from becoming a tool for stronger party to impose its one-sided choice on the weaker party, which reflects the pursuit of substantive justice.[41]

---

[35] Tian (2021), p. 15; 田静怡:《网络购物合同纠纷管辖权的问题与建议探讨》，《法制博览》，2021年3月，第15页。

[36] Liu and Hu (2012), p. 42.

[37] Liu and Hu (2012), p. 42.

[38] Yang (2012), p. 121. In this scenario in which the targeting test is fulfilled and the consumer does not make a choice, it is suggested that the consumer's home law or the law of the place of provision of goods or services, whichever is more favorable to consumers, shall apply.

[39] Xia (2010), p. 418; 夏雨:《论我国国际旅游法律制度的缺失与构建——以和平崛起为视角》，《武汉大学学报(哲学社会科学版)》，2010年第3期，第418页。

[40] Huang and Jiang (2011), p. 233; 黄进、姜茹娇，《〈中华人民共和国涉外民事关系法律适用法〉释义与分析》，法律出版社，2011年，第233页。

[41] Liu and Hu (2012), p. 43.

5.3.1 Unilateral Party Autonomy in Consumer Choice of Law Under Chinese Conflict of Laws Act

The unilateral party autonomy under Article 42 of the Chinese Conflict of Laws Act is based on the presumption that parties are unlikely to agree on a choice of law once a dispute has arisen. Article 42 does not aim to entirely exclude party autonomy from consumer contracts, except to prevent a choice of bad faith.[42] It in effect totally deprive the business party's right to choose applicable law and does not fully respect the mutual consent of both parties. This unilateral party autonomy is questionable, as it goes to another extreme. In *Xie Shixiong v. Qiu Lijuan et al,*[43] the court seized invoked Article 42 of the Chinese Conflict of Laws Act to justify the application of Chinese law. If the loan agreement were classified as a consumer contract, the unilateral choice of law should be granted to the borrower, as a consumer, rather than the lender. The statement that 'the lender Xie Shixiong explicitly chose the application of Chinese law and none of the parties raised an objection' indicates that the court upheld two-sided party autonomy based on implied consent, which is not explicitly stated in Article 42 of the Chinese Conflict of Laws Act. In this context, a reference to Article 41 of the Chinese Conflict of Laws Act regarding general contracts may be more appropriate.

The unilateral party autonomy granted to consumers aims to protect consumers as weaker parties and prevent them from passively accepting choice of law clause imposed by businesses that could put them at a disadvantage.[44] For instance, in a package travel contract, consumers usually do not negotiate with travel agents or tour operators on the pre-drafted contract and often find themselves in a take-it-or-leave-it position.[45] If businesses were allowed to choose the applicable law before a dispute arises, the potential risk is that all travel companies or businesses would include choice of law clauses in their standard contracts that are most convenient or beneficial for them, potentially providing minimal consumer protection or being inconvenient for consumers.[46] However, it remains debatable whether the business' freedom to choose applicable law should be totally deprived after a dispute arises and whether the law chosen by the consumer should be applied even if the business disagrees. Eliminating one party's right to choose the law applicable to disputes

---

[42] Tang (2007), pp. 113–136.

[43] *Xie Shixiong v. Qiu Lijuan et al*, Guangdong Province Foshan Municipality Intermediate People's Court, [2018] Yue 06 Min Chu No 177. 谢世雄与邱丽娟、林昌华民间借贷纠纷一审民事判决书, 民间借贷纠纷, 中华人民共和国广东省佛山市中级人民法院民 事 判 决 书,(2018)粤06民初177号。The court did not specifically classify the loan agreement between two individuals as a consumer contract.

[44] Yang (2012), p. 119.

[45] Tang (2009), pp. 8–11.

[46] A counter argument is that companies or businesses should be allowed to choose the law where goods or services are provided to reduce commercial risks, because it is unpredictable for the cross-border companies if consumers are entitled to file a lawsuit in their home state or habitual residence.

over contractual obligations is a gravely flawed party autonomy. Despite differences in bargaining power and financial status between consumers and businesses, it does not necessarily mean that the law chosen by the business party is always detrimental to consumers.[47] What if the law chosen by the business party can better protect the rights and interests of the consumer?[48] It is questionable to completely deprive the business's right to choose the applicable law.

5.3.2 *Limited Material Scope of Chosen Law*

If the targeting test is fulfilled, consumers may freely choose the law applicable under Article 42 of the Chinese Conflict of Laws Act. This choice is limited to the law of the consumer's habitual residence and the law of the place of provision of goods and services. If a consumer does not exercise this unilateral right to choose the applicable law, the default rule is the application of the law of the consumer's habitual residence. Although it seems more protective to consumers by granting consumers the right to choose applicable law, this unilateral party autonomy is limited to only one law, namely, the law of the place where goods or services are provided. It is assumed that the place where goods or services are provided usually has the closest connection with the consumer contract and is usually known to consumers or expected by consumers.[49] Furthermore, business operators are generally expected to know and abide by the laws of the place of provision of goods and services, making it more likely for them to accept the consumer's choice of this law, thereby facilitating dispute resolution.[50] This assumption may not hold true in all circumstances.

Firstly, unlike business operators who need to know the law of the place where goods or services are provided in order to conduct commercial activities for benefits in the long run, consumers purchasing goods or services for family or personal purposes may have limited or no knowledge of the law of the place where goods or services are provided.[51] Second, with the increasing prevalence of E-commerce in the digital economy, business operators may not know all the laws of the place where goods or services are provided. In complex international transactions, multiple places might be involved in a consumer contract, meaning that the place where goods or services are provided may not have the closest connection with the consumer contract. What if the parties want to choose the law of a third country,[52] rather

[47] Yang (2012), p. 119.

[48] Yang (2012), p. 119; Xu (2006), pp. 188–189; 许军珂:《国际私法上的意思自治》, 法律出版社，2006年，第188–189页。

[49] Tang et al. (2016), p. 232; Tang (2009), p. 208.

[50] Huang and Jiang (2011), p. 233.

[51] Huang and Jiang (2011), p. 233.

[52] Huang (2017), p. 31.

than the law of the consumer's habitual residence or the law of the place of provision of goods or services? Such free choice of law of a third country is not allowed under Chinese private international law. Article 42 of the Chinese Conflict of Laws Act only provides two connecting factors that designate two laws, completely excluding all other laws, even those having a closer connection with the consumer contract.[53] One of the reasons Chinese courts did not invoke Article 42 of the Chinese Conflict of Laws Act in determining the law applicable to package travel contracts is the limited scope of unilateral choice of law, in addition to the inapplicability of bilateral party autonomy and the closest connection principle.[54]

Secondly, when a consumer does not choose the law of the place where goods or services are provided, the law of the consumer's habitual residence applies directly in accordance with Article 42 of the Chinese Conflict of Laws Act. This article does not specify whether the consumer has the right to choose another law, such as the law of the place where the business is domiciled after the dispute arises.[55] This may not be in line with the favoring principle in the field of consumer protection.[56] The primary reason is that the level of consumer protection under the law of the consumer's country of habitual residence may be lower than that of the business's country of domicile.[57] The Chinese Consumer Protection Law may not provide sufficient protection to consumers in every aspect, especially in this fast-changing society and increasingly complicated transactions. In order to provide sufficient protection, it is advisable to allow consumers to choose the more favorable law after the dispute takes place.[58] Some scholars advocate for the addition of a principle that applies the law favorable to the protection of the consumer's rights and interests, in addition to the two laws provided in Article 42 of the Chinese Conflict of Laws Act.[59]

Thirdly, apart from being less favorable to consumers, the law of the place of provision of goods or services may not have relevant consumer substantive law rules. The application of the place of performance of the contract in certain circumstances may be unpredictable for both parties, thus undermining legal certainty and predictability. In some circumstances, the law of the country of the business's domicile, which has not been taken into account, may provide better protections. Some cross-border companies may prefer the application of their home law to their global consumers. This might be beneficial to consumers from particular countries, especially when the country of the consumer's habitual residence has no relevant substantive laws or provides a much lower level of

[53] Huang (2017), p. 31.

[54] Wang (2018), pp. 103–106; 王群,《海外旅游消费者权利保护机制探讨—基于<涉外民事关系法律适用法>视角》，《九江学院学报(社会科学版)》，2018年第1期，第103–106页。

[55] Fan (2014), p. 225, 范晓亮,《欧盟金融消费者合同法律适用规则研究》，《武大国际法评论》，2014年第16卷第2期，第225页。

[56] Liu (2005), pp. 89–91.

[57] Xu (2006), p. 144.

[58] Fan (2014), p. 225.

[59] Huang and Jiang (2011), p. 233.

protection to consumers. For instance, a Chinese tourist concludes a timeshare contract with a French business for the use of a Spanish holiday villa and sues the French defendant in a Chinese court. If the targeting test is fulfilled and the Chinese tourist does not choose to apply the law of the provision of services (Spanish law), the law of the consumer's habitual residence (Chinese law) will be applicable under Article 42 of the Chinese Conflict of Laws Act. There is no ground to apply French law (the law of the business's domicile) under Chinese consumer conflicts rules. Since Chinese law does not provide any specific provisions on timeshare contracts, the application of Chinese law may lead to no applicable substantive law. In this sense, the strict limitation of the material scope of the applicable law might also be abused by the business to prevent the consumer from being protected by a better law.

This is the case in *British Carnival Cruise*,[60] in which a Chinese tourist sued a British Carnival Cruise company seeking compensation for a swimming pool accident that occurred during the performance of a package travel contract. The British company had a representative office in Shanghai and had conducted commercial activities in China for several years. These factors may potentially constitute engagement in relevant commercial activities in China, as stipulated in Article 42 of the Chinese Conflict of Laws Act. In such cases, the law of the consumer's habitual residence shall apply unless the consumer chooses to apply the law of the place where the services are provided (Japanese law or Korean law). However, in reality, while the British cruise company chose to apply Chinese law, the Chinese tourist consumer chose to apply English law (the law where the British cruise company was domiciled), rather than the law of the place of provisions of services (Japanese law or Korean law). In this context, Article 42 of the Chinese Conflict of Laws Act will play a negative role by preventing consumers from relying on a more favorable law. This gives rise to the question of whether the material scope of the applicable law that a consumer can choose should be confined solely to the law of the place of provision of goods or services. This issue becomes particularly relevant when the place of provision of services is not limited to one country, such as in the case of package travel and car rental services which are provided across several countries. By confining the material scope of the chosen law to the law of the consumer's home country and the law of the place of provision of goods and services, it does not allow the parties to select other laws that may be more closely connected to the dispute. Such limitation, on one hand, may not enhance legal certainty and, on the other hand, may be detrimental to consumers, which goes against the objective of establishing protective consumer choice of law rules.

Fourthly, the limitations on the exercise of unilateral party autonomy under Article 42 of the Chinese Conflict of Laws Act appear to be incomplete. It does not

[60] The swimming pool accident on the cruise which causes the tort liability was arising out of, or at least in relation to the package travel contract. Although the cause of action chosen by the plaintiff was tort liability, consumer choice of law rules shall apply if the cause of action was contract liability. Chen (2021), pp. 626–647.

specify whether the mandatory provisions of the consumer's country of habitual residence shall still apply even if the consumer chooses the law of the place where goods or services are provided.[61] For instance, the consumer's unilateral choice of law might be irrational, as they may not fully understand or compare the consequences of applying different laws.[62] Furthermore, if the consumer agrees to apply the law designated in a choice of law clause pre-drafted by the operator in a standard contract, the exercise of the consumer's unilateral choice may lead to a less favorable law.[63] This will be discussed further in the section on bilateral party autonomy and mandatory provisions.

5.4 Lack of Interaction Between Article 41 and Article 42 of the Chinese Conflict of Laws Act

5.4.1 *Two-Sided Party Autonomy in General Contract Choice of Law Rules*

Under the general contract choice of law rules in Article 41 of the Chinese Conflict of Laws Act, parties in a contractual relationship may choose the law applicable to their contract; in the absence of a choice, the law that has the closest connection with the contract or best reflects the characteristic performance of the contract shall apply. According to Article 41 of the Chinese Conflict of Laws Act, there is no limitation on the material scope of the chosen law. This means that parties may even choose a law unrelated to the contract or dispute. Under Article 5 of the SPC Judicial Interpretation of the Chinese Conflict of Laws Act, the argument that the choice of law is invalid because the chosen law has no factual connection with the dispute will not be supported by Chinese courts. This article clarifies that the law chosen by the parties does not have to have a practical connection with the contract, Therefore, parties could choose a neutral law to govern their contractual obligations.[64] If the parties do not choose the applicable law, the court will decide which law has the closest connection with the contract or best reflects the characteristic performance of the contract.

[61] Tu (2011), pp. 11–23; 涂广建:《解读我国涉外民事关系法律适用法》，《时代法学》，2011年第2期，第11–23页; Wang (2014), p. 82; 土立武,《国际私法的强制性规则适用制度研究》，中国人民大学出版社年 2014 版，第 82 页。

[62] Wang (2021b), p. 15.

[63] Wang (2021b), p. 15; Wang (2021b), p. 19; 王璇:《我国涉外网络消费者合同的法律适用研究》，安徽财经大学硕士论文，2021年, 第19页.

[64] Tang et al. (2016), p. 212. The choose of competent court still requires a factual connection.

5.4.2 *Differences Between Contract and Consumer Choice of Law Rules*

The general contract choice of law rules and consumer choice of law rules in the Chinese Conflict of Laws Act differ in two aspects: the exercise of party autonomy and the application of the closest connection principle and characteristic performance principle. First, party autonomy differs between Article 41 and Article 42 of the Chinese Conflict of Laws Act. Article 41 adopts bilateral party autonomy, while Article 42 adopts unilateral party autonomy. Additionally, Article 41 does not limit the material scope of the chosen law, as the 'no practical connection criterion' allows parties to choose a law with no connection to the case.[65] Under Article 42, apart from the law of the consumer's habitual residence, the consumer's exercise of party autonomy is strictly limited to only one law: the law of the place of provision of goods or services. Moreover, the consumer may exercise unilateral choice of applicable law only when the business has engaged in commercial activities in the consumer's country of habitual residence. This limitation or condition means that consumers have less freedom to choose the applicable law under the special protective rule of Article 42 compared to the general contract rule of Article 41, which is undesirable and questionable.

Second, the closest connection principle and characteristic performance principle are not expressly stated in Article 42 regarding consumer choice of law rules. In the absence of the consumer's unilateral choice, the closest connection principle, which is otherwise applicable, has no role to play. This is problematic, especially when the dis-targeting test is fulfilled. The law of the place of provision of goods or services applies as a secondary default rule, regardless of its connection with the dispute. Just as the consumer is restrained to choose only the law of the place of provision of goods or services when the targeting test is fulfilled, the applicable law is also restricted to the law of the place of provision of goods or services when the targeting test is not fulfilled. What is the point of having the targeting or dis-targeting test as a condition if the law of the place of provision of goods or services applies in both cases? In increasingly complicated consumer transactions in the digital age, the place where goods or services are provided does not necessarily have the closest connection with the dispute in both targeting and dis-targeting contexts.

[65] This is implied in Article 7 of the SPC Judicial Interpretation of the Chinese Conflict of Laws Act. Xu (2013), pp. 24–34; 徐伟功,《法律选择中的意思自治原则在我国的运用》,《法学》, 2013年第9期, 第24–34页。

5.4.3 Relationship Between Article 41 and Article 42 of the Chinese Conflict of Laws Act

In principle, as a special rule, Article 42 on choice of law rules for consumer contracts should take precedence over Article 41 on choice of law rules for general contracts. However, there is a lack of interaction between these two provisions. Unlike Article 41 on contract conflicts rules, Article 42 on consumer conflicts rules considers the consumer's habitual residence as the primary connecting factor, limiting party autonomy in certain ways.[66] The general principles in Article 41, such as the closest connection principle and the characteristic performance principle, theoretically apply to all contractual obligations, including consumer contracts. Special consumer choice of law rules in Article 42, as an exception, take precedence over general contract choice of law rules in Article 41. Due to the absence of interaction between Article 41 and Article 42, general principles applied to contractual obligations could not apply to consumer contracts. There is a need to clarify the relationship between Article 41 and Article 42 of the Chinese Conflict of Laws Act.

Article 42 of the Chinese Conflict of Laws Act does not provide other flexible connecting factors. The strict application of the consumer's home law and the law of the place of provision of goods or services potentially excludes the law of another country that might have a closer connection with the dispute. In contrast, Article 41 of the Chinese Conflict of Laws Act designates the law that has the closest connection with the contract or best reflects the characteristic performance of the contractual obligation. Nevertheless, Article 42 of the Chinese Conflict of Laws Act does not refer to the application of contract choice of law rules when the dis-targeting test is fulfilled. Instead, it applies the law of the place of provision of goods or services as a default rule when the business does not engage in relevant commercial activities in the consumer's home country, regardless of whether it has the closest connection with the consumer contract. This lack of interaction between protective consumer choice of law rules and general contract choice of law rules raises questions about whether the closest connection principle should be completely excluded in determining the applicable law for consumer contracts.[67] Although Article 42 of the Chinese Conflict of Laws Act, as a special provision, takes priority over Article 41, Article 41 as a general provision should still apply to consumer contracts.[68] The question is when and under what conditions general contract choice of law rules may apply to determine the law applicable to consumer contracts.

[66] Weng (2014), p. 76; 翁玉真,《涉外消费权益的法律保护——兼评我国〈涉外民事关系法律适用法〉第 42 条》，《福建法学》2014 年第 2 期，第 76 页。

[67] The principle of the closest connection should be introduced into foreign-related consumer contracts to further increase the flexibility. Huang (2017), p. 31.

[68] Wang (2021b), p. 18.

5.4.4 *The Law of the Place of Provision of Goods and Services Under the Dis-targeting Test?*

Under Article 42 of the Chinese Conflict of Laws Act, the law of the place of provision of goods and services applies in two scenarios: first, when the targeting test is fulfilled and the consumer chooses such law, and second, when the targeting test is not fulfilled. The law of the place of provision of goods or services is applicable both when the business targets the consumer's home country and when the business does not target the consumer's home country. The place where goods or services are provided is an objective connecting factor which has a close connection with the operator's performance of contractual obligations.[69] The application of the law of the place of provision of goods or services generally corresponds to the operator's reasonable expectations and interests.[70] In the context of targeting activities, it is presumed that the consumer will choose the law of the place of provision of goods or services only if it provides a higher level of protection than the consumer's home law. In the context of dis-targeting activities, the question is whether the law of the place of provision of goods or services always has the closest connection with the consumer dispute, as presumed.

When the place of provision of goods or services is the same as the consumer's habitual residence, the unilateral right granted to the consumer to choose applicable law becomes meaningless. In such cases, the applicable law remains the same, regardless of the consumer's active or passive choice.[71] For instance, many transnational corporations have established direct-operated stores and flagship stores in mainland China to sell goods and provide services, such as Apple, LVMH selling luxury products, and companies selling luxury cars, among others.[72] Since the targeting test is fulfilled, Chinese law applies, either as the law of the consumer's habitual residence or as the law of the place of provision of goods or services, regardless of the consumer's choice. In these cases, under Article 42 of the Chinese Conflict of Laws Act, Chinese consumers have no right to choose any other laws, such as the law of the business' domicile which might be more favorable. Furthermore, if the place of provision of goods or services is in the consumer's habitual residence, it also means that the law of the consumer's habitual residence always applies, regardless of the business's targeting or dis-targeting activities. This is questionable, as it may not have the closest connection with the contract or correspond to the reasonable expectations of the parties. Applying the law of the place

[69] Such place is different from the place of conducting advertising and refers to the place of actual performance. Huang (2017), pp. 20–21.

[70] Such connecting factor is almost of the same weight of the law of the consumer's habitual residence in Chinese private international law, but it is not listed as a separate connecting factor in many other countries. Huang (2017), p. 20.

[71] Wang (2021b), p. 16.

[72] Wang (2021b), p. 16.

of provision of goods or services in both targeting and dis-targeting scenarios may ensure legal certainty at the cost of limiting legal flexibility.

5.4.5 The Closest Connection Principle

5.4.5.1 Legal Flexibility and Substantive Justice

The closest connection principle, which designates the law most closely connected to a particular case, has played a significant role in conflict-of-law rules.[73] Private international law endeavors to strike a balance between legal certainty and flexibility when it comes to the applicable law.[74] The flexibility in applying the law often has a direct impact on the fairness of the judgment, known as substantive justice.[75] The closest connection principle allows legal flexibility by granting judges the discretion to determine which law should apply. However, excessive flexibility in applying this principle, without any limitations, can always lead to the application of the forum law, which could be seen as an abuse.[76] The consumer choice of law rules in Article 42 of the Chinese Conflict of Laws Act also reflect the closest connection principle. A consumer contract might be concluded or performed in a place other than the consumer's habitual residence, but it mostly has a connection with the consumer's habitual residence.[77] The place of the consumer's habitual residence might be not only the place whether the consumer purchases goods or services but also the place where the operator conducts commercial activities, thus it is usually easier to be known for consumers and business operators.[78] The law of the consumer's habitual residence generally has the closest connection with the consumer contract.[79] The application of the consumer's home law is under the condition that the targeting test is fulfilled. If the targeting test is not fulfilled, the law of the place of provision of goods or services, which is presumed to have the closest connection with the contract, applies as a secondary default rule.[80] However, this may unduly limit the court's discretion in using the closest connection principle to designate

[73] Fang (2013), pp. 110–116; 方杰,《最密切联系原则考证》,《比较法研究》, 2013年第2期，第110–116页。

[74] Guo (2011), pp. 155–167; 郭玉军,《中国国际私法的立法反思及其完善-以<涉外民事关系法律适用法>为中心》，《清华法学》, 2011 年第5期，第155–167页。

[75] Han (2007), p. 96; 韩德培主编:《国际私法》，高等教育出版社2007年版，第96页。

[76] Ma (2016), pp. 15–23; 马志强:《最密切联系原则在中国的立法完善》,《当代法学》2016年第6期，第15–23页。

[77] Huang and Jiang (2011), p. 234.

[78] Huang and Jiang (2011), p. 234.

[79] Huang and Jiang (2011), p. 234.

[80] Tang et al. (2016), p. 232.

another law.[81] For instance, a Chinese tourist from Hong Kong concludes a package travel contract with a travel agency in mainland China for a trip to an EU country like Italy or the Netherlands. This tourist sues before a court in mainland China. The applicable law under Article 42 of the Chinese Conflict of Laws Act would be the law of the place of performance of the contract (Italian law or Dutch law), provided that the Chinese travel agency does not engage in commercial activities in Hong Kong. In this scenario, Chinese law, as the law of the business's domicile, may have a closer connection than the law of the place where the travel services were provided.

5.4.5.2 The Closest Connection Principle as an Exceptional Rule or Escape Clause

Article 2 of the Chinese Conflict of Laws Act has established the closest connection principle as a supplementary principle to address gaps left by the Chinese Conflict of Laws Act and other laws.[82] The place of the closest connection is an abstract concept and does not designate any specific law. Its application depends on the subjective analysis of the judge.[83] When a business does not specifically target the consumer's home country, and the parties involved have not chosen the applicable law, the closest connection principle can play a supplementary role in protecting the weaker parties.[84] However, the law of the place where goods or services are provided may not always have the closest connection with the consumer dispute, particularly in cases involving services rather than goods, such as cross-border travel services. Therefore, a strict application of the law of the place of provision of goods or services might turn out to be less favorable to consumers in certain situations.

While Article 2 of the Chinese Conflict of Laws Act acknowledges the supplementary nature of the closest connection principle, it has not become a general exceptional rule or an escape clause for all legal relationships.[85] To strengthen its role, the closest connection principle could be integrated into Article 42 on consumer choice of law rules. This could be achieved by expressly stating that when parties in a consumer contract do not choose the applicable law, the law of the country which has a closer connection with the contract should apply. Alternatively, an interaction could be established between Article 41 and Article 42 of the Chinese

[81] In the context of cross-border tourism, the law of the provision of travel service is a foreign law, which would increase the difficulty and burden of ascertaining the foreign law. Zhuang (2020), p. 29; 庄允,《我国涉外旅游纠纷法律适用问题研究》，山东大学硕士学位论文，2020年，第29页。

[82] Du (2011), p. 58; 杜涛,《涉外民事关系法律适用法释评》，中国法制出版社 2011年版，第58页。

[83] Du (2011), p. 334. Such ambiguity may easily lead to the application of the law which the judge is most familiar with, namely, the forum law.

[84] Weng (2014), pp. 75–79.

[85] Zhuang (2020), p. 34.

Conflict of Laws Act to allow the application of the closest connection principle, especially in the context of dis-targeting activities.

5.4.5.3 The Closest Connection Principle in Consumer Choice of Law Rules

In judicial practice, Chinese courts may determine the place which has the closest connection with a case by counting on the number of connecting factors and first see whether China has the closest connection.[86] Usually, Chinese courts only list connecting factors which have connection with China, without a comparison of the number or significance of connecting factors with other foreign countries.[87] This practice is also reflected in the application of the closest connection principle to package travel contracts, which has led to a frequent but wrong reference to Article 41. Under this principle, Chinese courts tend to exclusively list or analyze connecting factors related to China while neglecting those related to other foreign countries.[88] Regarding package travel contracts, Chinese law is usually applied, regardless of the quantity and quality of connecting factors with China.[89] For example, when a Chinese tourist travels abroad under a contract concluded with a Chinese travel agency, the contract has a closer connection with China.[90] Conversely, when a foreign tourist travels to China under a contract with a Chinese travel agency, the contract may have a closer connection with the foreign country. When it comes to one specific connecting factor, such as the place where goods and services are provided under Article 42 of the Chinese Conflict of Laws Act, it does not necessarily have the closest connection with the consumer contract in all circumstances.

Additionally, the place where goods and services are provided may not be limited to a single country but could span multiple countries. For instance, in a package travel contract, the place of the provision of services might be in several countries which all have a connection, rather than the closest connection, with the travel dispute. In *Cong Shuwan v. Zhongxin Travel Service Group*,[91] the tourist Liang Huifang signed an outbound travel contract with the defendant for a 15-day-5-country travel itinerary. While traveling in Switzerland, Liang Huifang developed symptoms of fatigue, weakness and other discomforts. After arriving in Paris, she was already

[86] Xiao (2008), p. 187; 肖永平,《法理学视野下的冲突法》，高等教育出版社，2008年版，第187页。

[87] Xiao (2008), p. 187.

[88] Zhuang (2020), p. 29.

[89] Zhuang (2020), p. 29.

[90] Zhuang (2020), p. 30.

[91] *Cong Shuwan v. Zhongxin Travel Service Group*, Liaoning Province Dalian Municipality Xigang DPC, (2017) Liao 0203 Min Chu No 4789. The plaintiffs Cong Shuwan and Cong Zhefeng were the deceased Liang Huifang's husband and son respectively. The plaintiffs sued the defendant Zhongxin Travel Service Group for the compensation of Liang Huifang's death and the refund of travel fee.

very ill and died in Paris later. In this package travel contract, the place of provision of services involves multiple countries, the application of the law of the provision of services is not certain nor predictable compared to other connecting factors, such as the consumer's domicile or the business's domicile. Similarly, in timeshare contracts, the place of performance or provision of services may be different every year, making it unpredictable for both parties. In *Wei Hong and An Yu v. Xi'an Diyawei Travel Tourism Project Development Co., Ltd., et al,*[92] the plaintiffs signed a contract with the first and second defendants for being a member of the second defendant in order to participate travel activities organized by the second defendant in Thailand, Europe, Bali and other places. According to the contract, the membership price was 88,000 RMB and the plaintiffs had the right of one-week vacation accommodation per year from January 2017 to December 2046. The membership of the club of the second defendant granted the plaintiffs the right of accommodation, the right of exchange, the right of gifting, the right of rent, the right of transfer, and the right of inheritance. Since the place of performance of a timeshare contract might change each year, the application of the law of provision of services is unpredictable for both parties and may not has the closest connection with the dispute.

The closest connection principle has played a role in determining the law applicable to consumer contracts in China prior to the enactment of the 2010 Chinese Conflict of Laws Act by virtue of Article 145 of the General Principle of Civil Law and Article 126 of the Contract Law.[93] These two provisions allowed the parties in a foreign-related contract to choose the law applicable to their contract; in the absence of such a choice, the law of the country which has the closest connection with the contract should apply.[94] The Supreme People's Court further clarified that the law of the country of the party whose performance of contractual obligations best reflects the nature of the contract should be applied.[95] Article 42 of the 2010 Chinese Conflict of Laws Act separates consumer contracts from general contracts by establishing a favorable consumer choice of law rule. Despite this, when the targeting test

[92] *Wei Hong and An Yu v. Xi'an Diyawei Travel Tourism Project Development Co., Ltd., et al,* Shaanxi Province Xi'an Municipality IPC, (2017) Shaan 01 Min Chu No 977. The plaintiffs Wei Hong and An Yu, domiciled in Shaanxi Province, sued the defendants (i) Xi'an Diyawei Travel Tourism Project Development Co., Ltd., domiciled in Shaanxi, (ii) Now Vacations, Co., Ltd., domiciled in HongKong, and (iii) Hambesi Hotel Development (Shanghai) Co., Ltd., domiciled in Pudong, Shanghai.

[93] The original texts are《民法通则》第145条: 涉外合同的当事人可以选择处理合同争议所适用的法律，法律另有规定的除外。涉外合同的当事人没有选择的，适用与合同有最密切联系的国家的法律。《合同法》第126条第1款: 涉外合同的当事人可以选择处理合同争议所适用的法律，但法律另有规定的除外。涉外合同的当事人没有选择的，适用与合同有最密切联系的国家的法律。

[94] These provisions do not impose a limitation on the right to choose applicable law. Due to the imbalance of bargaining power for parties in a consumer contract, the so-called party autonomy may turn out to reflect only the business operators' intention. Yang (2012), p. 8.

[95] The original text is 2007 年《最高人民法院关于审理涉外民事或商事合同纠纷案件法律适用若干问题的规定》第5条: 人民法院根据最密切联系原则确定合同争议应适用的法律时，应根据合同的特殊性质，以及某一方当事人履行的义务最能体现合同的本质特性等因素，确定与合同有最密切联系的国家或者地区的法律作为合同的准据法。

is not fulfilled, the application of the law of the place where goods or services are provided is questionable, as it may not always have the closest connection with the consumer contract. In cases where the business does not target the consumer's home country, it would be more reasonable to subject consumer contracts to general contract choice of law rules based on the closest connection principle or the characteristic performance principle. This can be achieved by establishing a connection between Article 41 and Article 42 of the Chinese Conflict of Laws Act. For instance, if the business has not engaged in commercial activities in the country of the consumer's habitual residence, the law applicable to a consumer contract should be determined under Article 41 of the Chinese Conflict of Laws Act. Alternatively, the closest connection principle could be integrated in Article 42 and applies when the business has not engaged in commercial activities in the consumer's habitual residence.

5.4.6 *Adding More Flexible Connecting Factors*

Article 42 of the Chinese Conflict of Laws Act restricts consumers to choosing only the law of their home country or the law of the place of provision of goods or services. This limitation on one-sided party autonomy actually closes the door for consumers regarding the possibility of applying other more favorable laws, such as the law of the business's domicile, the law of the consumer's domicile, the law of the common domicile of the parties, the law of the place of conclusion of the contract, the law of the place of registration or main business of a company, or the law that may have a closer connection with the dispute. The strict application of two connecting factors is at odds with the tendency of increasing flexibility in private international law concerning connecting factors, especially in matters of contractual obligations.[96]

Meanwhile, under Article 42 of the Chinese Conflict of Laws Act, if the place where goods or services are provided is also the consumer's habitual residence,[97] the consumer has no freedom to choose any other laws. It does not matter whether the consumer is granted unilateral right to choose applicable law,[98] as the two connecting factors essentially lead to the application of the same law. Consumers can only make a meaningful choice if the place of provision of goods or services differs from their habitual residence. The narrow material scope of unilateral party autonomy may fail to efficiently protect consumers' rights.[99] Therefore, there is a need to

---

[96] Xiao (2008), p. 59.

[97] For instance, if a Chinese consumer receives services in China which are provided by a foreign business.

[98] Jiang (2019), p. 30; 江威，《涉外消费者合同法律适用问题研究》，郑州大学硕士论文，2019，第30页。

[99] Jiang (2019), p. 31.

add more flexible connecting factors and expand the range of laws consumers can choose from.

Limiting the material scope of the chosen law may prevent business operators in consumer contracts from evading mandatory consumer protection rules through their choice of law. However, it also prevents business operators from choosing a law that is more favorable to consumer protection.[100] Article 42 of the Chinese Conflict of Laws Act offers only two connecting factors for consumers' unilateral party autonomy: the consumer's habitual residence as the primary connecting factor and the place of provision of goods and services as the secondary connecting factor. This limitation is overly strict and lacks reasonable flexibility, since it does not provide a broader range of applicable laws.[101] The legislator's intention was to protect the weaker party in a consumer contract and fully respect the weaker parties' right to choose applicable law.[102] If consumers are granted the unilateral right to choose the applicable law, they should be allowed to choose from a certain range of laws, instead of being confined to only one law.[103] However, giving consumers too many choices may undermine the protection of business operators' rights and interests.[104] Thus, it is more advisable to limit the territorial scope of the consumer's choice of law to the places with a connection to the consumer contract.[105] This connection requirement in the material scope of the applicable law unilaterally chosen by the consumer can help avoid overprotecting consumers while also safeguarding the reasonable expectations of operators. Having considered the closest connection principle and the characteristic performance doctrine, the following connecting factors might be relevant: the domicile of the parties, the place of registration or main business of a company, or the place of conclusion of the contract.[106]

5.4.7 Allowing Bilateral Party Autonomy in Special Consumer Choice of Law Rules

Many legal systems narrow the scope of party autonomy by excluding it from certain contracts, in whole or in part, such as consumer contracts, employee contracts and other contracts involving presumptively weak parties.[107] Under unilateral consumer choice of law rules, only the consumer can choose the applicable law, and

[100] Yang (2012), p. 119.

[101] Yang (2012), p. 119.

[102] Yang (2012), p. 119.

[103] Huang and Jiang (2011), p. 234.

[104] Huang and Jiang (2011), p. 234.

[105] Huang and Jiang (2011), p. 234.

[106] It makes sure that the chosen law has a connection with the transaction, instead of the law of a random third country. Wang (2021a), p. 32.

[107] Symeonides (2019), p. 3.

thus bears the obligation to ascertain a foreign law. The comparison between that foreign law and the domestic home law inevitably increases litigation costs for consumers.[108] In contrast, under bilateral party autonomy, if a foreign law is chosen, both parties (the consumer and the business) have the obligation to ascertain that foreign law.[109] Additionally, the parties may choose a law that has no actual connection with the consumer contract but offers better consumer protection.[110] In this regard, allowing two-sided party autonomy can expand the material scope of the law that can be applicable.

In fact, the draft proposal of the Chinese Conflict of Laws Act adopted two-sided party autonomy in consumer contracts and only limited the material scope of chosen law with the connection criterion. Specifically, Article 56 of the Proposal Draft and Explanation of the Chinese Conflict of Laws Act on the choice of law rules over consumption contracts states that: *For consumption contracts, the law of the consumer's habitual residence or the law of the place where goods or services are provided shall apply. The parties to a consumption contract may also choose a law that has a reasonable connection with consumption.* The 'reasonable connection' criterion might be used to expand the material scope of chosen law over consumer contracts. Article 42 of the Chinese Conflict of Laws Act should embrace bilateral party autonomy and expressly state that the parties may choose the law applicable to the consumer contract. This may correct the wrongful reference to other legal provisions to justify bilateral party autonomy over consumer contracts in judicial practice.[111]

In addition, the adoption of bilateral party autonomy may solve the dilemma in which the law of the consumer's habitual residence and the law of the provision of services have no relevant substantive laws. For instance, there are no substantive laws regarding timeshare contracts in China, when Chinese timeshare tourists conclude a timeshare contract with a business domiciled in Country A, the parties may choose the law of Country A as applicable law. Based on bilateral party autonomy, the parties may choose the law of the defendant's domicile, the law of the country in which the consumer and the business are domiciled, or the law of the place of registration or main business of a company. Moreover, the unilateral party autonomy granted to the consumer is based on the presumption that the parties can hardly reach an agreement after the occurrence of the dispute. In judicial practice, the consumer and the business may reach a choice of law agreement after the dispute arises.

As to the manner of the parties' choice, Article 3 of the Chinese Conflict of Laws Act states that the parties' choice of law must be made in an explicit manner. How

[108] Zhuang (2020), p. 31.

[109] Zhuang (2020), p. 31.

[110] Yang (2012), p. 119.

[111] Xia (2013), pp. 123–128; 夏雨：《涉外旅游合同法律适用规则探析》，《旅游学刊》，2013年第5期，第123–128页。

to interpret the wording 'explicit' is an issue.[112] The requirement of a contract being in written form has been abolished in China, as a contract may be made in writing, in an oral conversation, or in any other form.[113] In judicial practice, the parties who did not select the law applicable to their contract may invoke the law of the same country and neither has raised any objection to the choice of law. Whether such a choice constitutes an 'explicit' manner is a question. In terms of package travel contracts, most disputes involve a Chinese tour operator and a Chinese tourist who travels abroad; the parties may invoke the law of the same country, usually Chinese law, without any objection. The judges intend to confirm the validity of such a choice of law.

In *Liu Peilong v Kunming Kanghui Yonghui Travel Agency* case,[114] the plaintiff was an American citizen, and the accident happened in Thailand. The parties unanimously agreed to choose Chinese law as the applicable law to settle the dispute. The court referred to Article 41 of the Chinese Conflict of Laws Act to justify bilateral party autonomy and apply the parties' chosen law. The same goes for *Weihong v Xi'an Diyawei Tourism Project Development Co.*,[115] a Hong Kong-related (timeshare) contract dispute, in which the court respected the contractual parties' party autonomy by applying the law chosen by the party (Chinese mainland law) in accordance with Article 41 of the Chinese Conflict of Laws Act. It can be seen that in the absence of two-sided party autonomy in consumer choice of law rules under Article 42 of the Chinese Conflict of Laws Act, the courts have to resort to general contract choice of law rules in Article 41 of the Chinese Conflict of Laws Act to justify the application of the law chosen by the parties.

When it comes to package travel contracts, especially those in which a Chinese travel operator organizes Chinese tourists to travel abroad and a lawsuit is initiated in China after the tourist returns home, parties in many cases may reach an agreement on the applicable law after the dispute arises, namely Chinese law. Such a bilateral choice may correspond to the reasonable expectations of both parties and relieve the burden of ascertaining a foreign law for the parties and the court.[116] However, this bilateral party autonomy is not currently justified under the existing consumer choice of law rules, which explicitly limit the right to choose the applicable law to the consumer. The existence of bilateral party autonomy in judicial practice shows the need to embrace bilateral party autonomy. Nevertheless, whether

---

[112] He (2014), p. 165.

[113] He (2014), p. 165.

[114] *Liu Peilong v Kunming Kanghui Yonghui Travel Agency*, Kunming Railway IPC, (2017) Yun 71 Min Zhong No 11.

[115] *Weihong v Xian Diyawei Tourism Project Development Co., Ltd*, Shaanxi Province Xi'an Municipality IPC, (2017) Shan 01 Min Chu No 977.

[116] Due to heavy workload and higher requirement on qualification for the judges in China, there is a tendency to apply the forum law in judicial practice. After all, no matter how knowledgeable a judge is over his home law, he is always a beginner for a foreign law. Zhuang (2020), p. 28; Posner (1989), pp. 431–454.

the law chosen in a standard form contract can be considered as the result of exercising bilateral party autonomy remains a question.

In the context of the Internet and the digital economy, a consumer may already make a choice of applicable law by clicking 'agree' or 'accept' before concluding contracts with an operator,[117] often without knowing the legal consequences of their unconscious agreement. In judicial practice, judges might argue that the consumer has made a unilateral choice when signing the contract and, therefore, apply the law specified in the standard clause.[118] This means that unilateral party autonomy might be used to the disadvantage of the consumer. Similarly, the validity of bilateral party autonomy in the context of digital contracts is also questionable, considering that a consumer may not express his or her true intention via a click-wrap contract unilaterally provided by an operator.[119] The advantage of adopting two-sided party autonomy is that the court does not have to examine whether the business has engaged in relevant commercial activities in the consumer's country of habitual residence. However, the drawback is that the court needs to evaluate the validity of choice of law clauses. As to how to examine the validity of dispute resolution clauses, including choice of court clauses and choice of law clauses, please refer to the discussion in Chap. 9 on the validity of choice of court agreements.

5.5 Bilateral Party Autonomy and (Overriding) Mandatory Provisions

If Article 42 of the Chinese Conflict of Laws Act adopts bilateral party autonomy in the applicable law of consumer contracts, such exercise of party autonomy should be limited to prevent abuse.[120] Apart from limiting the material scope of the chosen law, this can be achieved by limiting the validity of the choice of law to prevent businesses from choosing the law with a lower level of consumer protection.[121] Many countries which do not limit the material scope of the chosen law do impose limitation on the validity of the chosen law through the mandatory provisions of the consumer's home law.[122] This means that if the law chosen by the parties provides more protection for consumers, it will take precedence. Consumer contracts are governed by a combination of the law chosen by the parties and the mandatory rules

[117] Wang (2021a), p. 27.

[118] Wang (2021a), p. 27.

[119] Wang (2021a), p. 24.

[120] Liu (2008), p. 314; 刘益灯，《跨国消费者保护的法律冲突及其解决对策》，法律出版社，2008年，第314页; Wang (2021b), p. 19.

[121] Yang (2012), p. 119.

[122] Countries include South Korea, Japan, Bulgaria, Liechtenstein, Ukraine, and Russia. Yang (2012), p. 118.

in the law of the consumer's habitual residence.[123] The consumer protection standard provided under the mandatory rules of the law of the consumer's habitual residence is the bottom line and ensures the minimum level of protection.[124]

Although Article 42 of the Chinese Conflict of Laws Act also aims to shield consumers from adverse consequences of a choice of law. It does not adopt the more favorable law approach by limiting the exercise of party autonomy through the mandatory provisions of the consumer's home law. Due to information or knowledge gaps, not all consumers will make an informed and rational choice of applicable law. If a consumer is unaware of certain mandatory provisions of the law of his or her home country, or if a business deliberately misleads the consumer, whether the mandatory provisions of the consumer's home law should apply if the chosen law undermines the mandatory protection afforded by the consumer's home law? Furthermore, at the heart of this question, it remains unclear whether provisions protecting consumer rights can be considered as mandatory provisions in Chinese private international law. If the answer is affirmative, another further question arises as to whether consumers not covered by protective consumer choice of law rules can invoke a protective provision via overriding mandatory provisions.

5.5.1 The Definition of Mandatory Provisions and Overriding Mandatory Provisions

In Chinese private international law, the definition of mandatory provisions is vague and its distinction with overriding mandatory provisions is blurry. To determine whether provisions protecting consumers can be qualified as mandatory provisions, it is necessary to first draw a clear distinction between these two definitions. Mandatory rules typically have two different types, domestic mandatory rules, which cannot be derogated by the parties' through their agreement, and international mandatory rules, also known as overriding mandatory rules, which override the effect of conflicts rules.[125]

Article 4 of the Chinese Conflict of Laws Act states that if there are mandatory provisions on foreign-related civil relations in Chinese law, these provisions shall apply directly. This application is mandatory and applies regardless of the law chosen by the parties, making them overriding mandatory provisions.[126] Article 8 of the SPC Judicial Interpretation of the Chinese Conflict of Laws Act further elaborates on what constitutes overriding mandatory provisions. Provisions involving employee

---

[123] Yang (2012), p. 118.

[124] Yang (2012), p. 118.

[125] Tang et al. (2016), p. 241, para. 8.85; The expression 'mandatory rules' which designates both concepts may cause confusion.

[126] Wang (2015), p. 25; 王立武，《国际私法的强制性规则适用制度研究》，中国人民大学出版社，2015年，第25页。

protection, food safety, environmental safety, financial safety, and anti-monopoly or anti-dumping measures, are expressly considered as overriding mandatory provisions under Article 8 and must apply directly without relying on the guidance of conflicts rules.

However, there appears to be a contradiction in the concept of 'mandatory rule' and its material scope as prescribed in Article 8 of the SPC Judicial Interpretation of the 2010 Chinese Conflict of Laws Act is self-contradictory. On one hand, it states that mandatory provisions apply directly without the need to refer to choice of law rules. This holds true for provisions related to foreign currency control and anti-monopoly or anti-dumping measures. On the other hand, it includes provisions related to the protection of employees, food security, and environment, which may also be subject to the choice of law rules in Article 42 (on employee contracts), Article 45 (on product liability), and Article 44 (on tort liability) of the 2010 Chinese Conflict of Laws Act respectively. This means that these provisions are not applicable directly without reference to choice of law rules, but apply as domestic mandatory rules. Therefore, the term 'mandatory rules' used in Article 4 of the Chinese Conflict of Laws Act and Article 8 of the SPC Judicial Interpretation of the Conflict of Laws Act encompasses both domestic mandatory rules and international mandatory rules. Given that the material scope of overriding mandatory provisions is clearly narrower than that of mandatory provisions, it is necessary to distinguish mandatory provisions from overriding mandatory provisions.

Overriding mandatory provisions, which are designed to safeguard a nation's economic or social order, designate a specific law for a particular legal relationship and do not permit the parties to choose their governing law.[127] These provisions seek to uphold the public interests or public policy of a nation, rather than protecting the interests of a specific group of people.[128] Although Chinese Labour Law prioritizes the protection of employees, it does not mean that Chinese law provides a better or the best protection to employees compared to the laws of other countries.[129] Consequently, the mandatory application of Chinese law may not always be advisable. Provisions related to employee contracts should be classified as protective mandatory provisions rather than overriding mandatory provisions.

[127] Wan (2011), p. 33; 万鄂湘主编,《〈中华人民共和国涉外民事关系法律适用法〉条文理解与适用》，中国法制出版社, 2011年版，第33页。

[128] Liu and Hu (2012), p. 44.

[129] Liu and Hu (2012), p. 44.

5.5.2 Provisions Protecting Employees or Consumers as Domestic Mandatory Provisions

The application of mandatory provisions is not just a choice of law rule, but also reflects a doctrine in which a country intervenes in the exercise of party autonomy by the contracting parties.[130] Some substantive provisions tend to provide more protection to the weaker contracting parties in order to strike a balance of interests between both parties, which constitute protective mandatory provisions or semi-overriding mandatory provisions.[131]

Under Article 8 of the SPC Judicial Interpretation of the Chinese Conflict of Laws Act, provisions protecting employees are considered overriding mandatory provisions. This means that party autonomy is not allowed, as these provisions have direct applicability. However, not all rules protecting employees are considered overriding mandatory rules. Some are simply mandatory in a domestic context and can be replaced by applicable foreign law.[132] For instance, provisions in Chinese Labour Contract Law that cover probation,[133] minimum wage standards,[134] and contractual penalties[135] are considered protective mandatory provisions or semi-overriding mandatory provisions in China.[136] If the parties in an employee contract choose to apply a foreign law which provides higher levels of protection to employees, such as a higher minimum salary, the chosen law shall apply.[137] Article 43 of the Chinese Conflict of Laws Act on employee choice of law rules also allows for the application of the law of the employee's workplace, the law of the place of the employer's main business, or the law of the dispatching place. The existence of Article 43 Chinese Conflict of Laws Act itself is evidence of the somewhat self-contradictory concept of 'mandatory rules' used in Article 43 Chinese Conflict of Laws Act and Article 8 of the SPC Judicial Interpretation of the Chinese Conflict of Laws Act. Therefore, it is essential to distinguish between (domestic) mandatory provisions, such as those involving employee protection, and overriding

[130] Wang (2015), p. 1; Michaels (2017), p. 421. A choice of law in contracts between parties with unequal bargaining power (consumer, employees) cannot deprive the weaker party of the mandatory protection by the law otherwise applicable. The question is whether the laws should be compared in their entirety or with regard to the result of their application in the particular case, which resembles macro and micro comparison in comparative law.

[131] Xiao and Long (2012), p. 111; 肖永平、龙威狄:《论中国国际私法中的强制性规范》,《中国社会科学》, 2012年第10期, 第111页; Zhong (2009), p. 44; 钟瑞栋,《民法中的强制性规范》, 法律出版社, 2009, 第44页。

[132] Tang et al. (2016), p. 242, para. 8.87.

[133] Article 19 of the Labour Contract Law of the PRC.

[134] Article 20 of the Labour Contract Law of the PRC.

[135] Article 22(2) of the Labour Contract Law of the PRC.

[136] Zhong (2009), p. 45.

[137] It is noticeable that Article 43 of the Chinese Conflict of Laws Act does not allow the law chosen by the parties, since the exercise of bilateral party autonomy is not explicitly prescribed in this provision.

(international) mandatory provisions set forth in Article 8 of the SPC Judicial Interpretation of the Chinese Conflict of Laws Act. Otherwise, the ambiguity between these two concepts may lead to confusion and misunderstanding, resulting in the excessive application of Chinese law in many situations.[138]

Another debatable point regarding Article 8 of the SPC Judicial Interpretation of the Chinese Conflict of Laws Act is its failure to address provisions related to consumer protection. Both consumers in consumer contracts and employees in employee contracts are weaker contracting parties deserving of special protection.[139] While the policy of protecting weaker parties encompasses both consumers and employees,[140] only provisions related to the protection of employees are regarded as (overriding) mandatory provisions.[141] Whether consumer protection provisions can be regarded as 'other circumstances' in Article 8 of the SPC Judicial Interpretation of the Chinese Conflict of Laws Act remains a topic open for discussion.[142] The omission of consumer protection provisions as mandatory provisions in Chinese private international law is questionable. While it could be argued that some consumer protection provisions related to food safety or public health may be classified as international mandatory provisions under Article 8 of the SPC Judicial Interpretation of the 2010 Chinese Conflict of Laws Act, not all consumer contracts involve the provision of food. Consumer contracts providing services or goods other than food are clearly not covered in the material scope. Like employee provisions in the Chinese Labour Contract Law, certain provisions in the Chinese Consumer Protection Law are mandatory provisions.[143] As discussed earlier, provisions in employee contracts or consumer contracts are of a private nature, while provisions related to foreign currency control, anti-monopoly or anti-dumping measures are of a public nature. Hence, it is more reasonable to classify provisions protecting employees and consumers, who are typically perceived as weaker contracting parties, as domestic mandatory provisions, rather than international mandatory provisions. The exercise of bilateral party autonomy in consumer choice of law rules can be limited by virtue of mandatory provisions to ensure that consumers are not deprived of the protection offered by their home law.[144]

[138] Tang et al. (2016), p. 244, para. 8.91.

[139] Qu (2009), p. 9.

[140] Tu (2016), p. 102, para. 192.

[141] Article 8 of the SPC Judicial Interpretation of the Chinese Conflict of Laws Act.

[142] Tang (2015), pp. 58–61; 汤霞,《论消费者权益保护之规定纳入直接适用的法的可行性——兼评<涉外民事关系法律适用法>第42条》, 《公民与法:法学版》, 2015年第4期, 第58–61页。

[143] Du (2011), p. 334.

[144] Zhuang (2020), p. 33.

5.5.3 *Overriding Mandatory Provisions as a Safety Valve for Excluded Consumers or Consumer Contracts*

The fact that provisions protecting consumers should be regarded as domestic mandatory provisions does not mean international mandatory provisions have no role to play in ensuring consumer protection. Although the mandatory provisions of the consumer's habitual residence can apply by virtue of Article 42 of the Chinese Conflict of Laws Act, the problem is that not all consumers or consumer contracts are covered by this protective regime. The material scope of consumer contracts covered by Article 42 of the Chinese Conflict of Laws Act is limited to consumers targeted by businesses.

For consumers and consumer contracts not falling within the scope of Article 42 of the Chinese Conflict of Laws Act, general contract choice of law rules come into play.[145] If the targeting test is not fulfilled, consumer contracts shall be governed by the law of the place of provision of goods or services under Article 42 of the Chinese Conflict of Laws Act. In these two scenarios, the question arises whether a consumer can invoke the protective rules of a country through overriding mandatory provisions in Article 4 of the Chinese Conflict of Laws Act, which would otherwise not apply. To answer this question, it is crucial to determine whether provisions protecting consumers can be considered overriding mandatory provisions.

The overriding mandatory provisions in private international law exist in the fields of both public law and private law.[146] Some overriding mandatory provisions have a dual nature (half-public and half-private), combining elements of both public and private interest, but most of them have the public nature.[147] The distinction between public interest and private interest is not always crystal clear. Article 8 of the SPC Judicial Interpretation of the Chinese Conflict of Laws Act expressly states that provisions involving financial safety, such as foreign exchange control and anti-monopoly or anti-dumping measures are (overriding) mandatory provisions. While this clear inclusion offers legal certainty, it may lack flexibility. Although Article 10 also provides an umbrella clause to include other provisions that should be recognized as (overriding) mandatory provisions, it lacks specific criteria.

In China, opinions vary on whether provisions protecting consumers, such as those in the Chinese Consumer Protection Law, qualify as overriding mandatory provisions. One opinion holds that such provisions do not fall within the scope of overriding mandatory provisions.[148] Another opinion asserts that consumer protection laws, just like foreign currency regulations, fall within the material scope of

---

[145] Article 41 of the Chinese Conflict of Laws Act, which designates first the law chosen by both parties and second the law which has the closest connection with the contract or best reflects the characteristic performance of the contract.

[146] Huang and Jiang (2011), p. 23.

[147] Huang and Jiang (2011), p. 23. The development of overriding mandatory provisions in private international law reflects the tendency of transforming private law into public law.

[148] Du (2011), p. 64.

overriding mandatory provisions.[149] It is advocated that consumer contracts should first be subject to the mandatory provisions in Article 4 of the Chinese Conflict of Laws Act before applying consumer choice of law rules in Article 42.[150] Protective mandatory provisions aimed at protecting weaker contracting parties, such as consumers and employees, should not be entirely excluded from the scope of overriding mandatory provisions.[151]

For instance, a consumer in a transport contract is excluded from the protective regime in Article 42 of the Chinese Conflict of Laws Act. In substantive law, the carrier in a carriage contract shall help passengers facing acute illness, childbirth, or distress during transportation.[152] Such obligation to rescue is mandatory for the carrier.[153] Additionally, the carrier is liable for damages resulting from the passenger's injury or death during transportation, unless the injury or death can be attributed to the passenger's personal health issues or the carrier proves that the injury or death was caused by the passenger's intentional or gross negligence.[154] Transport contracts do not fall within the material scope of consumer choice of law rules in Article 42 of the Chinese Conflict of Laws Act. Still, passengers in transport contracts are consumers requiring special legal protection. Protecting consumer interests is a requirement of implementing social public policy and serves the interests of society at large.[155] If parties reach an agreement that the carrier assumes responsibility for compensation in cases of personal injury or death, even in instances of gross negligence by the passenger, such an agreement is valid since it is more favorable to the passengers.[156] However, if the carrier and the passenger reaches an agreement that the carrier is not liable for compensation as long as the carrier can prove it has no gross negligence, and this is clearly more favorable to the carrier and detrimental to the passenger, such an agreement should be invalid.[157] Whether such protective mandatory provisions can be classified as overriding mandatory provisions depends on a case-by-case analysis by the judge, guided by national policy considerations.[158]

---

[149] Huang and Jiang (2011), p. 21.

[150] Huang and Jiang (2011), p. 23.

[151] Xiao and Long (2012), p. 111.

[152] Article 301 of the Chinese Contract Law.

[153] Xu (2010), p. 281; 许中缘,《民法强行性规范研究》，法律出版社，2010，第281页。

[154] Article 302(1) of the Chinese Contract Law. It has been replaced by Article 823 of the Civil Code of the PRC, which took effect on 1 January 2021.

[155] Zhong (2009), p. 44.

[156] Zhong (2009), p. 44.

[157] Zhong (2009), p. 44.

[158] Xiao and Long (2012), p. 111; Chen (2024a), p. 34.

5.5.4 Provisions Protecting Food and Public Health as Overriding Mandatory Provisions

Article 8 of the SPC Judicial Interpretation of the Chinese Conflict of Laws Act states that: *In any of the following situations, the provisions of law or administrative regulations involving the social-public interests of the PRC, which the parties may not exclude from their application through agreement and which are directly applicable to a foreign-related civil relation without the guidance of Conflict of Laws Act, are to be recognized by the people's courts as the mandatory provisions specified in Article 4 of the Chinese Conflict of Laws Act*:

(1) where protection of the rights and interests of workers is involved;
(2) where safety of food and public health is involved;
(3) where environmental safety is involved;
(4) where financial safety, such as foreign exchange control, is involved;
(5) where anti-monopoly or anti-dumping are involved; or
(6) other situations that should be recognized as mandatory provisions.[159]

Notably, Article 8(2) of the SPC Judicial Interpretation of the Chinese Conflict of Laws Act specifically mentions that provisions involving safety of food and public health (涉及食品或公共卫生安全的) can be classified as overriding mandatory provisions and apply directly without referring to choice of law rule. Although this provision does not explicitly refer to consumer contracts, disputes over the safety of food and public health could arise out of consumer contracts. The food poisoning case in *Li Lijun v. Guangzhou Yiyan Jiuding Catering Co., Ltd., et al*[160] serves as an example of disputes concerning food safety. Typical cases involving food safety issues published by the High People's Court of Hubei Province in 2024 include poisonous and harmful soybean products, weight loss drugs and coffee, beverages, and rice noodle rolls.[161] The Supreme People's Procuratorate, the State Administration

[159] The original text in Chinese reads as follows. 最高人民法院关于适用《中华人民共和国涉外民事关系法律适用法》若干问题的解释(一)第八条:有下列情形之一，涉及中华人民共和国社会公共利益、当事人不能通过约定排除适用、无需通过冲突规范指引而直接适用于涉外民事关系的法律、行政法规的规定，人民法院应当认定为涉外民事关系法律适用法第四条规定的强制性规定:
(一)涉及劳动者权益保护的;
(二)涉及食品或公共卫生安全的;
(三)涉及环境安全的;
(四)涉及外汇管制等金融安全的;
(五)涉及反垄断、反倾销的;
(六)应当认定为强制性规定的其他情形。

[160] *Li Lijun v. Guangzhou Yiyan Jiuding Catering Co., Ltd., et al,* Guangdong Province Guangzhou Municipality Intermediate People's Court, [2015] Hui Zhong Fa MIn Si Zhong Zi No 134; Guangdong Province Guangzhou Municipality Panyu District People's Court, [2015] Hui Pan Fa MIn Si Chu Zi No 12.

[161] Hubei Provincial High People's Court Releases Typical Cases of Food Safety Criminal Offenses (湖北省高级人民法院发布涉食品安全犯罪典型案例), http://hubeigy.hbfy.gov.cn/article/detail/2024/11/id/8212099.shtml, accessed on Jan 23, 2024.

for Market Regulation and the State Food and Drug Administration jointly released 15 typical cases involving issues of food and drug safety.[162] These cases involve selling expired, toxic, or harmful drugs, food, drinks and makeups, or those mixed with toxic and harmful non-food ingredients or additives, or cosmetics that do not meet hygiene standards. Although most of them are criminal or administrative cases, some cases also involve civil public interest litigation.

When it comes to consumer disputes in food and drug safety, each individual consumer contract which is supposed to involve only private interests between the parties may concern public interest. In another case involving food safety, when no individuals filed lawsuit, People's Procuratorate may initiate public interests litigation. For instance, a breakfast shop, selling buns, steamed bread, and fried dough sticks, operated by a person named Li in Lvchun County, was found through testing to have food items containing excessive chlorine elements. This seriously infringed on the health rights of unspecified majority of consumers (严重侵害了不特定多数人的健康权利). Given no organization or individual had initiated a civil public interest lawsuit, the Lvchun County People's Procuratorate filed a criminal case with civil public interest litigation (刑事附带民事公益诉讼) to protect consumers' legitimate rights and social public interests (为了维护广大消费者合法权益和保护社会公共利益).[163] This case concerns the application of Article 148 (2) of the Food Safety Law of PRC. Although this purely domestic case does not involve a foreign element and the application of a foreign law, it implies that if a consumer contract involves food safety, Article 148 (2) of the Food Safety Law may directly apply as overriding mandatory provisions.

For instance, if a foreign business target consumers in China and the food, drinks, cosmetics or drugs provided by that foreign business harmed the interests of unspecified majority of consumers (侵害了不特定多数消费者的利益), endangered personal safety of the public (危及社会公众的人身安全), and damaged social public interests (损害了社会公共利益), provisions protecting the food and drug safety of consumers, such as Article 148 (2) of the Food Safety Law, may have direct applicability as overriding mandatory provisions.

Although Article 8(2) of the SPC Judicial Interpretation of the Chinese Conflict of Laws Act does not explicitly mention consumer contracts, consumer contracts concerning food and drug provision may have been indirectly covered in this provision. If this is the case, why not establish a separate provision to cover consumer contracts, similar to how employee contracts are covered under Article 8(1) of the SPC Judicial Interpretation of the Chinese Conflict of Laws Act? In terms of safeguarding food and drug safety, protective mandatory provisions aimed at protecting consumers and offering relevant remedies and compensations could qualify as

[162] Typical cases of special actions to implement the "four most stringent" requirements for food and drug safety (落实食品药品安全"四个最严"要求专项行动典型案例), https://www.gov.cn/xinwen/2021-02/19/content_5587696.htm, accessed on Jan 23, 2024.

[163] Lvchun County: First Food Safety Criminal Case with Civil Public Interest Litigation was Heard Publicly (绿春县:首例涉食品领域刑事附带民事公益诉讼案公开审理), https://www.hhlc.gov.cn/info/3621/179491.htm, accessed on Jan 24, 2024.

overriding mandatory provisions. For instance, the 2008 melamine-tainted milk scandal and the 2018 vaccine scandal discussed in Chap. 2 on the classification of professional fake-fighters[164] highlight the public interests in protecting individual consumers. Private international law in China could play a role in safeguarding public interests in food and drug safety by expressly include consumer contracts in Article 8 of the SPC Judicial Interpretation of the Chinese Conflict of Laws Act. This can be done by establishing a new provision or including consumers in the existing provisions. For instance, Article 8(1) of the SPC Judicial Interpretation of the Chinese Conflict of Laws Act can be revised slightly as "*where protection of the rights and interests of workers or consumers is involved*". This could also include consumer disputes over provision of services, such as travel and tourism services, while public interests may also be involved.

5.5.5 Mandatory and Overriding Mandatory Provisions as Double Insurances in Consumer Protection

If Article 8(1) of the SPC Judicial Interpretation of the Chinese Conflict of Laws Act has changed to "*where protection of the rights and interests of workers or consumers is involved*", the question of how to apply mandatory and overriding mandatory provisions to protect consumers may arise. In short, mandatory and overriding mandatory provisions can act as double insurances in consumer protection,[165] depending on whether the targeting test and other conditions to apply Article 42 of the Chinese Conflict of Laws Act have been met.

Mandatory provisions apply to restrict the parties's choice of law when the targeting test and other conditions are met. When the targeting test other conditions are not met, excluded consumer contracts under Article 42 of the Chinese Conflict of Laws Act may still be protected by the mandatory provisions of the consumer's home law by virtue of overriding mandatory provisions. This can make sure that the public interests in consumer disputes over provision of goods or services will be protected.

5.6 Conclusions

The connecting factors set out in Article 42 of the Chinese Conflict of Laws Act are limited to two types: the place of the consumer's habitual residence and the place of the provision of goods or services. Under Article 42 of the Chinese Conflict of Laws

[164] These two cases involve defective products and faulty vaccines that affect the health of thousands of children in China.

[165] Chen (2024a), pp. 15–34.

Act, a consumer contract is governed either by the law of the consumer's habitual residence or the law of the place of provision of goods or services. Such limitations are overly rigid and may lead to no applicable law or a law having no substantial connection to the case. If these connecting factors happen to be in the same country, it means that the consumer has no choice, as the law of the consumer's habitual residence and the place of provision of goods or services applies anyway, regardless of the targeting test or dis targeting-test. This leaves no room for the application of the law of another country which may also have a close connection to the consumer dispute. If the exercise of party autonomy has to be limited to the consumer, it becomes necessary to introduce more flexible connecting factors, such as the law of the business' domicile, the law of the consumer's domicile, or the law of the conclusion of the contract.

Granting unilateral party autonomy solely to the consumer is a matter of debate. The consent of the business party should also be taken into account. While this one-sided party autonomy granted to the consumer aims to protect consumers as weaker parties, such a one-sided choice of law may not necessarily protect consumers in terms of their substantive rights due to the limited scope of applicable law the consumer can choose. This strict limitation may not adequately address the increasingly complex cross-border consumer disputes. Allowing for two-sided party autonomy could provide more choices for both consumers and businesses, corresponding to the reasonable expectations of both parties in certain situations. Article 56 of the Proposal Draft and Explanation of the Chinese Conflict of Laws Act expressly adopted two-sided party autonomy in consumer contracts and only limited the material scope of the chosen law with the connection criterion. It is necessary for Article 42 of the Chinese Conflict of Laws Act to embrace bilateral party autonomy. This approach can also ease the burden on consumers in ascertaining foreign laws under unilateral party autonomy.

There is a lack of interaction between special consumer choice of law rules in Article 42 of the Chinese Conflict of Laws Act and general contract choice of law rules in Article 41 Chinese Conflict of Laws Act. Since the law of the place of provision of goods or services does not always have the closest connection with the consumer contract in all circumstances, applying such a law may not align with the consumer's expectations in certain cases. Instead, if the targeting test is not fulfilled, it may be more advisable to apply general contract choice of law rules to determine the applicable law, rather than strictly applying the law of the place of provision of goods or services as a default rule.[166]

If Article 42 of the Chinese Conflict of Laws Act were to embrace bilateral party autonomy, both mandatory and overriding mandatory provisions could play a role and function as double insurance in terms of consumer protection. Currently, mandatory provisions do not play a role in consumer protection under Article 42 of the Chinese Conflict of Laws Act. Provisions protecting consumers should be considered mandatory provisions and could be used to limit the exercise of party

[166] Chen (2024b), pp. 73–77.

autonomy in China. Provisions protecting employees are classified as overriding mandatory provisions under Article 8 of the SPC Judicial Interpretation of the 2010 Chinese Conflict of Laws Act, which is questionable. There is a need to draw a distinction between mandatory and overriding mandatory provisions in China. Provisions protecting weaker parties, such as employees and consumers, are domestic mandatory provisions, instead of international mandatory provisions. Nonetheless, excluded consumers or consumer contracts under Article 42 of the Chinese Conflict of Laws Act may still be protected by the mandatory provisions of the consumer's home law by virtue of overriding mandatory provisions. To this end, Article 8(1) of the SPC Judicial Interpretation of the Chinese Conflict of Laws Act can be revised slightly as "*where protection of the rights and interests of workers or consumers is involved*". This would cover consumer disputes over provision of goods or services, while public interests may also be involved.

References

Barnhizer DD (2005) Inequality of bargaining power. Univ Colorado Law Rev 76:139–241

Chen Z (2021) Tort conflicts rules in cross-border multi-party litigation: which law has the closer or the closest connection? Maastricht J Eur Comp Law 5:626–647

Chen Z (2022) Jurisdiction and choice of law rules over electronic consumer contracts: the nexus between the concluded contract and the targeting activity. Maastricht J Eur Comp Law 3:406

Chen Z (2023) Internet, consumer contracts and private international law: what constitutes targeting activity test. Inf Commun Technol Law 1:23–44

Chen Z (2024a) Mandatory and overriding mandatory provisions as double insurances in consumer protection. Eur Law Rev 49:15–34

Chen Z (2024b) Consumer jurisdiction and choice of law rules in European and Chinese private international law. Chin J Transnatl Law 1:73–77

Du T (2011) Comments on Chinese Conflict of Laws Act. China Legal Publishing House, p 58; 杜涛,《涉外民事关系法律适用法释评》，中国法制出版社 2011 年版，第58页。

Fan X (2014) The law applicable to EU financial consumer contracts. Int Law Rev Wuhan Univ 16:225; 范晓亮,《欧盟金融消费者合同法律适用规则研究》，《武大国际法评论》，2014年第16卷第2期，第225页。

Fang J (2013) Research on the closest connection principle. Comp Law Res 2:110–116; 方杰,《最密切联系原则考证》,《比较法研究》, 2013年第2期，第110–116页。

Guo Y (2011) Legislative reflection and improvement of China's private international law—focusing on the law applicable to foreign-related civil relations. Tsinghua Univ Law J 5:155–167; 郭玉军,《中国国际私法的立法反思及其完善-以<涉外民事关系法律适用法>为中心》，《清华法学》, 2011 年第5期，第155–167页。

Han D (2007) International private law. Higher Education Press, p 96; 韩德培主编:《国际私法》，高等教育出版社2007年版，第96页。

Han D, Xiao Y (2014) Private international law, 3rd edn. Higher Education Press, pp 153–154; 韩德培、肖永平,《国际私法》(第三版)，高等教育出版社，2014年，第153–154页。

He Q (2014) Recent developments of new Chinese private international law with regard to contracts. In: Basedow J, Pissler KB (eds) Private international law in Mainland China, Taiwan and Europe. Mohr Siebeck, p 165

Hong L, Zong X (2014) Theory and practice of private international law. China Legal Publishing House, pp 282–283; 洪莉萍，宗绪志,《国际私法理论与实践探索》，中国法制出版社，2014年，第282–283页。

Huang W (2017) Provisions on the application of laws to foreign-related consumer contracts in China. Master's thesis, Huazhong Normal University, p 31; 黄文秀,《论我国关于涉外消费者合同法律适用之规定》, 华中师范大学硕士论文, 2017年, 第31页。

Huang J, Jiang R (2011) Understanding act of the PRC on the application of laws over foreign-related civil relationships. Law Press China, p 233; 黄进、姜茹娇,《〈中华人民共和国涉外民事关系法律适用法〉释义与分析》, 法律出版社, 2011年, 第233页。

Jiang W (2019) Research on the application of law for international consumer contracts. Zhengzhou University, p 30; 江威,《涉外消费者合同法律适用问题研究》, 郑州大学硕士论文, 2019, 第30页。

Liu Y (2005) Research on the legal system of international consumer protection. China Fangzheng Press, p 234; 刘益灯,《国际消费者保护法律制度研究》, 中国方正出版社, 2005, 第234页。

Liu Y (2008) The conflict of laws and its solution of the international consumer protection. Law Press China, p 314; 刘益灯,《跨国消费者保护的法律冲突及其解决对策》, 法律出版社, 2008年, 第314页。

Liu X, Hu D (2012) Several issues arising from the judicial practice related to the "Law of Application of Law for Foreign-related Civil Relations of the People's Republic of China". Chin Yearb Priv Int Law Comp Law 15:42; 刘晓红, 胡荻,《论我国〈涉外民事关系法律适用法〉的若干实践困境》,《中国国际私法与比较法年刊》, 2012年第15卷, 第42页。

Ma Z (2016) The legislative improvement of the closest connection principle in China. Contemp Law Rev 6:15–23; 马志强:《最密切联系原则在中国的立法完善》,《当代法学》2016年第6期, 第15–23页。

Michaels R (2017) Comparative law and private international law. In: Basedow J et al (eds) Encyclopedia of private international law. Edward Elgar Publishing, p 421

Posner RA (1989) Legislation and its interpretation: a primer. Nebraska Law Rev 68:431–454

Qu B (2009) The protection of the interests of weaker parties in private international law. Law Press China, p 8; 曲波,《 国际私法本体下弱者利益的保护问题》, 法律出版社, 2009年, 第8页。

Rosler H (2010) Protection of the weaker party in European contract law: standardized and individual inferiority in multi-level private law. Eur Rev Priv Law 18:729

Rühl G (2011) Consumer protection in choice of law. Cornell Int Law J 44:569

Symeonides SC (2019) The scope and limits of party autonomy in international contracts: a comparative analysis, p 3. https://ssrn.com/abstract=3359988

Tang Z (2007) Parties' choice of law in E-consumer contracts. J Priv Int Law 3:113–136

Tang Z (2009) Electronic consumer contracts in the conflicts of laws. Hart, pp 8–11

Tang X (2015) On the feasibility of incorporating the provisions of consumer protection into overriding mandatory provisions. Citizens Law 4:58–61; 汤霞,《论消费者权益保护之规定纳入直接适用的法的可行性——兼评<涉外民事关系法律适用法>第42条》,《公民与法:法学版》, 2015年第4期, 第58–61页。

Tang Z et al (2016) Conflict of laws in the People's Republic of China. Edward Elgar Publishing, p 233

Tian J (2021) Discussion on issues and suggestions on jurisdiction over online shopping contract disputes. Legal Expo 3:15; 田静怡:《网络购物合同纠纷管辖权的问题与建议探讨》,《法制博览》, 2021年3月, 第15页。

Tu G (2011) Interpretation of the law on the application of laws for foreign-related civil relations. Contemp Jurisprud 2:11–23; 涂广建:《解读我国涉外民事关系法律适用法〉》,《时代法学》, 2011年第2期, 第11–23页。

Tu G (2016) Private international law in China. Springer, p 102, para. 193

Wan X (2011) Interpretation and application of provisions of the Chinese Conflict of Laws Act. China Legal Publishing House, p 33; 万鄂湘主编,《〈中华人民共和国涉外民事关系法律适用法〉条文理解与适用》, 中国法制出版社, 2011年版, 第33页。

Wang L (2014) On the application of mandatory rules in private international law. China Renmin University Press, p 82; 王立武,《国际私法的强制性规则适用制度研究》, 中国人民大学出版社年 2014 版, 第 82 页。

Wang L (2015) On the application of mandatory rules of law in private international law. China Renmin University Press, p 25; 王立武，《国际私法的强制性规则适用制度研究》，中国人民大学出版社，2015年，第25页。
Wang Q (2018) Discussion on the protection mechanism of overseas tourist-consumer rights—based on the perspective of the law applicable to foreign-related civil relations. J Jiujiang Univ (Soc Sci Ed) 1:103–106; 王群,《海外旅游消费者权利保护机制探讨—基于<涉外民事关系法律适用法>视角》，《九江学院学报(社会科学版)》，2018年第1期，第103–106页。
Wang F (2021a) Research on the application of law for foreign-related consumer contracts. Yanshan University, p 30; 王芳,《涉外消费者合同的法律适用研究》，燕山大学硕士论文, 2021年, 第30页。
Wang X (2021b) Study on the law applicable to foreign-related online consumer contract. Anhui University of Finance & Economics, p 19; 王璇:《我国涉外网络消费者合同的法律适用研究》，安徽财经大学硕士论文，2021年, 第19页
Weng Y (2014) Legal protection of foreign-related consumer rights—comments on Article 42 of the Chinese Conflict of Laws Act. Fujian Leg Sci 2:76; 翁玉真,《涉外消费权益的法律保护——兼评我国〈涉外民事关系法律适用法〉第 42 条 》，《福建法学》2014 年第 2 期，第 76 页。
Xia Y (2010) On the deficiency and construction of the international tourism legal system in China. Wuhan Univ J (Philos Soc Sci) 3:418; 夏雨:《论我国国际旅游法律制度的缺失与构建——以和平崛起为视角》，《武汉大学学报(哲学社会科学版)》，2010年第3期，第418页。
Xia Y (2013) Analysis on the law applicable to foreign-related tourism contracts. J Tour 5:123–128; 夏雨: 《涉外旅游合同法律适用规则探析》，《旅游学刊》，2013年第5期，第123–128页。
Xiao Y (2008) Conflict of laws from a jurisprudence perspective. Higher Education Press, p 187; 肖永平,《法理学视野下的冲突法》，高等教育出版社, 2008年版，第187页。
Xiao Y (2017) Enhancing international credibility of Chinese judiciary: the tongs to jointly promote the BRI. Int Law Rev Wuhan Univ 1:16. 肖永平,《提升中国司法的国际公信力:共建"一带一路" 的抓手》，《武大国际法评论》，2017年第1卷第1期，第16页。
Xiao Y, Long W (2012) Mandatory provisions in Chinese private international law. China Acad J 10:111; 肖永平、 龙威狄:《论中国国际私法中的强制性规范》，《中国社会科学》，2012年第10期, 第111页。
Xu D (2004) Humanitarian care and the protection of the interests of the weak parties in international private law. Contemp Law Rev 5:18; 徐冬根，《人文关怀与国际私法中弱者利益保护》,《当代法学》, 2004年第5期，第18页。
Xu J (2006) Party autonomy in private international law. Law Press, pp 188–189; 许军珂: 《国际私法上的意思自治》, 法律出版社，2006年，第188–189页。
Xu Z (2010) Study on mandatory rules in civil law. Law Press China, p 281; 许中缘，《民法强行性规范研究》，法律出版社，2010，第281页。
Xu W (2013) Application of the principle of party autonomy over choice of law in China. Leg Sci 9:24–34; 徐伟功,《法律选择中的意思自治原则在我国的运用》，《法学》，2013年第9期，第24–34页。
Yang Y (2012) The law applicable to consumer contracts involving foreign elements in China. J Chongqing Technol Bus Univ (Soc Sci Ed) 2:119; 杨月萍:《论我国涉外消费者合同的法律适用及其完善》，《重庆工商大学学报(社会科学版)》，2012年第1期，第119页。
Yu Y (2011) Analysis of Article 42 of the Law on the application of laws in foreign-related civil relations - protection of consumers under Chinese private international law. Law Rev 2:65–70. 于颖:《〈涉外民事关系法律适用法〉第42条评析-我国国际私法对消费者之保护》，《法学评论》，2011年第2期，第65–70页。
Zhong R (2009) Mandatory provision in Chinese civil law. Law Press China, p 44; 钟瑞栋,《民法中的强制性规范》，法律出版社，2009，第44页。
Zhuang Y (2020) Research on the application of laws concerning foreign tourism disputes in China. Shandong University, p 29; 庄允,《我国涉外旅游纠纷法律适用问题研究》，山东大学硕士学位论文，2020年，第29页。

Chapter 6
Conclusions

6.1 Who Is a Consumer?

6.1.1 Combining the Negative and Positive Definition of Consumer?

A clear notion of consumer or consumer contract and the material scope of consumer protective rules may enhance consumer protection as well as increase legal certainty with regard to the application of consumer jurisdiction and choice of law rules. China adopts a positive definition of consumer. What is the meaning of 'a person' and 'daily consumption need' has been discussed in Chap. 2. In principle, the Chinese notion of consumer only covers natural persons. As an exception, certain categories of small or micro businesses, such as agricultural workers, are included. The notion of consumer in Chinese Consumer Protection Law expressly protects farmers as consumers. Although Article 2 of the 2016 Regulation for the Implementation of the Chinese Consumer Protection Law implies that legal persons or other organizations that purchase or use goods or receive services not for making a profit may also be protected as consumers, the notion of consumer in Chinese private international law shall not be construed in exactly the same meaning as that in substantive law. The term 'daily consumption needs' in China can be construed as meeting a person's 'personal, family or household needs'. In terms of the notion of consumer, a combination of negative and positive definition of consumer is proposed. Accordingly, a consumer may be defined as '*a natural person who, acting outside his or her trade or profession, concludes a contract with another person, acting within his or her trade or profession, for the purpose of private, household, family consumption*'.

Z. Chen, *Tourists, Consumer Contracts and Private International Law in China*, Ius Gentium: Comparative Perspectives on Law and Justice 123, https://doi.org/10.1007/978-3-031-87915-9_6

6.1.2 What Elements are Relevant to Determine Consumer Status?

How are the terms 'outside of his trade or profession' and 'daily consumption need' interpreted in relation to consumer status? Are factors the amount of money involved, the regularity of the activity, the economic gain or the risk of financial loss relevant? Chapter 2 concludes that factors such as transaction volume and economic gain are irrelevant to determine a person's consumer status in China. Whether the consumption involves luxury goods/services or a person is acting for the purpose of making a profit is not relevant to determine whether a person is qualified as a consumer in China. Professional consumers, such as private investors and consumer activists, should be protected as consumers. Professional fake-fighters are protected as consumers, provided they do not purchase goods for resale or business purposes and do not file malicious complaints or lawsuits. However, the experience of a person and the regularity of activities might be relevant to determine whether a person is a consumer. If a fake-fighter's frequency of purchasing goods and the volume clearly exceed the reasonable amounts of daily consumption, he may be disqualified as a consumer. Because of the complexity of real-life transactions, the question of who qualifies as a consumer is subject to further discussion and clarification.

6.1.3 Is a Dual-Purpose Contract Qualified as Consumer Contract?

For dual purpose contracts in which a person is acting partly outside her trade or profession and partly within her trade or profession, the main question arises as to are dual purpose contracts considered consumer contracts, and what criteria are used to determine this. Chinese courts tend to interpret dual purpose contracts more broadly by examining the primary purpose of the contract, evidenced by two cases analyzed in Chap. 2. Accordingly, the primary purpose of contract should be decisive in determining the legal nature of a dual purpose contract. In terms of multi-party litigation in which different parties have different purposes while concluding a contract, is the nature of the contract subject to separability? In China, the nature of the contract in multi-party litigation is not subject to separability. The primary purpose of one party may trump the accessary purpose of other parties.

Having considered national and international definitions of consumer, the notion of consumer in Article 42 of the 2010 Chinese Conflict of Laws Act (or Article 2 of the Consumer Protection Law) may combine the positive definition and negative definition by defining a consumer as '*a natural person who, acting outside his or her trade or profession, concludes a contract with another person, acting within his or her trade or profession, primarily for the purpose of private, household, family consumption*'.

6.1.4 Should the Assessment of Consumer Status Be Based on Static or Dynamic approach?

In principle, whether a person is qualified as a consumer should be examined on the basis of the objective circumstances at the time of conclusion of the contract. Such static approach, or *ex ante* approach, may ensure legal certainty and predictability as well as protect professionals acting in good faith. However, given that a person may change the purpose after the conclusion of the contract, especially considering the emergence of new kinds of contacts which entail the performance of a continuing obligation (duration contracts), such as social network contracts, the *ex ante* approach is not always advisable. Such deviation contracts may require a deviation of the traditional *ex ante* approach and embrace the dynamic or *ex post* approach. A dynamic approach could be adopted as a secondary rule to examine whether the predominantly private purpose has been changed to predominately professional. In this regard, it is unclear whether Chinese law will also embrace the dynamic approach. Since a person may change the initial private purpose to professional purpose, or vice versa, after the conclusion of the contract, a dynamic approach, albeit secondary to the static approach, should be adopted in China in order to make sure that consumer choice of law rules only apply to the weaker party.

6.1.5 Are Package Travel Tourists Consumers?

Package travel contracts are not expressly included in the material scope of Article 42 of the Chinese Conflict of Laws Act. In Chapter 4, the judicial practice in China shows that the material scope of Chinese consumer choice of law rules is quite limited, since only some service contracts, sale contracts and loan contracts are protected as consumer contracts. Package travel contracts involving a foreign element are governed by general jurisdiction and choice of law rules. A distinction needs to be drawn between service contract, travel contract and package travel contract. Travel contracts and package travel contracts in essence are service contracts, but only some service contracts and travel contracts are classified as package travel contracts. Since package travel contracts are classified as nameless contracts, consumer choice of law rules are not applied. Article 111(3) of the Chinese Tourism Law defines package travel contracts. Although such definition has its limitations, it is necessary to establish a separate provision under Article 42 of the Chinese Conflict of Laws Act to expressly include package travel contracts set forth in Article 111(3) of the Chinese Tourism Law. Alternatively, the Supreme People's Court may issue a judicial interpretation of Article 42 Chinese Conflicts Ac and clarify the notion of consumer contracts by explicitly including package travel contracts.

6.1.6 *Are Timeshare Tourists Consumers?*

Like package travel contracts, timeshare contracts are also not expressly included in the material scope of Article 42 of the Chinese Conflict of Laws Act. Instead, timeshare contracts, as nameless contracts, are governed by general jurisdiction and choice of law rules in Chinese judicial practice. The Chinese Tourism Law also does not define timeshare contracts. Chapter 4 concludes that timeshare contracts should be protected as consumer contracts and explicitly included in the material scope of consumer choice of law rules under Article 42 of the Chinese Conflict of Laws Act. To this end, it is crucial to provide a specific definition of timeshare contract and establish relevant provisions over timeshare contracts in Chinese substantive law by virtue of the Tourism Law, the Consumer Protection Law or the Chinese Civil Code. Alternatively, the Supreme People's Court may issue a judicial interpretation of Article 42 of the Chinese Conflict of Laws Act and clarify the notion of consumer contracts by explicitly including timeshare contracts.

6.2 How to Improve the Jurisdiction Rules over Consumer Contracts in China?

In the absence of a consumer jurisdiction rule in China, Chap. 3 focuses on the questions of what jurisdiction rules are applied to consumer contracts, what are the challenges and problems in judicial practice, and what can be done to enhance consumer protection. In judicial practice, general jurisdiction rules over domestic contracts in the Civil Procedure Law are applied to consumer contracts by Chinese courts. China lacks a specific consumer jurisdiction rule. This means that consumers are not granted with the jurisdictional privilege to sue or be sued by businesses in their home country's courts. The arising question is how to improve consumer jurisdiction rules in China.

6.2.1 *Establishing a New Consumer Jurisdiction Rule*

It is crucial to establish a specific consumer jurisdiction rule in China. The adoption of Article 31 of the Draft Model Law of Chinese Private International Law on consumer home jurisdiction rule would largely solve the problems existing in judicial practice. Many scholars have advocated the establishment of a consumer jurisdiction rule which grants the consumer the right to sue at the consumer's home jurisdiction. This can be achieved by establishing a new provision or amending current provisions in the Civil Procedure Law of the PRC or the SPC Judicial Interpretation of the Civil Procedure Law. In this regard, Article 280 of the Chinese Civil Procedure

Law (amendment draft) which proposes a protective consumer jurisdiction rule, which states that:

> a consumer's lawsuit against a business operator or a branch of a business operator whose domicile is not within the territory of the People's Republic of China, if the domicile of the consumer is within the territory of the People's Republic of China, it may be subject to the jurisdiction of the people's court of the consumer's domicile.

Such consumer home jurisdiction rule is also in line with the favorable consumer choice of law rules set forth in Article 42 of the Conflicts Law Act which designates the home law of the consumer. Meanwhile, the conditions of applying consumer jurisdiction rules need to be more specified to increase their functionality in judicial practice. For instance, it needs to clarify whether a consumer contract has to be concluded, what constitutes targeting or dis-targeting test and whether a causal link is required. In principle, the conclusion of a written consumer contract should be a pre-condition. However, other factors may substitute the lack of a written contract and justify the existence of a de facto contractual relationship. The dis-targeting test indicates that a causal link is not required. As to the determination of a foreign element, the fact that the performance of the contract is in a foreign country may constitute a foreign element under Article 1 of the SPC Judicial Interpretation of the Chinese Conflict of Laws Act, regardless of whether the contract is performed or not. In this regard, the Chinese courts should be more consistent when identifying a foreign element to ensure that alike cases are treated likely.

6.2.2 Restricting the Validity of Choice of Court Agreements Procedurally and Substantively

As to the validity of choice of court agreements in standard consumer contracts, different courts may have different opinions. The Civil Procedure Law does not specify whether a choice of court agreement in a consumer contract is effective. The second paragraph of Article 280 of the Chinese Civil Procedure Law (amendment draft) expressly addresses the validity of choice of court agreement in consumer contracts, which reads that:

> Where a business operator uses standard terms to sign a jurisdiction agreement with consumers but fails to perform the obligation of informing or explaining in a reasonable manner, consumers may claim that the terms do not become the content of the contract. If it is obviously inconvenient for a consumer to file a lawsuit under the jurisdiction agreement, the consumer may claim that the clause is invalid.

This provision puts restrictions on the choice of court agreement inserted in standard terms. The business operator has the obligation to inform or explain reasonably to the consumer about the jurisdiction clause inserted in standard terms, failing that, the consumer may claim the jurisdiction clause does not constitute part of the consumer contract. Meanwhile, even if a business reasonably informs or explains the jurisdiction clause to the consumer, such clause is still invalid provided that it is obviously inconvenient for the consumer. Consumers are protected from business operators in bad faith both procedurally and substantively. This proposal is beneficial to consumers in foreign-related litigation. Adopting it would be a big step forward in Chinese private international law over consumer protection. Unfortunately, the final text of the 2023 Civil Procedure Law did not adopt this provision.

6.3 What are Applicable Law Rules Over Consumer Contracts in China?

Article 42 of the Chinese Conflict of Laws Act ensures that a consumer contract in principle is governed by the law of the consumer' habitual residence and the exercise of party autonomy is limited. The application of this consumer applicable law rule is subject to targeting test in China. The arising question includes how does China handle excluded consumer contracts? Should party autonomy in consumer contracts under Article 42 of the Chinese Conflict of Laws Act be limited to unilateral exercise by consumers, or should it allow for two-sided party autonomy? Is there a need for more flexible connecting factors? When the targeting test is not fulfilled, should general contract choice of law rules in Article 41 of the Chinese Conflict of Laws Act apply? What role mandatory and overriding mandatory provisions play in consumer protection? Is there a need to distinguish between mandatory and overriding mandatory provisions in China, especially concerning provisions protecting weaker parties like employees and consumers? These questions are addressed in Chap. 5.

6.3.1 Embracing Bilateral Party Autonomy

The exercise of party autonomy is limited both in China under Article 42 of the Chinese Conflict Act. The Chinese approach only allows consumers to choose applicable law unilaterally, limiting the material scope to only the consumer's home law and the law of the place of provision of goods or services. It seems more favorable to the consumer, as the consumer may choose the applicable law unilaterally. However, the limited material scope of the chosen law may be detrimental to the consumer. Such limitation is too strict and may lead to no applicable law or a law having no substantial connection with the dispute in some cases, such as in the context of package travel or timeshare contracts. If the goods or services are provided in the consumer's home country, it means that the consumer has no choice to choose any other laws, because the consumer's habitual residence and the place of the provision of goods or services applies anyway, regardless of the targeting test or dis targeting-test.

If the exercise of party autonomy has to be limited to the consumer, it is necessary to add more flexible connecting factors. Expanding the material scope of the chosen law to those which have a connection with the dispute is also subject to the condition that the business could reasonably expect the application of such law. Alternatively, Article 42 of the Chinese Conflict of Laws Act could also embrace bilateral party autonomy and confine the chosen law with mandatory provisions of the consumer's home country. Allowing two-sided party autonomy after the dispute arises may provide more choices for consumers and businesses. It reflects the respect of the parties's will in contractual obligations. The law chosen by both parties after the dispute arises usually corresponds to the reasonable expectations of the parties. Due to the limited bargaining power of consumers, such two-sided party autonomy could be limited by mandatory provisions or the connection criterion. Article 56 of the Proposal Draft and Explanation of the Chinese Conflict of Laws Act expressly adopted two-sided party autonomy in consumer contracts and only limited the material scope of chosen law with the connection criterion.

6.3.2 Establishing an Interaction with General Contract Choice of Law Rules

In China, if the targeting test is not fulfilled, consumer choice of law rules still apply, which designates the law of the place of provision of goods or services. However, the place of provision of goods or services does not necessarily have a close connection with the consumer dispute in every circumstance. When the business does not engage in commercial activities in the consumer's habitual residence, it is better to determine the law applicable to a consumer contract under general contract choice of law rules in Article 41, instead of applying the law of the place of provision of goods or services without any exception under Article 42. Thus, it is necessary to establish an interaction between consumer choice of law rules in Article 42 of the Chinese Conflict of Laws Act and contract choice of law rules of Article 41 of the Chinese Conflict of Laws Act. A possible proposal to amend Article 42 of the Chinese Conflict of Laws Act would be as follows: *Provided that the business does not engage in relevant commercial or soliciting activities, the law applicable to the consumer contract will be determined by contract choice of law rules in Article 41 Chinese Conflict of Laws Act.*

6.3.3 Consumer Rules as Mandatory Provisions and Overriding Mandatory Provisions as the Safety Valve

In China, the boundary between mandatory and overriding mandatory provisions is unclear. Whereas provisions on employee contracts are considered as mandatory provisions set forth in Article 8 of the SPC Judicial Interpretation of the Chinese Conflict of Laws Act, provisions on consumer protection are not expressly included. Consumers, just like employees, are weaker parties and should be protected under the mandatory provisions set forth in Article 8 of the SPC Judicial Interpretation of the Chinese Conflict of Laws Act. Both mandatory and overriding mandatory provisions could also play a role and function as double insurances in terms of consumer protection in China. To this end, there is a need to draw a distinction between mandatory and overriding mandatory provisions in China. Provisions protecting weaker parties, such as employees and consumers, are domestic mandatory provisions, instead of international mandatory provisions.

6.4 Legislative Suggestions

In China, in terms of the notion of consumer, a combination of negative and positive definition of consumer is proposed. Accordingly, a consumer may be defined as '*a natural person who, acting outside his or her trade or profession, concludes a contract with another person, acting within his or her trade or profession, primarily for the purpose of private, household, family consumption*'.

Package travel and timeshare contracts are not expressly included in the material scope of Article 42 of the Chinese Conflict of Laws Act. These contracts are classified as nameless contracts and governed by general jurisdiction and choice of law rules in judicial practice. To protect these contracts as consumer contracts, it is necessary to establish a separate provision under Article 42 of the Chinese Conflict of Laws Act to expressly include package travel contracts set forth in Article 111(3) of the Chinese Tourism Law. The definition of timeshare contracts could be provided in Chinese substantive law by virtue of the Tourism Law, the Consumer Protection Law or the Chinese Civil Code before the express inclusion in Article 42 of the Chinese Conflict of Laws Act. Alternatively, the Supreme People's Court may issue a judicial interpretation of Article 42 Chinese Conflicts Ac and clarify the notion of consumer contracts by explicitly including package travel and timeshare contracts.

In China, it is crucial to establish a specific consumer jurisdiction rule. In this regard, adopting Article 280 of the Chinese Civil Procedure Law (amendment draft) could be a solution. It proposes a protective consumer jurisdiction rule, which states that: *a consumer's lawsuit against a business operator or a branch of a business operator whose domicile is not within the territory of the People's Republic of China, if the domicile of the consumer is within the territory of the People's Republic of China, it may be subject to the jurisdiction of the people's court of the consumer's domicile.* Meanwhile, the conditions of applying consumer jurisdiction rules need to be more specified, such as what constitutes targeting test and dis-targeting test, to increase their functionality in judicial practice.

As to the validity of choice of court agreements in standard consumer contracts, it is expressly addressed in the second paragraph of Article 280 of the Chinese Civil Procedure Law (amendment draft), which reads that: *Where a business operator uses standard terms to sign a jurisdiction agreement with consumers but fails to perform the obligation of informing or explaining in a reasonable manner, consumers may claim that the terms do not become the content of the contract. If it is obviously inconvenient for a consumer to file a lawsuit under the jurisdiction agreement, the consumer may claim that the clause is invalid.* This provision puts restrictions on the choice of court agreement inserted in standard terms. Consumers are protected from business operators in bad faith both procedurally and substantively. Adopting this provision would be a big step forward in Chinese private international law over consumer protection.

In terms of the exercise of party autonomy, Article 42 of the Chinese Conflict of Laws Act could embrace bilateral party autonomy and confine the chosen law with mandatory provisions of the consumer's home country. If the exercise of party autonomy has to be limited to the consumer, it is necessary to add more flexible connecting factors and expand the material scope of the chosen law to those which have a connection with the dispute.

It remains a question to what extent and when China would make amendments as suggested with regard to consumer jurisdiction and choice of law rules. These legislative suggestions are merely academic proposals for legislators to take into consideration for future legal reform. Even if the proposals are adopted, some issues still require ongoing discussion due to the complexity of real-life transactions and the fast development of technology. In a broader context, this study on consumer rules in China is meaningful in the sense that it may provide inspiration and guidance for other countries facing similar questions and challenges.

If the targeting test is not fulfilled, consumer choice of law rules still apply under Article 42 of the Chinese Conflict of Laws Act, designating the law of the place of provision of goods or services. Since it does not always have a close connection with the consumer dispute, it is better to determine the law applicable to a consumer contract under general contract choice of law rules in Article 41. To this end, it is necessary to establish an interaction between consumer choice of law rules in Article 42 of the Chinese Conflict of Laws Act and contract choice of law rules in Article 41 of the Chinese Conflict of Laws Act. A possible proposal to amend Article 42 of the Chinese Conflict of Laws Act would be as follows: *Provided that the business does not engage in relevant commercial or soliciting activities, the law appli cable to the consumer contract will be determined by contract choice of law rules in Article 41 Chinese Conflict of Laws Act.* Give the importance of targeting test as a condition and the development of new personalized advertising strategies in tourism industry, such as recommendations system, Generative AI, social media, and influencer marketing, the Supreme People's Court could issue judicial interpretations to clarify what constitutes the targeting test.

Both mandatory and overriding mandatory provisions could play a role, albeit a very limited one, in consumer protection in China. There is a need to draw a clear distinction between mandatory and overriding mandatory provisions. Provisions protecting weaker parties, such as employees and consumers, are domestic mandatory provisions, instead of international mandatory provisions. Mandatory provisions apply to restrict the parties's choice of law when the targeting test is met. When the targeting test is not met, excluded consumer contracts under Article 42 of the Chinese Conflict of Laws Act may still be protected by the mandatory provisions of the consumer's home law by virtue of overriding mandatory provisions. To this end, Article 8(1) of the SPC Judicial Interpretation of the Chinese Conflict of Laws Act can be revised slightly as "*where protection of the rights and interests of workers or consumers is involved*". This would cover consumer disputes over provision of goods or services, while public interests may also be involved.

These legislative suggestions could provide more legal certainty as to who is qualified as a consumer and what jurisdiction and choice of law rules apply to a consumer contract. Compared to existing rules, the proposed protective provisions or more favorable approach could help achieve a higher level of consumer protection. However, it remains a question as regards to what extent and when China can make an amendment as suggested with regard to consumer jurisdiction and choice of law rules. These legislative suggestions are merely academic proposals for legislators to take into consideration for future legal reform. Even if the proposals are adopted, some issues still require ongoing discussion due to the complexity of real-life transactions and the fast development of technology. In a broader context, this study on consumer rules in China is meaningful in the sense that it may provide inspiration and guidance for other countries facing similar questions and challenges.

The manufacturer's authorised representative in the EU is Springer Nature Customer Service Centre GmbH, Europaplatz 3, 69115 Heidelberg, Germany. If you have any concerns regarding our products, please contact ProductSafety@springernature.com

Printed and bound by CPI Group (UK) Ltd, Croydon, CR0 4YY
01/10/2026
02225950-0006